Italian Bel Canto
in the Age of
Vocal Science

*The evolution of the art
and the science of singing*

JOSEPH TALIA

Other books by this author:
A History of Vocal Pedagogy: Intuition and Science
Vocal Science for Elite Singers

First published 2019 by:
Australian Academic Press Group Pty. Ltd., Australia
www.australianacademicpress.com.au

Copyright © 2019 Joseph Talia

Copying for educational purposes
The *Australian Copyright Act 1968* (Cwlth) allows a maximum of one chapter or 10% of this book, whichever is the greater, to be reproduced and/or communicated by any educational institution for its educational purposes provided that the educational institution (or the body that administers it) has given a remuneration notice to Copyright Agency Limited (CAL) under the Act.
For details of the CAL licence for educational institutions contact:
Copyright Agency Limited, 19/157 Liverpool Street, Sydney, NSW 2000.
E-mail info@copyright.com.au

Production and communication for other purposes
Except as permitted under the Act, for example a fair dealing for the purposes of study, research, criticism or review, no part of this book may be reproduced, stored in a retrieval system, or transmitted in any form or by any means electronic, mechanical, photocopying, recording or otherwise without prior written permission of the copyright holder.

 A catalogue record for this book is available from the National Library of Australia

Italian Bel Canto in the Age of Vocal Science

ISBN   9781925644258 (paperback)
ISBN   9781925644296 (hardback)
ISBN   9781925644265 (ebook)

Publisher: Stephen May
Copy editing: Rhonda McPherson
Cover design: Luke Harris, Working Type Studio
Typesetting: Australian Academic Press
Printing: Lightning Source

Foreword

Italian Bel Canto in the Age of Vocal Science is the third and final volume in Dr Talia's trilogy that begins with Gianni Maffei in 1562 and ends with contemporary Italian authors as late as 1917. This trilogy is dedicated to revealing the complex art of singing and to the development of vocal science. This book is the conclusion of a profound, prolonged and exhaustive study through a kaleidoscope of evolving aesthetic, scientific and musical evolution responsible for generating the two preceding works by the same author, *A History of Vocal Pedagogy Intuition and Science (2017),* and *Vocal Science for Elite Singers (2018).*

The objective of the work is to critically evaluate the Italian school of bel canto, the culmination of the harmonious fusion between the old school, the present school and modern vocal science.

The structure of the volume is articulated in two sections: the first is dedicated to the periods of bel canto, that is, the Baroque period, dominated by the presence of the castrati who covered the role of singers, teachers, and composers; the second bel canto period is represented by the influence of the immense genius of Rossini, reformer of opera and bel canto.

The second section of the book comprises of an exhaustive examination of the prevailing conditions for Italian bel canto over the last fifty years and fills an enormous gap in our knowledge regarding the evolution of the modern school. The book includes elaborate chapters on respiration, voice production (voice source), registration, vocal attack (onset), resonance and articulation of the voice.

The inspiration for the book, as affirmed by the author, originated in his passionate research.

> The idea of this book came to me whilst translating certain selections from the Italian literature into English for my previous books. It occurred to me that there were a number of excellent Italian authors who were exploring and writing about contemporary vocal research in Italy. However, their books were not available in English despite the fact that these writers are in direct line to Porpora, Manuel Garcia, Francesco Lamperti and Mathilde Marchesi.

Italian Bel Canto in the Age of Vocal Science considers and analyses the evolution of the art and the science of singing, examining it from various points of view and through the perspective of pedagogues of the last fifty years. In so doing it throws light on the vocal research conducted in present day Italy.

These studies were conducted by first rate Italian scientists and have been integrated in the singing studios by excellent teachers and authors.

Before Dr Talia's intervention, no one had investigated how much and in what manner Italian singing teachers are introducing modern vocal science into their teaching, and no one had studied in depth the content and influence that vocal science research has exercised over them.

The author does not surrender to the temptation of confining the Italian school to the past on the basis of its deep historical roots, its past achievements and jubilant celebrations. On the contrary, Dr Talia describes the present school as a singular, luxurious, and thriving scene in which an increasing number of authoritative scientists dedicated to vocal research are following in the footsteps of Professor Carlo Meano in his book *The Human Voice in Speech and Song*. Their investigations have produced a vast scientific literature which has been assimilated into the Italian singing studios by singers and singing teachers, many of whom are fine authors in their own right, demonstrating a profound understanding of the fusion between vocal science and the teaching of voice.

Dr Talia's clear narrative reveals how these teachers have guided, with assured hand, the transformation of the Italian bel canto school, based on empiricism and tradition, into a school that adheres to scientific principles. They have confronted the technico/physiological question by opening the discussion with respect to the principles and practices of the past century, and the strong progress made by vocal researchers and phoneticians, all with a renewed critical attitude.

In this sense, they have attempted to overturn the empirical spirit that characterised a great many bel canto teachers of the past.

There, alongside the stylistic and interpretative concepts and precepts imposed by such grand figures as Farinelli, Caffarelli, Pistocchi, Bernacchi, Carestini, Senesino, Garcia, Colbran, Malibran and the methods of singing of the eighteenth century, we find the flourishing of vocal science. The new authors focus their attention on the acquisition of the modern psycho-pedagogy, on phonetics and vocal physiology upon which scientific knowledge we base the study of voice, ushering in recent discoveries and the continued progress of medical science. As the author rightly observes, they are committed to weaving the essential connections between the art of singing and the scientific descriptions able to explain and deepen the fascinating vocal phenomenon of voice production, applied for the purpose of artistry.

The vocal phenomenon considered as biological activity must be well understood and evaluated, until it can fulfil its purpose in full and perfect efficiency. The study of expression must go back to the exact cause that determine and sharpen the possibilities.

Dr Talia's clear treatment is combined by a fascinating and lively style, confronting a number of crucial arguments, revealing and critically examining from different points of view and perspectives. Dr Talia explores in a masterly fashion the journey undertaken by the old empirical school of bel canto, with its proven techniques, superb vocalizzi, ornaments, and celebrated *fioritura*, towards the confluence of the modern Italian singing school dominated by scientific knowledge and objective physiology and methodology.

The time has come for Italian bel canto to study in depth the various problems associated with diverse didactic methodologies, to dispense with the intractability of scientific culture and the sparse dissemination of the latter in the practice of singing. It is time to address the prevailing chaos both at the level of concepts and terminology. We must try to restructure the point of view of traditional didactic by incorporating scientific discoveries, a reconciliation which is only possible if we consider that those who wish to learn how to sing are already complex human beings, and not scientific equations.

Scientific knowledge can help to formulate and comprehend the fundamental principles in a more complete manner, define the use of an exact terminology, and better determine the sonorous potential. It can also define unimaginable resources and limits of both voice and vocal art.

> There are many excellent authors who have written a great number of erudite books, demonstrating an excellent knowledge of both the old school and contemporary science. In fact, it would not be an exaggeration to claim that their knowledge is the equal of any of their contemporaries anywhere in the world. The problem that we all have, which is not a national but rather an international one, is how do we propagate this knowledge amongst teachers who are less enthusiastic about the physiological and scientific progress being made through vocal science then they should be. This is not an Italian phenomenon, but rather an international one, simply because there is no remedy for ignorance and self-satisfied complacency, nor is there a cure for arrogance, and people who have been infected with the malady known as "I know it all".

Today, more than ever before, we must aim to strike a balance between the scientific approach, which regards man as an equation, and the old traditional pedagogy that considers him a person. Man is governed by natural laws, but it is through the essence of his humanity that he is enriched in a manner that can't be measured or evaluated.

When all the knowledge of the vocal mechanism, and all the artistic ability of the singers is utilised, then the result cannot be anything other than a greater comprehension and a higher enjoyment of the vocal art. Singing is an art. But just as science without art lacks the essence: the spark, the flame, the impression, the divine, so too, art without science remains most assuredly incomplete. The voice with its mechanism, its emission, its countless modifications, constitutes a science.

Italian Belcanto in the Age of Vocal Science reveals itself as an indispensable work, aimed not only at singers and singing teachers, but also at serious disciples of singing and those perennial seekers of that ineffable and elusive vocal freedom. It is also a book for all those who have an interest in voice, vocal technique and the art of singing. Its aims are in line with Dr Talia's conviction that,

> There is an understanding that it takes more than a good voice and a good technique to make a wonderful career.It takes temperament, intelligence, subtlety, musicality, and a strong winning psychology.This is a school that understands that ultimately it is the richness of our humanity that makes each performance a unique experience.

Dr. Maria Luisa Sanchez Carbone

Author of *Vox arcana, Teoria e pratica della voce* (2005); *La voce. Mille esercizi e vocalizzi per educarla, esercitarla, perfezionarla* (2010); *Il mondo del canto. Vivere e sopravvivere* (2017).

Contents

Foreword iii
Preface: Rationale for writing this book xiii

Chapter 1: Italian Bel Canto in the Age of Vocal Science 1
Effectiveness or Efficiency 6

Chapter 2: What is Italian Bel Canto? 13

Chapter 3: Bel Canto Schools of the First Golden Age 15
Scarlatti and Bel Canto 15
Antonio Pistocchi and Bel Canto 18

Chapter 4: Nicola Porpora and the Neapolitan School 21
Antonio Bernacchi and Bel Canto 27

Chapter 5: The Naples of Caffarelli and Farinelli 33
Farinelli, Carlo Broschi 35
Summary and Analysis of the Porpora Method 37
Conclusion to the First Golden Age of Singing 38

Chapter 6: The Second Golden Age of Bel Canto 41
Rossini and the Golden Age of Bel Canto 42
    Gioachino Rossini 45
        La Pietra di Paragone 50
        Tancredi 50
        L'occasione fa il ladro 50
        L'italiana in Algeria 51
        Il Turco in Italia 51
Rossini's Neapolitan Sojourn 53
        La Gazetta 54
        Elisabetta Regina d'Inghilterra 56
        La Gazetta 56
        Otello: Naples 1816 56
        Armida 57
        La Donna del Lago 57
        Semiramide 59

Guillaume Tell 64
   Rossini's Influence on Opera 65
   Rossini's Effect on Singing... 68
Pre-Rossinian Vocal Characteristics...73

Chapter 7: Italian Vocal Pedagogy in the 21st Century 75
Respiration in the Age of Bel Canto 79

Chapter 8: Pronunciation and Articulation 91
Lamperti on Pronunciation and Resonance 92
   Resonance and Articulation 92
   Enrico Delle Sedie and the Scientific Approach to Resonance 93
   Vowel Chart 93

Chapter 9: Vocal Pedagogy: Art or Science?..97
Characteristics of a Good Singing Teacher 99

Chapter 10: The State of Contemporary Vocal Pedagogy in Italy.........103
Vocal Pedagogy in Chaos..103
The Famous Singing Teacher 106
The Triumph of Nature and Science Over Incompetence.........................111
Summary 118

Chapter 11: Respiration in the Contemporary Italian School.................121
Anatomy of Respiration 124
   Inspiratory Muscles: The Diaphragm and External Intercostal Muscles 124
   The Thorax...124
   The Sternum 125
   The Diaphragm 126
The Intercostal Muscles 130
   Internal and External Intercostals...130
The Diaphragm and External Intercostals: Inspiratory Muscles..............................133
The Abdominals and Internal Intercostals: Expiratory Muscles..............................133
   The Abdominal Girdle...134
   The Lungs 135
The Importance of Respiration in The Italian School of Singing 138
   Rachele Maragliano Mori on Breathing 138
   Normal Respiration 140
   Instinctive and Volitional Respiration 148

About Appoggio 151
Appoggio and Sostegno 151
Exchange of Gases Guaranteeing Life 153
The 'Belly In' and 'Belly Out' Strategies 157
Fussi and Magnani on Sostegno and Appoggio 158
Interaction Between Sostegno and Appoggio 162
Appoggio or Sostegno 164
Clavicular Respiration 166
Abdominal Respiration or Affondo 168
Elastic Recoil Force 170

Conclusions 171
Definition of Appoggio 172

Chapter 12: The Development of the Appoggio System......................177

The Mechanics of Appoggio 178
Summary..187
Conclusions 187

Chapter 13: Laryngeal Physiology and the Vibratory System 191

Carlo Meano 194
Summary of Meano's Work 201
Historical Perspective — Oskar Schindler 201
Schindler Next Interprets Raul Husson's Neurochronaxic Theory.....................203
Marco Galignano 207
The Hypothesis of the Mechanical Workings of the Vocal Folds 208
The Neurochronaxic Theory 209
The Aerodynamic Theory 209
The Myoelastic/Aerodynamic 209
General Description 213

Chapter 14: Building the Instrument 215

The Cartilages 215
The Thyroid Cartilage 215
The Cricoid Cartilage 216
The Arytenoid Cartilages 217
The Epiglottic Cartilages...217
Marco Galignano and Cartilages...217
The Arytenoids 218

Anatomy and Physiology of the Vibratory System: Larynx 218
   The Cartilages 218
   The Crcioid Cartilage 219
   The Thyroid Cartilage..220
   The Arytenoid Cartilages 220
   The Extrinsic Laryngeal Muscles 221
   The Intrinsic Muscles of the Larynx..222
   The Posterior Cricoarytenoid Muscle 222
   The Interarytenoid Transverse Muscles 222
   The Oblique Interarytenoid Muscle 223
   The Aryepiglottic Muscle 223
   The Thyroarytenoid Muscle Superior...223
   The Inferior Arytenoid Muscle 223
   The Suspensory Mechanism: The Connection to the Hyoid Bone....................223
   The Infrahyoid Muscles 224
   The Suprahyoid Muscles 224
   Interaction Between the Thyroarytenoid and Cricothyroid Muscles 225
   The Cricothyroid Muscle 225
   The Thyroarytenoid Muscles 226
   The Vocal Folds...229
   The Lateral Cricoarytenoid Muscle 231
   Posterior Cricoarytenoid Muscle..231
   The Interarytenoid Muscles..231
   Frequency...232
   Falsetto 233
   Lowering the Frequency 233
   Intensity 234
   Breathy and Pressed Phonation 235
   Pressed Voice 236
   Conclusions to Quality: Vocal Timbre 237

Chapter 15: Vocal Quality and Registers 239

Registers 242
   Register Terminology 243
Antonio Juvarra..248
   The Larynx 250
   The Vibrator..250
Juvarra on the Vocal Registers and Passaggio 251

Covering	251
A 21st Century Scientific View of Registers	256
Fussi and Magnani 2015 on Vocal Registers	257
Medium Register	262
Transition From the Empirical System Towards the Scientific Method	265

Chapter 16: Modern Masters on Registers 267

The Low Registers	268
Medium or Mixed Voice	269
The Higher Register	270
Damiani on Registers	271
Registers and Voice Classification	273
Heavy Register	273
Chest Register	273
Mixed Register	274
Sanchez Carbone on Registers	275
Chest Register	278
High Register	279
Medium Register	279
Mixed Register	281
Conclusions to Register	283

Chapter 17: Vocal Onset in the Modern Italian School 285

Prephonatory Preparation, Breathing and Focal Points	287
Prephonatory Preparation: Timing and Coordination	291
Ideal Onset Begins With Apnea	292
Psychological Aspects of Vocal Attack	293
Conclusions to the Italian Approach	293
Conclusions	294
Voice Quality Ensuing From Vocal Onset	295
The Elite Singer's Zone	297

Chapter 18: The Physiological Elements of Supraglottic Events 301

The Vocal Tract	301
The Pharynx	303
Righini on Sound Waves and Formants	306
Definition and Importance of Resonators	307
The Tongue	308

Bruno and Paperi on the Tongue 313
The Lips 314
Soft Palate 317
Definition and Importance of Resonators 319
    Absorbent Function 323
    Inertial Impedance Function 323
    Proprioceptive Function 324
Vocal Timbre 327
Formants and Vocal Tract Resonances 329
Formants and Formant Tuning 332
    Antonio Juvarra on Formants 332
    Matching Formants in the Female Voice 333
    Damiani on Vowel Formants 334
    Formants and Timbres 335
    The Singer's Formant 335
Conclusions 336

Chapter 19: Consonants and Articulation 339
The Oropharynx 340
Nasopharynx 341
Conclusions to Consonants 345
Final Conclusions 346

Appendix A: Muscles of Respiration 349

Appendix B: Laryngeal Musculature 359

Appendix C: Head and Neck Muscles 367

Bibliography 379

Preface

Rationale for Writing this Book

It was in the process of translating certain selections from the Italian literature into English for my previous books *A History of Vocal Pedagogy: Intuition and Science (2017)* and *Vocal Science for Elite Singers (2018)* that it occurred to me that there was a distinctive hole in our knowledge of the Italian school. The truth is that there are a number of English-speaking authors, myself included, who have written at length on the Old Italian School, and many of us who had also written on vocal science, but no-one had written on how contemporary practitioners of Italian *bel canto* are integrating modern science into their teaching. Nobody had explored the impact that vocal research being performed in the Italian laboratories of today was having on modern Italian singing masters.

It also occurred to me that there is a great temptation to confine the Italian school to the past, believing that because of its deep historical roots and in spite of its glory days, the Italian bel canto school has become irrelevant.

Nothing could be further from the truth. An appreciation of the past does not mean that Italians live in the past, but rather that they have a better perspective of the present and a more intuitive understanding of the future.

My research revealed a thriving scene in which more and more vocal science is being investigated by first-rate scientists following in the footsteps of Carlo Meano's *The Human Voice in Speech and Song* (1964), English edition (1967). These include Oskar Schindler, Franco Fussi, Franco Gilardone, Silvana Magnani, Giovanna Bruno and Giovanni Ruoppolo, producing first class research, which has since been assimilated into the Italian singing studio by excellent teachers. Authors such as Rachele Maragliano Mori, Nanda Mari, Antonio Juvarra, Bruno and Paperi, Battaglia Damiani, and Maria Luisa Sanchez Carbone, and more recently, Delfo Menicucci (2011) have given lucid explanation of the physiology and science of singing, whilst also integrating science into their teaching. It is true that most of these authors still speak of the old school with great affection but that is only because they are desirous of bringing forward many of the proven techniques of that august institution. However, they teach those techniques in a very different way to their predecessors. Not only do they incorporate an increasing amount of science into their teachings, but they also use a very different and more precise scientific language to teach it.

Undoubtedly, there is a hangover from the Bel Canto School in the modern Italian School, but it does not prevent these modern teachers from moving forward towards the twenty first century, informing, enriching and humanising their teaching. It provides the foundations for the new Italian School by applying proven and successful techniques in a more direct, scientific way. Above all it provides the Italian school with a sense of continuity, a sense that history naturally evolves and that there is no need for damaging revolutions. They have seen it all before: they know that history has its own means of illuminating genuinely brilliant and durable ideas and eliminating those that appeared full of sparkle and glitter but ultimately lack substance.

The Modern Italian School aims to incorporate and assimilate, not divide. It understands that it takes more than a good voice and a good technique to make a wonderful career. It considers the importance of temperament, intelligence, subtlety, musicality, and psychology. It appreciates a richly nuanced performance, and knows that ultimately it is the richness of our humanity that makes each performance a unique experience.

Chapter 1

Italian Bel Canto
In the Age of Vocal Science

Notwithstanding the fact that the very best Italian Schools have embraced science whole heartedly, there is a continuing debate with respect to the amount of vocal science singing teachers should introduce into their studio. In addition, the big question remains as to how vocal science may best be utilised in order to consistently obtain the highest results. My personal opinion is shaped by a strong belief that being in possession of a large body of scientific and physiological knowledge is not just useful, it is indispensable. I am also aware that many teachers are already using this knowledge to describe the instrument and explain its function.

I applaud these teachers! However, I believe that this growing body of work is too powerful a tool to remain chronically either misunderstood or underutilised, which is the situation we are confronting today. Using this knowledge as a physiological explanatory tool is a step forward from where we have been, but it is nowhere near enough. To limit ourselves to this function would be an incredible waste of an extraordinary resource. In a world where sports science has been utilised to consistently break world records, I do not believe that singers can be satisfied to use vocal science as a descriptive and explanatory tool. Vocal science should expect and demand similar outcomes to those achieved through sports science. The objective should be to build the instrument, enhance endurance and develop stamina, all with a view to improving technique and optimising performance. For too long singers have been spectators at sports arenas, cheering athletes as they break world records, whilst they themselves have been largely content to just meander on a journey to nowhere. For too long we have been content to be far too cautious. If we are to achieve enduring glory in our art, we must be adventurous, passionate and have a strong appetite for creating exciting performances. I understand that some singers have not been endowed by nature with either the instrument or the psychology to withstand these demands, and I am sympathetic. I remain convinced that those who are genuinely passionate will find a place for themselves in the arts. I do not, however, believe that that place should be in the opera stages of the world. The other issue that I want to bring up is the issue of vocal health and performance. Here again we can learn a great deal from sports medicine. In elite sports, they have a straightforward philosophy, which dictates procedure. The philosophy is simple, if you are fit and step into the arena, you are obliged to give it your all, if you are not fit, you will not be picked for the team or the sport you participate in. It is a philosophy that singers would do well to adapt. If you are not well, do not perform, because you will disappoint your audience and also increase the risk of doing yourself damage.

You do not have to perform at full throttle throughout the performance, but a great voice should be fully developed and used vigorously, but also gently, with flexibly, agility and ornamentation as required by the composer. These demands are de rigueur in a substantial career and should not be eschewed by any singer worthy of an international career. I remain convinced that singers have a great deal to learn from sports medicine, sports psychology, sports training and performance expectations.

And that is why I believe that vocal science is absolutely critical to the production of elite singers and artists. We need to inspire artists to do their best if we are to defer the introduction of microphones in the opera houses of the world, something that is already happening as we speak. This will have enormous consequences for vocal culture and the way we educate the human voice.

I am not going to argue the merits and importance of developing a wide vocal range, and a high level of vocal intensity and carrying power as required for the opera house. I have already done it in my *History of Vocal Pedagogy: Intuition and Science* (2017), and in my *Vocal Science for Elite Singers* (2018). The rise of the little voice is something that has concerned me as well as many great singers of the recent past including Pavarotti, Corelli, Hines and Horne. Indeed, it should concern all of us who are trying to preserve our art form as we have known it for centuries. Let me make it clear that it takes a special instrument to sustain an enduring and elite singing career, but a good technique, considerable muscular athleticism, an excellent mind, and the wisdom to make good decisions are even more critical to long-term success.

Too often singers and their teachers believe that wrapping their vocal folds in cotton wool is the only way to preserve the voice. That is absolutely false. Great singers typically utilise a wide vocal range and varying levels of intensity from piano to fortissimo, with the ability to execute all sorts of ornaments, sustaining this for many years. Sutherland, Freni, Caballe, Horne, Taddei, Cappuccilli, Bruson, Nucci, Bergonzi, Corelli, Pavarotti and

Domingo all had very long careers and they never left you with a sense that they were saving the voice for a rainy day.

At this point of the discussion, if you were living in Italy in the mid-seventies, you would be made aware in no uncertain manner that all of these singers were taught with the empirical method, with the exception of Horne who studied with William Vennard, and was taught the scientific method.

This is a position that you would have to readily concede, whilst also pointing out the disadvantages of the empirical method, which includes the fact that training takes twice as long, and is therefore twice as expensive and, if badly taught, can ruin voices. It also involved a great deal of guesswork, which means a less direct journey to success. In the end, you would probably find much agreement that if you were a responsible teacher who was devoted to serving the art, whilst doing the best for your students, you would probably make it your business to obtain as much knowledge as possible.

The best paradigm to adopt would be one in which the principles and the sound world of the old Italian bel canto school should become the guiding objective, but the way forward should be informed by a deep knowledge of science and physiology which will enlighten our path and ensure a more direct and objective route to success.

One of the problems that we have is that vocal scientists and some singing teachers have been aggressively promoting the idea that vocal science should replace the empirical system. Consequently, too many teachers are still trying to juxtapose vocal science and empiricism, but that is a false equivalency, simply because even though there is some overlap vocal science and empiricism serve quite a different purpose. The physiological and scientific aspects of singing, which I regard as indispensible, are much more relevant to voice production rather than singing. A greater knowledge of how the instrument works and how we may manoeuvre it to attain the sounds we wish to produce can only be a good thing. If we gain a deep knowledge of how the instrument works, we are in a better position to send more precise, incisive messages from the frontal cortex via the nervous system to the muscle fibres. It is from here that we can generate a programme of exercises that will build stamina and endurance, as well as agility and flexibility for that particular instrument.

I feel very strongly that a singing teacher needs to be more than just a vocal coach, they need to have the knowledge required to develop voices; that is our raison d'être. The first responsibility of a singing teacher is to provide the student with an excellent technique, designed to yield maximum output for least effort. For this to occur, however, we must develop a programme of exercises and vocalizzi specifically designed to build the vocal instrument by strengthening all the relevant muscles and developing elasticity, resilience, stamina, flexibility and endurance. It is only after we build the instrument that we can concentrate on artistic and aesthetic refinement. Although the need for elegance and taste should be instilled during the developmental phase, intense concentration on artistry and expression should be deferred until a solid technique has been established. Even then, we must continue to monitor technique.

This beneficial development and sequencing of technique and artistry does not downgrade the importance of teaching 'bel canto techniques' to a student. Students still must learn canto spianato and flexibility, agility, legato, portamenti, staccato and all sorts of ornamentation; they still have to blend registers and develop vocal dynamics, they still have to extend they range, and learn how to spin a phrase with meaning and emotion. They still have to develop they musicianship and powers of interpretation, so what are we arguing about, science is never going to replace the art of singing but it can help an awful lot with the anatomical and physiological aspects of voice production.

In the sixties and seventies, this debate between the empirical and scientific method was raging everywhere, but it was particularly intense in Italy, the place where solo singing began, and where its immense history is recognised. It is also a country renowned for its preoccupation with volume, amplitude and intensity on one hand, and agility and virtuosity on the other. This system of vocal pedagogy has produced the greatest singers in history through the judicial employment of the empirical system of voice education — the didactic system in which knowledge is passed down from one generation to the next in a very personal way.

There is little doubt that the accumulation and proliferation of scientific and physiological knowledge are having a beneficial effect everywhere, including Italy. But the Italians view this development as more of an evolution rather than revolution. They understand the importance of a good vocal technique, but their primary objective remains one of creating exciting theatrical performances of opera, which involves sharing an emotional experience with their audience.

The case for the benefits of optimising performance through vocal science and objective knowledge has not been made convincingly to the contemporary Italian master, who ultimately wants to provide exciting, magnetic, and mesmerising performances. Consequently, those of us who wish to propagate the scientific method into every music school need to do more than just explain how the instrument works. That may have been sufficient at the beginning of the scientific era, when every conscientious teacher longed to know how the instrument works, but those days are long gone. We need to recall that the volume of vocal science, the scope of its proliferation, and the ease of its dissemination, ensure that this knowledge is readily available, but it has to be used properly.

We could argue that one of vocal sciences great, and often underestimated achievements, is the fact that by taking the guesswork out of the equation it has almost eliminated the senseless, passionate arguments that spawned extreme theories. These arguments, whilst creating a great deal of fermentation, were ultimately destructive, often turning well-meaning colleagues into enemies. Without claiming perfect knowledge, most vocal scientists would agree that we now know how the instrument works. The fact that our knowledge is still far from perfect cannot to be used as an excuse for paralysis.

If we are going to serve the art of singing that we feel so passionately about, we need to embrace the responsibility of using vocal science in a manner that enhances our teaching, taking it into the level of elite singing that nurtures our student's aspiration to greatness. Competence is no longer acceptable. Our aim should be to create a sense of magic and excitement by optimising critical performance indicators.

Until we are able to achieve this standard through vocal science, the argument from some Italian singing circles will persist as follows: 'If we are still producing the greatest singers in the world, why should we change?' Why should we change to a method that engenders anaemic performances when the old school produced Callas, Tebaldi, Freni, Cabballe, Sills and Sutherland, not to mention Caruso, Gigli, Bijorling, Del Monaco, Corelli, Bergonzi, Di Stefano, Domingo and Pavarotti. The list could go on and on. It is not just the singing teachers who rebel against this type of anaemic performance, but also the singers themselves, not to mention the audience. Too often we tend to forget that great artists, like great athletes, don't spare themselves. Their first and ultimate desire is to set their audiences on fire with emotions, and everything else is secondary. Callas, Di Stefano, Del Monaco and Beverly Sills are all unrepentant about their so-called accesses. When pressed, they all agreed that they were happy to take some years off their careers in order to create convincing and exciting characters for the stage.

The above anecdotal evidence is supported by a study published by Harm Schutte. In an interesting piece of research, Schutte enquired about vocal efficiency in the professional male voice. The study found that questions of efficiency and energy preservation came a very poor second in comparison to the desired quality. This inefficiency was notable in the lower male voices, including bass and baritone voices, but it was even more accentuated in the tenor voice. In particular, he found that when singing in the higher register at high intensity, the tenor voice required a much higher level of subglottal pressure, which was expected, but the real interesting and perhaps unexpected finding was and the tenor did not use the larynx efficiently [Schutte, 1984: 267].

Harm Schutte concluded that:

> The results actually mean that the tenors put more energy in the larynx to obtain the desired good-quality tone. They apparently only achieve a good 'ring' with high subglottal pressure [Schutte, 1984: 271].

My own conclusions, which are supported by fifty years in the theatre, support Schutte's findings. Further I contend that too many singers and singing teachers fail to comprehend how physical the act of singing really is, nor do they understand the importance of psychology in terms of determination and perseverance, but also developing a winning psychology with respect to the management of one's career. Unless you are driven to be the best you can be, unless you are motivated by the love of the art and your desire to serve it, then you should leave the field. Again, I must reiterate that being driven to do well does not exclude an intelligent, logical approach towards your art, and a graceful approach towards your colleagues.

Effectiveness or Efficiency

Schutte's study confirms that in the battle between conflicting desires, that is, between efficiency and effectiveness, efficiency comes a poor second to vocal quality, and musical expression. Studies also revealed that what was true of the male subjects was equally true of the great sopranos. For instance, the American soprano Beverly Sills made a compelling case for the supremacy of artistic and emotional expression over vocal efficiency. Sills contends that there are two ways of doing things:

> You can wrap your vocal cords in cotton and just stand and sing pretty, or you can really let loose, make a character, scream when you have to scream, yell, pound the table, I did all those things. I chose that route.

> About ten or eleven years ago, when I made a cover of one of the national magazines, I said in their story that I would rather have ten or twelve exciting years than fifteen or twenty dull ones. I made that choice; I never walked out of the theatre where I had an ounce (of energy) left [Sills, 2006].

Both the scientific study above and Beverly Sills's cogent argument give us cause for contemplation. Nonetheless, it is important to recognise the context of this argument, which sprang from the rivalry between Maria Callas's and Joan Sutherland. Callas's more fanatical fans, encouraged by their idol's performance philosophy, came to abhor Sutherland's more controlled and less theatrical performing style.

I believe that Sills' argument is based on a false premise. The truth is that you can be a great singing actress and a great singer who is in possession of a fantastic technique. This is the natural domain of vocal science; that is, we need to help these people who are amongst the most natural, complete and probably amongst the greatest of their generation to achieve their artistic vision and dreams without ruining themselves.

Callas was another example of a magnetic stage animal, with a tremendous artistic vision but lacking the technical knowledge to achieve it safely. She experienced serious vocal problems, but not, as has been widely asserted by her fans, because she was a great singing actress prepared to jeopardise her career in order to bring authentic characters and emotions to the stage. Callas's deterioration can be traced back to three elements: the first was an over-emphasis on impostazione (placement), which in later years she unwisely, and perhaps unintentionally, separated from breathing and articulation strategy; and the second was that her teacher, De Hidalgo, had taught her the sostegno breathing technique which was more appropriate for the bel canto repertoire she began with, but definitely not adequate for the dramatic singing she moved to later. The third problem was related to her weight loss, which had a negative impact not so much on her voice as is often asserted but rather on her breathing and psychology.

Just returning to Callas's sostegno breathing strategy for a moment: this was based on a the 'up and in' system of the old Italian school which emphasised breath flow as opposed to breath pressure. This respiratory strategy is generally inadequate for dramatic singing, which success essentially requires the implementation of the appoggio 'down and out' strategy. In Callas's case there was a double jeopardy, because even within the sostegno strategy, the volume of breath flow was insufficient for most of her high register. Consequently, the breath flow was insufficient to fill the space between the vocal folds that acts as a cushion or as protective shock absorber. Callas produced a hard, metallic, straight sound with few overtones, which unfortunately but predictably developed into a tremolo, or a wobble. Joan Sutherland, whilst careful not to mention Callas, describes the difference in breathing strategy not only most eloquently, but also correctly:

> You have to make some muscular effort to control the compressed air, but you still have to control the issue of that air ... You don't sing with breath, but rather on the breath, and you let as little escape as possible to project the sound' [Sutherland, Opera News, 1998: 20].

With respect to Callas, we recall that she was singing Beethoven's Leonora, Santuzza, and Tosca in her late teens, and Gioconda, Turandot, Isolde, and Brünnhilde in her early twenties, all with a tenuous dramatic technique. It was Serafin who guided her back to the bel canto repertoire. However other aspects of her life, including weight loss, which effected respiration, and an unhealthy compulsion to join the jest set exacerbated the difficulties ensuing from an unbalanced technique.

Sadly, Callas was not the only one of her generation to have a very short career. The 1950s and 1960s ushered in a whole generation of great artists whose careers were shortened through lack of discipline and poor technique. Amongst them we find, not only Callas, but also Di Stefano, Beverly Sills, Renata Scotto, Vittoria de Los Angeles and to a lesser extent Tito Gobbi, Mario Del Monaco, and Renata Tebaldi, although the latter had a genuine medical problem which impacted on her breathing, especially in her later years. I must say that in her early career, Tebaldi's voice was absolutely divine. It remains regrettable that in time the balance between appoggio and impostazione shifted towards a greater reliance on impostazione to compensate for a reduced level of effective appoggio.

With the exception of Mario Del Monaco, who employed an extreme version of the Melocchi affondo School, which was characterised by an excessively lowered larynx and very high levels of subglottal pressure, most other Italian singers suffered from insufficient subglottal pressure and an ineffective laryngeal position.

These inefficiencies reflect the absence of precise objective knowledge, which is associated with the empirical system of vocal pedagogy. Notwithstanding the limitations connected with the empirical system, the paradigm is still highly prized in Italy. In fact, in some cases it is positively cherished. Consequently, when authors such as Rachele Maragliano Mori ask the salient question, 'what is the prevalent pedagogical paradigm dominating our century?' Her answer is that,

> For now, technically, it is still a tributary of the past without serious aspirations towards modernization, or a desire to link its glorious past from which it cannot, and should not be separated, with the evolution of style such as always occurs in every era. This (separation) represents a significant part of the cause of the disorientation of the contemporary Italian School of singing [Mori, 1970:10].

Mori seems to be implying that there is a lot of tension in the Italian school between the evolutionary and revolutionary forces. She suggests a schism between the past and the present and concedes that the Italian school could not and should not be separated from its glorious past.

The glorious past she is referring to here of course is its inseparable connection to the bel canto school. The Golden Ages of Bel Canto: the first refers to the age of those incomparable artists and phenomenal singers, the great castrati, and the second refers to the final and halcyon days of bel canto: the age of Rossini and to a lesser extent the romantic bel canto of Donizetti and Bellini. This is a valid hypothesis to which I adhere to, and which will be discussed at length in these pages.

Bruno and Paperi provide us with a vivid and compelling account of the present state of singing in Italy in comparison to previous movements such as the bel canto era of Tosi and Mancini. These authors provide us with a paradigm that includes the tensions between the revolutionary and evolutionary trajectory during the various Golden Ages of singing. Here is what these authors believe with respect to these tensions:

> All sorts of controversies and uncertainties arising from different schools have reduced the evolutionary aspects of singing to an unplanned almost unintentional process. Even today, notwithstanding our superior knowledge, the attacks provoked through discussions concerning vocal science, style and practice remain as animated as ever. In fact, we can say that to a large degree the strength of the Italian School lies in the certainty it has attained from a tradition that over time has proven its ability to change and evolve. As the above suggests, we all feel a little complicit in the Italo/European musical programme [Bruno & Paperi, 2001: 71].

Bruno and Paperi use Panofka's comments to show the fragmentation of the prevailing environment of the time. Panofka declares that every professor has his own system which he believes in and is absolutely convinced is the best. According to Bruno and Paperi, the strength of Panofka's statement lies in the fact that when we examine the very best singers of our day we discover that they do not all have the same respiratory technique, or use the resonators in the same way, or share the same musical response or taste as provoked by the same text. What these singers have achieved, however, is a sense of personal balance through the harmonious interplay between the internal and external tensions of the body. This was realised irrespective of whether the singer resonated with the merits or the provenance of a particular school, which was often the result of a teacher's affinity with a certain repertoire, or a technique borrowed from another vocal model. Bruno and Paperi argue that this has always been the case, even during Tosi and Mancini's time [Bruno & Paperi, 2001: 71].

The above notwithstanding, we can say that in general, Italians see the old school as evolving rather than experiencing a break with the past through revolution. Italians are by nature not an artistically fearful people. After all, they were able to reconcile the García revolution, and later accommodate the Mandl/Lamperti appoggio contribution to and later still the

Curtis/de Reszke attack. As a result, the better Italian teachers view the proliferation of science and physiology as another evolutionary phase rather than a revolutionary reform. In other words, they experience empiricism and science on a continuum; that is, contemporary vocal science is the natural next step for the art of singing, but its glitter is not so compelling that they feel the necessity to adopt it immediately, or in its entirety. These teachers would rather spend time analysing the various issues spawned by vocal science so as to carefully choose to adopt or reject certain elements, rather than introduce them randomly only to reject them later. Their attitude reveals a healthy suspicion of what they often refer to as excessive progress. They are desirous of incorporating vocal science into their work but they are not relying on the next fashionable bauble to help them produce great singers, because they believe that they can already do that. On the other hand, this current and younger generation of teachers is increasingly open to vocal science, believing that it too has something to contribute.

With respect to the balance between how much science and how much empiricism to utilise in the studio, the Italian singing fraternity seems to be divided.

It is not that these teachers do not have or do not desire a theoretical base to their teaching, but rather that they feel they have a proven theoretical foundation based on the work of the old masters. Many of them are tremendously intelligent and extremely cultured, and well read. They have literally been brought up on the theories of Giovanni Maffei, Zarlino, and Lodovico Zacchoni, Caccini. Peri and Monteverdi. Their work is characterised by early attempts to codify the rules that govern the production of the human voice. Of these, only Maffei, being a medical practitioner, viewed the vocal instrument through the eyes of the scientist and physician. The others were able to correctly describe the type of sound that the early singers were producing, whilst also giving much good advice with respect to attitude, refinement, physical grooming, posture, and performance practise. They also tried to connect cause and effect, but not always successfully, simply because they lacked the necessary objective knowledge. Theirs was a world of trial and error, analyse, repeating what worked and correcting what did not.

In this respect, I agree with Duey (1951) that in this period even though much of the anatomical discoveries were complete, the way the intrinsic muscles influenced voice production was not well understood. Consequently, any emphasis on the physiological aspects of phonation before 1800 was based on false or incomplete theories. From the above therefore, we conclude that the most successful schools of singing were based only on their empirical nature, but also the keen vocal intuition, and ear of the individual teachers, and the theoretical base provided by the early masters.

The most successful period, according to Rossini, was the one dominated by the teachings of the castrati, which coincides with the early murmurings of vocal science. These included such figures as Antonio Bernacchi and his Bolognese School students, and Nicola Porpora and his Neapolitan School.

These legendary figures understood that singing was not only a physical act but also contained psychological, musical and emotional elements, but they had not yet at conquered the physiological and scientific aspects of singing. These famous singers had achieved great success as teachers under the empirical system, and they approached singing as a practical art and therefore used breathing exercises, pronunciation drills, register blending, messa di voce and staccato exercises to produce the great singers of their generation. The thing to remember here is that there was no such thing as a myoelestic/aerodynamic theory and no one had been able to observe the vocal folds in action; that only happened in 1855 the year García discovered the laryngoscope. Everything was based on experiential observation, theorising and subjective conclusions. Fortunately, there was sufficient collective agreement based on these conclusions to establish a number of valuable precepts. On a practical level, they mainly studied breathing by performing light physical exercises, and articulation through a regime of repeated recitation of vowels and consonants, all of which culminated in a prolonged study of Vocalizzi, which were the dominant coordinating tool to achieve their vocal objectives.

Consequently, we can say that they enjoyed the advantages of a growing theoretical foundation, which, although not based on scientific method, drew widely on theories of the old masters based on empirical evidence. Nonetheless, on a positive level, this was the era that spawned teachers such as Porpora's Neapolitan School and the Pistocchi/Bernacchi Bolognese School, and they students such as Mancini, Ansani, Lablache, García Père and Fils, Corri, Guarducci, and Mengozzi.

This was also the period that would come to be widely known as the halcyon days of bel canto. That fabled period of music making that reached its zenith with Porpora, Bernacchi and Handel but which many argue began earlier with Cavalli, Cesti, Rossi and Scarlatti. Either way, the concept of bel canto and what it stands for is not something that the Italians can or wish to circumvent.

It is clear from Mori's comments above that the Italian School is very closely connected to the past, and that in her opinion, and mine for that matter, it should remain so. The world, however, is inexorably moving forward and scientific knowledge is no longer something that they can escape. Over the last fifty years, it has become the dominant teaching paradigm. So, the Italian School is stuck on he horns of a dilemma. This dilemma, can best be described as empiricism versus science and physiology, and is not a predicament that can be easily solved. Consequently, in this book we are going to analyse both paradigms in an effort to find a way forward that maximises the benefits of both. We need to address these issues directly, honestly and with clarity. Let us begin by analysing the old bel canto school, and from there move forward thorough a deep study of the scientific developments that have occurred in the Italian school in the last fifty years. I trust that you will enjoy the journey.

Chapter 2

What is Italian Bel Canto?

The term *bel canto* simply means beautiful singing. However, for singers, bel canto refers to a mythical, legendary style of singing that denotes the highest technical and aesthetic achievement in vocal culture. This style of singing also signifies a highly expressive and emotional sound, combined with a gloriously ornamented style (canto *fiorito*), which is alternated and contrasted with a firm impeccable legato (*canto spianato*). Bel canto refers to the complex of vocal ideals and style that every school of singing claims to teach, but very few are able to define it means let alone execute it.

I admit that trying to pin down the origins of bel canto has proven rather difficult, although it is now widely believed that the Baroque and that otherworldly sound of the castrati was the impulse for its emergence. In part, this confusion came because of the term was coined long after the Halcyon era it was meant to describe. Let us examine these and other issues relating to bel canto.

We begin by stating that bel canto means different things to different people. The major differences, however, seem to relate to the period and the style of music making we are referring to: most authors seem to believe that Rossini is the composer that best represents the halcyon days of bel canto, with Donizetti, and Bellini representing the romantic bel canto period. Other writers include the high Baroque period dominated by the castrati as the highpoint of bel canto. In general, Italian authors seem to regard Rossini as the last of the great bel canto composers, although Celletti and Bruno and Paperi believe that even the later Rossini operas were going in a different direction. I concur, and certainly by the time we arrive at the later Bellini and Donizetti, a period which is now 'called romantic bel canto, it is clear that opera is moving away from Rossini and more towards Verdi. Even though, Bellini and Donizetti, cover extraordinarily well the two pillars of be canto, that is, *canto fiorito* and *canto spianato*, which represent a smooth legato, alternated with virtuosic agility, *passaggi* and trills. This was a somewhat different and more dramatically expressive path, less a sequel for Rossini, than a precursor to Verdi. If we adopt this paradigm, Donizetti than becomes a much more pivotal and innovative composer than originally thought. This paradigm shift requires a re-evaluation of Donizetti's work, one in which he created a new paradigm that was later brought to fruition by Giuseppe Verdi.

This clearly has repercussions for repertoire and structure: the earlier period of bel canto was dominated by the late Baroque da capo ABA aria; whilst the later classical/romantic period is dominated by the cavatina/cabaletta form of the romantic period, and structure of the music. Bel canto style of singing also refers to the ornamentation utilised in this particular period.

I agree with Celletti and Sanchez Carbone that there were in fact two Golden Ages of Bel Canto: the first coincided with the rise of the castrato voice which was well served by virtuosi composers such as Hass, Porpora, Broschi (Farinelli's brother) and above all George Fredrick Handel; the second Golden Age coincided with the rise of the normal as opposed to the mutilated voice and this coincided with Rossini's reign and the at the decline of the castrato voice, and the rise of the tenor, contralto and soprano voices.

This was the period that spawned Giuditta Pasta, Isabella Colbran, Maria Malibran, Domenico Donzelli, Andrea Nozzari, Emanuel García, and Giacomo and Giovanni David to name but a few. These great artists were followed by the next generation of artists such as Grisi, Rubini, and Lablache.

Let us examine more closely and more deeply, both of these two Golden Ages.

Chapter 3

Bel Canto Schools of the First Golden Age

The two most important Italian schools of this period were the Neapolitan school and the Bolognese school. They were well served by their respective disciples Nicola Porpora and Antonio Bernacchi. Although adversarial, these schools combined to bring the art of singing to such an unprecedented level of perfection that we still refer to this epoch as the Golden Age of Bel Canto.

It is an interesting twist of fate that two young boys from Palermo, Sicily, born within a year of each other, both moved north in a quest to make their fortune, and achieved so much more than anyone thought possible. It is a testament to their enormous gifts and perseverance that they were able to alter the course of their art to such a degree. It would seem that Alessandro Scarlatti (1660–1725) was destined to become the foremost opera composer of his generation, and Antonio Pistocchi (1659–1726), the most famous singing teacher of his generation.

Scarlatti and Bel Canto

Scarlatti was the son of a Sicilian tenor, and when things became even more difficult than usual as a result of a horrendous famine, the family decided to move north to Rome. Scarlatti arrived in Rome in 1672, where he furthered his musical education studying with Carissimi. In 1678, at the age of eighteen he married Antonia Maria Anzaloni, a Roman girl who would eventually present him with ten children, including their son, Domenico Scarlatti, a master of the harpsichord, and an outstanding composer.

Alessandro's first opera *Gli equivoci nel Sembiante* was produced in Rome in 1679 when Scarlatti was only eighteen. The work was so successful that it not only established him as a composer of considerable originality and promise, but also secured the patronage of Queen Christina of Sweden who was then residing in Rome. Queen Christina became his great champion at a time when he desperately needed one. She not only appointed him as Her Majesty's Maestro di Cappella, but her patronage and strong advocacy ensured a number of other commissions. This would not have been easy, because Scarlatti was persona non-grata with the Catholic Church, the biggest employer of artists and musicians. The Church was not happy that his sister had been conducting an affair with a priest. The young Scarlatti was grateful for the Queen's help and honoured her with his opera *L'honesta negli Amori* (1680). This arrangement, which produced a number of major works including several operas, lasted until 1684 when Scarlatti was appointed to the prestigious position of Maestro di Cappella to the Viceroy of Naples.

Scarlatti's appointment was controversial, simply because there was strong evidence that it was politically motivated. Especially suspicious, was the fact that it occurred simultaneously with the promotion of his brother Francesco to the position of first violin of the Vice Royal Orchestra. It was later revealed that their sister Melchiorra, who was a lovely soprano in her own right, was the mistress of Don Giovanni de Leone, the Secretary of Justice to the viceroy. Everything points to the fact that it was her influence that provided the much needed patronage for her brothers' rise to prominence. That notwithstanding, it would be a brave person today who would suggest that Scarlatti was not the right man for the position. It is worth recalling that Dent declares that Scarlatti as not only one of the most influential opera composers of his generation, but rather as one of the most important composer in the entire history of opera. He provided the bridge between that early pioneering generation and the Golden Age that follows, which was dominated by Handel, Porpora, Vinci, Rossi and Hasse [Dent in Groves, 1973: 449].

Scarlatti wrote over forty operas in Naples, most of which were either performed at Court or the Teatro San Bartolomeo: he remained there until 1702. For sixteen years his main preoccupation was producing operas either for the Royal theatre San Bartolomeo, or for the court at the Royal Palace. Scarlatti was very busy and very much in demand, a situation that led to short cuts and by his lofty standards, inferior work. By 1702 he was disillusioned and disappointed. Consequently, he saw his departure from Naples as a blessing. He was aware that he had not been maximising his creativity and that his personal musical standards had been lowered. There were good reasons for this: he was in constant demand and had to deliver new works just to satisfy his masters, but also there were financial difficulties which were the result of unpaid remuneration. The other reason for his departure was the unforeseen political change due to the Spanish war of succession, which made the political situation unstable and his personal position less secure and more intolerable. Scarlatti moved to Florence where over the next two years he wrote four operas for the Medici court. As successful as these operas were, they failed to produce the hoped for permanent appointment at the Florentine court. Consequently, he left for Rome where he attained an appointment with Cardinal Pietro Ottobene, who was also responsible for his appointment as

Maestro di Cappella at Santa Maria Maggiore in 1907. In Rome, he was elected as a member of the Arcadian Academy.

The following year found Scarlatti in Venice where he supervised the staging of two of his grand operas especially produced for the Venetian Festival. The first was *Il Trionfo della Liberta,* and the second was *Il Mitridate Eupatore*, which is still considered one of his best works.

The political situation having being resolved, it was almost inevitable that Scarlatti would be lured back to Naples, the scene of his earliest and greatest successes, but not before negotiating a far better contract than his previous one.

Now at the peak of his creative power and famed throughout Europe, Scarlatti produced work of great brilliance such as *Tigrane* (1715), which although less interesting than his later operas was nonetheless effective. In many respects, his later works such as *Il Triofo dell'onore* (1718), *Telemaco* (1718), *Marco Attilio Regalo* (1719), and *La Griselda* (1721), were the product of 'a leisured man mellowed by success, not the hurried output of one struggling to retain the favour of his patrons at any sacrifice of artistic ideals' [Dent in Groves, 1973: 448].

This is especially evident in his later operas in which Scarlatti further developed the ternary form of the aria and generated a more sophisticated harmonic structure through the increased usage of chromatic passages.He also developed the size of the orchestra, and enhanced its importance through a more sophisticated orchestration, especially through the bolder use of the strings, and more innovative use of the woodwinds. Finally, he expanded the range of the human voice both in the high and lower register, whilst simultaneously increasing the vocal dynamic range and expanding its coloratura capabilities.

Dent declares that no composer did more than Scarlatti to establish Neapolitan opera, and I agree. He has deservedly been called the father of Neapolitan Opera, and it appears to me that this 'sobriquet' is not at all exaggerated.

However, his contribution did not end there, as he did a great deal for music composition by teaching and influencing Porpora, Hasse, Hayden and his own son Domenico Scarlatti. He influenced music in general and singing in particular through his work with the students at the conservatorium of Santo Anofrio. Scarlatti's music and style left a huge imprint on Naples, one that no young composer could escape. There is also much evidence suggesting that Scarlatti helped Porpora and other composers with the staging of their early operas at the San Bartolomeo. In this way, Scarlatti nurtured the next generation of Neapolitan composers.Porpora went on to become one of the most influential opera composers, and certainly the singing teacher not only of the next generation, but also the 18th century.

Antonio Pistocchi and Bel Canto

Antonio Pistocchi (1659–1726) was a singer composer and librettist. He was born in Palermo, Sicily. His father was a violinist, and having attained a position as a musician attached to the Cathedral, the family moved north to Bologna. He was a child prodigy both as a singer and a composer, and by the age of five his precocious gifts had brought him to the attention of both the Grand Duke of Tuscany and the Cardinal-Legate of Bologna. His first compositions 'Capricci Puerili' were published when Pistocchi was only eight years old. He was also a vocal prodigy. From all accounts, his voice was a remarkably beautiful boy soprano, and it was at this stage that he began singing in the Cathedral choir with his father. It certainly helped to give the boy a wonderful foundation not only in voice but also in harmony. Unfortunately, neither he nor his father seem to have taken Cathedral duties too seriously as they spent most of their time playing and singing in second rung theatres and courtly houses all over the countryside. It would not come as a surprise to anyone who was aware of the degenerate lifestyle led by many travelling musicians at this time, that in due course through some unfortunate and unforeseen circumstance the young Pistocchi lost his beautiful soprano voice, leaving him no choice but to concentrate on composition.

The problem was that at this point in time composition was not a lucrative profession and having experienced the freedom, the fun, and the good life on tour with his father. Pistocchi would not easily have become accustomed to a more disciplined and less opulent lifestyle. Consequently, as predicted, he made a failed attempt to return to the stage as a singer. It was probably at this stage that he realised that if he wanted to be an artist of consequence he would have to obtain a serious technique that would allow him to perform consistently to the levels dictated by his naturally prodigious talent. This would require a level of discipline that he had not been able to master hitherto.

This failure seemed to be the necessary spark for him to develop his gifts.Finally, the disciplined and assiduous work seemed to pay dividends and he emerged from the musical wilderness as a wonderful and mature contralto, allowing him to forge an international career and refine the art vocal art. Antonio Pistocchi endowed the vocal art with a level of musicianly virtuosity and refinement that had hitherto being missing in the Italian school. Having found his voice and fulfilled his promise, Pistocchi became one of the outstanding castrato contraltos of his generation. Tosi regarded him very highly, believing him to be the possessor of a great voice and inimitable taste.

He became Maestro di Cappella for the Duke of Ansbach from 1696–1700, after which he founded a singing school in Bologna. His ideas on voice would prove both influential and enduring, coming down from generation to generation through Bernacchi and his students, Carestini, Senesino, Mancini and are still influential today.

To proclaim Pistocchi as the founder of the Bolognese school is to do him an injustice. Pistocchi was much more than that. He was not only a great singer and composer, but a far-sighted genius who recognised the need for a school of singing built on sound empirical principles and capable of systematically addressing the emerging problems and technical difficulties spawned by the new generation of operatic composers. He understood in a way that most did not that, if the Italian School were to achieve greatness, it should develop not only technical skill and dexterity, but also elegance, refinement and emotional expression. In this respect, he was very forward looking, seeing way beyond his own generation, and anticipating the post Scarlatti era of composers which included Hasse, Porpora and above all, Georg Handel. These post Scarlatti composers wrote music of considerable sophistication, deploying a greater vocal and dynamic range, combined with greater musical complexity and character development. Their operas were at an altogether a greater level of difficulty than anything written by their predecessors.

Pistocchi's vocal ideals remained the quest for beauty of tone, vocal control (through the breath), agility and ornamentation. An excellent technician, he combined an instrumental virtuosity (mainly influenced by strings) with singing of inimitable taste and refinement. These qualities soon catapulted him into the first rank of international singing teachers, the corollary of which was to cement the reputation of the Bolognese school as the most influential in Europe. The only school to seriously rival it was the Neapolitan School of Nicola Porpora, which will be addressed in the next section.

Pistocchi's immediate successors were his most successful students, including Antonio Bernacchi, Antonio Pasi, Annibali Pio Fabri, and Domenico Gizzi, many of whom further developed and disseminated his principles throughout Europe. The most influential and respected contributors were the scholars Padre Martini, and Antonio Bernacchi who taught Carestini and Senesino, other contributors were the mezzo soprano castrato Domenico Gizzi who taught the famous castrato Gizziello, and many others. Their collective influence was immense: Padre Martini, especially, was one of the most respected and beloved musical scholars of the age, and Bernacchi taught not only Senesino, Carestini, and Antonio Raff, but significantly, he also taught Giambattista Mancini, whose *Riflessione sul canto Figurato* was not only the most influential book of its generation, but remains so even today. The tenor Bernardo Mengozzi, who under the guidance of Cherubini wrote the controversial but still influential *Method du Chant* for the Paris Conservatoire also made a vital contribution.

In addition, we can say that the two Sicilian boys who migrated north for the purpose of making their fortune, certainly managed to do much more than that: they left an indelible mark on the history of opera and singing. Their influence went far beyond their own remarkable careers.Scarlatti left an indelible influence on Nicola Porpora in Naples, whilst Pistocchi did the same for Antonio Bernacchi in Bologna. The result was the creation of the two finest singing schools of the age. The Bolognese and Neapolitan Schools combined to produce the greatest singers of the era, an epoch that undoubtedly represents the zenith of the first Golden Age of Bel Canto.

History would confirm that Antonio Bernacchi was destined to become one of the greatest teachers of the 18th century. Unfortunately for him, one of his contemporaries was even better, and that teacher was Nicola Porpora who is widely regarded as the finest singing teacher of all time. I certainly concur with Christiansen when he states that Porpora was 'indisputably the greatest singing teacher of the eighteenth century' [Christiansen, 1995: 22]. And I would remind my reader that there are many who would argue that Porpora was the greatest singing teacher of all time. As Henry Pleasants puts it, 'he was irascible, difficult and even exasperating, but there has never been a teacher who produced such an array of legendary singers, ranging from castrati such as Farinelli, Caffarelli, Porporino, Appiani, Salimbeni, and female sopranos such as Caterina Gabrielli, and Regina Mingotti, to the great Basso Antonio Mantagna', to name but a few [Pleasants, 1983: 66]. And if this were not enough, he was also a serious competitor for the affection of the English public along with that great creative genius George Frederick Handel. Let me hasten to add that Porpora did not possess the creative genius of Handel, but he was a very good composer.His influence not only on the above listed singing students, but also on the composer Joseph Hayden, and the librettist Pietro Antonio Metastasio (1698–1782) was very great indeed. A close analysis of Porpora's career reveals a remarkable man of music and song, who was one of the forces of nature of his generation: a generation that included Vivaldi, Bach, Handel, Vinci, Leo and Hasse. All of contributed significantly to the Second Golden Age of Bel Canto, which coincided with the rise of the castrato voice.

Chapter 4

Nicola Porpora
and the Neapolitan School

Porpora was the giant of eighteenth century Italian opera and vocal pedagogy. I like Frank Walker's sobriquet of Nicola Porpora, which suggests that 'he was the greatest singing teacher amongst composers and the greatest composer amongst singing teachers' [Groves, 1973: 1879]. Some people think that this was not much of a compliment, but when you consider that at that time almost all teachers were also composers, it puts it in perspective. Porpora may have been an irascible old man, but following in Scarlatti's footsteps he along with Pergolesi, Durante, Jomelli and Cimarosa was one of the geniuses responsible for elevating the Neapolitan school to international prominence. More specifically, Porpora was responsible for the formation of some of the greatest singers in vocal history. Whilst most of his operas have been forgotten, his achievements as a vocal pedagogue have become legendary, as evinced by the mythical status of many of his students. Singers like Farinelli, Caffarelli, Porporino, Salimbeni, Mingotti, Gabrielli, Hasse, Hayden and Metastasio who are still household names. They were the superstars of late Baroque, men and women who have been vested with the glow of mythology.

Nicola Porpora was born in Naples in 1686, and studied with Greco and later with Scarlatti. He was the son of Carlo Porpora, a bookseller and Caterina di Costanzo. At the age of ten he was enrolled as a paying student to the conservatorium of *Gesu Christo dei Poveri*, but by the third year the family fell on hard times and was no longer in a position to support him financially. Porpora therefore joined a program that was created for gifted boys whose families lacked the means to pay fees.

His first opera *Aggripina* (1708) was produced at the Royal Palace, Naples, and was repeated a few days later at the Teatro San Bartolomeo. His next two Operas *Flavio Anicio Olibrio* (1711), and *Basilio re d'oriente* (1713), were both produced at Naples and these performances were almost certainly authorised by Alessandro Scarlatti who had a virtual monopoly on the Teatro San Bartolomeo. His next opera *Arianna e Teseo* was performed at the Court Theatre in Vienna in 1714 and repeated there in 1717.

In July 1715 Porpora was appointed Maestro of the *Conservatorio di Sant'Onofrio*. He was also giving singing lessons to private students and such was his success that he quickly gained a reputation as being unrivalled throughout Europe [Groves, 1973: 876]. This was also the period in which he affirmed himself as a major opera composer not only in Italy but also throughout Europe and later England.

From 1726 to 1731 Porpora established himself in Venice, where he not only produced a number of successful operas but was also appointed to the position of Maestro do Cappella for the *Ospedale degli Incurabile*.

In 1733, he was called to London to establish and act as principal composer for, a new company called the 'Opera of the Nobility'. He built a formidable company, which was led by his former student Farinelli. The results were majestic! For a time, the 'Opera of the Nobility' did not just rival Handel's company but actually surpassed it. Time, however, would prove that this kind of rivalry would ruin both companies, simply because there was insufficient audience to support them.

George Frederick Handel (1685–1759), German by birth, Italian in style and English by adoption, was certainly the greatest composer of the period, and one of the greatest composers of all time. He eventually vanquished Porpora as a composer, but there was nothing he could do to mitigate Porpora's superiority with respect to the art of singing. When it came to singing, Porpora had no rivals.

Unfortunately, Porpora left no written documentation, barring some vocalizzi and of course his operas and oratorios. Consequently, we have no direct knowledge of how the Neapolitan School managed to become so dominant. However, some important elements of his brilliant technique may be deciphered from other people's writings (such as those of Agricola), his own compositions and vocalises, the breathing exercises he reputedly gave his students, and the embodiment of his teaching, which resided in his students.

What we discover from an analysis of the above documentation is that his technique, is first and foremost founded on an excellent command of breathing, vocal emission, articulation and resonance, registration and ornamentation. His emphasis on the importance of breathing was matched only by his vehemence in inculcating the other pillars of the Italian School, especially articulation, pronunciation, and resonation, not to mention register blending and messa di voce. Agricola informs us that amongst Porpora's many accomplishments as a singing teacher, was 'his insistence on clear and correct pronunciation' [Agricola, 1757: 81].

Let us review some of his breathing technique; Cappelletto, Farinelli's biographer states clearly, that

> the foundation of Porpora's Neapolitan School was built first, second and always, on a great emphasis on the art of breathing: to learn the art of dilating the chest and renewing the breath was highly prized. The castrati assumed a rigorous regime of breathing exercises intended to develop the chest and lungs to exceptional dimensions. Farinelli was certainly a great example of this philosophy and technique [Cappelletto, 1995: 9].

According to tradition, Porpora provided Farinelli respiratory exercises that were built on a cycle of inspiration, suspension and expiration, and will be further examined below. We also know through his compositions and vocalises, and through the demands he made on his students, including Farinelli and Caffarelli, that Porpora was a perfectionist with respect to the human voice. Finally, we should note that notwithstanding the fact that many of his students possessed very extensive vocals range, it is significant that his compositions are primarily centred on the medium/mixed voice. This is proof positive that Porpora, in common with many other singers and singing teachers before and after him, believed that the middle/mixed register is the spiritual home of the voice.

Let us elaborate on each of these points.

The first thing to note about these breathing exercises is that they are progressive and that Porpora designed them to achieve breath capacity and control. Miller informs us 'that notwithstanding the lack of written historical corroboration, tradition maintains that Farinelli daily practised the following exercises for long periods of time' [Miller, 1986: 31].

The exercises referred to are a cyclical breathing drill with an inspiratory phase, a suspension phase and an expiratory phase. Each phase is performed silently, with open lips and glottis and free of undue tension either in the vocal tract or the thorax region.

The inspiratory phase consists of a complete but unforced expansion of the ribs, the umbilical/epigastric area and the lumbar region. We achieve this whilst inhaling for five seconds.

The suspension phase consists of retaining the expanded position of the rib cage, the umbilical epigastric area, and the lumbar area, which anchors down the diaphragm. This should be achieved without either adding to the breath or exhaling.

The exhalation phase consists of trying to retain the inspiratory position established during the suspension phase, that is, the relatively high sternum, the expansion of the rib cage and the umbilical/epigastric region as well as the lumbar region. These should not move substantially until the very end of the cyclic phase or phrase.

The exercise grows exponentially in difficulty as an additional second is joined to each phase of the cycle.

Consequently, we begin by inhaling for five seconds, suspending for five seconds, exhaling for five seconds, followed by inhaling for six seconds, suspending for six seconds, exhaling for six seconds; this is followed by inhaling for seven seconds and so on up to twelve seconds or more.

The last phase is designed to maintain the inspiratory position as long as possible without depressing the ribcage, which would automatically draw the diaphragm in an ascending excursion and lead to a total collapse of breath control.

Finally, I should report that Carlo Vitale (2000) in the preface to his publication of Farinelli's letters describes his daily study routine. According to Vitale, in addition to his musical, literary and vocal studies, Farinelli performed wore a lead vest around his thorax whilst performing important physical exercises that were designed to build his breathing muscles and organs [Vitali, 2000: 50].

Porpora believed that silent breathing exercises he could train and strengthen Farinelli's respiratory musculature without tiring the voice. Miller states some teachers attribute Farinelli's outstanding breath control and ability to renew breath silently and imperceptibly to these exercises [Miller, 1986: 31].

Porpora's vocalises provide us with further indications about his teaching methods. These were designed to stretch and develop the breathing apparatus, establish a seamless legato line, and rehearse the twin pillars of bel canto, agility and cantabile (sostenuto). Some passages in Porpora's operas are long and complicated, and display a blend of agility, bravura and cantabile passages far beyond the capacity of all but the greatest singers of the twentieth century.

The above evidence reveals a methodical, strict and unrelentingly disciplined training technique that was strictly enforced through well-established principles and techniques. Porpora was never one to pander to his students: he insisted on an increasingly progressive interpretation of the same or similar exercises year after year, simply because they achieved his goal. He knew that in order to overcome certain defects you were required to constantly practise particular passages [Blom in Groves, 1973: 802].

It is well established that Porpora was a difficult personality, but I am not sure whether he was naturally unpleasant or whether he was just a hard taskmaster. We do know, however, that he was definitely uncompromising in his principles and standards, and unrelenting in his drive to greatness. It is well documented that he kept Caffarelli on the same page of vocal exercises for six years, at which time, legend has it, that Caffarelli summoned the courage to ask the master whether he might start working on a song, a request that Porpora ignored. By the end of that year he surprised Caffarelli by saying,

'Go, my son, you have no more to learn. You are the first singer of Italy and of the world' [Pleasants, 1983: 67]. According to Henry Pleasants, he had spoken the truth, because soon Caffarelli would indeed be recognised as the finest singer in Europe.

It is interesting to note that Porpora never altered his opinion with respect to Caffarelli's singing; to the very end, even though he became increasingly aware of the flaws in his character, he maintained that Caffarelli was the greatest singer he had ever heard. And this in an era when great singing was heard everywhere, and not least among his own students, including Farinelli (Carlo Broschi), Regina Mingotti, and Caterina Gabrielli and many other legendary students. If in the long run, Farinelli undoubtedly outstripped Caffarelli's achievement as an artist, but this does not indicate that Porpora was wrong in his assessment of the two great singers. It is simply a reminder that there is much more to being a great artist than being a great singer. From a vocal point of view, I am reluctant to question Porpora's judgement, but I remain convinced that in the end it is how you conduct yourself and manage your career that makes all the difference. The fact remains that Farinelli epitomises 'the castrato par excellence', the embodiment of Porpora's teaching, and the measure by which all other singers are judged.

I like Heriot's contrasting and clear description of these giants of singing. He states that Farinelli remains widely recognised as the greatest singer of all time, and Caffarelli was undoubtedly his greatest rival. I must emphasise that, in my view, it would be wrong to underestimate Caffarelli's singing just because in later life he became a highly dislikeable character. At his best, Caffarelli was by all accounts a truly great singer, and a worthy rival for Farinelli. His character-flaws tell us an awful lot: the first thing to note is that they certainly proved detrimental to his career, but on the other hand it also reminds us that he must have been an extraordinary singer to persuade managements to suffer his mischievous behaviour.

Let us examine Caffarelli's character and singing.

Caffarelli was born Gaetano Majorano in Bitonto near Bari in 1710, and came from a family of considerable substance. That his parents were well off may be evinced by two anecdotes related to us by Henry Pleasants and John Rosselli respectively. Pleasants suggests that upon her marriage, Majorano's sister was settled with a considerable dowry, and that informs the socio-economic status of the family. On the other hand, John Rosselli contends that Majorano's grandmother pledged 'the income of two vineyards towards his education so that he could study grammar and especially music'. Given the economic strength of the family it is unlikely that they would have sold their son into castration for material gain, as was often the case at that time with more impoverished parents and households. There is no doubt that many of these poor but gifted boys were sold off by unconscionable parents for economic reasons, but that was not the case with Gaetano Majorano's family. In fact, both Pleasants and Rosselli suggest that the strong-willed twelve-year old Majorano may well have driven the decision himself. Rosselli suggests that the young Majorano was determined to study singing, 'to which he is said to have a great inclination, desiring to have himself castrated and become a eunuch' [Rosselli, 1995: 38].

Here is how Heriot describes the character and rivalry of both Farinelli and Caffarelli:

> Caffarelli, the almost exact contemporary and greatest rival of Farinelli, offers, as a man, the most striking contrast imaginable with that great singer. Where Farinelli was gentle, courteous, and unassuming, Caffarelli was capricious, proud, and quarrelsome; Whereas Farinelli was the perfect courtier and confidant to Kings, Caffarelli cared nothing for any man, and his insubordination in an age of flatterers, often landed him in serious trouble. He exhibits, in fact, the perfect type of 'the prima donna temperament', and it is doubtless his career, above all else, that has earned the castrati their reputation for ridiculous and insupportable vanity [Heriot, 1956: 141].

I admire Henry Pleasant's cogent description of the contrasting characters and rivalry of our two major protagonists. I would, however, take this opportunity to add one or two observations of my own. Having examined the cumulative evidence, one can only conclude that over time Caffarelli became a highly dislikeable character, but I don't think we can say that he didn't care for anybody. I think that assessment is too brutal and does not align with the fact that as a young man he seemed to have enjoyed a good relationship with his family and teachers. In fact, the evidence is that Porpora was genuinely fond of him. We can also assume that he got along very well with his family and his grandmother in particular, or she would not have provided the money and resources for his study.

So, I think we can say that Caffarelli was definitely selective with whom he chose to share his better nature. My other observation is that unfortunately for Caffarelli, although his family was reasonably well off, they didn't have a great deal of finesse, or breeding, that sense of refined diplomacy that was second nature to the Farinelli's. Let us recall that Farinelli's father was a senior diplomat and a public figure, and that Farinelli himself would have absorbed much of this behaviour by osmosis. This observation does not diminish the fact that Farinelli was by nature a more refined, softer grained, and more elegant personality that intuitively understood that getting along with people was important. Caffarelli, on the other hand, was an altogether more aggressive, a combative character, who was always ready to fight a duel or get into a heated argument. These are not qualities that would endear our protagonist to anybody.

The more we learn about Caffarelli, the more we realise that once having left Porpora's studio he was almost impossible to teach. On the other hand, Farinelli remained the eternal student. I here refer to two well-documented events that led to major enhancement of Farinelli's performance. The first event was the competitive duel with Antonio Bernacchi, and the second refers to his assimilation of the counsel offered by Emperor Charles VI. Let us elaborate on these events.

The first thing to note is that in terms of natural quality and beauty of tone, not to mention vocal and dynamic range, and flexibility, both Farinelli and Caffarelli would have sung Bernacchi off the stage: their natural gifts were altogether in another league.

The difference between the two artists was that Farinelli not only understood that he could learn something from Bernacchi, but he also had the courage and humility to ask for the knowledge. These were not qualities that we could associate with Caffarelli.

Antonio Bernacchi and Bel Canto

Let us deliberate on Porpora's great contemporary, Antonio Bernacchi and his fabulous career. Bernacchi (1685–1756) was a mezzo soprano castrato who constructed and conducted a spectacular career both as a singer and singing master. His future, however, had not always been so promising or assured. In fact, his voice had been so seriously damaged by inferior teaching that for a time it was very uncertain as to whether he would have a career at all. It was the great Pistocchi who first healed his voice and then gave him the technique that turned him into a legendary singer and teacher. Consequently, the two shared a close relationship and that is probably the reason why Pistocchi later felt that he could reproach his student for what he considered to be an unbridled emphasis on prodigious technique at the expense of sensuousness, beauty of tone, style and emotion. Truth to tell, Bernacchi was only furthering Pistocchi's earlier innovation of executing cadenzas and ornaments in an instrumental manner, but whereas Pistocchi had introduced the notion of imitating the uninterrupted legato line of stringed instruments, Bernacchi now went further by imitating the acrobatic pyrotechnics of flutes and oboes. Pistocchi is alleged to have chastised his former student with the following rebuke: 'Tristo a me, Io t'ho insegnato a cantare, e tu vuoi suonare' (Sad am I because I taught you how to sing, and all you want to do is play).

The above anecdote notwithstanding, Bernacchi's greatness within his chosen paradigm remains unassailable; nor can we deny that 'Bernacchi's character was in general noble and generous, and that historically he is one of the most important singers who ever lived' [Heriot, 1956: 90].

Bernacchi made his debut in Genoa in 1703 and ended by singing successfully throughout Italy and Europe. His was not by nature the most glorious of voices, but with diligent study he obtained an exceptional technique, which allowed him to perform miraculous acrobatics. In 1727, in open competition, he defeated the young Farinelli with a flurry of roulades of uncommon brilliance. He was clearly a singer of great technical virtuosity, but lacked pathos and subtlety, elements that possibly contributed to his failure to conquer all. For instance, when Handel called him to London in 1729 to replace Senesino, Bernacchi failed to please. Burney found his singing artificial.

Farinelli for his part accepted defeat with grace, asking Bernacchi to teach him, a request to which the older man acceded. Bernacchi's school became celebrated throughout Europe and his students include Guarducci, Carestini, Senesino, Raaff, and Gianbattista Mancini. Mancini would produce an enduring legacy far greater than could have been achieved through his own singing by writing down the techniques and precepts of the Bernacchi School. Mancini's book *Riflessione Pratiche sopra Il Canto Figurato,* or Reflections on Figured Singing (1774 enlarged in 1777), went on to become one of the pillars of vocal pedagogy and will be examined in this book through the prism of Rachele Maragliano Mori's glance.

Farinelli was much younger and was not lacking in confidence, but he was extremely intelligent and understood immediately that Bernacchi's coloratura was more sophisticated. He perceived instantly that his execution of agility was more robust and that he was able to generate greater power in his cantabile especially in the middle (mixed) voice, and he was willing to ask for help.

The young Farinelli possessed a genuinely sweet nature, which was imbued with a great deal of humility. These were qualities that easily persuaded the older artist to share his secrets with the younger man. So, Farinelli was the recipient of a vastly superior technique with respect to singing agility in full chest voice, with a more rounded, robust sound than he had previously utilised. Singers had become accustomed to producing a penetrating, substantial tone in the cantabile, but combined this with a finer more lyrical sound for agility. It was quite daring of Bernacchi to introduce an entirely new paradigm for the execution of coloratura and ornamentation.

There is no question that later in his career, when the voice became worn, overtaxed and threadbare, Bernacchi naturally reverted back to his original breathy, veiled sound that he had at the beginning of his studies with Pistocchi. Consequently, he found it difficult to penetrate over an orchestra.

Henry Pleasants describes this development most eloquently:

> It may have been this frailty that prompted Bernacchi to sing his divisions with a full chest voice instead of the lighter head or mixed voice previously considered more suitable for such rapid and florid passages. And it was this devise, presumably, that

enabled him to compete successfully a few years earlier with the younger and more generously endowed Farinelli. The practice was followed by his students, and constituted one of his most important and enduring innovations [Pleasants, 1983: 62].

Recalling that Bernacchi damaged his voice as a young singer makes it easy to agree with Henry Pleasant's notion that it was the lack of purity and brilliance of tone that motivated him to experiment. Even though Bernacchi managed to recover much of his vocal health with Pistocchi's teaching, the truth is that his voice was never quite the same again. Consequently, we can say that his medium, mixed register was always a little breathy, resulting in a dull, opaque, tattered tone that lacked the brilliance (squillo) to carry over an orchestra. It was most probably this lack of brilliance and penetration that led him to adopt the strategy of using a predominantly chest voice, relative to medium and head register in the first place.

Meanwhile, it is almost certain that Bernacchi's more extreme experimentation led to a sense of alienation from his master Pistocchi. Exasperated, Pistocchi chastised him with this legendary epithet quoted above. That Bernacchi was able to forge an international career with a previously damaged instrument and considerable vocal limitations, was quite miraculous and a testament to his willpower. Time, however, would prove that it is too difficult to maintain such giddy heights with a damaged instrument, especially when you have a limited talent and are prone to experimentation. In these circumstances, you need to be at your best all the time to compensate for natures deficiencies, and that is a big burden for any artist to carry.

Soon, the detrimental effect of his inferior vocal instrument and experimentation began to manifest themselves and the critics of the day made it clear that his glory days were indeed short; his voice grew thin, breathy, and lacking in brilliance. These are typically the symptoms of an imperfect glottal adduction, producing a breathy/sound admixture, which prevents the breath flow from being efficiently converted into acoustic energy. It would not be long before his students Senesino and Carestini were preferred over their master. It is almost certain that it was Bernacchi's experimentation with a limited instrument that led to the disapproval of his master as well as his early demise.

It is clear that Bernacchi's experimentation was not just aesthetic but rather born out of a desire to circumvent the problems associated with a damaged voice. It is now well-accepted that repeated vocal fold trauma impacts the epithelium and the superficial layer of the lamina propria (Reinke's space) much more than any of the deep layers of the vocal folds [Hirano, 1988: 5]. In fact, it has been well established that very rarely are these deeper layers, or the body of the vocal folds damaged. Consequently, we can state with confidence that any vocal fold damage is generally confined to the cover, which is prone to scarring, rather than either the vocal ligaments or the body of the vocal folds (thyroarytenoid). In conclusion, we can say that this scarring of the tissue prevented a firm closure of the vocal fold tissue, impairing agility, soft singing and excess to the head register. In the circumstances, the vocal bands do not adduct properly, resulting in a breathy, dull sound lacking in brilliance.

In the end, adopting a predominantly chest voice (thyroarytenoid dominant) production would have been an easy decision for Bernacchi. There was a precedent for this strategy in the writings of Caccini, Peri and many early Italian writers who believed that nobility of tone could not be attained from falsetto.

Bernacchi discovered that concentrating his efforts on the chest voice he would not only avoid the problems with the passaggio into head register, but would also attain a cleaner, rounder, more brilliant sound in the medium (mixed) voice.

This rounder, fuller sound, which was a predominantly vocalis muscle production (chest voice strategy), that Bernacchi's gifted to Farinelli. It was an indication of the magnitude of his genius that Farinelli adapted the strategy in such a way that it became uniquely his. He balanced the chest register with a seamless passaggio into head register (voce complete), the technique taught him by Porpora. This allowed him to take advantage of Bernacchi's chest register technique whilst maintaining the equilibrium of the instrument, which allowed him to sing a three-octave range with refined dynamics and virtuosic agility, with easy access into head voice.It is a credit to him that he was able to maintain this well into old age.

The next event to consider is Charles VI chastising Farinelli for his extraordinary but unrelenting feats of vocal acrobatics clearly aimed at dazzling his audience.

Pleasant's reports that the Emperor Charles the VI Admonished the great singer, 'those gigantic strides, those never-ending notes and passages, only surprise; and it is now time for you to please; you are too lavish with the gifts that nature has endowed you; if you wish to reach the heart you must take a more plain and simple road' [Pleasants, 1983: 74]. These few words, and the pause for reflection they caused, were sufficient to change Farinelli's entire manner of singing. From this period on, he adopted a more moving and expressive style aimed at reaching the heart of his listener rather than dazzling them with acrobatics. This was a change with far reaching consequences not only for Farinelli but also, because he was such an influential figure, for the art of singing in general.

These events and the effect they had on Farinelli inform us that this was not a singer who was ego driven, but rather an artist who, along with many other great artists, was always in a state of becoming. He knew intuitively that seeking clarity as a means of improving his craft meant respect for learning and developing. He was a genuine artist who understood in a way that Caffarelli never could that the art is more important than the individual, and that artists should act like a High Priest in the service of art. The attitude and dedication, not just the vocal gifts, were probably the defining differences between Farinelli and Caffarelli.

Before examining the most salient and elements of Porpora's vocal technique it may be interesting to explore the musical environment of the Neapolitan school during the Baroque period.

Chapter 5

The Naples of Caffarelli and Farinelli

Roberto de Simone provides us with a very good description of the Neapolitan environment that produced these great singers and musicians. He explains that the musical world of the Baroque in Naples was essentially built around the four conservatoriums, *Santa Maria di Loreto, Santo Anofrio, I Poveri di Gesú Christo,* and *La Pietá dei Turchini.*

These institutions were a great idea, and founded by people with a compassionate heart for the sole purpose of helping children that were less fortunate than their own. The talent they produced was and remains unique in the annals of music and singing. But that does not reflect the hardships that these students had to undergo in order to achieve their objectives. Not that the people in charge were cruel or even unkind, on the contrary, they did the best they could with very scant resources. Life was hard for the Neapolitans at that time, and conditions were primitive and difficult. The dormitory was overcrowded, and the tiny, simple beds doubled as a settee during the day. The common rehearsal room was totally inadequate with too many students playing different instruments very loudly in the same space at the same time. The food was what the institutions could afford and certainly edible but not always nutritious. What is remarkable, given the conditions of their lives, was how these boys were able to achieve such majestic results. These boys really earned their greatness; it was not offered on a platter. Anyone with a sense of justice would be thrilled that some of them became legendary figures in their chosen profession.

De Simone continues:

> These conservatoriums were founded by certain pious individuals interested in rescuing young people who had been abandoned by their families or were orphaned as a result of plagues or other natural disasters. These boys were taught music, and in particular singing, which provided them with a source of employment in churches and private residences. It also allowed them to perform at funeral ceremonies, carnival parties and at other occasions where they would sing to an instrumental accompaniment [de Simone, 2004].

It is clear from the above that there was great demand for music in Naples during the Baroque era. Unlike the German school, which developed in a more instrumental symphonic form, the Neapolitan school privileged the theatrical and vocal aspects of music, which were best expressed in operas and oratorios. As a result, the singing schools of the Neapolitan conservatories flourished, producing the greatest castrati and composers of the age.

Riccardo Muti, the international conductor who graduated from the St Pietro a Majiella Conservatorium, informs us that the Neapolitan world of the four conservatoriums which educated these children was also responsible for producing outstanding artists such as Durante, Porpora, Leo, Jomelli, Cimarosa, Paisiello, Pergolesi, Spontini and other singers of a similar calibre. He elaborates:

> These children wandered the streets ... Each conservatorium dressed differently to distinguish them from the other schools. Some wore white, or had turquoise sleeves, or wore blue caps. And they walked the streets begging for alms, going to funerals and ceremonies, and all of Naples resounded to the songs of these lads, some of whom grew up to become Caffarelli, or Farinelli, the great singers who graced the courts of all of Europe [Muti, 2004].

Muti explains that Naples always was and remains a very theatrical city, and consequently, it is not surprising that it took the operatic form to its heart:

> Naples is to this day a city theatre. Every corner of the old historical Naples, that is, the Naples of Pergolesi and Scarlatti and other great composers, reminds one of a city theatre. This theatricality has never changed, and remains embodied in the music of these composers. This typically Neapolitan theatricality is certainly present in the sublime and melancholic melodies of Pergolesi. Theatricality here does not mean spectacle or triviality: it is a gesture which becomes action, a gesture that expresses something. [Muti, 2004].

Muti explains that in this sense the whole world is theatre, and that in this theatrical world Naples remains more theatrical than any other city on earth.

I think there is no better way of introducing Farinelli, arguably the greatest singer of all time, than by allowing the present representative of that fabled tradition, Riccardo Muti, to describe the city and its broader social and musical environment in which he began his career.

Farinelli is a perfect example of an artist who revolutionised his art without ever intending to do so; his singing was simply a manifestation of his personal greatness. Collectively, these artists- Farinelli, Caffarelli, Porpora, Metastasio, Pistocchi, Bernacchi, Carestini, and the composers Hass and Handel - represent the evolution of vocal music, vocal pedagogy and the composition of opera in the Baroque.

In returning to Farinelli, we can say with confidence that when an artist of the stature and genius of a Farinelli emerges, he influences not only his immediate art, but also music making in general, including composition. He demonstrated through his art what was possible by transcending the prevailing practice of his day. Several disparate eighteenth-century writers including Metastasio, Mancini, Goudar and Burney identify Farinelli as the inspirational catalyst who propelled vocal music towards a new florid style of composition and who established performance characteristics which, especially after 1730, came to be increasingly associated with *Opera Seria*. This further evinces the notion of evolution and of interdependence between the creative and performing artists, and how one can influence the other.

The most representative artist of this period of *bel canto*, that is, the First Golden Age, is undoubtedly Carlo Broschi, better known as Farinelli. Let us look at his life and art as an example of what the great castrati could ultimately achieve.

Farinelli, Carlo Broschi

Coming from an entirely superior background, Farinelli was a very different character to most of the boys who were castrated at the time in order to satisfy the demand from the church for high male voices. In this way, as we saw above, there were certain similarities between Farinelli and Caffarelli, the main one being that they came from families that were quite well off. This was dramatically different to the majority of boys who underwent castration with the objective of improving their socio-economic status.

Farinelli came from a noble family, his father holding the post of Royal Viceroy at Maretea and Cisternino between 1706 and 1709. Salvatore Broschi was also a fine musician, and was probably responsible for Farinelli's early training, which was later completed by Porpora. It is rumoured that the Broschi family may have fallen on difficult times as a consequence of a scandal created by Salvatore Broschi, and that it was this desperate search for an amelioration of fortune that led to recognition that Farinelli's talent may well be the means to restore the family's fortunes.

What we do know is, that in spite all the controversies, Farinelli's breeding and character came through not only in his art but also in his private life. Farinelli possessed many extraordinary qualities, including an excellent character, generosity of spirit, refinement and elegance, all lauded by commentators and contemporary colleagues alike.

Farinelli remained respectful and cognisant of Porpora, but according to Carlo Vitali, this recognition never translated into genuine affection. Farinelli, however, felt a responsibility towards his old master, and on many occasions, when Porpora became impecunious, he would send him money. This was generous, but not unusual for the period. There was an unwritten covenant that if you were one of the lucky youngsters to make it in a big way, you would never forget the people who helped you to achieve fame and fortune. Consequently, the ones who were lucky enough to achieve great success were generous in their recognition, often even changing their names in honour of their teachers or patrons (as with Porporino and Giziello).

Your mentors were acknowledged to have given you a blueprint to success, sharing their lifetime's work and dedication, and nurturing you in your time of need. The great artists of every generation have always known this, and history is replete with their generous acknowledgement of the men and women who have helped them achieve the greatness of which they were capable. Porpora was undoubtedly an irascible old man, but his students never forgot that he was a force of nature when they most needed it.

Vitali continues the Porpora story by vividly describing Farinelli's training regime. He emphasises that Porpora would impose as much discipline on his students as was commensurate with their discernible talent. For the young Carlo Broschi, the curriculum consisted of daily exercises on a dozen or so solfeggi designed to acquire the technique of clean emission and true intonation. This regime continued for the first year, at which time it was deemed that he had acquired the basics of vocal technique and could now move forward to a further four-year course designed to perfect his unique talent. This included of musical theory, sight reading, interpretation, expressive mime, poetic and dramatic literature, and physical exercises, which we may recall were performed with lead weights designed to strengthen the chest, and gain control over respiration [Vitali, 2000: 50–51].

Having completed Porpora's programme at the age of seventeen, Farinelli was finally ready to make his debut in the serenade *Angelica e Medoro* composed by Porpora to a text by one of his other students, Pietro Metastasio, who would soon become the foremost librettist of the 18th century. The whole enterprise was a great success, but the sensation of the evening was definitely Farinelli. Soon he would vanquish a particularly talented and powerful trumpet player in a musical duel and in the process evinced his extraordinary breathing prowess, taking the first step towards his legendary status.

The story of Farinelli's duel with the trumpet has been told and retold many times. This version comes to us from Burney's history:

> After severally swelling a note, in which each manifested the power of his lungs, and tried to rival the other in brilliancy and force, they had both a swell and shake together, by thirds, which was continued so long, while the audience eagerly awaited the event, that both seemed to be exhausted; and, in fact, the trumpeter, wholly spent, gave it up…when Farinelli, with a smile on his countenance … broke out all at once in the same breath, with fresh vigour, and not only swelled and shook the note, but ran the most rapid and difficult divisions.

Farinelli himself recalls the great attention paid to breathing in his training, but he does not give many details about the exercises. His influence, in any case, remains enormous. He demonstrated what was humanly possible and in the process provided us with a glimpse into our own potential. Giambattista

Mancini in his book of *Riflessione* (1774–1777) also makes much of Farinelli's breathing and singing:

> The art of knowing how to conserve and take in the breath with reserve and neatness, without ever becoming noticeable to anyone, began and ended with him; very perfect intonation, spinning out the voice and swelling the voice, his portamento, the unity, the surprising agility, his singing to the heart and his gracious manner and perfect and rare trill, were all equal excellences in him…His voice was considered surprising because perfect, strong and sonorous in its quality, and rich in its range from the deepest low notes to the high, the equal of which has not been heard in our time [Mancini, 1776: 46].

Quantz, in his description of Farinelli's singing also refers to his extraordinary breath control. He describes his singing as having the following characteristics: 'the voice was (a) penetrating, full, rich, bright and a well-modulated soprano … his intonation was pure, his trill beautiful, his breath control extraordinary and his throat very agile' [Quantz in Christiansen, 1995: 22].

Farinelli achieved these fabled results by performing silent breathing exercises every day and for long periods of time. He believed that he could train the musculature responsible for breathing without tiring the voice. Some teachers, according to Miller, attribute Farinelli's outstanding breath control and ability to renew breath silently and imperceptibly to these exercises [Miller, 1986: 31].

Farinelli is a perfect example of an artist who revolutionised his art without ever intending to do so; his singing was simply a manifestation of his personal greatness. Collectively, these artists (Farinelli, Porpora, Metastasio and others) represent the evolution of vocal music, vocal pedagogy and the composition of opera. When an artist of the stature and genius of a Farinelli emerges, he influences not only his immediate art, but also music making in general, including composition. He demonstrated through his art what was possible by transcending the prevailing practice of his day. Several disparate 18th century writers including Metastasio, Mancini, Goudar and Burney identify Farinelli as the inspirational catalyst who propelled vocal music towards a new florid style of composition and who established performance characteristics which, especially after 1730, came to be increasingly associated with *opera seria*. This further evinces the notion of evolution and of interdependence between the creative and performing artists, and how one can influence the other.

Summary and Analysis of the Porpora Method

I have demonstrated that whilst Porpora left no written documentation regarding his teaching, there are a number of secondary sources such as biographers and other researchers ready to attest to the importance he placed on breathing, and his insistence on clear and correct pronunciation. The results attained by his students were so spectacular that they leave no room for speculation. I believe we can assume that his students must have been very well drilled not only vocally but also with respect to renewing, conserving and dosing out the breath for a considerable time (breath management). Tradition tells us that his students resorted not only to breathing exercises but also to physical exercises to strengthen the chest and thorax muscles. Agricola contends that Porpora's concentration on pronunciation (i.e. articulation and resonation) was the equal of his emphasis on breathing. It is also clear from the sound his students produced that there was considerable subglottal pressure and a concomitant glottal resistance, leading to a penetrating, brilliant, powerful and rounded sound. We also know that the full breath practised by his students must have been connected to a lowering of the diaphragm, leading to a comfortably low larynx, and a round and full tone. These sounds were accompanied by evenness in the vibrancy of tone and consistency of resonance. Porpora also insisted on agility, ornamentation and above all *messa di voce*, all of which must have originated with great breath control and glottal resistance

Bruno and Paperi believe that it has always been so. Even if we confine ourselves to an analysis of some of Tosi's strategies or even Mancini's for that matter, we still encounter many of today's problems, which are generally informed by our habitual and stylistic characteristics, and which reflect our many various choices [Bruno & Paperi, 2001: 71].

Conclusion to the First Golden Age of Singing

The first Golden Age of Bel Canto was dominated by the 'poetics of wonder', which was a cultural movement characterised by a sense of wonder, fantasy and other-worldliness. These qualities were privileged over reality. This was also a period dominated by the castrati, whose entire persona and not just their phenomenal voices was tailor made for this broader cultural phenomenon.

For instance, both Tosi (1723) and Mancini (1774) recommend the robust chest so as not to stiffen the muscles of the throat to the detriment of the sound. These authors subscribed to and demonstrated through their work, albeit in a confused manner, the idea that singers should maintain the tonus of the thorax muscles during singing in order to maintain freedom at the laryngeal level. Perfectly valid, in fact, some would say necessary conclusion. If we were to interpret this to the letter today, we could conclude that this is a directive from a teacher to use excessive force, if need be, so as to prevent the collapse of the thorax during the singing of a phrase. They may be some teachers today that would recommend such muscular behaviour. Bruno and Paperi admit in fact, that they have chosen to give this directive the most benevolent expressive interpretation, suggesting that these masters simply want to reinforce the idea of maintaining a certain physical tonus during singing, but with particular emphasis on the thorax [Bruno & Paperi, 2001: 71].

Chapter 6

The Second Golden Age of Bel Canto

Bruno and Paperi believe that we cannot discuss the evolution of bel canto without reference to Rossini, even though his vocality changed considerably over time relative to the demands made in his early operas. Rossini's vocality would renew and revitalise itself from his very first operas, it still represents the final manifestation of the bel canto of the 18th century, as proclaimed by both his predecessors and contemporaries. The beginning of Rossini's career was marked by innovation and creativity, and perhaps it is because of his innovations that Rossini's raise to the first rank of composers indicated the beginning of what would become the end of the previous Age of Bel Canto. The Age in which the castrati had reigned supreme, but now Rossini began to break with the past by casting female contraltos in parts that were traditionally sung by castrati, and then enforcing the soprani supremacy whilst bringing into being both the high brilliant tenor (Giovanni David & Giambattista Rubini), and the low baritenor (Andrea Nozzari, Domenico Donzelli and Garcia Peré). We should recall that these were singers of substance whose gifts and sense of aesthetic taste went far beyond trying to stupefy their audiences through the boldness of their performances and the ardour of their interpretation. These singers insisted on using the music's melodic graces, in a manner that not only embellished the phrase, but also added expression, enhancing and nurturing it with their personal vocal colour.

It is clear from the above discussion that we cannot separate the pedagogy from the epoch that spawns it. As we saw above, Rossini quickly substituted the castrato with the contralto voice (often in the lover's parts), and for a number of years maintained a noble musical language, although often a little stylised and hermetic. This represented a style of coloratura, which was associated with instrumental music, a primary element of which was the use four-quarter notes (semiquavers) for each syllable. Bruno and Paperi remind us that we should not be under the misapprehension that the emphasis on coloratura did in anyway indicate the neglect of *canto spianato* [Bruno & Paperi, 2001: 74].

Bruno and Paperi provide us with an excellent account of the changing face and style of bel canto. They give us a wonderfully vivid description of the bel canto characteristics associated with the pre-Rossinian period, before launching into a narration of Rossini's contribution to the Age of Bel Canto, not only musically but also vocally. This was followed by an excellent description of the stylistic requirements of the romantic period. These authors emphasise the difficulty of adapting the pre-Rossinian bel canto style to a more languid, more robust and increasingly more onerous style of 'romantic bel canto' period.

According to Bruno and Paperi the most important characteristics of bel canto are as follows:

> A clean attack, followed by a clear and luminous sound on the breath, combined with a fluid emission, which is both delicate and stimulating. Other important characteristic of bel canto are the use of crescendo and diminuendo, the use of *filato* (spinning) sounds, a refined forte/piano, an elegant legato, a portamento and a pathetic accent that modulate the execution of the 'fioritura' and stylized singing (canto di maniera). These qualities are complemented by an instrumental type agility, which expression, often full of tension is never vulgar or forced, but rather always accompanied by good taste. This produces a sharp and incisive sound quality, and a recitative that is distinctly pronounced but flexible, followed by a free, and clear articulation of the text [Bruno & Paperi, 2001: 74].

Bruno and Paperi emphasise the overall quest for perfection.

According to these authors, in time, Rossini experienced a personal evolution that brought him much closer to the world of French opera, the world of Spontini and Cherubini, an encounter that was marked by mutual and beneficial influence. These French/Italian composers used a more elastic emission, a more imperious declamation, and longer more sustained, bountiful melodies. These were more reminiscent of a style that originated with Gluck, including the use of the baritenor. The historical conditions of singing had changed as a consequence of the discord occurring within the pedagogy of that time. It was at this point that Rossini wrote the composer Giovanni Pacini commenting on the state of the art of music. Rossini declared that 'this art (music) which alone has its foundation in ideals and sentiment cannot be separated from the influence of the times that we live in' [Bruno & Paperi, 2001: 73].

The above historical narrative by Bruno and Paperi only serves to prepare us for the second Golden Age of Bel Canto.

Rossini and the Golden Age of Bel Canto

Celletti declares that the second Golden Age of Bel Canto coincided with the rise of the normal as opposed to the mutilated voice. This occurred at the time when the castrato voice was in decline and the tenor, soprano, and especially the contralto voices were increasingly celebrated. Let us be very clear about what occurred in this time of transition. This was not about audiences losing interest in the castrato voice, or lacking an appreciation of its unique qualities, because that was certainly not the case.

Rossini himself recorded the sensation that these unique vocal sounds had inspired in him. Here is how Rossini described its effect of the castrati on him:

> I have never forgotten them. The purity, the miraculous flexibility of those voices and, above all, their profoundly penetrating accents — all that moved and fascinated me more than I can tell you. I should add that I myself wrote a role for them, one of the last but not the least —Velluti. That was in my opera *Aureliano in Palmira* [Rossini in Osborne, 2007: 13].

According to Osborne, Rossini lamented not only the passing of the castrati as singers but also decried the end of their unparalleled contribution to the teaching of singing.In a conversation with Wagner, he confessed that in his opinion the castrati were incomparable teachers who in connection with the church had 'developed master schools', which, because they produced the finest singers in Europe were not only very prestigious but also very much in demand. Young singers were yearning to gain entry into these institutions. The changing political situation ensured that these master schools were either supressed or replaced by new conservatoires. These new musical institutions developed their own valuable traditions, but in the process failed to preserve the techniques and traditions associated with bel canto [Osborne, 2007: 13–14].

Much of the political backlash was centred on the church's involvement with the controversy raging with respect to the mutilation of thousands of young boys for the purpose of preserving the freshness and uniqueness of their premutated voice. This ensured not only its uniqueness, but also the conservation of its naturally penetrating and thrilling sound.The whole issue was about managing the moral outrage regarding the act of castration, which highlighted the concomitant moral dilemma relating to the prohibition of women singing in church. The notion that the church could morally justify the castration of young boys rather than having women take their rightful place in its musical life was no longer tenable. It was now well accepted that for the last two centuries the church had tacitly condoned the practice. These two moral issues combined to threaten irreparable damage, and something had to be done about it. The first amendment came in the form of a strong repudiation of the barbarous practise; the second amendment granted women their rightful place in religious musical life. Soon women were not only singing in church, but were also utilising their considerable gifts in court and on the public stages. In a moment of perspicacious clarity, Rossini could see the future and began to recast his operas around the normal voice, replacing the male soprano with the tenor, and the male contralto with the female mezzo or contralto.

Celletti (2001), Fussi and Magnani (1996), Bruno and Paperi (2001), and Sanchez Carbone (20025) all believe that we cannot discuss the evolution of bel canto without reference to Rossini. More specifically, Bruno and Paperi suggest that even though Rossini's vocality would renew and revitalise itself over time, and the difference between his early operas and the later ones was and remains significant in its complexity, it still represents the final manifestation of the bel canto of the 18th century. However, it must be said that this style of bel canto had undergone minor reforms enacted by his predecessors and some contemporaries [Bruno & Paperi, 2001: 73].

Rossini's early career was marked by innovation and creativity, and it is perhaps because of these innovations that he rose quickly to the first rank of composers. He signalled the beginning of the end of the previous Golden Age in which the castrato had reigned supremely. As with all endings, they only serve to create space for new beginnings, and Rossini was at hand to enable these new beginnings. He transformed the world of the early 19th century Italian opera. He began by substituting the female contralto voice in parts that would traditionally have been sung and played by a contralto castrato voice.

Bruno and Paperi remind us that these 'were singers whose gifts go far beyond astonishing their audiences through the boldness, and the ardour of their performances. These singers also insisted on using their melodic graces, and the manner of embellishing a phrase and sensing the expression in a way that enhanced and nurtured not only the phrase, but also favourably displayed their personal vocal colour' [Bruno & Paperi, 2001: 73].

These authors suggest that it is clear from the above that Rossini's innovations cannot be separated from the pedagogy of the epoch. Rossini rapidly substituted the castrato with the female contralto (often in the lover's role), but he maintained a noble musical language, although it was a little stylised and hermetic, and some have said that he remained a little aloof and removed. These authors believe that he represented a style of coloratura generally associated with instrumental music, a primary element of which was the use four semi quaver notes for each syllable. It should be understood that the emphasis on coloratura did not indicate the neglect of *canto spianato* [Bruno & Paperi, 2001: 73].

Over time Rossini cautiously underwent a personal evolution that brought him much closer to the world of French opera, the world of Spontini and Cherubini, an encounter marked by mutual and beneficial influence. These French/Italian composers used a more elastic emission, a more imperious declamation and longer more sustained, and bountiful melodies. These were more reminiscent of a style that originated with Gluck, including the use of the baritenor. The historical conditions of singing had changed due to the discord with the pedagogy of the moment. It was at this point that Rossini wrote the composer Pacini commenting on the state of the art of music. Rossini declares that 'this art (music) which alone has its foundation in ideals and sentiment cannot be separated from the influence of the times that we live in' [Bruno & Paperi, 2001: 73].

Sanchez Carbone supports Bruno and Paperi's argument, but goes further, declaring Rossini as the last authentic bel canto composer. She rightly believes that after Rossini, composers concentrated on 'romantic bel canto', an epoch that led to the reduction of two important elements of bel canto singing, namely coloratura and invention. This had the effect of privileging the more direct expressive elements of singing [Sanchez Carbone, 2005: 724].

Celletti corroborates Sanchez Carbone. He contends that Rossini was not only the dominant composer of his age, but he was also the transformational composer of his era. Celletti believes that Rossini not only inherited the bel canto tradition, but that he also nurtured it and eventually transformed it. By the end of his sphere of dominance he had prepared the groundwork for romantic bel canto to such a degree that it was difficult to refer to the Bellini and Donizetti operas (except for a few) as bel canto operas. Celletti makes a compelling argument that:

> The right of the opera historian to speak of bel canto, whether for or against, begins to decline, either positively or in a polemical sense. When the hot-headed fan in the gallery or the professional biographer, refers to a soprano who makes an impeccable job of the runs in Traviata, or tenor who tosses off a top note in Tosca, as a bel canto singer, it is simply a misnomer. In fact, the moment opera begins to admit realism and to advocate it in place of abstraction, stylization, and ambivalence of timbre, bel canto is on the wane [Celletti, 1991: 10].

I agree with Celletti's conclusions, but I would also caution that there is a very wide interlude between Rossini, and Verdi and Puccini. A much better comparison would have been to cite his immediate successors, Donizetti and Bellini. Their work, I believe, would provide us with a much more suitable comparison between Rossini's bel canto and the Donizetti Bellini paradigm that followed, now widely referred to as romantic bel canto. The authoritative opinion declares Rossini as the last and arguably the greatest of the bel canto composers. Consequently, we are under an obligation to address his work and his era.

Gioachino Rossini

The second Golden Age of Bel Canto began at the start of the 19th century, which incidentally also coincided with the rise of Rossini and the decline of the castrato in Italian musical life, paving the way for Donizetti and Bellini, composers whose work signalled the beginning of the romantic period. All three composers were, in very different ways, giants of Italian musical culture, but the most important in terms of the history of bel canto was undoubtedly Gioachino Antonio Rossini. The authoritative opinion, of writers such as Fussi and Magnani (1994), Celletti (1999), Bruno and Paperi (2001) and Sanchez Carbone (2005) is that Rossini represents the zenith of the second golden age of bel canto. It was Rossini who, during his French period, which was best represented by *Guillaume Tell* (1829), pointed the way to the Romantic Movement that follows. The romantic period was advanced by Donizetti and Bellini, and brought to fruition by Verdi.

Gioachino Rossini was born in Pesaro on the Adriatic coast of Italy on the 29 February 1792. Rossini was not only destined to change the world of Italian opera but also (and even more importantly for those of us who love singing), he was destined to bring the art of bel canto to unprecedented heights.

Rossini's father Giuseppe was a competent professional horn and trumpet player. His mother Anna Guarini was a singer of minor principal parts or seconda Donna, as they were sometimes referred to. The couple married in September 1791, Gioachino was born in February 1792, and no sooner was he settled with his grandparents than his parents resumed their itinerant musical careers, Giuseppe playing the horn in the opera orchestra and Anna singing on stage.

The responsibility of rearing the young Gioachino fell on his maternal grandmother Lucia Guadarini, and one of her daughters [Kendall, 1992: 11].

From about the age of ten his mother began taking him on the road. On tour with his parents, he realised not only how exciting a lifestyle this could be, but also how educational. This became a rehearsal for his later life and by the time he was fourteen, music and the theatre were in his blood. The rather organic conditions that prevailed in the theatre, especially on tour, suited the young Rossini very well because he was from all accounts a spirited young man who was quite adapt at getting into a fair bit of mischief if not outright trouble. Richard Osborn describes him as 'a high-spirited scamp, much given to stone-throwing and the raiding of the cruets in the cathedral sanctuary' [Osborn, 1995: 6].

In 1802 the family moved to Giuseppe's ancestral home in Lugo and it was here that Giuseppe began the young Gioachino's musical education. Giuseppe personally taught him to play the horn, whilst the local canon, Giuseppe Malerbi, taught him composition and singing. Malerbi proved not only an excellent musical instructor, but he also possessed an extensive musical library which was well patronised by the young Gioachino [Gossett, 1983: 4].

At some point in 1807 Anna developed vocal problems that forced her into premature retirement from the stage. Anna did very well with her singing, but there is evidence that her technique had been at best tenuous and incomplete, and at worse courting disaster. At any rate, this appears to have being the impetus for the family moving back to Bologna. It was here that Gioachino resumed his studies with Padre Angelo Tesei, under whose tutelage he made tremendous progress.

So naturally gifted and so advanced were his vocal and Musical studies that in 1806, at the age of fourteen, Gioachino was admitted to the famous Liceo musicale where he studied singing, piano, cello and counterpoint.His theoretical studies were undertaken with the director of the Liceo, Padre Stanislao Mattei, who was the successor to the famous Padre Martini. It was at the Liceo that the young Rossini embarked on a prolonged study of composers of the classical period, in particular Hayden and Mozart. The latter became and remained forever his idol.

It was also during this period that Rossini, following in his father's footsteps, gained admission to the famous Accademia Filarmonica in Bologna. This was an amazing achievement for the young composer, but there was a precedent for this singular honour. Nearly forty years earlier, in 1770, another 14-year-old had been so honoured by the Accademia Filarmonica, namely Amadeus Wolfgang Mozart.

There is no question that from a very early age Rossini displayed a precocious and remarkable musical gift.It would not be long before he was ready to take centre stage, filling the void left by the death of Cimarosa and the retirement of Paisiello.Other composers such as the German Johannes Simone Mayer (1763–1845) and Ferdinand Paer (1771–1839) had temporarily occupied that space, introducing a new orchestral richness whilst simultaneously constructing longer and more complex scenic sequences than had hitherto been used in Italian opera. Nonetheless Stendhal believed that it was not until Rossini took centre stage that Italian opera found an exponent capable of bringing these disparate elements together in a synergistic whole which was greater than its parts.

Rossini had been composing for many years before his big opportunity in opera arrived. Indeed, some of the string quartets he composed at the age of twelve are still highly regarded. In fact, many of Rossini's youthful compositions are still extant. Amongst the more memorable ones are the six sonatas a quattro, performed at Agostino Triossi's home in Ravenna. He had also composed masses and oratorio, sung parts in opera as a boy soprano and been engaged as maestro al cembalo in operatic productions. He composed some sacred music and a successful cantata, *Il pianto d'Armonia sulla morte d'Orfeo*, which won him a prize at the Liceo and was performed there at an academic convocation in 1808. However, his best preparation as an opera composer came in the form of a piecemeal opera composition known as *Demetrio and Polibio*. Domenico Mombelli, artistic director of a touring company, commissioned the opera. Mombelli, who was a fine tenor, joined with his two daughters to form the nucleus of a touring opera company. Rossini never saw the complete libretto of the opera so he had no idea of the characterisation or the interrelationships between characters. However, what he was able to achieve with the individual pieces and ensembles that were commissioned was nothing short of inspirational. In particular the duet 'Questo cuor ti giura amore' and the quartet 'D'onami omai Seveno' can only be described as the youthful work of a musical genius. Rossini later recycled this particularly inspired music in some of his other operas, but it was the original setting that moved Stendhal to declare that had Rossini not written anything else but this duet and the quartet from *Demetrio and Polibio*, Cimarosa and Mozart would have welcomed him as their equal [Stendhal in Gossett, 1983:11].

We can see from the above that Rossini had considerable knowledge and experience of the operatic milieu. He was aware of the structures and traditions of the theatre. In large part this was the result of his personal experience in the theatre, but also the result of all that time spent on the road with his parents. Let us recall that his parents and many of their friends were theatre people, all of which was marvellous preparation for this most difficult profession. Therefore, when his opportunity came he was in an excellent position to take advantage of it.

His first opportunity came when a composer who had been hired for the Teatro San Moisè in Venice broke his contract at rather short notice. The San Moisè was a small theatre, employing only six singers, a small orchestra and no chorus. It specialised in producing farces that generally ran for about 90 minutes and were performed on one simple set with modest costumes. It was a wonderful place for Rossini to learn his craft.

Fortunately for Rossini, when the news broke that the original composer of the proposed farce would not be honouring the contract, Giovanni and Rosa Morandi recommended the young Rossini for the commission. The Morandis were not only influential singers, but also close friends of the Rossini family, and therefore very much aware of Gioachino's extraordinary gifts.

After some deliberation, Rossini was contracted to write the one act farce based on a libretto by Gaetano Rossi (1774–1855). The opera was *La cambiale di Matrimonio*, the plot of which was designed to poke fun at the North American materialistic, commercially based culture. The opera depicts a world where everything is bought and sold, including love. The story is centres on a wealthy Canadian by the name of Slook who has written to Tobias Mill an English gentleman, requesting that he find him a wife. Tobias is scornful of the idea, until he reads at the bottom of the letter that the mandatory dowry that would normally come with such marriage arrangement is not required. Suddenly, Mill sees an opportunity to marry off his daughter Fanny without providing a dowry. Proving that materialistic greed has no national boundaries or particular moral imperatives.

Even though this is Rossini's first opera buffa, and the secco recitatives are rather long, the music he lavishes on it as absolutely lovely. Amongst the highlights, we find Slook's aria, the duet between Slook and Mill, and Fanny's aria 'Vorrei spiegarvi il giubilo'. *La Cambiale di Matrimonio* is a youthful work, Rossini being only eighteen, and whilst its format is old fashioned, there is no mistaking its musical originality and its effervescent and contagious sparkle. Although we can hear the slightly tentative tone, and the influence of Mozart, and Cimarosa, there is no mistaking Rossini's distinctively new direction and the remarkably original musical voice.

As a result of this success, Rossini received a great many offers, not only from the Teatro San Mosè, but also from his home city of Bologna.

Consequently, 1811 found Rossini in Bologna where his new opera, *L'equivico stravagante*, with a libretto by Gaetano Gasparini, was given its premiere. The opera was too risqué for the sensors, as well as lacking in patriotic fervour. The attempt to avoid army service did not go down well. The opera was a complete failure, and was withdrawn after three performances.Fortunately, for Rossini, the failure was attributed to an unpalatable libretto rather than the music, mitigating his disappointment. At any rate, Rossini refused to allow this disappointment to deter him from his single-minded course. He concentrated instead on the positive, such as his fateful meeting with Marietta (Maria) Marcolini, an important prima donna of her day. From contemporary accounts, their relationship went far beyond the professional and indicated an important phase of Rossini's musical and professional life. Kendal confirms that at this stage of his development 'Rossini seems to have been attractive to and attracted by, women in his younger days' [Kendall, 1992: 27].

At any rate, Rossini had little time to ponder the situation simply because he was due to deliver *L'inganno Felice* to the Teatro Moisè in Venice. As successful as *La cambiale di matrimonio* had been, *L'inganno Felice* with a libretto by Giuseppe Foppa, became his first genuine hit.

Rossini's next farce for the San Moisè was *La Scala di Seta*, which opened in May 1812. *La Scala di Seta* is best remembered today for its magnificent overture, but in truth what follows in the opera is every bit its equal. In particular, Giulia's aria, 'Il mio ben sospiro e chiamo' is a fine aria accompanied by a rich and complex orchestration, including a haunting solo for cor anglais. The duet between Giulia and Germano is a masterpiece, as is Germano's aria with its shifting mood ranging from buffoonery to lyricism, and some ensembles are also of a very high calibre.

La Pietra di Paragone

La Pietra di paragone was written for La Scala in Milan and opened in September 1812, was Rossini's first enormously successful full-length masterpiece. The opera received 53 performances in its first season.

Rossini was introduced to La Scala in Milan by his then lover Maria Marcolini, and her colleague Filippo Galli. These artists believed in Rossini's extraordinary talent and they were sufficiently influential to make a difference. *La Pietra di Paragone* is a story of the idle wealthy at play. The major protagonist of the opera, Count Asdrubale, refers to the touchstone of the play, which in his mind is the test of emotional sincerity.

The wit, the fluency, the elegance, the sophistication and the modernity of this opera were remarkable for its time and are still in evidence today.

Its immense success was very well deserved.

Tancredi

With *Tancredi*, Rossini achieved two major objectives. It was the first great work of his maturity, and as such it produced a new paradigm for *opera seria*. Rossini consolidated and refined this new paradigm until over time it became the favoured paradigm of future Italian composers.

Musically, *Tancredi* is a wonderfully fresh and innovative score with a great deal of drama and pathos. Most people associate *Tancredi* with the aria 'Di Tanti Palpiti', but *Tancredi* is much more than that. For me, one of the most exquisite moments in a score that is full of glorious moments comes in the form of Amenaide's aria 'Ah, che il morir non e'. This is a remarkable piece of writing for such a young composer, and in many respects because of its refinement of spirit, simplicity of expression and depth and sincerity of emotion, it looks forward to the romantic bel canto that follows Rossini.

Philip Gossett suggests that when we look forward to *Semiramide*, which was Rossini's last Italian opera, we see that, although considerably more developed, there is nothing in *Semiramide* that does not have its roots in *Tancredi*. Stendhal regarded it as one of the young composers crowning and defining achievements. *Tancredi* is a tragic masterpiece! Stendhal believed it to be one of the composer's great achievements.

L'occasione Fa Il Ladro

L'occasione fa il ladro was performed at the Teatro San Moisè in November 1812, and enjoyed a great success. This is a seriously beautiful score that manages to vividly depict the individual characters, and delineate the interrelationships with the most devastating clarity, and simplicity of manner.

L'Italiana in Algeria

L'Italiana in Algeri is undoubtedly a comic masterpiece. Many of the arias such as Lindoro's 'L'anguir per una bella', one of the most ravishing arias in the score, and because of its high lying tessitura, also one of the most difficult, is justly famous. Isabella's 'Cruda sorte', 'Colui che adoro', and 'Pensa Alla Patria' are not just wonderful musical examples, which they are, but they also help to establish her character. Memorable also, is Haly's 'Le Femmini d'Italia', and Mustafa's 'Gia d'insolito ardore nel petto agitare'.

Il Turco in Italia

Il Turco in Italia premiered at La Scala, Milan in 1816 and was not a great success, which was a disappointment not only for Rossini. The opera's failure does not lie with Rossini's music or the opera, which is one of the composer's most beautifully crafted early operas, but rather with the sophisticated Milanese audience. They felt aggrieved because they unfairly believed that *Il Turco in Italia* was a sequel to *L'Italiana in Algeri*, which it decidedly was not. It is true that there may have been one or two short familiar motifs, but unlike many of Rossini's operas which are characterised by a great deal of self-borrowing, *Il Turco in Italia* was a substantially new composition, and very sophisticated at that.

Il Turco in Italia is a very well constructed and crafted opera. It is innovative in its structure, with the Pirandellian character of the poet not only obtaining his story from real live situations, but in the process also superimposing himself in the story and directing its outcome. Musically, it is original and quite different to *L'Italiana*. In style, sophistication and wit, it recalls *La pietra di paragone* more than *L'Italiana in Algeri*.

Richard Osborne's comments are representative of the authoritative opinion with respect to *Il Turco in Italia*. Osborne suggest that:

> *Il Turco in Italia* is quite unlike its predecessor. Very much an ensemble piece, it is one of Rossini's most sophisticated and succinct essays in the comic style. If there was a problem with the opera, it was that it was not properly finished. The Lotus lands of the Belgiojoso estate had clearly taken their toll. Rossini eventually put matters right, removing or editing the assistant's work for what proved to be a rapturously received new production at Rome's Teatro Valle in November 1815. This was not the first occasion, nor would it be the last, on which he completed a work, as it were, in stages [Osborne, 2007: 27].

The following year, Rossini wrote *Aureliano in Palmiera* (1813), and the year after *Sigsmondo* (1814), both of which possessed interesting and quite beautiful moments, but neither had the consistency and the dramatic intensity to achieve the success that of *La Pietra di Paragone* (1812), *L'Italiana in Algeri* (1813), or *Il Turco in Italia* (1814). In fact, if in addition to the already mention trio with the five farces he wrote for the Teatro San Moisè in Venice, we are led to conclude that much of Rossini's success came from his opera buffa. I agree with Philip Gossett that both *Demitrio and Polibio (1808)*, and *Ciro in Babilonia* (1812) were at the very least inconsistent. In fact, his only major success with *opera seria* came through *Tancredi* (1813), which as discussed above was an extraordinary work from such a young composer. This was a propitious time for Rossini, because within a few months he followed *Tancredi* with another masterpiece, *L'Italiana in Algeri* (1813), which was an immense success. So, Rossini in the space of a few months had produced two contrasting masterpieces *Trancredi*, which was an *opera seria*, and *L'Italiana in Algeri*, an *opera buffa*.

Kendall contends that what is generally true about *Tancredi's* music, however, is that it has an engaging fluency and freshness, and offers the singers wonderful opportunities for bel canto [Kendall, 1992: 43].

Philip Gossett writes about Rossini's reforms with respect to *opera seria* in general and *Tancredi* in particular, central to Rossini's reform, though, is the internal expansion of the musical unit. The simpler forms of *Tancredi* are pressed far beyond their original confines to incorporate extended dramatic action and diverse musical elements [Gossett, 1983: 41].

With respect to formal innovations, Gossett believes that Rossini handles the diverse situations with flexibility and effectively. He states that:

> The lines are clear, the melodies crystalline, the rhythms vital without been exaggerated, the harmonies simple but with enough chromatic inflections to keep the attention. Orchestral writing is kept in perfect control, with the wind offering numerous colouristic solos. Heroic and idyllic moods dominate, and Rossini captured well the pseudo-Arcadian spirit [Gossett, 1983: 21].

With respect to *L'Italiana in Algeri*, Gossett suggests that with Rossini the lines between *opera seria* and *opera buffa* are often blurred. For instance, he mentions that traditionally there is little space within the *opera buffa* genre for an aria such as 'Pensi alla Patria', but in *L'Italiana in Algeri* it works very well. Gossett continues:

> Nor does the orchestration differ greatly between the genres. The ease with which a single overture could introduce a serious or comic opera is well known. This confounding of types, particularly the rhythmic vitality injected from the *opera buffa* into *opera seria* and the introduction of more noble sentiments into stock buffo figures, is central to an understanding of Rossini's music and its effect on his contemporaries [Gossett, 1983: 22].

At this point, we can state unequivocally that *Tancredi* and *L'Italiana in Algeri* were the first Rossini operas to achieve international success.Following *Tancredi* and *L'Italiana in Algeri*, Rossini's international fame was assured, or as Osborne suggests, after the twin successes of *Tancredi* and *L'Italiana in*

Algeri, in the spring of 1813. He would leave the city a made man [Osborne, 2007: 18]. Rossini was only twenty-one.

Rossini's Neapolitan Sojourn

In 1815 the impresario Domenico Barbaja beckoned Rossini to Naples, where he would reside for the next seven years. This was a tremendously productive period for Rossini, not only producing 10 operas for Naples, but also writing such masterpieces as *Il Barbiere di Siviglia* (1816) and *La Cenerentola* (1817) for Rome.

Domenico Barbaja (1778–1841) was born in Milan into very difficult circumstances. His family was very poor indeed, and his education was virtually nonexistent. He began his working life as lowly waiter, but Barbaja was touched by genius. He was driven to rise above his miserable circumstances, and this fostered his creative imagination, and his sense of innovation. Above all he was able to turn his creativity into action and action into material success. Just like a magician, he was able to create, innovate and manifest success.Everything he touched turned to gold.

It all began with his discovery of a new coffee recipe. He found that by mixing whipped cream with coffee and chocolate, he could produce what came to be known as a Barbajata. The discovery lifted him out of poverty and made him a small fortune. Barbaja, however, was not one to let the grass grow under his feet. He soon began searching for new ideas and opportunities. He discovered that there was a close structural relationship between the operatic theatres and gambling, and that it was the gambling that made the real money. That connection was forged at the beginning of commercial opera in Venice, where the Teatro San Moisè was connected with the casino of the *ridotto*.

Theatres were not just sites for culture, but also social centres where patrons used their boxes to entertain friends, conduct romances, conclude business deals, and yes, they also gambled.

This created a situation in which impresarios, who were capable of staging a season worthy of the San Carlo in Naples and La Scala in Milan, were granted a monopoly. They also yielded the greatest return from gambling. Even though Barbaja was happy to preside over this gambling empire, he was also eager to further develop it.For instance, Kendall informs us that 'when the roulette wheel, a French invention, appeared in Italy, it was Barbaja who introduced it to La Scala in the Carnival season of 1805' [Kendall, 1992: 57].

Barbaja understood that if he wanted to keep his monopoly on the theatres he was responsible for, he had to invest heavily on producing excellent opera.

Consequently, he engaged a stable, 78-piece orchestra, comprising some of the best musicians in Italy, as well as an excellent and substantial chorus, and a stable of some of the best principal singers in Europe. Amongst these were, the tenors Andrea Nozzari (1776–1832), Domenico Donzelli (1790–1873), Giovanni David (1790–1864), Emanuel del Puopolo García (1775–1832), and the dramatic soprano Isabella Colbran (1785–1845) who was not only a worthy Diva, but also Barbaja's mistress and later Rossini's muse.

Colbran was the *prima donna assoluta*, of the San Carlo Theatre in Naples. She was born in Madrid, Spain in 1785, and following intense study with Paraja, Marinelli, and Crescentini, made her debut in Spain before migrating to Italy. She made her Italian debut in Bologna in 1807, and the following year saw her at La Scala in Milan. In 1809 she returned to Bologna, and then on to Venice for her debut at La Fenice. 1810 saw her Roman debut and then finally in 1811 her long awaited debut at the San Carlo in Naples. Historically, this represented a fateful new beginning for Colbran as she was destined to rule supremely at the famed theatre for over a decade. It was here that she met and later became Barbaja's mistress and Rossini's muse. Later still, she would become Rossini's muse, mistress and later his first wife. She created nine of the ten dramatic soprano roles for him over the next decade, having enormous influence on the way he wrote for the voice. Being a highly dramatic soprano, Colbran was particularly memorable in tragic roles such as Giulia in Spontini's *La Vestale* (1805) and Medea in Mayr's *Medea in Corinte* (1813). For Rossini, she created nine memorable heroines, including *Elisabetta Regina d'Inghilterra* (1815), *Otello* (1816) *Armida* (1817), *Mose in Egitto* (1818) *Ricciardo e Zoraide* (1818), *Ermione* (1819), *La Donna del Lago* (1819), *Maometto II* (1820) and *Zelmira* (1822).

We will learn that in addition to creating a beautiful and sustained cantilena in the cavatina section of her arias, Rossini's coloratura passages, influenced by Colbran, became increasingly complex allowing her to shine. Stendhal was convinced that this departure was a *faux pas* for Rossini in particular, and for singers in general. Celletti muses on the reasons for these developments.

La Gazetta

Nine of these operas would establish Rossini as a composer of *opera seria,* but the tenth *La Gazetta* was a delightful *opera buffa* or *opera giocosa* and it served its purpose admirably. Rossini had met with some resentment when he arrived in Naples, mainly because the city was such an operatic centre and Neapolitan composers had been so dominant that it was difficult for anyone born in other parts of Italy to be considered the next Cimarosa or Paisiello. Rossini's new opera, *La Gazzetta* gave him the opportunity not only to produce an *opera buffa*, but also to use some of his best material from other operas that were unlikely to be produced in Naples. The most important element of the equation was the opportunity to utilise the famous buffo cantante, Carlo Casaccia as Don Pomponio. Casaccia was the scion of the most popular singing dynasty in Naples, and for this production, he had the role translated into Neapolitan, so that Casaccia could bring some local colour to the piece. Osborne informs us that this was a decision that he almost immediately regretted. Overall, however, the gesture was probably an intelligent manoeuvre. Rossini was not just a musical genius, he was also extremely canny and his life is replete with incidents in which he was not only making good decisions that contributed to his artistic success, but also to his financial prosperity.

Consequently, he refused to take chances in Naples. His first two operas abound with efficacious self-borrowings from other operas, thereby ensuring his success in this great musical centre. A decade later, he would follow the same strategy in Paris.

Before elaborating on Rossini's first success in Naples, *Elisabetta Regina d'Inghilterra* (1815), we should recall two relevant facts: the first is that Rossini was a star of opera, or what the Italians called a *compositore di cartellone* at a very young age. This title was typically reserved for established composers whose name recognition alone would be enough to draw a large audience irrespective of the singers involved.

The second issue to recall is that for Stendhal, Rossini's early work such as *La Pietra di Paragone* (1812), *Tancredi* (1813) and *L'Italiana in Algeri* (1813) represented the apotheoses of his work, citing the spontaneous freshness and inspired outpouring of his *Tancredi* to support his stance. I would also include *L'Italiana in Algeri* and *Il Turco in Italia* in that category. I agree that these were certainly admirable works for what they were and they certainly contained a great deal of vitality, spontaneity, freshness, and naturalness, as well as a high level of technical proficiency. *Tancredi*, especially, contains some exquisite moments. Having said that, they lack the sophistication, the maturity and refinement that came with his later offerings whether it be the *opera buffa* as in *Il Barbieri*, opera semiseria such as *Cenerentola* or his *opera seria* such as *Otello* (1816), *Armida* (1817), *Ermione* (1819), *La Donna del Lago* (1819), *Maometto II* (1820), *Matilde di Shabran* (1821), *Zelmira* (1822) or *Semiramide* (1823), not to mention *Le Comte* Ory (1828), and *Guillaume Tell* (1829).

Let me make it clear that I will not be analysing all of these operas in miniscule detail because that is not the purpose of this book. I will however, examine Rossini's impact on bel canto singing. I would also remind my reader that Rossini was by all accounts a lovely lyric baritone in his own right, and that he had been brought up around singing even before becoming a composer. We have already discussed the fact that following the international success of *Tancredi* and *L'Italiana in Algeri*, Rossini quickly became a maestro di *cartellone*. What happened during his Neapolitan sojourn with its flexibility to work for Rome, Milan and other centres would make him a very famous and wealthy man.

Elisabetta Regina d'Inghilterra

Elisabetta Regina d'Inghilterra was the first Rossini opera to be staged in Naples in August 1815. The opera tells the story of the relationship between the Earl of Leicester and Queen Elisabeth I. It is a story of love, jealousy and betrayal. There is a certain amount of self-borrowing in this opera, but much of the original music is outstanding and displays a newly found gravitas. Specifically, the two arias for Elisabeth 'Quant'é grato all'alma mia', and 'Fellon la pena avrai' are both excellent, as is Norfolk's aria 'Deh! Troncati i ceppi suoi', and Leicester's aria in act II, Della cieca fortuna'. The duet between Elisabeth and Leicester also displays a new maturity, the beginning of a deeper understanding of the human condition, something that would deepen further in his next *opera seria*, Otello.

La Gazetta

The second opera for Naples was *La Gazetta*. This was an *opera buffa* that was at least as derivative as *Elisabetta*. The story is about a father, Don Pomponio who places an advertisement in the Gazetta hoping to find a husband for his wayward headstrong daughter, Lisette. Don Pomponio is unaware that Lisette has already chosen a lover. His name was Filippo, the owner of the inn in which they have been staying.

The sophistication, the wit, the mixture of vitality and elegance of this opera reminds one of *La Pietra di Paragone*, an opera in which the lovers also find each other and live happily ever after. However, Rossini's Neapolitan sojourn was all about *opera seria* and not the buffa genre.

Otello: Naples 1816

Having recaptured Cypres from the Turks, *Otello* returns victorious to Venice, where he is feted for his services to the Venetian Republic. As a reward for his bravery, the Doge grants him citizenship. Whilst most Venetians are genuinely happy for him, Elmiro, Desdemona's father, and his friends Jago, and Rodrigo see him as an upstart African whose rise is to be regretted. They prejudices notwithstanding, Otello is hailed as a Venetian hero. He expresses his gratitude in the 'A si per voi gia sento nuovo valor nel petto'.

There is so much that is original and inventive in *Otello's* including Rodrigo's aria in act II, 'Cosa sento' and a number of duets and trios that bring a new and tremendous energy to the stage. All of the above is valid, but the music tat unites all critics in their praise of this opera is reserved for the last act. There is a great deal of agreement that the last act of *Otello* with its strophic willow song 'Assisa a pie d'un salice' is simply outstanding. It announces Rossini not only as an original composer but also as an altogether more dramatic voice in Italian *opera seria*. *Otello* points the way forward to a more dramatic, forceful and expressive style of Italian opera, one that influences the next generation of composers.

Armida

Armida: Naples, 2017. The curtain goes up on a group of Paladin Knights who are led by Goffredo on a crusade to Jerusalem. In an aria of heroic of dimensions (Ardite all'ira), Godfredo asks his Knights to prepare a hero's farewell for their late leader Dudone, and also to prepare for the election of a new leader.

Armida is a unique opera amongst the composer's output. It is a work that reveals are darker side of the composer who had become very famous for farces and *opera buffa* and had within that genre been quite removed, more the observer than the participant.

In *Armida*, Rossini demonstrates the darker more sensual part of his nature. In It, he contrasts the well-intentioned, heroic, clarity of the Paladin Knights with the darker side of the human condition represented by the supernatural forces surrounding Armida. Forces that in some way have come to dominate Armida herself. Certainly, Rossini has not written anything more overtly passionate and sensuous than the love duets between Armida and Rinaldo, 'Amor…possente nome!' 'Ah! Non possio restire', and 'Soave catene' and nothing more brilliant than 'D'Amore il dolce impero', and the finale to Armida is as dramatic as any music he has written. Speculation has been rife for two centuries with respect to the depth of passion and emotion portrayed in this opera. It is widely believed that much of it was driven by Rossini's love for his leading lady, Isabella Colbran, his muse and lover. It therefore seems to me a plausible and valid theory.

La Donna del Lago

La Donna del Lago: Naples, 1819. The grace, the beauty, the humanity of Elena's character is so deeply ingrained that it seems to spring from the very air she breathes. Elena seems to be the offspring of the very lochs she was born and raised in. These natural elements seem to have contributed to her nature and fame as 'The Lady of the Lake'. This is undoubtedly the most romantic of Rossini's operas, and in it he weaves a magical and idyllic musical world worthy of one of the greatest composers in the history of opera at the peak of his powers. Right from the very beginning of the opera, Elena haunts us with the simplicity of her barcarolle 'Oh mattutini albori!' Until the end of the opera with her great rondo 'Tanti affetti in tal momento', Elena remains the epitome of extraordinary feminine strength, and kindness. Malcom's aria 'Mura felice' is also an excellent piece of work.

Following the success of *La Donna del Lago* 1919, Rossini decided to become more adventurers and experimental. He was after all an artist on the quest to growth and Naples had placed tremendous resources at his disposal and given him the artistic freedom to test himself and his audience, in short, the opportunity to develop his enormous gifts and grow as an artist. Rossini was extraordinarily intelligent and having attained the lie of the land, he became increasingly aware that the Neapolitan public although very cultured, were also a little on the conservative side.

Mind you, it has to be said that with the exception of Ermione they had followed Rossini loyal and with nonstinting admiration through his ongoing innovation. For instance, the holistic and composed-through style associated with last act of *Otello*, and ending with his *Manoetto Secondo* (1820) and his last opera for Naples, *Zelmira* (1821).

By 1820, Rossini was most performed and famous opera composer in Europe. He was a celebrated artist in his prime and at the peak of his creativity. For the last decade, he had been enormously assiduous, and working extremely hard at his craft (composing up to three operas a year), but it was not all work, he also played enthusiastically. He later truncated that to two operas a year, and then eventually one. But whilst the quantity may have been reduced, the quality had become even more opulent.

His offering for the San Carlo season of 1820 was *Maometto Secondo*, an opera that despite its original failure would remain close to his heart.

Maometto Secondo is essentially a love story set against a backdrop of war and its destructive consequence, not only in terms of destroying cities and properties, but also the ravages of homes, heart and cultural identity.

The plot centres on our heroine Anna who whilst in Corinth had fallen in love with a handsome young man by the name of Uberto, and it is only now that she discovers that he had deceived her and in fact, he was her father's sworn enemy, *Maometto Secondo*. And now, his army has surrounded her city threatening to burn and destroy it.

It is at this moment, when her father and his men set out to defend the city that, Maometto and his men break the sanctuary of a church and he immediately recognises her. Aware of his deception, she breaks down in tears. He is genuinely moved, and in a moment of tenderness offers to marry her and provide her with a life of luxury. She rejects him, and he orders his men to assault the citadel. Fearing for her life, she asks him for an assurance for her safety, and in an act of love, he provides her with the Impirial seal of authority.

This notwithstanding, Anna concludes that romantic love is simply not enough. She believes that love of family and country, and old fashion virtues such as duty and responsibility are after all more important. Consequently, it is her sense of duty that leads her to deliver Maometto's Impirial seal to her father, providing him and his men with safe passage throughout the city.

Driven by this sense of duty, she concludes that leads her to conclude that it is better to die rather than surrender to the enemy she loves.

It is not possible to speak about each of Rossini's 39 operas in a book in which the concentration is not on Rossini's operas per se, but rather on the effect Rossini and his music had on Italian bel canto. However, having come all this way, it would be a piety not to say a few words about *Semiramide*, Rossini's last Italian opera. There is certain symmetry about Rossini's Italian career, it began in Venice with La cambiale di matrimonio and ended there with *Semiramide* in 1923.

Semiramide

Semiramide is a grand opera in the true sense of the word. When the curtain goes up, we discover that Queen Semiramide is ruling Babylonia as a temporary substitute for her dead husband, King Nino. At this point, neither the audience nor the Babylonians know that the King's his ambitious wife Semiramide and her lover Assur have murdered Nino in order to seize power. Hidden from Semiramide, was the fact that before being slain, King Nino had managed to spirit his young son Arsace to safety. Now, Arsace has returned to avenge his father. Semiramide, not realising that the disguised young man is really her son, falls in love with him. This situation is destined to end badly and it does.

Semiramide is a mature, sophisticated dramatic opera, composed on a grand scale, with a number of large, thrilling choruses and ensembles, not to mention extraordinary arias and duets. Musically, *Semiramide* is an inspired mature work with many particularly memorable moments such as Arsace's 'Eccomi alfine in Babilonia', and Semiramide's aria 'Bel raggio lusinghier', not to mention the duets for Semiramide and Arsace 'Alle piu care imagine' in act 1, and 'Giorno d'orrore' in Act 2. Arsace's aria 'In si barabara sciagura', Idreno's aria 'Dove, dove il cimento', and Assur's Aria and scena 'Il di gia cade' are also much admired.

Semiramide (1823) marks the end of Rossini's Italian career.

He was not yet 31, and had already attained the distinction of being a legendary composer. He was a superstar: famous beyond his wildest dreams, wealthy beyond all expectations, the most celebrated composer in Europe. In large part, his accumulated wealth was the result of considerable fees, but he was also a shrewd investor. Many of his lucrative investments involved his impresario, Domenico Barbaja. Barbaja was the impresario with the Midas touch, a great intuition for success and a genius for making money.

Rossini's was sought out by all the glitterati; his genius for music was universally admired, but so too was his acerbic sense of humour and wit.He was the life of the party and high society could not get enough of him.

Professionally, his journey was no less spectacular. He had begun as a composer of one act farces for the Teatro san Moisé in Venice, and had gone on to conquer the operatic citadels of the world.

Rossini had made his reputation as a composer of *opera buffa* or as it is sometimes called, *opera giocosa*. These included such operas as *L'Italiana in Algeri, Il Turco in Italia, Il Barbiere di Siviglia*, and the *quasi-seria La Cenerentola*. The last two were composed simultaneously with his *opera seria* for Naples. These operas were written for the Teatro San Carlo in Naples, and became a great success. Unlike other Italian theatres, the San Carlo had a stable orchestra and chorus, and ensemble of excellent singers on its roster. This meant that Rossini was able write for specific voices, which he had become very familiar with, thereby reversing the process of writing his opera and then looking for a cast that could sing it. In addition, we can say that these were great singers, and in many were inspirational. His debut opera for the San Carlo was *Elisabetta Regina d'Inghilterra*, starring the reigning Queen of the San Carlo, the inspirational, Isabella Angela Colbran. It was a great success, and one that would be replicated many times with operas such as *Otello, Ermione, La Donna del Lago, Armida and Zelmira*.

He followed this wonderful period in Naples with *Semiramide*, in Venice, and after a sojourn in Vienna where he and Isabella made a small fortune, it was off to England and then finally his French period.

August 1824 saw Rossini in Paris, where he was offered and accepted the position of director of the Théâtre-Italien. He also signed a contract to restage for Paris some of his established Italian operas, compose some new ones for Paris and stage operas by new composers. He did all three of these by staging such operas as *La Donna del Lago, Zelmira* and *Semiramide*, staging operas by Donizetti and Bellini and above all presiding over the debut of Meyerbeer's phenomenal success *Il Crociato in Egitto*.

Rossini's first opera for Paris was *Il Viaggio a Reims*, more a cantata than an opera, really, but the music was splendid, characterised by an extraordinarily melodic vein, energetic rhythm, and a fantastic drive, not to mention a sense of great fun. It helped that Rossini had some of the greatest singers in Europe at his disposal, including Giuditta Pasta and Domenico Donzelli. The production was supported by lavish sets and costumes and forty ballet dancers.

Rossini wrote the opera for the coronation of Charles X, and it was undoubtedly the highlight of the season, a fabulous success, universally praised in all reviews. Rossini, however, was aware that the opera was inextricably linked with that particular event, and it was therefore unlikely to see the light of day again. Consequently, he determined to use much of the music for his first authentic French opera, *Le Comte Ory*.

Before setting his first opera in French, Rossini set out to learn the intricacies of the French language. Authorities such as Philip Gossett and Osborne agree that Rossini had a bit of a struggle with French prosody and declamatory style, the type of nuanced language critical for setting an operatic score [Osborne, 2007: 93].

Whilst he was waiting to conquer the intricacies of French declamation, Rossini did what he always did in these circumstances: he opted to revise one of his established operatic scores rather than compose a new one. In this instance, he withheld two of his operas from performance at the Théâtre-Italien, the first was *Maometto Secondo*, which was destined to become *Le Siège de Corinthe* in French, and the second was *Mosè in Egitto*, which was already well known in Paris, and was very successful as *Moïse et Pharaon*.

Maometto Secondo was one of Rossini's favourite compositions. He loved the music and found the characters sympathetic, and above all he believed in the opera: its failure really hurt. He felt that the Neapolitan audience had failed to comprehend its grandeur, its audacity and the ground-breaking innovations discussed above. For instance, Rossini understood how difficult it is to develop a traditional terzetto into what he called a terzettone, which in turn evolved into a 30-minute scena, whilst still retaining the attention of the audience, and he knew how well he had accomplished this feat. Frustratingly, he also knew he was well ahead of his time and could not control the verdict of the opera connoisseurs. He was determined that the revisions for Paris would reconnect the opera to its Parisienne public.

According to Osborne, for eighteen months, Rossini toiled in preparation for his critical encounter with his Parisienne audience. That first encounter with the Parisienne establishment came with the premiere of *Le Siège de Corinthe* on October 9th, 1826.

He changed the time and place of the action and some of the plot lines and suddenly a transformation to *Le Siège in Corinthe*.

Osborne (2007) contends that both the *Le Siège de Corinthe* and the *Moise et Pharaon* had much in common. More specifically, Rossini managed to link both of his early Parisienne operas:

With the most fashionable political cause of the decade, Greece's fight for independence. A preoccupation with classical antiquity, and Byron's death in Greece in 1824, had already inflamed pro-Greek and anti-Turkish sentiment [Osborne, 2007: 100].

Rossini was always very clever, even when he was being audacious and adventurers, as he was with *Ermione* and *Maometto Secondo*, and later with *Guillaume Tell*, he knew deep down that the audience may not be able to follow him, and notwithstanding the possibility of disappointment, he created something knew and of a monumental stature. Some people don't understand why an artist of his stature would court disappointment? The answer is simply, because artists like Rossini need to grow. You can't just stand still and be the Peter Pan of your generation: you need to grow through experimentation, innovation, creativity and breaking new ground. And now, he knew that linking his opera to the Greek cause for independence would make his work more relevant and topical, leading to greater popularity.

Having linked his work with a fashionable cause, Rossini began to simplify his bel canto *fioritura*, replacing it with an increasingly plain vocal line (canto spianato).The extremes of dramatic declamation, music experimentation and audacity, give way to a quest of narrowing the gap between the declamatory line and florid passages [Gossett, 1983: 49].

The other major differences in *Le Siège de Corinthe* (1826) relative to *Maometto Secondo*, was the fact that there are fewer arias, and those arias that are retained are considerably less important. The importance of the aria was substituted by an increased number of large unit scenes for solo voices and choruses. Rossini adopted a similar approach to *Mosè in Eggitto*, cutting three of the four original arias, whilst increasing the number of unit scenes, thereby transforming the opera into *Moïse et Pharaon (1827)*.

Having made a wonderful success with the revisions that transformed two of his Italian operas into *Le Siège de Corinthe* and *Moïse et Pharaon*, Rossini knew that the next step would be to write operas that were conceived for a French audience and not just in the French language, but more importantly in the French idiom.

The surprise package came in the form of *Comte Ory*, his first truly French opera, although it must be said that at least fifty percent of the music was derived from his comedy *Il Viaggio a Reims*. What he salvaged from *Il Viaggio a Riems* was excellent, but the new music he wrote for the *Comte Ory* was splendid.

In fact, we can say that *Le Comte Ory* (1828) marked Rossini's return to his most humorous past. The opera is one of Rossini's wittiest; it has a wonderful vitality and energy about it. In short it is Rossini at his delightful best, especially the new duet for the first act between Isolier and the countess Adele. The opera is set during the Crusades and it centres on the amorous adventures of Comte Ory. This is a man who, like Don Juan, on whom it was modelled, is addicted to women.

At the beginning of the opera the audience discovers that the count Formoutiers has left his castle for in favour of the Crusades, leaving his sister Countess Adele in charge of their castle. Adele is well served by her companion and stewardess, Ragonde.

Ragonde soon announces to Comte Ory that all the women in the town have taken a vow of chastity whilst their men away at war.

This vow does not deter Comte Ory from seizing the opportunity to seduce as many lonely women as he can manage.

With this in mind, he disguises himself into a Hermit, a wise holy man dispensing advice on matters of the heart. His guise meets with considerable success with the town folks. Ragonde consults him for herself and then reveals that her mistress, the Countess Adele, wishes to consult him. Comte Ory is beside himself with the delight at the prospect of seducing countess Adele.

Meanwhile, Comte Ory's page, Isolier, not recognising his master in his guise as a Hermit, asks for romantic advise, and in the interim reveals more than he had intended. He tells the hermit of his love for countess Adele, and of his plan to attain entry to the castle by disguising himself as female pilgrim 'Une dame de haut parage'.

No sooner has Isolier left the Hermit than the countess arrives to consult him. She confesses to the fact that since her brother and his men have left, she has been seized by Melancholy, and unable to find any delight in life 'En proie a la tristesse'.

In spite of her protestation, the Hermit's solution is simple, 'trust me, the best thing that could happen to you is that you fall in love again'.

The second act opens with a chorus and a bitter storm raging outside.

A sound piercing through the storm reveals a group of nuns requesting sanctuary from Comte Ory's wicked intention. Asylum having being granted, sister Collette is expressing her appreciation of the countesses' kindness, whilst advancing the count's cause 'Ah! Quel respect Madame'. Isolier becomes aware that Ory is in the process of seducing the countess and manages to gain entry to her rooms, whereupon he reveals the truth about Comte Ory 'A la faveur de cette nuit obscure'.

The whole event turns into a hilarious adventure and all of it accompanied by some the most wonderful music Rossini ever wrote, especially the duet and trio in the second act, but also the duet between Isolier and Ory in the first act. Rossini had conquered Paris with a French Opera.

Guillaume Tell

The curtain goes up on an idyllic rustic scene. It is the day of the Sheppard's Festival and the village people are preparing for the festivities, including the celebrations for the newlyweds. From the shores of Lake Lucerne, we hear a boatman's alluring love song. It all adds to the colour and harmony of the local community, or so it seems on the surface. When we look a little deeper, we see that William Tell is not part of the group. He stands to the side with a critical eye and is more than a little disillusioned with the Austrian oppression of his country. Melcthal arrives to bless the newlyweds and at the same time rebukes his own son Arnold for not taking a wife.

Arnold is visibly upset about his father's reaction, but he is not prepared to marry. William invites both Melcthal and Arnold back to his place. On the way, Arnold takes advantage of a private moment to explain to William why he can't get married. Sometime ago, he saved a beautiful young woman from almost certain death in an avalanche. Her name was Mathilde, and the couple fell in love. The problem is that she happened to be an Austrian Princess, and the Austrians are seeing by the Swiss as a symbol of oppression, which in the case of the Austrian Governor, Gesler, is absolutely right. He is more than a symbol, he is in fact a sadistic tyrant.Arnold is in emotional turmoil. He is a patriot who hates the oppressive Austrians, and yet, he has fallen in love with one of their noble daughters.

William listens carefully, but when Arnold is about to leave, he asks him to stay and during the conversation William talks him into joining the rebellion against the Austrians.

When they return to the city square, they see Leuthold, one of the herdsman, running towards them pleading for help to flee the governor's soldiers. He has killed one of Gesler's men because he was about to violate his daughter, and now he is facing certain death. William, who is both an outstanding archer and an excellent sailor, agrees to make the dangerous crossing over Lake Lucerne and to safety.

Gesler's soldiers are prepared to take drastic action to ascertain the identity of the person taking Leuthold to safety. Melcthal exhorts the villagers to be brave and refuses to speak, as a result he consequently is thrown into prison.

Meanwhile Arnold meets with Mathilde and the couple confess their love for each other whilst swearing to find a way around their difficulties.No sooner has Mathilde left Arnold than William and Walter arrive, chastising Arnold for romancing an Austrian after all that has happened. Arnold accuses them of spying on him and threatens to switch sides, but when Walter announces that the Austrians have killed his father, Arnold is at first devastated and then is moved to swear vengeance.

The stage is set for revenge, betrayal and the rediscovery of true village values and love, the ingredients for one of the grandest of grand operas.

Philip Gossett contends that Rossini was able to weave pastoral elements into this historical drama about patriotic deeds carried by superbly drawn characters. Ensembles dominate the opera but they serve the drama well. The whole is crowned by some of Rossini's most inspired music.

Further, Gossett believes that:

> The opera must be heard as the towering entity it is too be properly appreciated. Carefully written, harmonically daring, melodically purged of excessive ornamentation, orchestrally opulent, *Guillaume Tell* represents a final purification of Rossini's style [Gossett, 1983: 52].

Guillaume Tell is by any measure a masterpiece. It is therefore difficult to understand why it marked Rossini's Swan song to the world of opera. The reasons for his premature retirement are many and varied, first and foremost, there was Rossini failing health, he was suffering from venereal disease contracted in his youth and it was having a devastating effect not only on his physical health, but also on his mental health. It is well known that *Guillaume Tell* cost him a great deal of energy leaving him quite depleted. In large part, writing William Tell made him realise that he was not well enough to undertake such monumental works. At the same time, he received word that the pension bestowed on him by Charles X would be honoured. Truth to tell he was a very wealthy man even without it, so there was no question that he realised that he did not have to work anymore. Finally, there was the struggle to bring his audience along with his new vision for opera. There was no question that Rossini was way ahead of his time, and it was a struggle to be understood and appreciated. In the end, I think it became easier to say no then undertake new contracts, which would undoubtedly have further depleted his resources.

Rossini's Influence on Opera

Having spent considerable time analysing Rossini's brilliant output, and the impact that he had on Italian bel canto, I find myself in agreement with Stendhal, Celletti, Gossett and Osborne.

I agree with Stendhal's assessment of Rossini's early operas, they are new, original, and a wonderfully spontaneous outpouring of creative flair and wit, crowned with vivid imagination and intellectual sparkle.

Having said that, I don't agree that these early operas, good as they are, represent the zenith of Rossini's creativity, but they were the foundation upon which he rose to greatness. The enthralling question remains, 'was Rossini a reformer'?

The answer is undoubtedly yes, but not for the reasons most people attribute to him. Too often the fact that Rossini wrote his own ornamentation, variations and cadenzas for his da capo arias is considered as being an innovation, a breakthrough. Rossini, however, was not a fanatic with respect to having his variations and ornaments sung exactly as he wrote them. In fact, there is evidence that he congratulated some singers, including Henrietta Sontag, for their originality and good taste with respect to the variations they introduced into his ornamentation.

Both Celletti and Philip Gossett believe that too much has been said about this, and the issue has been misunderstood. Often, Velluti's excessive ornamentation of Rossini's music is cited as the case that set Rossini onto the path of writing his own cadenzas in order to control excesses. Celletti makes a compelling argument that Rossini was not trying to punish Velluti or other singers, but rather he was trying to protect his music from excesses and banality. He also believed that much of his ornamentation was an integral part of his melody, which spoke very much to character and expression. So, Rossini wrote his ornamentation not to punish singers but rather to develop and express his artistic vision and characterisation. In fact, the delightful thing about Rossini is that he always remains a little detached and is never didactic.He was not prone to intellectual revelations or manifestos brimming with reformist zeal. He just did what his creativity dictated in order to remain musically authentic and artistically expressive. What he did possess in abundance, which is not often spoken about, was a very rich humanity, allowing him to extrapolate many important truths about the human condition. Consequently, his work is laced with a sense of understanding rather than judgement. He stands a little apart like a demigod, observing and understanding rather than judging. In so doing, Rossini did in fact reform opera, but he did so by adding to its attractiveness through a sense of energy, fun and excitement rather than a heavy-handed dictatorial approach. This was particularly so with early farces for the Teatro San Moisè in Venice. These were designed to be a fun and entertaining. In fact, when he offered something that was a bit more sophisticated, the whole thing backfired, as it did for instance, with *Il signor* Bruschino. He discovered that his audience did not want sophistication, but rather fun and entertainment. Philip Gossett believes that these early farces were delightful, in part, because they possessed a certain simplicity. Gossett suggests that these early works were less florid than his later operas, and in this he is supported by no less an authority than Rodolfo Celletti. Gossett also advances the idea that especially in his early works, the singers themselves would have improvised much of the ornamentation, especially repeated passages. This practise that became increasingly rare after Aureliano in Palmira. Nonetheless, the style of composition would have imposed certain limitations on how far the singer could ornament the piece. Gossett suggests that:

> Alongside the comic elements in the sentimental vein that pervades much of Rossini's *opera buffa*. Floreville's opening solo in the introduction of *Il Signor Bruschino*, 'Deh! Tu m'assisti, amore! Isabella's 'Perche del tuo seno' in *L'inganno felice*, or the cavatina of Bernice in *L'occasione fa il ladro*, 'Vicino e il momento che sposa saro' are all lovely examples. Rossini's vocal lines here are less florid than in his later operas. Although some ornamentation would have been applied by singers, particularly in repeated passages, the style imposes limitation. Isabella in *L'inganno felice'* could hardly sing in the vein of such heroines as *Semiramide* or *Elisabetta, Regina d'Inghilterra*. The simplicity and balance of these melodic periods, which avoid the deformations that give Rossini's later melodies such variety, help explain their freshness and appeal [Gossett, 1983: 13].

In the end, one is compelled to conclude that Rossini undoubtedly reformed opera, but he did so naturally, and spontaneously through the power of his creativity, rather than in any calculating intellectual manner. He used to advantage his inventive melodic vein, and the clarity, energy and verve of his rhythmic impulses. In addition, he reformed opera by closing the gap between *oper seria* and *opera giocosa*, achieved by reshaping the drive of the concertato pieces and the finales of *opera seria*. This was particularly so for the concertatos at the end of an act. Rossini developed a technique in which the concertatos begin lento and piano but gradually perform a crescendo and accelerando, working their way up to what seems to be more an uproarious and hilarious racket. Osborne reminds us that too often today we forget how unusually loud Rossini's operas were for their time. He also refers to Rossini's famous finales in which there is a constant increase in tempo and loudness promising to surge out of control.

Another important innovation as that Rossini imbued *opera giocosa* with the same florid and sumptuous language that had previously been bestowed on *opera seria*, whilst providing *opera seria* with the rhythmic verve associated with *opera giocosa*. Further, Rossini introduced an element of nobility to the buffo characters that populated his *opera giocosa*, a nobility of character that had hitherto been associated with and confined to the characters inhabiting *opera seria*. At the same time, he introduced a certain vitality and energy into *opera seria* through the introduction of rhythmic drive and declamation which was traditionally connected with the fun and hilarity of *opera giocosa*.

Gossett elaborates further on these points:

> The stretta of an *opera seria* would never adopt the 'bum bum' fracas of *L'Italiana*, there is really scarce difference in character between the close of the first-act finale in the serious *Aureliano in Palmira* and the comic *Il turco in Italia*. Nor does the orches-

tration differ greatly between the genres. This confounding of types, particularly the rhythmic vitality injected from the opera buffa into the seria and the introduction of more noble sentiments into stock buffo figures, is central to an understanding of Rossini's music and its effects on his contemporaries [Gossett, 1983: 22].

What is very clear from the literature is that notwithstanding the sense of fun, energy and chaos, Rossini's characters seem to stand on a pedestal, way above normal human beings, therefore remaining outside human experience and relatively distant from reality. Rossini would never apologise for this approach, simply because in truth he never aimed for realism. He loved the world of fantasy, and realism and verisimilitude were anathema to him. Clearly all of these attitudes and philosophical positions were very well depicted in his music [Celletti, 1996: 137–8].

The authoritative opinion suggests that, as a result of an increasingly sophisticated compositional style, Rossini's melody became progressively more ornate. Celletti suggests that, in contrast to the earlier philosophical position of the Camerata, a position in which the word reigned supremely, Rossini reversed the paradigm by assigning the central expressive role to the melody.In this instance, the melody was born complete with various types of ornamentation. These ornaments were not mere embellishments, they were designed to create mood and express sentiments such as love, anger, hatred, joy and retribution. Stendhal believed that it was primarily this emphasis on melody and ornamentation that became the most compelling reason for the popularity and subsequent international success of Italian opera. When melody reigns, he assures us, the audience does not need to be in command of the language, let alone the text, to understand and appreciate the piece. This happens automatically, simply because the melody and ornamentation fuse into a constituent element of storytelling. Rossini's extraordinary reputation and popularity was largely the result of fabulous melodies and expressive ornamentations [Celletti, 1996:137–8].

His compositional style also included an incisive and energetic rhythmic drive, and an increasingly sophisticated, brilliant and edgy orchestration. The chorus, which in his early operas had begun by commenting on the action, very much in the style of a Greek chorus, would in time become a central character in its own right. Finally, in his later operas he was able to bring together many of the techniques that he had developed over time in a most propitious and synergistic manner [Gossett, 1983: 22, 42].

Rossini's Effect on Singing

The authoritative opinion, including Fussi & Magnani [1994], Bruno & Paperi [2001] and Sanchez Carbone [2005] have all declared Rossini as the last and greatest of the bel canto composers. His glorious melodies demanding *canto spianato*, which was juxtaposed with *canto fiorito*, represent the zenith of Italian bel canto.

Rossini was a fine baritone in his own right, but he also had the good fortune to be surrounded with the greatest singers of his age.

Rossini was trained as a singer in the style of the period prior to his own compositional influence. That was the era when the castrati dominated the stages of the world and many of the princely and ducal palaces, as well as the cathedrals. Rossini himself confesses to never having beard such an appealing and celestial sound as that that came out of the castrati's throat.

According to Bruno and Paperi the most important characteristics are:

> A clean attack, a clear and luminous sound on the breath, fluid emission, which is both delicate and stimulating, a characteristic use of crescendo and diminuendo, filato (spinning) sounds, a refined fp [forte/piano], an elegant legato, a portamento and pathetic accent that provides various highlights within the phrasing, the capacity to modulate the execution of the 'fioritura' and stylized singing (canto di maniera).

These qualities are complemented by an instrumental type agility, which is expressive but never forced, and often full of tension but without ever being vulgar or forced and a certain taste for sharp and incisive sound quality, and a recitative that is distinctly pronounced but flexible, followed by a loose, and clear articulation of the text.

All of the above had been sustained and advanced by Rossini, with masterly internal instrumentation balanced with talented geometry [Bruno and Paperi, 2001: 74].

Sanchez Carbone adds her considerable voice to the discussion when she reminds us of two important pedagogical elements in this period:

The first suggests that this was a completely empirical system of teaching voice, a system that was characterised by its incessant trial and error, which was essentially founded on the precision and acuity of hearing (ear) both the teacher and the students.

The second pedagogical indication was founded on imaginative teaching and psychological expediency across a figurative and imaginative language, based on suggestion and psychological metaphors [Sanchez Carbone, 2005: 724–5].

Following this period, Rossini himself found a new style and language with the 'Siege of Corinth', 'Mosè', and Guillaume Tell, but he is not convinced about the divisions that arise between the vocal schools and the characteristics of the new theatrical productions.

Nonetheless, it is clear that he did not foresee where singing might have been going when he composed his *Guillaume Tell*, and certainly he was appalled when Gilbert Duprez sang the high Cs in *Guillaume Tell* from the chest by in the 1837 season of his *Guillaume Tell*. Rossini had been brought up on a high register that sounded more like a supported falsetto, but with the minimal amount of vocalis muscle involvement, the result of considerable subglottal pressure required to supported what is widely recognises as a supported falsetto.

Rossini virtually created the contralto voice, and was also responsible for the development of the dramatic coloratura soprano. He also placed the tenor voice centre stage, and in so doing further redefined it into two categories, the first as a high *tenor di grazia,* and the second as a darker dramatic tenor, which came to be known as a *baritenor.*

He developed vocal virtuosity, especially in his Neapolitan operas, to an unprecedented level of complexity, agility and ornamental virtuosity. Finally, he developed his orchestration and the scope of the vocal ensemble to incorporate much long scenic units, such as the terzettone in Maometto Secondo, which allowed him to delve into his characters at greater depth, whilst being musically innovative in closing the gap between opera buffa and opera seria. These reforms meant that to a large degree the orchestra, chorus and ensembles came to dominate his later operas at the expense of the number of arias, which became not only rare but also less important. This was especially so of his French operas, Le Siege de Corinthe and Guillaume *Tell*, but it had actually begun these reforms with *Maometto Secondo.*

Bruno and Paperi support the above contention with their suggestion that Rossini advanced and sustained these techniques 'with his masterly orchestration, and balanced internal geometry'. In fact, Rossini developed a completely new language for his later operas, *Le Siege de Corinthe, Mosè,* and *William Tell* [Bruno & Paperi, 2001: 74].

he above is an important description of Rossini's development, but it does not tell us what Rossini himself thoughty about the situation. And yet, there is good evidence that he had strong opinions on the decline and renewal of vocal pedagogy.

Fussi and Magnani report that in discussing the state of Italian singing with Wagner in 1860, Rossini declared that the decadence of bel canto singing could be traced back to the demise of the castrati.

He believed that the singers who graduated from these fabled schools acquired not only an excellent vocal technique, but also a solid musical foundation. This allowed them to improvise ornamentations and execute variations designed to enhance the mood of the composition and the effectiveness of the role in accordance with the practice of their time.

Fussi and Magnani conclude that the bel canto method of voice production is still as valid today as it ever was. In fact, they believe that the theories and pedagogy associated with the 17th and 18th century contains many ideas that are still an essential part of the very best Italian schools. These authors believe that Manuel García Fils was amongst the teachers who represent a didactic bridge between bel canto and the Rossini, Bellini and Donizetti era. García was Spanish by birth, a belcantist through education and training, but French in spirit. In presenting his *Memoire* to the Academie of Science in Paris, 1841, García stressed the importance of conscious objective knowledge and the physiological laws of voice production designed to regulate vocal emission [Fussi & Magnani, 1994: 95].

Sanchez Carbone concurs with Fussi and Magnani, suggesting that at the beginning of the eighteen hundreds some composers were still providing us with singing exercises in keeping with the altered style of the bel canto school, but by now the bel canto aesthetic was well and truly out dated.

Rossini, according to Sanchez Carbone, was the last authentic bel canto composer, after which we encounter the romantic bel canto renewal that reduced some of Rossini's major singing components such as coloratura and improvisation, whilst privileging the aspects that are more directly expressive. The bel canto renaissance consists of a phenomenon, which is purely dedicated to the recovery of that classical school of singing. Bel canto therefore, is a modality that squeezes all of the possibilities from the human voice [Sanchez Carbone, 2005: 724].

Fussi and Magnani contend that at this point we were gradually moving towards a romantic, dramatic vocalisation, where the 'nervous and muscular exaggerations' so abhorred by Rossini guaranteed the efficiency of the vocal instrument, which was placed at the service of a declaimed psychological expressivity and the concepts of beauty of tone. The latter refers to a quality of tone that remains even throughout the range, and is combined with prodigious embellishments, flexibility and smoothness.

Bruno and Paperi (2001) support Fussi and Magnani's point of view also, but they also appear to move seamlessly from the stylistic characteristics associated with Rossini to those of the 'romantic bel canto period'. According to these authors, it was the 'romantic bel canto period' which elicited two transformational events: The first referred to the historical fact that during the 17th and 18th century, the castrati occupied the central position in the world of opera. Their influence was immense, and not only because they dominated the stages and courts of Europe, but also because they increasingly came to dominate vocal education, mainly through their leadership of the conservatoires, but also by the knowledge proliferated in vocal treatises, such as those written by Pier Francesco Tosi and Giovanni Battista Mancini, both influential castrati.

The second major transformation occurred in the early part of the 19th century, when the castrati relinquished the central position in opera to sopranos, contraltos and tenors. It was during this period that we discovered a new type of human interpreter: an interpreter capable of displaying great ecstasy, sadness, anguish and romantic vigour. These sentiments were expressed with a languid vocal style, a style that ranged from dreaming, through to thrusting and ardent. All too often these interpreters confronted the high register with force, which had the effect of giving that register less clarity and completeness. It also intervened with the possibilities of communicating sentiments with a more flexible and varies range of expression. Let us examine the specific differences between the romantic period and that which precedes it [Bruno & Paperi, 2001: 74].

According to Bruno and Paperi, the 'romantic bel canto period' was characterised by a smoother and cleaner attack on the breath, which itself was a little deeper. This period utilised a different type of *ornamentation*, privileging a style that began with Bellini, and which later found it impetus in the French style of Spontini: a style that developed an expansive and powerful vocal line which used a different type of legato. It also utilised a deeper type of respiration that in a great interpreter always generates great expressivity.

This was the type of music that was more apt at maximising the possibilities of the human voice, whilst simultaneously finding the true value of the theatrical language, and the scenic movement. It is a different way of accentuating the expressivity of the voice [Bruno & Paperi, 2001: 74].

The recitatives were often long, allowing singers to display their romantic declamatory capacity, which frequently privileged darker timbres over clear ones. There was also a certain empathy and disposition for dramatic passages, often displaying exaggerated emphasis, although, still a long distance from the future verismo. The top C5 from the chest attributed to the tenor Domenico Donzelli, the last of the baritonal tenors, and Gilbert Duprez, is understood as a supported falsetto with a modest participation of the resonance associated with the inferior part of the larynx. This was very different to the appoggiato attack, fired and epitomised by the vocality of a Caruso [Bruno & Paperi, 2001: 75].

Fussi and Magnani believe that before arriving at this point, Italian singing schools had to reinvent themselves in the image of the 18th century. This served as preparation for a style of virtuosic singing in which particular attention was given to diction, articulation and expression. This renewed emphasis on articulation and expression provides the drive for Bernardo Mengozzi's *Method du Chant* (1800), the official method for the Paris Conservatoire.

In his method Mengozzi enunciates for the first time two fundamental principles or concepts that connect this method to the old bel canto school. The first of these relates to the *voce di mezzo,* or mixed register, which today is referred to as the medium register sitting as it does between the chest and head registers. The second principal refers to the emphasis on demanding vocal comfort (*comodita*) during the execution of *canto spianato* and agility [Fussi & Magnani, 1994: 96].

Fussi and Magnani are not sure whether these were a musical style or pedagogical criteria, but they are certain that the fame of Italian music of this period might be directly attributed to the excellence of Italian singers. These are sentiments that echoed Stendhal's conclusions in *La Vie de Rossini*.

These authors confirm that as opera increased in popularity, composers took advantage of the technical possibilities inherent in the art of bel canto, producing operas of great beauty and complexity that came with elaborate ornamentation and bravura passages *fioritura*, forcing singers to sustain long phrases with ease whilst varying intensity at their discretion.

They were also great musicians, gifted with considerable powers of improvisation and the imagination and creativity to embellish a melody line and in the process, promote a deeper understanding of vocal instrument and its capability.

These bel canto pedagogues established a line of demarcation between chest and falsetto register, and gradually progressed into producing gifted voices of great beauty, resonant quality, and a wide vocal range, whilst also conforming a predetermined model of vocal technique [Fussi & Magnani, 1994: 97].

Post-Rossinian Vocal Characteristics

Having catalogued the qualities required by the pre-Rossinian repertoire, let us ask what were the aesthetic and technical requirements of the Rossinian period?

In the first decade of the 1800s singing teachers seemed to be quite perplexed and not at all sure how to adapt the traditional technique of the Italian school to the new style of singing which privileged a more spontaneous expression of sentiments, utilising a vocality that in turn counterpoised great emotions with melancholic abandon. This new taste and colour evolving from the discovery of new scenic word (*La parola scenica*), a mode of expression that was more fervent, filled with abrupt suspensions, and pauses that were loaded with sad amorous anxiety.

Bruno and Paperi cannot understand why Italian teachers failed to adapt the traditional technique to the new circumstances without forgetting the past.

They failed to confront the challenges posed by the new tessitura, which was both higher and fuller, relative to that of Rossini. According to these authors, they should have confronted the challenge of the new phonic requirements head on. They must have known that the use of a unison accompaniment with heavier sonority would impede expressive flexibility and rubato. Certainly, they retained the taste for damping the sound (smorzatura), the suggestive mezza voce, the ecstatic vocality that only a few great interpreters are capable of executing.It became important to produce a new generation of singers with a vocal technique that avoided vocal fatigue, or partial weakening of the lower register, which was made more difficult by the increasingly onerous use of the high register, combined with a much fuller orchestral sonority. These teachers could not accept the difference between the old school and the new artistic values affecting theatrical productions. This was mainly due to the fact that the operas presented were mainly contemporary operas, unlike today. Consequently, it was the composers, who, confronted with the indifference from the teachers and writers of the period, began to demand a more declamatory style, and therefore a different use of the vocal line [Bruno & Paperi, 2001: 74–5].

Chapter 7

Italian Vocal Pedagogy in the 21st Century

Finally, we come to the more contemporary period which represents the scope of this book, a period beginning in 1966, the year Carlo Meano published his excellent book *The Human Voice in Speech and Song* (1966) in Italian, William Vennard (1967), D. Ralph Appelman (1967), and Frederick Husler and Yvonne Rodd-Marling (1965); to contemporary times, and is comprised of Richard Miller (1986), Berton Coffin (1986), Arnold Rose (1976), and in Italy, which is the focus of this particular book, by Carlo Meano (1964), Rachele Maragliano Mori (1970), Nanda Mari (1975), Oskar Schindler and Nanda Mari (1986), Antonio Juvarra (1987), Franco Fussi and Silvia Magnani (1994; 2003; 2015), Giovanna Bruno and Valerio Paperi (2001), Daniela Battaglia Damiani (2003) and Maria Luisa Sanchez Carbone, (2005), Delfo Menicucci (2011) and Marco Galigliano (2012).

In this book, we are going to concentrate on the transition from the empirical method of producing voice to the more physiological and scientific model of voice production. This transition of the Italian school involves the very successful and famous singing teachers who taught singing mainly through the empirical system, because that is what they were taught, but who were also sufficiently intelligent and inquisitive to seek out and incorporate the scientific knowledge available. This includes the great contemporary teachers who have essentially made the transition to a more physiological and scientific method of teaching voice.

The older authors we have chosen to examine were all highly invested in adopting scientific knowledge, however, they were naturally and emotionally more attached to the empirical school, because for generations that is all that was available to them. On the other hand, the present generation of authors remains respectful of its predecessors but is moving inexorably towards a more physiological and scientific system. Authors such as Mori (1970), Mari (1975), Juvarra (1987), Fussi and Magnani (1994), Bruno and Paperi (2001), Damiani Battaglia (2003) and Sanchez Carbone (2005 & 2017), and Menicucci (2011) Galigliano (2013) and Fussi & Magnani (2015 & 2017) all have an excellent command of the physiological and scientific aspects, whilst also embracing the psychological, aesthetic and emotional aspects of singing.

This more holistic approach seems to pervade not only the Italian singing studio but also the Italian scientific laboratory. Vocal scientists such as Meano, Schindler, Bruno, Fussi, and Gilardone, Fussi and Magnani, likewise address a broader spectrum of artistic criteria including not only aesthetic aspects but also the emotional and psychological elements of singing.

What is particularly appealing about the Italian school relative to other schools is its richness of humanity, its holistic approach, and its genuine effort at completeness, including issues of psychology and temperament. The Italians know only too well that you can't turn back the clock and that you can't change the findings of a scientific paper or article, and frankly serious teachers have no desire to do that, they would much rather incorporate that knowledge into their teaching whilst still managing a more holistic approach. They achieve this by integrating science with a number of intangibles that combine to have a great impact on the quality of sound. With this more human approach the Italians are able to better balance science, empiricism and history, the physical with the mental, the physiological with the psychological, the intellectual with the emotional, and the profane with the divine.

In order to better understand the present situation in Italy and appreciate how the Italian school evolved to it is present state, we need to know a little about its history. The guiding principle of the Old Italian masters was embodied in Gaspare Pacchierotti's dictum *Chi sa respirare e pronunciare sa cantare* (He who knows how to breathe and pronounce knows how to sing). This simple dictum would over time be transformed into the most sophisticated and complete vocal paradigm known in the history of singing. (In the following pages, we will elaborate on this and other important principles of the old school).

By the time the model was completed it included such elements as posture, register, onset, and a deep study of articulation, resonation, and *messa di voce* and all matter of *ornamentaion* and *sfumature.* It was this quest for completeness that transformed the school into a holistic paradigm in which component ideas were endowed with a universality that caused them to be transferred from one generation to the next, albeit in a modified form. The modifications were necessary simply because musical styles and taste were constantly changing, as were the size of operatic theatres, rising orchestral pitch, and the constant march of emerging scientific knowledge, a situation that demanded flexibility of thought, creative solutions, and where necessary, modification and adaptation of technique.

Notwithstanding the fact that the Italians prefer to think of the old school as an amorphous evolving phenomenon, it remains a reality that from the point of view of vocal technique, there were several distinct developments that led to a realignment of the empirical school and set it on the path to the contemporary scientific method of voice production fused with the technique of bel canto, a fusion which is becoming even more pervasive today. It is true that some of these discoveries were evolutionary, whilst others were revolutionary: all of them, however, left an indelible mark on the art of singing. The most important amongst these and the ones that constituted the biggest breaks with the past were as follows:

The first realignment came in 1855 with Manuel García's invention of the laryngoscope, which set the art of singing on a hitherto unforeseen trajectory. For the first time in vocal history, García's discovery allowed us to study the vocal folds at work, but more than that it redirected the emphasis onto the physiological study of the vocal instrument. Whereas in the past we understood that subglottal and supraglottal events had an enormous impact on the voice source, it now became possible to study the influence on the glottis in a more direct and objective way.

The second revolutionary break with the past came also in 1855 when Dr. Louis Mandl of Paris discovered that many of the cases presenting with wobbly less desirous voices were due to a very poor and high breathing technique. Mandl's work on low diaphragmatic breathing was promoted by Behnke and Browne in England, but the real breakthrough came when Francesco Lamperti, that irascible Italian genius, adopted Mandl's work by combining his emphasis on the downward movement of the diaphragm with his own emphasis on the balancing lateral movement of the lower costals (ribs), all the while maintaining the inspiratory position for an unusually long time.

The third revolutionary development came in the form of *singing in the Masque,* advocated by Dr. Holbrook Curtis of New York and the great Polish tenor, Jean de Reszke. Up to this time, the Italian School worked on the assumption that if the variable subglottal pressure was just enough to induce the correct amount of glottal resistance and a relatively complete closure of the vocal folds as required by García's firm closure or *coup de glotte,* and then add the supraglottal resonators, the issuing soundworld would be in keeping with Italian 'bel canto. That is, the work of the articulators was shaped in a manner that essentially formed pure and undistorted vowels especially in the lower to upper middle register, then the voice would ring forward in a pure, brilliant tone, rich in upper harmonics and perfect chiaro/scuro.

Not at all, said Holbrook Curtis, the vocal folds should not close completely and the breath should remain quite relaxed. In fact, the vocal folds should not even close sufficiently to collide at all, which closure was a prerequisite for García's *coup de glotte',* but rather they should have a loose setting, the breath should be more relaxed and the soundwaves should be directed towards the 'masque'. In what became an inseparable partnership, the tenor Jean de Reszke named this technique the *Chanter dans le Masque* Method. We will presently elaborate at length on this method, but for now let me say that I agree philosophically with Antonio Juvarra when he says that 'in singing it is often not one or the other but rather one and the other'. We will see that this inclusive philosophy remains indispensable to the art of singing.

Having earlier enumerated the component parts that constitute the framework required for great singing, such as breathing, pronunciation, resonation, articulation, register-blending, onset and all manner of ornamentation, we are now going to re-examine those elements in depth and also include some of the components that have become prominent since. One of the most important of these elements is without doubt the concept of *impostazione* or voice placement, which although mentioned in passing by Lamperti in 1864, English translation (c. 1883), it was not properly emphasised until the end of the 19th century, but has nonetheless become a major element of contemporary vocal technique.

If we are going not only to understand but also to assess how far the contemporary Italian singing teacher has progressed in terms of adopting tangible scientific knowledge into the historical Italian school, we must not only have a historical perspective of what the great Italian masters taught in the past, but also how that knowledge is transitioning from the age of bel canto into the age of vocal science. In particular we need to assess the progress in the designated areas mentioned above, which are not only cardinal but also enduring. This, then, becomes a framework by which scientific progress can be assessed; it also becomes a new and influential framework for the teaching of bel canto technique through a science.

We will begin by examining in more detail each of these evolutionary and revolutionary developments signalled above.

As discussed previously, perhaps the best place to start is with Pacchierotti's primary model *Chi sa respirare e pronunciare sa cantare* which so many of the great masters of the past subscribed to. In fact, in his excellent work exploring the thoughts of the great masters of singing between 1777 and 1927, Monahan found that there was not a single authority of any weight who failed to endorse Pacchierotti's statement. Further, he found that the Old Italian masters subscribed to the theory that 'the art of singing is the art of breathing' [Monahan, 1978: 46]. When these statements are combined with that other famous Italian adage, *Si canta come si parla*, it is easy to realise that we have the nucleus of a systematic model of singing. Given the above model, let us then follow the developments as they occur, by placing breathing first followed by pronunciation, articulation and resonation, register, vocal onset and so on.

Respiration in the Age of Bel Canto

In accordance with this we will begin by analysing the breathing components of the model. We will then continue by examining the early Bernacchi/Mengozzi *sostegno* system, which will then be followed by an exploration of the Mandl/Lamperti *appoggio* system. We then compare and assess the contribution made to voice education by each distinctive system.

The *sostegno* system was very well suited for the more lyrical and dramatically less onerous singing of the middle and late Baroque, but the *appoggio* system of breath management is definitely more appropriate to the dramatic demands made by Wagner, Verdi, Puccini and much of the Verismo repertoire. It is important to remember that the evolution of *appoggio* was also the result of changing musical style.

In an attempt to clarify the difference between the two distinctive systems of breath management, Rachele Maragliani Mori, noted author, teacher, singer and collaborator of leading composers of her day, such as Malipiero and Pizzetti, shared her thoughts in her excellent book *'Coscienza della Voce'* (1970).

Mori differentiates between objective and subjective *appoggio* and then proceeds to deal with the objective diaphragmatic *appoggio*. She does so by contrasting and comparing the objective focal points of both the *sostegno* and *appoggio* systems; the latter, she found, is the result of 'very deep breathing which is attained by swelling the abdomen and then stopping the breath neatly before beginning the emission of the sound, whilst maintaining the dilated position of the abdomen as long as possible' [Mori, 1970: 70].

On the other hand, the '*sostegno* system' of breath management is a very different system. *Sostegno* demands 'the retraction of the abdomen whilst dilating the base of the thorax'. According to Mori, this represents 'the model professed by García, Bonnier, and Lehmann, which they define as the *appoggio* based on low costal breathing.' This breathing system involves the moderate rising of the chest, the dilation of the lower thorax, and the lowering of the trachea; significantly, these are typically physiological responses that favour an open throated sound that favours the lower pharyngeal resonance cavity [Mori, 1970: 70].

This *sostegno* breathing system was used by the bel canto singers of the past, which they aptly described as the *sostegno del petto* or sustaining the chest', was characterised by the maintenance of a moderately high chest position. This characteristic chest position was subsequently used as a prop to support not only the chest, but also the whole breathing apparatus. These bel canto singers were also dedicated to the proposition that a moderately high chest position should be accomplished without either hardening the chest or exerting undue pressure. The *sostegno* system of breath management was the classical school's universal system of support, representing the defining characteristic of both the Pistocchi/Bernacchi Bolognese school and Porpora's Neapolitan school.

I applaud Mori's attempt to differentiate between these two distinctive breath management systems. Unfortunately, and much as I admire Mori's work overall, in this area it remains rather incomplete, especially with respect to creating an intellectual and theoretical framework by which we may assess the contemporary Italian masters. In my view, the real difference between the two systems lies in the fact that the *appoggio* system' is a far more complete system than *sostegno*. *Appoggio* involves not only the vertical muscles of breathing between the epigastrium and the umbilicus that impact on the vertical relationship between the diaphragm and the abdominals, but also encompasses considerable lateral, anterior/posterior and lumbar/dorsal expansion. It also engages the whole region around the floating ribs, that is, the area between the tenth rib and the iliac crest. The '*appoggio* system' of breath management is characterised by a firm outward leaning action against the anterior, lateral, and dorsal respiratory muscles (the lifebuoy analogy). In a developed instrument, the singer can generally afford to concentrate on one focal point, say against the abdominal girdle, which is comprised of the lateral oblique, the transversus and rectus abdominus muscles, and the other focal points should respond automatically. This muscle configuration offers not only a natural resistance to the lateral expansion, but it also involves the downward movement of the diaphragm which co-contraction pushes the abdominal viscera outward creating an antagonistic resistance to the upward thrust of the contracting abdominal muscles. However, the biggest difference between the two systems is the fact that in the '*appoggio* system' the inspiratory muscles are able to maintain their expanded position against the natural recoil forces exerted by the expiratory muscles for an unusually long period of time. Another major difference between the two systems is that whilst 'subglottal pressure' and the concomitant level of 'glottal adduction' are substantially high in both systems, these forces are better managed with the predominantly descending orientation of the '*appoggio* system' with its concomitant lowering of the larynx rather than the ascending orientation of the '*sostegno* system'. It remains a fact that whilst *sostegno* has predominantly an ascending orientation which essentially emphasises the function of abdominal muscles pushing the diaphragm back into the thorax, *appoggio* has a descending and even more importantly a balancing lateral and dorsal orientation which pressure is used to compress the breath flow against the resistance of the vocal folds. Both of these systems are safe when properly executed, but the second is safer because the airflow is dosed out indirectly by creating a downward/lateral pressure as opposed to pushing the air directly upward against the vocal folds: the latter can lead to excessive airflow with a concomitant congestion of the vocal folds.

In an effort to accommodate the distinction between the two systems, some contemporary Italian schools have developed an elegant solution which emphasises the simultaneous co-contraction of the diaphragmatic /abdominal muscles, whereby they combine the downward pressure exerted by the descending movement of the diaphragm, which they refer to as *appoggio*, with the ascending pressure exerted by the abdominal muscles pushing the diaphragm upward into the thorax, which phase they refer to as *sostegno*. Unfortunately, there is no mention of either lateral expansion or anterior/posterior movement, and no indication of the level within the thorax where these antagonistic forces meet. This can be variable depending on whether the diaphragm or abdominals dominate the co-contraction. If diaphragmatic contraction dominates, then the level at which the two antagonistic forces meet within the thorax will be lower; on the other hand, if the abdominal muscles dominate by contracting firmly upwards a flaccid or more lightly contracting diaphragm, then the level at which the co-contraction occurs within the thorax will be higher.

We can see from the above that this idea of a simultaneous enactment of the *sostegno/appoggio* system is not at all straightforward. Nonetheless, this is indeed a sophisticated paradigm and it certainly demonstrates the possibilities of co-contraction, which is a major characteristic of the '*appoggio* system', but it is not necessarily a satisfactory or complete description of either system'. Consequently, it does a disservice to both and is therefore a misrepresentation of both systems. The truth is that the *sostegno* and *appoggio* systems are two very different systems of breath control, each emphasising very different muscular configurations, philosophical attitudes, and stylistic outcomes. The closest paradigm equivalent we have in the English lexicon are the 'up and in' system of breath management standing in for *sostegno* and the 'down and out' system, which is not sufficiently complete to be called *appoggio*, but which can, when not abused by the plunging diaphragm, be a useful short term compromise. It is important to understand that a plunging diaphragm generally signifies the absence of the combined lateral and anterior/posterior expansion, the elements of breathing strategy that ensure equilibrium in the *appoggio* system.

But even these don't do the Italian systems justice, because *appoggio* which means to lean against something, incorporates not only laryngeal *appoggio*, but also the various resonatory focal points, that is, areas of resonance, including the *appoggio sul petto*, '*appoggio* of the chest' and even *appoggio della nuca*, '*appoggio* at the nape of the neck', the latter focal point being concentrated at the back of the neck.

The focal point that, I believe corresponds to the *appoggio sul petto*, has been widely used by many famous Italian singers. This focal point, with its characteristic high chest and expanded thorax, is often referred to as *appoggio*, but it is in fact the epitome of the *sostegno* system. Having established this position, Italians then directed the breath pressure to the focal point immediately below the breastbone. This was described most elegantly by Luisa Tetrazzini, widely believed to be the Diva of her generation and one of the great divas of all time. Tetrazzini said that:

> In singing I always feel as if I were forcing my breath against my chest, and, just as in the exercises according to Delsarte you will find the chest leads in all physical movements, so in singing you should feel this firm support of the chest on the highest as well as the lowest notes'. The immediate pressure of the air should be felt more against the chest. This feeling of singing against the chest with the weight of air pressing up against it is known as 'breath support,' and in Italian we have even a better word, *appoggio*, which is breath prop [Tetrazzini, 1909: 14–15].

Whilst Tetrazzini's is amongst the most concise and precise descriptions of the breathing system, but it is not actually a description of *appoggio*.

It is a simply a more contemporary and elegant version of *sostegno*.

If we compare Tetrazzini's description with Mori's sostegno paradigm, and Lamperti's description of *appoggio*, we will see that Tetrazzini has more in common with Mori's *sostegno* than with Lamperti's classical model of *appoggio*.

However, the most significant and controversial description of the 'sostegno system' of breath management has come down to us via Bernardo Mengozzi, in his *Méthode du Chant* for the Paris Conservatoire. Mengozzi was a direct descendant of the Bernacchi School via his teacher, the castrato Tommaso Guarducci. Consequently, his description of the 'sostegno system' was by and large in line with the Bernacchi School. However, he also paved the way for one of the greatest misunderstandings of *sostegno* [Duey, 1951: 109].

With respect to Mengozzi's description of *sostegno*, I tend to agree with Antonio Juvarra's suggestion that Mengozzi's overly prescribed description of *sostegno* had moved too far from its roots in the Bernacchi School. The words that most offend are as follows: 'In the action of breathing for the purpose of singing, in inhaling, it is necessary to flatten the body and make it rise again quickly, while swelling and lifting the chest'.

This interpretation of *sostegno* was worlds apart from the description provided by his great predecessor, Giambattista Mancini (1774). Mancini recommended a more flexible, more organic, less prescriptive and more balanced approach, eschewing all manner of rigidity and inflexibility. It is also interesting to reflect on the fact that Mancini concentrates far more on the process of expiration rather than the prescriptive, unnatural, and pre-emptive inspiratory technique recommended by Mengozzi. Mancini exhorts the young singer 'to derive and sustain the voice from the natural strength of the chest'. He also counsels the student 'to conserve the breath with such good economy that in his progress he will accustom the bellows of the voice to regulate, graduate and hold back the breath, and it will render him master of taking, re-taking and letting go of the voice, and not to take the breath only when prompted by necessity of pain and fatigue' [Mancini, 1774: 31, 41].

In the absence of the level of physiological and scientific knowledge available today, we can see that Mancini's more natural and organic approach is far more appropriate than Mengozzi's more rigidly prescriptive method. Even today, when we have far more definitive knowledge, it is wise for teachers to be on guard about individual differences and the need to induce rather than force what they believe to be correct breath management. However, this flexible approach needs to be achieved within the physiologically correct framework, and there should be nothing nebulous about that framework. We should not only know how it works, but we should also be able to hear the end results of the contraction or relaxation of particular muscle groups in the sound. A very good singing teacher can hear immediately the vocal effects induced by certain muscular manoeuvres. Rachele Maragliano Mori likewise recommended a more flexible approach to the *sostegno* system. Mori confirmed that the *sostegno* technique utilised by the castrati and *belcantists* was based on retracting the abdomen whilst inflating the lower thorax and sustaining the chest. But here is the rub. In contrast to Mengozzi, Rachele Maragliano Mori, as did Mancini before her, condemns rigidity and demands flexibility. Mori exhorts the student to 'sustain the chest without hardening the musculature, and without applying particular pressure on the chest' [Mori, 1970: 70].

Mori is in line with Mancini who had long ago discovered that it was possible to be systematic without becoming rigid. When you consider that subglottal pressure, vocal fold shape and vocal tract configuration necessarily alter with every change in intensity, vowel, timbre, and pitch, and that all are a function of muscular contraction, we can appreciate the need for elasticity and flexibility within the entire muscular complex associated with singing. Consequently, we can confirm that in singing the entire muscular complex is in a constant state of dynamic change, and that these alterations are based on muscular flexibility whilst retaining muscular tonus.

These subglottal alterations are further complicated by the concomitant changes in glottal resistance, the result of varying glottal adduction, and by the effect of supraglottal inertial reactance, both of which demand a particular and substantial pressure in order to overcome these resistances and impedances.

A close analysis of these facts leads to the inevitable conclusion that a natural and healthy use of the vocal instrument, no matter how powerfully it is deployed, does not lead to rigidity. On the contrary, the healthy use of the vocal instrument demands constant, dynamic and automatic alterations in pressure and muscular contraction, which leads to a state of dynamic flexibility. These flexible and often subtle changes in breath pressure serve not only to strengthen the relevant muscular complex but also the direct relationship between subglottic pressure and frequency, intensity, timbre and register. These changes, however, should never be jerky leading to a stentorian sound.

Consequently, we conclude that whilst it is widely accepted that breathing has a direct relationship with intensity, and a less direct relationship with pitch (frequency), the latter being primarily a function of the intrinsic laryngeal muscles, unfortunately there is only tenuous recognition of the equally direct relationship between the breath and vocal quality, or timbre. Quality is the result of the closing quotient and abrupt closure of the vocal folds, which skew the sound wave and heighten the higher partials at the expense of the fundamental and lower harmonics. The combination and relative strength of these harmonic partials is at the heart of voice quality or timbre. Mancini understood intuitively that naturalness and mobility is the key to success in a way that Mengozzi never did. Having set the scene, let us return to Mengozzi's description of *sostegno* breathing system.

To his credit, Mengozzi did acknowledge the need to compress the breath during expiration, and even though it is not explicitly stated, this suggests that both authors had an understanding of muscular contraction and its relationship to vocal fold resistance. Mengozzi also recommends exercises for holding the air as long as possible, which coincidentally also epitomises the *appoggio* system. Celletti confirms that this style of breathing, which was known as *Il sostegno della Voce* was standard for the Italian Vocal School for over one hundred and fifty years and could be traced back to the Bernacchi School [Celletti, 2000: 73]. *Sostegno* was eventually largely displaced by the *appoggio* system of breath management, but not before producing some of the finest and most virtuosic singers in the history of opera: with the era of the castrati the vocal world would never be the same again. Celletti is particularly informative on this era in general and the castrati in particular. The following narrative goes to the heart of Celletti's research on the castrati:

> Through the effect of orchiectomy, the castrato voice retained the ring, the freshness, and the carrying power of the boy's voice. Among the secondary manifestations was the appearance of pseudo-feminine characteristics (inhibited growth of the beard) and the so-called keel chest, with expansion of the rib cage, leaving more space for the

development of the lungs. Subjected as he was to assiduous and extremely strenuous vocal exercises, the boy castrato acquired an abnormal lung capacity, which had a direct impact on his ability to hold the breath for a long time, and on the power of his tone. This exceptional mastery of breath control and breathing power, combined with his assiduous training, was responsible for the flexibility, the soft edge, the agility, the wide range, the ease of legato, and other qualities which, although common to all the great singers of the eighteenth and the early nineteenth century, were nevertheless present in a more spontaneous and marked way in some castrati. In particular, the castrati took great pains with the so-called 'singing on the breath' method [Celletti, 2000: 109].

Celletti mounts a compelling argument for the *sostegno* system of breath management. He believes that it was an integral part of the Italian school of singing that for generations produced the most accomplished, virtuosic and artistic singers in the world. The question then as now is 'why change?' And the answer is, because the times are changing, and with that come new styles and different demands. The world is a very different place, moving at an infinitely faster pace, with very different economic imperatives, driven by temperamentally different humans, who are required to perform a variety of styles on demand.

Truth to tell, however, this has been a long time in the making; it is not a new phenomenon, just faster paced and more intense. Each succeeding generation of composers kept making new demands on their singers, and vocal technique had to change to accommodate these new stylistic requirements.In fact, the dramatic demands introduced by Verdi and Wagner created havoc for many singers, generating a crisis of confidence in the technique of the old school, and an urgency for a new technical model: a vocal technique that would accommodate the new and dramatic style of music.

In an effort to overcome this crisis, scientists, medical doctors and singing teachers came together to develop new techniques, including a new system of breath management, which is now best known as the '*appoggio* system' of breath management. This new breath strategy was designed to eliminate a number of vocal problems attributed to incorrect breathing in part as a result of the pervasive use of the corset.

Francesco Lamperti, and that other great titan of 19th century singing, Manuel García (1805–1906), and the illustrious Mathilde Marchesi (1821–1913), all confirm their belief that without an excellent technique it is impossible to express emotions and execute intelligent aesthetic decisions. García's response to the problem is to advise the singer that, 'to dominate the material difficulties of his art, he must have a thorough knowledge of the mechanism of all these parts to the point of isolating or combining their actions, according to need' [García, 1841: Lxiv].

Having expressed the need for an excellent vocal technique in general, their response to the problem is very different. Turning to breath management, García believes that the breath holds the entire instrument under its control, exerting 'the greatest influence on the character of the performance and can make it calm or trembling, connected or detached, energetic or lifeless, expressive or devoid of expression' [García, 1872: 35].

Francesco Lamperti, García's great contemporary, however, took a different path and in the end made a much greater contribution to the new style of singing than García ever did. Lamperti, like García, was totally devoted to the bel canto repertoire and style of singing, and like García lamented the passing of this era, which gradually superseded the music that both masters had come to adore. Lamperti writes, 'It is a sad thing, but nonetheless an undeniable truth, that the art of singing is in a terrible state of decadence. At the time the music of Rossini was in vogue, and was presented in all the theatres, was it possible, think you, for a man, though gifted with a beautiful voice and musical ability, to sing that music without knowing how to breathe well? Certainly not!' [Lamperti, 1883: 2].

In a similar vein to Lamperti, García contends that:

> It would not be difficult to trace the causes of the decline of the florid style. Let it suffice, however, to mention, as one of the most important, the disappearance of the race of great singers who, besides originating the art, carried it to its highest point of excellence. The impresario, influenced by the exigencies of the modern prima donna, has been constrained to offer less gifted and accomplished virtuosi to the composer, who in turn has been compelled to simplify the role of the voice and to rely more and more upon orchestral effects. Thus, singing is becoming as much a lost art as the manufacture of mandarin china or the varnish used by the old masters [García, 1894: iv].

It's hard to believe that these lamentations pertain to an era that had spawned Adelina Patti, the de Reszke brothers, Enrico Caruso, Lilli Lehmann, Luisa Tetrazzini, Nellie Melba, Alessandro Bonci, Giuseppe Amato, Antonio Scotti and other artists of that calibre. I can only assume that even geniuses such as García and Lamperti need to remain aware that the times are changing and every era is nostalgically recalled as the passing of a Golden Age. The truth is that every age produces its share of genius, phenomenal artists, and creative thinkers. Consequently, we conclude that the García/Lamperti era was no different. It is just that the geniuses were not Mozart, Rossini, Bellini, or Donizetti, but if we are going to be honest, Verdi, Wagner, Berlioz and Puccini were not indifferent composers either: they were just different, and required a different style of singing.

Having said that, and notwithstanding the lamentations, it remains a fact that whilst García grudgingly made some inevitable changes to his breathing technique to accommodate the dramatic repertoire, it was Lamperti who proved the real revolutionary in this respect: he created the *appoggio* system of breath management, which was based on Louis Mandl's research. Mandl had created the 'down and out' system which he called *lutte vocal,* but it was Lamperti who modified it to involve a more holistic approach which included the internal and external intercostal as well as the lateral/lumbar/dorsal expansion of the lower floating ribs, which restored equilibrium to the plunging down and out system introduced by Mandl, transforming it into the fully fledged *appoggio* system. By the time he had introduced resonance focal points into his *appoggio* system, Lamperti's *appoggio* strategy had developed into and still remains the most important and influential innovation in the systematic development of breath control in the history of singing.

Lamperti's greatest contribution, however, was the application of the *appoggio* method of *lotta vocale,* which he defines as 'the support afforded to the voice by the muscles of the chest, especially the diaphragm, acting upon the air contained in the lungs' [Lamperti, 1883: 14].

The following is an elaboration of Lamperti's *appoggio* system in action:

> To sustain a given note the air should be expelled slowly; to attain this end, the respiratory (inspiratory) muscles, by continuing their action, strive to retain the air in the lungs, and oppose their action to that of the expiratory muscles, which, at the same time, drive it out for the production of the note. There is thus established a balance of power between these two agents, which is called the lutte vocale, or vocal struggle. On the retention of this equilibrium depends the just emission of the voice, and by means of it alone can true expression be given to the sound produced [Lamperti, 1883: 25].

This is as accurate and eloquent a description of supported and expressive singing as any in the literature. More importantly it makes the significant connection between the vocal support system and voice quality. I would go a step further and suggest that in Lamperti's system, engaging the 'lotta vocale', defined as the simultaneous contraction of the internal and external intercostal muscles and the abdominal/ diaphragmatic muscles, imparts an emotional tinge to the sound that cannot be attained by any other means.

Thus, in his *appoggio* system, Lamperti describes not only breath management technique but also a support system based on the antagonistic forces constituted by the internal and external muscles of breathing. Lamperti's whole system is based on antagonistic muscular equilibrium, and a subtle dosing of the breath.

Singing *appoggiato* for Lamperti meant that all the notes throughout the range and across registers could be produced with a column of air over which the singer had complete command. The singer achieved this by holding back the breath through the antagonistic *lotta vocale* and not allowing any more air to escape the lungs than was absolutely necessary for the formation of the note. This should be done without straining the breath, frowning, contracting the tongue or a fixed expression of the eyes, but merely by demanding the external intercostal muscles oppose the internals in a balanced and equilibrated manner, whilst simultaneously inducing an antagonistic relationship between the diaphragm and the abdominals. Lamperti's theory of the vocal support system is still very relevant today and was recently scientifically validated by Johann Sundberg (1993).

Lamperti is clear about the advantages of the *appoggio,* stating that, it is only by singing with the voice *ben appoggiata* that the student will discover the true character and capabilities of his voice.

This statement is often quoted in the literature, but very rarely deeply examined. More often it is accepted at face value, and because there is such widespread acceptance of the concept that the vocal instrument should be well supported, or *ben appoggiata*, the normal reaction is to accept it without deep examination. The typical reaction is to say, 'of course the instrument should be well supported.' It goes without saying.

Well it doesn't go without saying at all; the statement requires a deep and serious analysis. In my view, what Lamperti is referring to here is much more than the technical aspects of voice production, he is referring to one of his many unique ideas: in this case he is exploring the idea that for every level of intensity and pitch 'the breath pressure must be greater than the force required to produce the particular sound' so that the work is always accomplished by the breathing muscles and not the throat [Lamperti, 1883: 19]. Even more importantly he is referring to the idea that when the breath force is consistently superior to that required for the production of a particular sound, a certain trust develops between the singer and his support system, allowing the singer to trust the breath, get out of the way and in so doing liberate the true nature of the voice quality and its optimal natural timbre. This can only happen when the singer has definite and tangible knowledge of the breath pressure required for each note on every vowel in any register. It also helps immensely when the singer has subconsciously memorised the various resonance focal points where the proprioceptive resonance vibrations are likely to impinge, and is able to guide the voice decisively towards the focal point without force, without unnatural pressure, but rather by giving it direction, whilst ensuring the focused vibrations of the high register are not excessively diffused.

In conclusion, I believe that what Lamperti was referring to here is not the generic support of the vocal instrument, but rather the precisely balanced use of the breath in such a manner as to induce a perfect harmonic series at the vocal fold level, and a perfect relationship between the fundamental and the overtones of that particular voice, depending on the voice quality the singer is aiming to produce.

Just a reminder that this natural personal timbre is not fixed, and may be altered to suit the musical and expressive requirements envisaged by the composer, as well as those imposed by the situational, emotional and motivational characteristics of the particular personality depicted.

However, it is the inherent vocal timbre of a particular voice that will dictate the limits of how far the timbre or rather the interrelationship within the harmonic series may be altered, which in turn either limits or expands the repertoire that she may sing, and the level of success she may achieve. Lamperti believes this concept of *voce appoggiata* is critical to the art of singing. In fact, he contends and I agree with him, that 'In this, in my idea, lies the great secret of the art of singing' [Lamperti, 1883: 14].

Lamperti recommends that the student should inhale slowly (only for the first inspiration) because a slow inhalation lasts longer. He also suggests that the singer should fill his lungs to around eighty per cent capacity before attacking the sound. Anything below that 80% level of capacity will have the effect of emitting a sound that is unsteady and wanting in feeling. His 80% theory has also recently been validated scientifically. Lamperti states that:

> He who does not support his voice in the manner here indicated does not sing; he may be able to emit loud, resonant sounds; but they will be without expression, they will never be living sounds, by which he can convey the emotions of the soul or express the various feelings of the human passions. Expression is wholly wanting in a voice not *appoggiata* (leaned upon or against) [Lamperti, 1883: 14].

This concludes our examination of the *appoggio* and *sostegno* system and consequently our analysis of the *chi sa respirare* section of our introduction. We will now turn to the introduction of *chi sa pronunciare*.

Chapter 8

Pronunciation and Articulation

The effect of the *appoggio* system on both voice and expression accounts for the 'he who knows how to breathe' aspects of singing; we now need to address the pronunciation aspect of our dictum. With regards to pronunciation, and the closely related subject of resonance, García contends that:

> The singer should then shape the instrument from the glottis to the lips by modifying the pharynx, the pillars, the arch of the palate, the tongue, the separation of the jaws, and that of the lips in such a way as to direct the sonorous waves against the osseous part of the mouth, which amplifies the tone and is favourable to the emission [García, 1855: 37].

García contends that in the process of manipulating the articulators we change the formants of the vocal tract and by so doing we alter the vowels. He confirms that, 'There is an intimate relationship between various vowels and the various conformations of the pharynx' [García, 1847: 29, 37].

He elaborates that as a result of its mobility the mouth can modify its diameter, its length, and its interior shape. And therefore, 'each of the forms which it assumes becomes a different mould in which the voice receives in its passage a determined sonority. The vowels are thus the result of the modifications which the tone receives from the vocal tube while traversing it' [García, 1847: 3].

Consequently, what the ear hears is no more than the oral representation of the shape in which the singer has held the vocal tube whilst driving the air through it. It then follows that if the flexible tube (tract) can undergo a multifarious number of different shapes, it must also be capable of an almost unlimited number of subtly different vowels [García, 1847: 3].

Just a reminder that the phenomenon García is referring to above is the now scientifically proven theory that the different shapes of the vocal tract are responsible for the different formants (resonances) of the vocal tract and that the frequency of these formants is the product of the infinite positions adopted by the articulators. It is the combination of first and second formant frequencies that are responsible for producing the different vowels. The first formant frequency, which is mainly associated with the pharyngeal cavity, has a frequency range of between 250 Hz and 700 Hz, whilst the second formant generally associated with the mouth and the masque has a frequency range between 700 and 2500. The cluster of the third, fourth and fifth, formants produce what is best known as the singing formant, which contains a frequency range around 3000 Hz. The singing formant is product of a lowered larynx and a narrowed laryngeal tube, which together are responsible for what the Italians call the 'squillo' of the voice, and vocal scientists refer to as the 'singing formant' which accounts for the constant 'ring' of the voice irrespective of the vowel being sung. It is this ring, this brilliance provided by the singing formant that furnishes the voice with the ability to carry over a full orchestra in a large theatre. These formants are best characteried as areas of concentration of acoustic energy, which are responsible for the formations of the various vowels and which are the result of the infinite variations and combinations of positions adopted by the articulators such as the tongue, the lips, the mandible, the soft palate and the pharynx.

Lamperti on Pronunciation and Resonance
Resonance and Articulation

With respect to resonance and pronunciation Lamperti believes that:

> The mouth should be in the smiling position, the lips drawn sufficiently tight to merely show the upper row of the teeth so that the sound striking on a hard surface may enhance the intensity, ring and brilliance of the voice. With respect to the tongue, Lamperti advocates an extended tongue so as to achieve the largest possible space in the mouth, leaving an easy open throat [Lamperti, 1964: 11–12].

Lamperti concludes that there are two principal vocal qualities: the open quality and the closed, which are the equivalent of García's clear and sombre, or chiaroscuro paradigm, which both authors associate with the position of the pharynx and soft palate. Lamperti, however, does not go as far as García in his recognition of the glottal settings (midline compression, and progressive occlusion), which settings determine the production of a brilliant or veiled sound. Lamperti more than García warns against the *voce bianca* (white voice) or *voce sguaita* (splayed voice). He nonetheless exhorts the student to practice on the moderately open quality, especially on the [A] vowel, simply because it is easier to detect faults. He also suggests that it is also less fatiguing and allows the singer to produce the high notes with greater ease and sweetness.

Lamperti also believes that the [A] vowel provides the singing voice with brilliance and carrying power. In contrast, however, if the singer allows the sound to deteriorate into an [0] vowel, the tone, though impressive in a small space, will lack brilliance and carrying power in the larger space. Finally, Lamperti warns that trying to strengthen a weak middle register, especially in the soprano voice, can be quite difficult. He suggests that the singer should concentrate on the medium register rather than emphasise either the high notes or the lower ones, because such emphasis can further weaken the middle voice [Lamperti, 1964: 11–12].

Enrico Delle Sedie and the Scientific Approach to Resonance

Enrico Delle Sedie was born at Livorno in 1824 and debuted in Verdi's *Nabbuco* in 1851. He appeared with success in Rome, Milan, Vienna, Paris and London. In 1867, he was asked by Auber to undertake a professorship of singing at the Paris Conservatoire with the specific task of remodelling that institution. In 1874, he published a large work called *L'Art Lyrique*, published into English in 1885 as the *Complete Method of Singing*.

Delle Sedie begins his vocal method with a lengthy exposition on the physiology of the singing voice in which he invokes the research of the then most influential physician in Paris, the Hungarian Dr Louis Mandl, whose work is already familiar to us. Even more importantly, he was the first author to seriously explore Hermann Helmholtz's cutting-edge work on the *Sensations of Sound* (1863).

Delle Sedie combined his own considerable singing experience, observations from his teaching, and the scientific influence of Helmholtz, Koenig, Bolza and other early voice researchers preoccupied with the resonance of vowels.

Vowel Chart

Until Delle Sedie amended the situation, Helmholtz's research had been largely ignored, inexplicably even by García. It is a measure of Delle Sedie's intellectual inquisitiveness that he took these developments seriously. Inspired by Helmholtz's work on vowels and resonance, he developed a vowel resonance and modification chart based on his own experience, and observations with his students.

Bertin Coffin, who over one hundred years later developed the definitive vowel chart in his *Overtones of Bel Canto*, believed that Delle Sedie's vowel chart was highly applicable even though the limitations in the chart were due to the primitive means of observations. Nonetheless, the text contains a number of astute observations with respect to vowel resonances.

Delle Sedie believed that any method that contradicted acoustic principle would fatigue the respiratory system, and greatly impair the sonority, flexibility, and mellowness of the voice.

I strongly subscribe to the ideas expressed by the Garcías, the Lampertis and Delle Sedie with respect to technical excellence. I would only add that although technique is very important in terms of the gross adjustments of the vocal musculature, the fine adjustments are the function of an artist's deep emotional involvement, which achievement is facilitated only by engaging the antagonistic forces of the breathing muscles. In conclusion then, I would argue that whilst the gross adjustments are a function of good vocal technique, the finer adjustments are induced by a refined aesthetic sensitivity, combined with great musicality, intelligence and deep emotional involvement.

The argument for emotional involvement has been fuelled by some of the greatest singing teachers of all time. It does not mean that the student should abdicate responsibility for the difficult and patient work necessary to obtain a sound technique on the basis of substituting a little emotion. I believe that a good technique is indispensable to the art of singing. However, a good technique by itself is not enough; more is required. The singer must possess a high level of intelligence, a charismatic personality, and the ability to engage the human emotions through her aesthetic faculties. Consequently, I urge the student to strive for an excellent vocal technique, and then superimpose emotions and artistic intelligence upon it. The singer must learn to find ways of simultaneously engaging vocal technique, emotions, musicality and intelligence.

Further, I confess that although I maintain that beautiful singing is founded on the dictum of the traditional Italian school, 'He who knows how to breathe and pronounce knows how to sing', I admit that this formula espoused by the bel canto singers does not constitute a complete and true picture of all the elements required to sustain a grand operatic career. Amongst the other elements necessary for a big career are 'range extension' through register blending, 'dynamic development' through 'messa di voce' exercises, 'vocal resonance', 'musicality', 'text appreciation', 'ornamentation', 'character development' and 'dramatic expression'.

The Masters of the Old Italian School understood that breathing and articulation would produce beautiful singing but only in a limited range, usually the spoken part of the voice, that is, chest and lower mixed register. Some masters, including Maffei, Zacconi and Caccini, (all writing between the 1560s and 1602), were prepared to accept those limitations in order to maintain their preferred sound-world. However, the demands made on the voice by Scarlatti, Cavalli, Cesti, and later Vivaldi, Porpora and Handel, ensured that the next generation of authors, including Tosi and Mancini, pleaded with the singing masters of their generation to do everything in their power to also develop the mixed voice and head register, knowing that without these blended registers the student was doomed to a limited range and a mediocre career.

By the late 16th century, Tosi and many of his contemporaries knew that the only safe way of extending the vocal range was not to extend the chest register but rather to negotiate the *passaggio* into head register. This was arduous and often ungrateful work for both student and teacher. They finally derived a successful formula for blending the registers. This technique was based on judicious vowel modification, a comfortably low larynx, and resonance balancing, which they called chiaroscuro. This also meant that the singer had to develop sufficient vocal command to be able to sing a number of critical notes in either register. This technique resulted in an equalised, homogenised, and consistently vibrant sound throughout the range, combined with what Lodovico Zacconi referred to as *voce mordente* or pungent quality.

Another myth that needs to be exploded is the modern notion that somehow in the Baroque period singers were producing ethereal, virginal and disembodied types of sound. That is not so! What these masters were aiming for was a full-bodied sound that was well sustained, constantly vibrant and capable of a full dynamic range, from the softest tone to a powerful and ringing sound. This was not in any way related to the Cathedral choirboy sound that would later be associated with the English School. In fact, the Italian School never tolerated the English Cathedral sound even in the early madrigals. Cornelius Reid spent much of his life researching the teaching of the old masters only to conclude that:

> Every voice ... was known to be able to produce resonant tones over a wide pitch range as well as possess the ability to swell and diminish fluently. Power and resonance were definite factors, and a smooth, even transition from one extreme of range and intensity to its opposite indicated that the balance and co-ordination within the vocal mechanism were in correct adjustment [Reid, 1974: 21].

These masters also knew that none of the above vocal objectives could be achieved without excellent breath management, which at the stage of history under discussion was represented by the *sostegno* system of breath management.

Following a period in which text and diction reigned supreme, but only over a rather small range, the old masters came to terms with the fact that in order to have a substantial career, it was necessary for the singer to develop the mixed register which alone would facilitate the *passaggio* into head register, ensuring a smooth transition between them.

The debate on vocal registers, however, rages on even today. The unanswered question remains: Are registers essentially, as García suggests, purely a 'glottal phenomenon'? or do they, as Lamperti suggests, include supraglottal events? Most commentators today have concluded that registers are an essentially glottal phenomenon; that is, they are the result of vocal fold adjustments, but with an understanding that supraglottal events play a significant part in either facilitating or hindering a smooth transition between registers.

The other area we will address in these pages is the very important issue of vocal onset, including García's controversial *coup de glotte,* which will be dealt with in a later chapter.In addition to onset there is an emphasis on the importance of good posture to voice production. The old masters also dealt with '*messa di voce, portamento, mordents, passaggi,* 'trills', *coloratura* techniques and other ornaments. All of these were analysed through the overarching framework of human emotions, musicality, artistic intelligence, impeccable taste and aesthetic refinement.

In this book, we intend to examine in considerable detail elements of breathing, onset, resonation, articulation, registers and range extension, intensity, pitch and vocal quality and a whole array of ornamentation. We will achieve this firstly through the theoretical aspects as seen through the prism of contemporary Italian vocal literature, and secondly through interviews, and case studies with contemporary singing masters, and audits of the Italian singing studio.

Chapter 9

Vocal Pedagogy: Art or Science?

Nanda Mari (1975) examines the making of singing teachers, and concludes that we can all teach what we know and have learned mechanically, but the best teachers also develop a high level of intuition.

The above comments from Nanda Mari suggest that whilst it is not difficult to become a singing teacher and teach what we have learned mechanically, the objective of becoming a very good or even great singing teacher seems to remain elusive. The reason for this is seems to be that a great singing teacher needs to transcend technical and scientific knowledge, she is required to tap into her creativity, intuition, and where available, a touch of genius which is not readily accessible to the average singing teacher.

Maria Sanchez Carbone (2005), lovely singer of Baroque music, excellent pianist, author and teacher, whose stated objective is to reconcile the empirical knowledge of the old school with the contemporary scientific knowledge of our time, also makes a compelling argument in favour of teaching vocal science and proven knowledge ahead of esoteric, and fantastic explanations.She argues that 'In singing, as with art in general, that which is less complex and more direct renders better and more beautiful results' [Sanchez Carbone, 2005: 369].

The above resonates with many teachers and authors, including this one, because too often simple, objective and direct explanations are undermined by complicated imagery, which although frequently creative, has nothing to do with objective knowledge. I also identify with Sanchez Carbone's view that when she states that:

> Pedagogical methods that refuse to consider the physiology and acoustics of the singing voice often invent complicated systems based on the conviction that it is too difficult to learn how the voice really functions, and a fear that real knowledge may bring us to an emission that is really unnatural. Whereas the true quest of vocal pedagogy is in fact the avoidance of complex manoeuvrers in the knowledge that they must be actuated by the tongue, the mouth, and throat, and that they must allowed to collaborate with the various elements that constitute the vocal apparatus to conform harmoniously with the laws of nature [Sanchez Carbone: 2005: 370].

Having urged her reader to adopt as much science and physiology as is practical in their practice, Mari then acknowledges the limitations of the scientific method with respect to singing and art, but that notwithstanding, she still considers that science's knowledge-based, simple, more straightforward message is far better than creative imagery. On the other hand, and in line with Meano (1967), Juvarra (1987), and Fussi and Gilardoni (1994), she believes that 'subjective sensations' can be a very useful training tool, provided that neither the teacher nor the student confuses their subjective sensations with the source. These sensations are purely subjective and always an indication of a healthy and aesthetically pleasing production.

Thirty years later, in her monumental *Vox Arcana* (2005), Sanchez Carbone would agree with Mari, by stating that 'to sing well is difficult but more arduous and problematic still is teaching the art of singing' [Sanchez Carbone, 2005: 14].

The above is not the only point of agreement between Nanda Mari and Sanchez Carbone: another is that they in line with Juvarra, Fussi and Magnani and Battaglia Damiani all believe that the conquest of science benefits the art of singing. Consequently, Mari declares that:

> The study of vocal technique is not an art, but rather a science, possession of which may bring us closer to the art, inasmuch as it allows us to express ourselves more deeply, more completely, and above all with greater freedom. So as to ensure that this new scientific knowledge bears fruit, we need to bring a real passion and a deep dedication to the craft [Mari, 1975: 21].

Sanchez Carbone (2005) would not only agree with Mari, but also with Rachele Maragliano Mori (1970), not only with respect to singing and science, but also with singing as art. All three authors agree that singing is both science and art, but insist that before becoming an artist, the singer must first conquer the science.

To this point we have concentrated on the points of agreement between the important Italian authors, and there is certainly much agreement amongst them, now, however, we must address rare points of disagreement. One such point arises on the issue pertaining to the connection between teaching singing and books. Mori, Juvarra, Seidner, Damiani, and Sanchez Carbone all appreciate the richness of ideas contained in books, but they still insist on the experienced ear of the teacher for the implementation of these ideas; Mari, as discussed earlier, proclaims books as next to useless. Only because, according to her it has all been said before and often very well, and still too many singers make horrible sounds and too many singing teachers make even worse teachers.

Out of the contemporary authors, the only one that is inclined towards Mari's pessimism is Battaglia Damiani (2003). Damiani, a contemporary of Sanchez Carbone's, concurs with the statement connecting vocal ideas and the need to collaborate with a good singing teacher, but she does so with considerable reservations about the current trends in singing, irrespective of whether they involve the scientific method or the empirical knowledge. Damiani agrees with the notion that you can't learn singing from a treatise, because in her view the indispensable element in the study of singing is still a very good teacher. In addition, Damiani concurs with Mori, Juvarra and Sanchez Carbone, lamenting the paucity of excellent books, in which many interesting ideas may be explored.

Damiani insists that the time has come to broaden the vocal paradigm and review and question many of the long-held conventions with respect to vocal technique.She believes that what appears to be definite today may yet change tomorrow, that is, things are constantly changing and developing. Damiani continues:

> If we admit individual difference in the physiological mechanism involved in voice production, then in a sense we must review and bring up to date the prevalent concept of vocal technique, which at the moment, although supported in concept by scientific knowledge, appears to have a single string to its bow and a rigid nature [Damiani, 2003: 4]. In fact, we continue to present this paradigm as the only true respiratory and phonatory mechanism, both on the didactic and scientific plane, and this can produce disastrous effects on voices that are still in the process of being formed. If Pavarotti is right when he affirms that today we are losing 80% of aspiring singers along the way (whereas a few decades ago it was only 50%) then we must admit the necessity for a critical revision of vocal didactics and scientific myths that in these last decades have reigned without encountering opposition [Damiani, 2003: 4].

I am sympathetic to Damiani's plea for greater flexibility within the respiratory and phonatory paradigm, I even share her scepticism about 'scientific myths', which I have also addressed in my previous books under the heading of 'exaggerated scientific claims', however, in the end my conclusions are that we must adhere to a general physiological paradigm even as we question some of the science behind the particular model and demanding more flexibility within the paradigm. Consequently, in the end my views are more in line with Sanchez Carbone than they are with Damiani.

Characteristics of a Good Singing Teacher

Nanda Mari examines what she believes are the indispensable requirements for an excellent singing teacher and concludes the following.

> The best singing teachers are those who combine erudition and science with a high level of intuition. That is, the kind of intuitive personality for whom teaching appears to be an improvisation involving a sense of creativity [Mari, 1975: 18].

In contrast to Damiani, Sanchez Carbone does not appear to have the same concerns about so called 'scientific myths', but rather concentrates on what must be done to induce a good vocal technique. She also adds her considerable voice, believing that the singer cannot achieve her artistic goals without proper technique. However, in line with the above authors, she concludes that the successful implementation of vocal ideas and techniques can best be achieved under the supervision of an experienced and competent teacher. Sanchez Carbone understands that it is difficult to enumerate the qualities required by a good singing teacher. Nonetheless, she delineates these relevant qualities as far as possible. These are her thoughts:

> The duty of the singing teacher is extremely delicate and must go beyond the attainment of a secure and vast body of knowledge, incorporating also a clear and efficient didactic style capable of transmitting fundamental vocal principles based on a physiological and natural emission. The teacher must also have a deep capacity for analysing, studying and respecting individual physiology and also to discover, understand and resolve problems of a physical and psychic nature for every student [Sanchez Carbone, 2005: 16].

Sanchez Carbone remains strong on the need for the full development and implementation of vocal ideals and techniques, but she believes that these are best accomplished under the supervision of an excellent teacher.

Franco Fussi supports Sanchez Carbone in her conviction that the teacher's ear remains indispensable. Fussi also developed his own description of desirable characteristics associated with a good teacher.

Franco Fussi, in an excellent preface to Delfo Menicucci's (2011) book *Scuola di Canto Lirico e Moderno* states that, the main task of a singing teacher is certainly not that of writing books but rather that of guiding and nurturing his students towards the fulfilment of their potential. Fussi believes that Talent can be a fragile commodity that requires the guidance of a mature individual who is fully aware of its potential and limitations and uses that knowledge to bring talent to fruition. Further, he states that:

> The emergence of motivation and talent requires considerable nurturing. In order to understand the student's personality, the teacher must not only be a good psychologist and an incisive mentor, but he must also have a good command of specific vocal techniques such as impostazione or (vocal placement), combined with the traditional 'didactic imagery' … We know that no teacher sets out to ruin even one single voice: and one of the best ways to avoid this danger is to apply the knowledge of physiology and the acoustic rules associated with the production of the singing voice, in order to help the student to avoid the stressful use of the vocal instrument [Fussi in Menicucci, 2011: 17].

Following Fussi's contribution above, let us return to Sanchez Carbone, who having extolled the virtuous of a good teacher as being superior to those of a good singer, then attempts to establish a number of criteria by which a good teacher may be judged. In a passage that recalls Damiani, Sanchez Carbone prioritises problems of a physiological and psychic nature with particular emphasis on individual physiology.

However, whereas Damiani concludes on a sceptical note with respect to vocal science, Sanchez Carbone in line with most other authors, myself included, urges its unconditional embrace of vocal science.

Sanchez Carbone maintains that the time has come to confront the problems arising from training the voice under the various didactic methods, and in complete contrast to Damiani, she asks us to dispense with the suspicions erected around the scientific paradigm and its effectiveness. It is time to end the prevailing chaos at both the conceptual and terminological level, by engaging with vocal science.

I propose that we should conclude this section with a statement from Rachele Maragliano Mori's excellent (1970) book *Coscienza Della Voce*.

Referring to contemporary vocal pedagogy, Maragliano Mori informs us that too often teachers today disparage the great masters of the past by implying that they left nothing of value because their treatises lack specificity. Mori agrees that sometimes the onerous task of adequate expression made some teachers a little cautious with explicit language, but still maintains that for those who are prepared to read between the lines they will find that the knowledge of the old masters is in evidence, as are their pedagogical concepts and how much they detested ignorance in their students. In general Mori agrees with Mancini's sense of organic naturalness and his statement that 'Art can only be conquered through striving and hard labour' [Mancini 1777: 225].

Mori's final statement above concludes this section of our investigation into the Italian singing school, confirming an emerging pattern with respect to Italian vocal pedagogy. It would seem that whilst the older authors such as Mori, Mari and the scientist Carlo Meano embrace and make excellent use of the then available science, you sense that they and the audience they are writing for are essentially still steeped in empiricism in a way that goes far beyond the intellectual to include also an emotional and philosophical element; whereas, this latest generation of authors such Juvarra, Bruno and Paperi, Battaglia Damiani, Sanchez Carbone and Franco Fussi et al. are respectful of the past whilst moving inexorably towards incorporating a greater volume of more sophisticated science whilst remaining respectful of an empiricism which is receding further into the past.

Chapter 10

The State of Contemporary Vocal Pedagogy in Italy

Vocal Pedagogy in Chaos

As we saw in the previous section, Juvarra (1987), Bruno and Paperi (2001) and Sanchez Carbone (2005) and to a lesser extent Damiani, all lament three elements of Italian vocal pedagogy: the first is the lack of quality teaching; the second relates to the indifference shown with respect to a more objective scientific technique; and the third pertains to the lack of personal research amongst teachers of their generation.

This situation above suggests to me that Italian vocal pedagogy is still driven by vocal imagery and subjective sensations, whereas the above listed authors believe that it is time to ground it in scientific knowledge and transmit it in a manner that achieves direct and consistently reproducible results.

With respect to this particular issue I agree not only with Juvarra, but also with Giovanni Acciai who wrote the elegant and perspicacious forward to Vox Arcana, Maria Sanchez Carbone's 2005 publication. In the Forward, Giovanni Acciai, like Juvarra twenty years earlier, laments the standard of teaching in Italy, and the small number of Italians who are doing serious voice research at the turn of the twenty-first century, not to mention the small number of informative books available. It would appear that, if we believe Acciai's following comments, not much has changed in Italy in the last 25 years.

Acciai first addresses the necessity to clear the decks of all 'stupidity and the unbearable nonsense disseminated by bad singers and good for nothing teachers, whose only art consists of trying to convince singers of the validity of their particular technique' [Acciai, in Sanchez Carbone, 2005: viii]

He then expresses his disappointment at the fact that 'even a cursory glance at the latest bibliographies leads to a troubling, not to mention confronting discomfort at the paucity of studies available in the didactic material relating to voice. This situation is exacerbated by an embarrassing silence with respect to specialist material published on vocal pedagogy' [Acciai, in Sanchez Carbone, 2005: 2].

Acciai's comments in many respects mirror Juvarra's ideas 20 years earlier. Juvarra had also lamented the state of teaching, believing that 'undoubtedly many teachers fall into the category of dangerous charlatans' [Juvarra, 1987: 4].Juvarra was also concerned about the lack of progress with respect to adopting scientific vocal knowledge.

As a consequence of this state of play, Juvarra deplored the growing list of vocal victims both in and out of music conservatoriums, not to mention talented people whose careers on the stage are cut short as a result of technical deficiencies. Sadly, recriminations do not gain anyone a career, but there is no doubt, according to Juvarra, that much damage is caused by 'dangerous, harmful teachers' [1987: 4].

Twelve years later in her second book *Il Mondo del Canto*, Maria Sanchez Carbone seems a little exasperated by the lack of progress, and who can blame her. She contends that:

> It would appear that one of the prerequisites for becoming a singing teacher is to completely ignore the minimum of anatomy, and the characteristics and limits of the vocal instrument ... The teaching of singing has been assumed by fantastic entities that, let us say it, are frequently dishonest, slaves to a blind empiricism, supporters of a didactic that is foreign to any systematic programme designed to develop one's vocal potential [Sanchez Carbone, 2017: 232].

Sanchez Carbone also acknowledges the chaotic state of Italian vocal pedagogy. She is astounded at the number of contrasting and discordant views expressed not only in the literature but also amongst teachers. More worrisome still are the number of singing teachers who would elevate their personal theories to the status of dogma if they could. This is especially true with respect to the vain attempts to explain laryngeal function; attempts that only lead to further confusion. Sanchez Carbone believes that it is always useful to know the various aspects of the numerous and competing singing techniques, as even many theories that as of now remain unproven are still worthy of serious consideration. (I agree with Sanchez Carbone that there is something to be obtained from each of the many different theories, but I feel that this type of exploratory work should be left to people who have an excellent knowledge of how the instrument really works. Absent this knowledge, too much experimentation can only lead to confusion both for the teacher as well as the student.)

She proceeds to predicate her theory that:

> All vocal practitioners, whether they are singers, singing teachers, choristers, choir directors, should have a broad preparation, which is deepened in various and numerous disciplines, a technical competence that has been derived from a binding condition that constitutes the only prerequisite for a serious career either as a singer or teacher. [Sanchez Carbone, 2017: 212].

The responsible singing teacher should attend a number of seminars, read the literature and attend master classes with famous singers, but at some point, teachers must make specific and intelligent choices, and these choices can only be made on the basis of real knowledge, that is, a scientific knowledge centred on how the instrument really works in order to attain a free and secure vocal technique. (This can only happen when the singer has considered a systematic approach to vocal technique, which is the most secure path to the art of singing.)

Sanchez Carbone also believes that much of vocal technique is grounded on erroneous conclusions. In these circumstances Sanchez Carbone rightly asks:

> Would it be such a strange and absurd idea if teachers, vocal technicians, or whosoever assumes the role of teacher were to receive the minimum amount of a broad and precise knowledge of vocal physiology? How can one not be amazed by the fact that there are no initiatives in place to instruct and prepare singing teachers? [Sanchez Carbone, 2005: 6].

Sanchez Carbone believes that absent the suggested teacher training, singing teachers can only teach their students what they have learned and experienced during the course of their own careers. Sanchez Carbone refuses to question their knowledge or preparation, and besides, she asks, 'what good would it do to criticise them and their profession. Wouldn't it be better to furnish them with the elements that would ensure a solid teaching technique, which would inform them, prepare them and facilitate the achievement of their teaching objectives' [Sanchez Carbone, 2005: 7].

In summary, we can say that there is a lot of genuine concern amongst major Italian teachers and authors; not so much for their own work and careers, because the very best in every country will always thrive, but rather for the general pedagogical situation in Italy. There is considerable tension in Italian pedagogy between contemporary scientific knowledge and historical empirical knowledge. Many blame the above tension on the lack of available literature, as well as the lack of teacher training, and the lack of research, but none of this is true. The real problem is an unwillingness to embrace change, adopt scientific research, and move towards a more objective methodology that clarifies real knowledge, and eliminates the present state of chaos. All of which, in a fast changing environment in which the scientific method is becoming the dominant paradigm, places Italian vocal pedagogy in danger of relinquishing its competitive advantage, relative to a more balanced pedagogy grounded in scientific knowledge, combined with didactic techniques inherited from the historical Italian school.

The Famous Singing Teacher

The other problem that vocal pedagogy has to contend with is an overabundance of famous singers who have turned to teaching. These former stars of opera are very happy to give an opinion on everything, for a price of course, but most of the time their opinions are neither systematic, nor too considered. Too often, these are based on their own sensations, which are difficult to duplicate without the appropriate breath pressure, the correct configuration of the vocal folds, and the appropriate adjustments of the articulators, which complete the process of impostazione.

Thus, as Juvarra rightly states (1987), the bad singing teacher is not the only disaster that may befall a student, the famous singer turned teacher can be just as dangerous. Often, these outstanding personalities and very gifted singers enjoy major careers based on exceptional natural gifts. The problem is that singers with such natural gifts and instinctive technique are often unable to translate their intuition and naturalness into a systematic and objective vocal technique. This type of technique, which is essentially based on imitation, can serve a natural artist very well until something goes wrong, and something always goes wrong. At this point, the whole edifice falls over like a house of cards, simply because this technique is bereft of an objective theoretical and intellectual framework, meaning that we are back to 'analysing sensations and imitating teachers'. These are the very elements that objective knowledge is aiming to replace. Consequently, we can say that being a great artist is excellent, but in terms of teaching, being a great technician with an outstanding body of work based on scientific and physiological knowledge combined with a broad range of empirical knowledge is even better. There is now much agreement that great artists do not necessarily make great teachers.

As with Juvarra above, Sanchez Carbone and Nanda Mari also make a compelling argument for the need to differentiate and decouple the relative value of the great artist from that of the great teacher, as the two are not synonymous. Sanchez Carbone argues cogently that:

> Having been famous artists and esteemed interpreters is not sufficient to guarantee one's ability to transmit that which is a synthesis of multiple and composite respiratory combinations, muscular, physical, psychological, mental and intuitive. All these operational functions should converge not only in the intent of emitting sound, but also in that of creating a resonant voice of particular beauty and power, born of optimum articulation for the purpose of making the voice the most harmonious of all instruments, simply because it is the only instrument capable of uniting text and music [Sanchez Carbone, 2005: 14].

Nanda Mari adds her considerable voice in support of Juvarra and Sanchez Carbone, whilst adding a few twists of her own:

> It is not always necessary to have had a great career in order to attain the experience that very often benefits others when we succeed in transmitting it to them. On the contrary, those who have had the good fortune of being above all nature's student have found, as a second part of good fortune, a teacher who has not been able to ruin that which nature has bestowed upon them. Often, they experience few problems, and at the very least, certainly not the problems of those who have constructed their voices with intuition and patience, overcoming the doubts and uncertainty of a technique that although very natural remains essentially unknowable [Mari, 1975: 16].

I agree with Sanchez Carbone that it is not necessary to be a famous singer with a glorious international career in order to teach an excellent vocal technique capable of transforming the voice into a most harmonious instrument. I also agree with Mari that it is not necessary to be a famous singer to help others. On the contrary, if that glorious career comes easily as a result of great talent combines with immense good fortune, chances are that the recipient of such good fortune cannot transmit that formula to the student. The above represents two sides of the same coin.

Having established that there are essentially no extraordinary benefits to learning singing from a famous singer relative to a good professional singing teacher, Antonio Juvarra then treats another prevalent vocal dysfunction. This problem is the consequence of an underdeveloped instrument due to unrealistic understanding of the demands made on the human voice by an operatic career. According to Juvarra, this type of emission, which although quite pleasant aesthetically, especially when not placed under pressure, which is often the case in a conservatorium setting, crumbles very quickly under the pressures imposed by the exigencies of a demanding operatic career. Juvarra suggests, and I agree with him, that the singer doesn't know how good their technique really is until they put it under pressure. While many singers make lovely sounds in a small room, singing chamber music, it takes a singer of consequence to put the voice under pressure in a demanding role, in a major theatre over a big orchestra and emerge unscathed.

Juvarra also warns against any method that concentrates on localising sensations at the laryngeal level, that is, inducing feelings of tenderness or sensations of soreness around the larynx or pharynx. These sensations and feelings are too often erroneously attributed to the pain of muscular development. The rationale is that of imposing a greater load on the instrument in order to strengthen the intrinsic laryngeal muscles [Juvarra, 1987: 4]. Sanchez Carbone is likewise concerned about localised sensations, especially around the larynx. Whilst laryngeal rigidity is clearly her primary concern, Sanchez Carbone also demonstrates considerable reservations with the technique associated with pointing the voice towards the mask with an overly tight and inflexible a focus.

The truth is that both the intrinsic and extrinsic laryngeal muscles do in most cases need to be strengthened, but this needs to be accomplished through a judicious and gradual process and not by adding pressure and tension at the vocal fold level. The singer must avoid at all costs any tension at the laryngeal or pharyngeal level. If it doesn't feel right, that is, if the sensations manifest themselves in the larynx, then there is a good chance that you are doing something wrong.

Finally, Juvarra makes a strong argument against the notion that a pleasant sound is always correlated with correct vocal technique. In fact, he believes that:

> An acceptable quality of sound on a purely aesthetic level does not necessarily signal the absolute correctness of emission. On the other hand, the number of singing teachers sufficiently gifted with a diagnostic ear capable of distinguishing the difference between a beautiful sound which is also correct from a sound which is also beautiful but incorrect, purely and only on the basis of acoustic quality, is absolutely rare [Juvarra, 1987: 4].

Unfortunately, these gifted teachers are often confused with inferior teachers who, bereft of such gifts, proceed to hide behind arbitrary methods, which are then credited to the traditional Italian school [Juvarra, 1987: 4].

> In such anarchic conditions where every vocal method contradicts another, it is extremely easy to perpetuate very harmful absurdities with respect to vocal technique. In these circumstances, it is more important than ever to avail oneself of the contribution made possible by scientific and didactic research in order to properly evaluate correct technique from that which is indeed ruinous [Juvarra, 1987: 4].

Juvarra laments the fact that in his opinion Italians teachers have been lagging way behind the times in terms of research and development in the area of vocal science. In this opinion, Juvarra is completely in line with Sanchez Carbone above.

To back up his argument, Juvarra brings two points to our attention:

> The first point refers to the small number of books published on singing in Italy and the fact that those that are published seem to have a distinctly historical flavour.

> The second point refers to the fact that Italian teachers do not traditionally prioritize their attendance of singing conferences and vocal seminars. Specifically, he cites the fact that the Voice Conference in Rotterdam boasted only two Italian attendees, and neither of these was a singing teacher [Juvarra, 1987: 5].

In fairness, I have to say that what was true in the mid 1980s is no longer relevant in 2015. Italians now have published a number of excellent books on singing and they attend and host important voice conferences on a regular basis.

And, whilst I am generally in agreement with Juvarra, I don't think either of these two points are a particularly strong demonstration of his thesis. The truth is that books with a historical bent can be very useful in terms of tracing the systematic development of ideas and vocal techniques which, when properly executed can prioritise enduring ideas ahead of fashionable but vanishing moments. Real knowledge and good ideas endure, undergoing innovation and becoming even more valuable over time. Juvarra himself knows this because in his excellent book *I Segreti del Bel Canto* (2006), he actually analysed the teaching of the old masters dating back to the sixteenth century. With respect to the second point, I don't think one can say that because teachers don't attend scientific voice conferences they don't consume scientific output. I think a better measure would be the number of teachers who study intensively the published proceedings from these conferences at their leisure, and read the books on vocal science and physiology that have proliferated in Italy over the last three decades. My feeling is that there are many more of the latter than the handful of teachers who actually attend conferences.

However, and keeping in mind that Juvarra's commentary refers to the situation in 1987, I do agree with him that the paucity of vocal pedagogy books published in Italy right up to that point, was indeed regrettable. He was right to lament the fact that Italy, the land of art and song, produced such a small number of distinguished publications during the period from the fifties to the nineties. This distressing situation denoted a lack of vital interest and robust intellectual debate with respect to systematising a theoretical framework for vocal pedagogy courses. However, more recently, there have been a number of excellent books on singing penned by Italian authors including Juvarra's himself. We will meet these authors, analyse their work, and quote them liberally throughout this book. The only comment I would make at this point is that it is not the number of books that are written, but the quality and authority of the work contained in them. I consider the thirty or so books, many excerpts have been translated and quoted in these pages, to be of a very high level indeed.

Analysing the situation in his 1987 book, Juvarra advanced a number of theories for what he saw as a dismal literary effort. The most prominent was based on the idealistic nature of Italian teachers and artists, whereby some feel that science should not intrude on the purity of the art of singing. I think there is some truth in Juvarra's thesis, but I believe there are also other forces at work, including an overreliance on historical pedagogy, and a reluctance to undertake a new and difficult journey which begins with the study of anatomy and physiology and is followed by a serious study of the constantly growing scientific literature associated with contemporary vocal pedagogy.

The conquest of this highly technical material and the sheer volume of research being performed internationally and now available everywhere represents a major challenge for up to 90% of singing teachers. It generally takes years to assimilate all the knowledge in a practical manner into one's teaching.

Having acknowledged the difficulty of keeping up to date, there is no alternative. One cannot hope to be at the leading edge of one's profession, whatever that profession happens to be, without making an effort to keep up to date.

In addition to the time constraints involved in keeping up to date, I believe that this literary failure on the part of the Italian pedagogue has its roots in the previously secretive nature of Italian vocal pedagogy. Retaining control over hard won knowledge and maintaining secrecy over what were regarded as unique and valuable techniques was an important part of the profession in the distant past. These were seen as the elements that gave some singing teachers the competitive edge. I like Sanchez Carbone's treatment of this issue. She maintains that:

> To achieve a high level of performance, whatever the original gifts, there are no secrets. The indispensable elements are infinite patience, assiduity, regularity, constancy, and application; these are the ingredients that ensure the miracle of singing. The teacher who treats the discoveries pertaining to the technical aspects of singing as his secret, or affirms that to subscribe to his personal method may obviate all difficulties to be found in the present vocal technique, demonstrates a lack of knowledge of the voice as an instrument, and displays his ignorance of comparative pedagogy. Vocal or physical tricks don't produce a secure vocal technique, only ability and talent can achieve that. He who assumes the right to substitute real knowledge with some mysterious personal method is nothing more than a charlatan [Sanchez Carbone, 2005: 4].

I agree with Sanchez Carbone. It is clear that, in Italy, some part of that primitive notion relating to the guardianship of ideas is still present, although it appears to be gradually receding, giving way to more open discussion. It must be said that most of the secretive teachers are the delusional ones who believe they have developed or discovered special techniques, but which they are never prepared to submit to scientific scrutiny.

In reality, the opposite is true. The really special teachers are the ones who do the painstaking research year in year out, those who agonise over the most appropriate structure for their books, struggle with establishing themes, privileging certain ideas above others, prioritising certain issues over others, and then struggling with the difficulties of language to provide clarity and meaning for the reader. And finally, these are the people who suffer the anxieties and insecurities of wondering whether their work is ever good enough to publish. They are not interested in keeping secrets; they just struggle to put it all down on paper, and make meaningful sense of it.

In our case, we make reference to the already quoted authors in these pages. The man and women who are providing structure and given new meaning to the contemporary Italian school. And in so doing are not only giving it continuing relevance, but also providing it with new direction, and making sense of the chaos that has reigned supremely in Italian vocal pedagogy. These authors achieve this order out of chaos through a fusion of vocal science, experimentation associated with empiricism, and the wisdom of the Italian historical school.

The Triumph of Nature and Science Over Incompetence

Finally, I am pleased to report that Juvarra, that previously trenchant critic of Italian vocal pedagogy asserts that even in Italy things are changing with respect to vocal pedagogy. Juvarra concludes that 'more and more, the Italian singers tend to consider themselves as professionals in the same sense as instrumentalists. Consequently, they are becoming aware of the need for books on vocal technique. Books, that although lacking the verbal magic potion, can help in concrete ways to understand issues and resolve problems on the basis of scientific theory' [Juvarra, 1987: 5].

In the twenty and more years following Juvarra's publication of *Il Canto e le sue Tecniche* or *Singing and its Techniques* (1987). Italians have published a number of important books that have had the effect of moving Italian vocal pedagogy forward in a more scientific and systematic way.

However, the really interesting element in all of this is the fact that the criteria for good singing have not changed. According to Juvarra, 'The objective for teachers and singers alike is to produce an easy and natural singing voice, just as it was hundreds of years ago' [Juvarra, 1987: 6].

Sanchez Carbone for instance, contends that 'the only technique to be taught is that which is founded on the principle that only an easy, natural and correct emission is worth teaching. Sanchez Carbone suggests that this idea, which she believes encourages naturalness, is simple to advocate but extremely difficult to achieve' [Sanchez Carbone, 2005: 15].

She relates this type of vocal production to one that has a tendency towards physical and mental relaxation, which she describes as 'the total absence of any undesirable sensations such as unnatural constrictions or vocal fatigue, making this the only method capable of inducing the correct *appoggio* of the sound and disposition of the larynx' [Sanchez Carbone, 2005: 15].

Nanda Mari also remains convinced that the quality of the voice is insufficient for success. She places much more emphasis on mental agility and intelligence.

Having held the singer to a high standard for her performance, Mari holds the teacher to an even higher standard:

> That notwithstanding, there are those who still believe that as long as the voice is in good order and resonant, they have all they need for a successful debut. All of which leads one to believe that much of the criticism levelled at singers with respect to a lack of general culture should more rightly be attributed to the even more scarce astuteness

of the teacher, many of whom, deprived of modern culture, and above all else of good sense and good will, leave the student in the same condition they found him in, throwing him into the fray, a triumph of stubbornness and primitive destiny [Mari, 1975: 26].

Mari laments the lack of comprehension with respect to the criteria necessary for success. She contends that not even the teacher's discrete knowledge, which is now readily available, nor the student's vocal talent, which has now been declared as insufficient, is enough to guarantee success. Mari believes that it is the combination of the student's intelligent and unique application to the task and the teacher's ability to deploy that knowledge and inspire the student to greater efforts that makes all the difference. As I have written in the previous pages, the better teachers are not only adopting a more open stance, but they are also going to great pains to become proficient in the areas of science, anatomy, physiology, acoustics and the physics of singing. They are also prepared to undertake the onerous task of recording their thoughts and techniques for posterity. Consequently, whilst for over twenty years there were only a handful of highly esteemed books on singing, such as Meano's *Human Voice* (1966), Mori's *Coscienza Della Voce* (1970) and Mari's *Canto e Voce* (1975), more recently an increasing number of excellent books have been published in Italy. This new generation of books is characterised by an excellent command of contemporary scientific knowledge, which is in most cases combined with the best of the historical school. The leading lights in this area include Mari and Schindler (1986), Juvarra (1987; 2006), Fussi and Magnani (1994; 2003; 2008), Bruno and Paperi (2001), Battaglia Damiani (2003), Sanchez Carbone (2005), and Fussi and Gilardone (2009). This is a considerable improvement relative to past efforts, especially since it is accompanied by an unprecedented number of academic papers. Even so, we find that Battaglia Damiani, for instance, whilst displaying an excellent command of the scientific material in her books, which should not come as a surprise, given that she was trained as a speech therapist (phonetician) as well as a singer, remains a little circumspect, stating that whilst we are now in possession of thousands of acoustic studies with respect to musical instruments, they only serve to remind us that even today no one has been able to build a violin better than some of the ancient violinmakers. She readily admits that we still build good instruments, but feels that they do not reach the level of perfection and refinement we had reached in the past. Damiani then makes a compelling parallel argument for the similarities between the early violinmakers and the early singing masters, inasmuch as neither had the scientific knowledge we have today, and yet both achieved unsurpassed results.

She argues persuasively that although modern scientific techniques such as fibroscopy, stroboscopy, and magnetic resonance imaging (MRI) have developed enormously, providing us with previously unimaginable information, this new knowledge is no substitute for the educated ear of the teacher.

I agree with Damiani when she states that there is no substitute for the educated ear, but I also believe that this process of education is more interactive than previously thought. I am impressed with the linkages drawn by Fussi and Magnani with respect to listening intuitively and seeing the vocal apparatus:

> He who has gained a deep knowledge and understanding of the physiology of voice will soon learn that through listening one can learn to 'See' the vocal apparatus in its operational functional. This deep understanding of the vocal mechanism reveals the relationship between listening and intuition and the subsequent objective evidence issuing from scientific inquiry [2015, 42].

I agree that the teacher's ear can be stimulated and educated not only through a deep understanding of vocal physiology, but also by the experience of eliciting different sounds in the studio but also by being made increasingly aware of how sound is produced through a long and deep study of the physics of singing. This should begin with the original disturbance, through to compressions and rarefaction stage, producing a sound wave comprised of a fundamental and its integer harmonics, which are finally matched to the enhancing frequencies of the resonator (harmonic partials of the sound wave with formants). Also important is the knowledge of how different acoustic outcomes are achieved through control of particular muscle groups. It is true that the educated ear becomes increasingly tuned by knowing what to listen for. However, it can also be stimulated by phonetic and acoustic knowledge, including a deep study of spectrograms designed to further inform the listening. Knowing how to listen and what to listen for leads to a more sophisticated analysis of sound. Mari, back in (1975), had already made a compelling argument for the benefits ensuing from knowledge. She states that it is only by knowing the cause that one may attain the effect and vice versa. She continues:

> Moreover, it is by making the student aware of the means at his disposal that the major and flexible possibilities will be revealed to him; for as well as one may drive his motor vehicle, he will always drive it even better when he attains an intimate knowledge of the engine and its function. If for no other reason than that in the process one acquires particular details that ignorance certainly can never bestow [Mari, 1970; 75: 24].

Mari is absolutely right to explore this philosophy. However, I don't think she goes far enough, because for a true artist it is not enough to have the possibilities revealed: the true artist is more interested in expanding those possibilities and pushing barriers. Let us return to Damiani who strengthens her argument with respect to the limits of science by citing such authorities as Hirano, Righini, and Wolfram Seidner. However, Hirano's famous (1988) quote which she cites is both generous and self-deprecating, not to mention that nearly thirty years later it is almost certainly out of date. In 1988, Hirano wrote, 'Finally it must be admitted that the science is far behind the art. Our knowledge of the vocal mechanism in singing is very limited' [Hirano (1988) in Damiani, 2003: 212].

I am not at all convinced that this statement still applies. I believe we have come a long way since Hirano made that now famous statement in 1988. And more importantly, many of the missing pieces of the jigsaw puzzle have been put in place, allowing us to deduce more easily the place and value of those pieces that are still missing. Consequently, I think the excuse of incomplete and unreliable scientific knowledge is no longer valid. Frankly, I don't believe there was ever a time when this excuse was valid as a reason for not engaging with science, simply because, in my view, knowledge is generally cumulative, every additional piece of knowledge based information making us better teachers and more complete artists.

As a community, we are in danger of becoming too fixated on the idea of the spectacular discovery, such as the invention of the Laryngoscope, stroboscopy, spectrum analysis and electromyography, and we tend to forget that most practical knowledge is built from one generation to the next, and should be gradually tested and assimilated into our teaching not as it becomes available, but rather as it becomes applicable. It is not just about new discoveries, its also about making the most of what is already available, optimising one's opportunities now.

I sometimes despair when I hear my colleagues making excuses and blaming incomplete knowledge for their personal deficiencies. It is only politeness that prevents me from reminding them that our predecessors produced some of the greatest singers and artists of all time with only a tenth of the knowledge we have available today. Ours is still called the Art of singing, informed by vocal science. If all you aim to do is teach vocal science without an ambition to transcend it, then you are doomed to be ordinary and so are your students. The reason being that in large part, Art is meant to transcend conscious knowledge. My advice is to make a real effort to conquer the considerable body of knowledge available to us and then fill in the gaps with imagination, creativity and great passion.

Damiani continues by citing Righini, one of Italy's leading acousticians. Righini wrote in 1972:

> To accept the contribution of scientific musical research does not mean that we extend the physics data upon the music itself: we cannot in the case of singing always apply

indiscriminately the results of scientific research to vocal technique. The singing master remains indispensable [Righini in Damiani, 2003: 212].

I agree with the above statement. Essentially, all knowledge is only as good as the teacher's ability to apply it, but before that we must make intelligent choices of what elements we concentrate our efforts on. In the end, we can read as many books and academic papers as we like, but if we can't convert that knowledge into a comprehensive, physiologically healthy and acoustically exciting school of singing, the material we read will be of little value. I refer my reader to Nanda Mari's statement, contending that what separates the great teacher from the good one is that quite separate to erudition, the great teacher possesses a highly developed level of intuition [Mari, 1970: 18]. I concur, and believe that part of this intuition relates to an innate knowledge of how far to push certain issues whilst still remaining healthy and stylistically tasteful.

Damiani further strengthens the case by citing Wolfram Seidner (1985), who expresses his position with compelling elegance when he contends that phoneticians, singing teachers and singers cannot hide behind scientific apparatus believing that such instruments can substitute for hearing, sight, sensibility and artistic judgment. You can only use such instruments as subsidiary tools, simply because they can never accurately measure the incredibly varied sounds of the vocal instrument, nor can they ever capture the magic of the singing voice [Damiani, 2003: 212].

Authors such as Meano, Mori, Mari, Juvarra, Damiani, Sanchez Carbone and Fussi and Magnani have one thing in common, they believe in and support science, they understand and appreciate its importance but they are all painfully aware of its artistic limitations. There is broad agreement that science is transformed into art only when its application is entrusted to a truly imaginative and creative artist able to transcend the facts.

Sanchez Carbone argues cogently for a vocal pedagogy grounded on scientific knowledge ahead of imaginative and esoteric explanations. She accepts certain limitations associated with vocal science, but still believes that science offers more direct and simple explanations, and therefore provides more incisive instructions, and more elegant results.

I find myself agreeing in essence with both Sanchez Carbone and Battaglia Damiani, simply because what they are saying represent two sides of the same coin. I believe that Damiani is right to remain sceptical of exaggerated claims made by certain scientists and teachers with respect to the efficacy of science. Similarly, I don't believe that scientific knowledge alone necessarily makes better singers or builds better violins, but science still has a major role to play with respect to muscular function and its resulting vocal quality. There is no doubt that throughout Italy there are factions of the teaching fraternity, including Damiani, who remain sceptical about scientific knowledge, claiming that it remains incomplete and warning against its indiscriminate and unquestioning use. My concern with this argument does not apply to the intelligent, well informed, sincerely questioning teacher, but rather the lazy, ignorant teacher, looking for an excuse to do nothing. On this account, I am with Sanchez Carbone. The responsible singing teacher should avail herself of contemporary science, examine it diligently, synthesise it and simplify its application, and above all don't look for excuses to do nothing.

The evidence is that exceptional singing teachers everywhere, but especially in Italy remain a little cautious with respect to overinflated claims made about new discoveries. However, their caution does not mean that the very best and responsible teachers are not prepared to examine, and even experiment with new ideas; it simply means that they are not prepared to adopt these ideas unconditionally until they become convinced that they may be beneficially incorporated into their teaching. Exceptional teachers are always on a quest for knowledge, always consulting their intuition, recalling their previous experience, questioning accepted wisdom, re-examining previous conclusions, and always asking the perennial question for singing teachers: where is this type of sound or this vocal idea likely to lead us not only aesthetically but also physiologically?I believe that beyond tangible knowledge the singing teachers should develop a sixth sense of where a particular sound or technique is likely to lead not just in the next few months but in the next 20 years. To the extent that the teacher is able to correctly predict such outcomes, he or she will be welcomed or refused a place in the pantheon of historically great singing masters.

I maintain that questioning not only contemporary scientific knowledge but also many of the precepts of the historical school is not only the responsibility, but also the duty of the singing teacher. It is important, however, that this questioning does not lead to a state of mind that opposes everything, finding little of value in anything new or old for that matter. The questioning needs to take the form of a genuine and open-minded examination of knowledge, with a view to adopting and not rejecting. The process cannot be allowed to disintegrate into a state of inertia, and a paralysing of initiative.

I also believe that the imagination, creativity and genius we bring to the strategic deployment of this ever-increasing body of knowledge, both historical and scientific, remain indispensable.

Having said that, I must admit that I also agree with Sanchez Carbone when she suggests that too many teachers tend to ignore the information revolution. For some of these teachers, it would appear that time has stood still not just for decades, but for centuries.As we argued earlier, they hide their ignorance behind erroneous concepts. The truth is that scientific knowledge is not limiting; it doesn't stifle creativity, and it does not get in the way of intuition and imagination. Some teachers even claim that singing is essentially an athletic activity and the singer should therefore concentrate on its physical execution. According to these teachers, the singer should essentially just practice and vocalise and leave the theorising to others.

I think these teachers are in denial and conveniently forget that singing is neither a purely athletic and technical activity nor purely an artistic, creative and intellectual endeavour, it is actually both, the final objective of which is to facilitate emotional expression.And in fairness, I must say that the best schools of singing do move with the times, they do incorporate new scientific knowledge whilst preserving the best of the old ideas and techniques. In this respect, there is good agreement with Sanchez Carbone when she insists 'that the artistic aspects of singing cannot be achieved without the necessary technical proficiency, and systematic vocal technique and artistic expression are inseparable' [Sanchez Carbone, 2005: 6].

I would only add that the fulfilment of this objective requires intelligence, meticulous planning, creative imagination and impeccable execution.

Such teachers know that really great artists don't leave anything up to chance: every detail is considered, artistic choices are made, performance solutions are planned and flawlessly executed, and audience reaction anticipated.What great artists refuse to do is to cut themselves off from a substantial body of knowledge, whether it is scientific or historical performance practices.

The idea is to conceive a grand artistic vision, followed by the development of an architectural blueprint designed to deploy that artistic vision. At this point the artist must not only rehearse what she is attempting to achieve technically, but also rehearse the aesthetic, artistic and emotional message she wishes to convey to the audience. The effect the singer wishes to obtain by applying the blueprint must be rehearsed until it becomes second nature, so that what to the artist is a well rehearsed performance becomes for the audience a spontaneous artistic and emotional expression.

Notwithstanding the importance of the architectural blueprint, there is no denying that the human instrument is a physical instrument that needs to be assembled every time the singer plans to use it. Consequently, we can state that since the human body is our instrument, it is the responsibility and duty of every artist to keep it in good shape.

Rachele Maragliano Mori (1970) argues cogently with respect to the singer's physical wellbeing:

> The responsible singer knows the importance of maintaining:
>
> A responsive instrument; he also knows that this responsiveness is closely tied to physical wellbeing, and that just as he must perform gymnastic exercises every morning

to maintain the elasticity of the muscles at the service of the voice, he must also perform the appropriate exercises in order to maintain the relaxation, elasticity and the flexibility of the organs that collaborate in the function of speech [Mori, 1970: 37].

Following many years of discussion, Sanchez Carbone continues in the same vein:

> The vocal instrument is mechanically very different to other instruments whose form and structure are determined by the mastery of the artisan who builds them, while the vocal instrument is created and moulded by the singer each time she uses it. The singer's instrument is comprised entirely of his body and he must learn not only how it works but also how best to use it. In order to achieve a balance between antagonistic forces in a most relaxed manner, the singer must utilize every technique at her disposal, be it empirical or scientific, physiological or psychological, or intellectual or emotional [Sanchez Carbone, 2005: 249].

Summary

In conclusion, the contemporary Italian singing master has a wondrous vocal historical framework to use for her teaching. It is comforting to know that a school based on such a simple dictum as *chi sa respirare e pronunciare sa cantare* when combined with new developments and a liberal but controlled level of emotion can achieve such majestic results. Nonetheless, contemporary Italian pedagogues have a number of issues that they are working through. There are constant tensions between their respect for past glories and their desire to break new ground by incorporating new physiological, psychological and scientific knowledge. Although most writers agree that singing is a physical practice and cannot therefore be learned from reading books, many of the leading teachers in Italy lament the current quality of vocal pedagogy. They are particularly critical of lazy teachers who do not make a serious effort to improve their knowledge base by reading academic articles and books, and those who do not seek the exchange of ideas by attending seminars and conferences. Some masters have in the past lamented the lack of available literature, although that is no longer the case. It is now more a question of how these authoritative books are used. The concern is that there are still too many lazy teachers refusing to read, consider and share this knowledge. The lack of teacher training is also of concern, especially with respect to physiology, anatomy, and the scientific preparation of students, especially those who are planning to teach.

Having performed a situation analysis for the teaching of the Italian vocal art, we are now able to say that in the sixties and seventies and to a declining extent even today there was considerable resistance in Italy to the advancement of vocal science. Italy is a country that has for generations produced the greatest singers in the world under the empirical system; it is therefore not surprising that it has been slow to react to the advances in science and physiology. However, as vocal science marches on its way forward, its enormous strides can no longer be ignored and consequently resistance to its knowledge based and systematic approach is fading. Over time, as more and more serious authors understand that embracing science is not a vote for declining creativity, as was earlier feared, but rather a freeing of the artistic and creative process, more and more teachers are embracing the inevitable advances in vocal science.Those enlightened teachers who have moved to adopt this new knowledge, as many of the authors here cited demonstrate, have gained greater command of the subject and as a result have evolved into better teachers.

Chapter 11

Respiration in the Contemporary Italian School

In the working formula of the historical Italian school already discussed, that is, *'chi sa respirare e pronunciare sa cantare',* the breathing aspects are cited first followed by pronunciation, articulation and then other areas important elements of singing, such as onset and registration. And since it is widely accepted that breath management is the motor force of the entire vocal instrument, I believe it is appropriate to deepen our knowledge of respiration as is taught in the 21st century Italian school of singing.

Every contemporary Italian author over the last fifty years, more specifically since Meano's work in 1967, has emphasised the importance of respiration with respect to singing, and almost as many have made the connection between respiration, and posture and the resulting vocal quality.

This connection between posture and respiration is nothing new, in fact, it has a history that can be traced back to the very first author to adopt a physiological approach to singing: the sixteenth century physician, Giovanni Maffei. In his excellent 2006 book, *The Art of Bel Canto in the Italian Baroque,* Forman emphasises the fact that writing in 1564, Maffei insists on good posture, suggesting 'that the singer should stand still and firmly on his feet'. Maffei also recommends the use of the mirror as a reminder that 'the mouth should be opened naturally and there should be no movement in other parts of the body. Nor should one fidget with his hands or unduly move his feet' [Forman, 2006: 179].

Porpora's Neapolitan School exhorted students to improve posture. Tosi, Berard, Lablache, García, Stockhausen and Marchesi all follow in the footsteps of Mancini, who famously said that 'I always acted as a dancing master, calling my students one by one before me, I would say, Son, pay attention carefully ... lift the head ... don't bend it forward...don't throw it back...but upright as is natural; thus the parts of the throat remain supple; because if you hang the head forward, the parts of the throat [the neck] stretch suddenly, and they stretch if you lean it back.' [Mancini, 1774: 30].

Contemporary Italian authors are no less sanguine about Posture. Mori (1970), Fussi and Magnani (1994), Bruno and Paperi (1999) all prize posture highly. Sanchez Carbone contends that, 'In the correct and active respiration, the expert singer ensures that the clavicles are in a horizontal position, the shoulders are projected back and the thorax is very open, almost as if, the fingertips turn into levers that raise the thoracic cavity and open it laterally' [Sanchez Carbone, 2005: 49].

Bruno and Paperi (2001) suggest that before concentrating on the end product of a good respiration, that is, artistic singing, we should consider strategies designed to achieve better physical posture and a good predisposition to the human communication represented in the act of singing. According to them 'When our body is straight, firm and agile, we gain confidence in its ability to respond flexibly to the requirements of the music' [Bruno & Paperi, 2001: 86]. Bruno and Paperi recommend gymnastic and other physical exercises designed to develop the body in order to progressively find our own expressive internal rhythm.

They exhort singers to exercise the body by adopting a regime designed to strengthen respiration. In addition to gymnastics, they recommend various styles of swimming, including aquafitness and aquatraining. They also suggest dancing both classical and modern, aerobics and anything else that serves to educate and render the musculature flexible and tonic.

We have argued above that the concept of posture is an important element of voice production has been with us for centuries. The difference between then and now is that contemporary authors have not just continued the recognition of posture but have actually subscribed to complete systems of postural alignment. Authors such as Fussi and Magnani (2003), Battaglia Damiani (2003), and Maria Sanchez Carbone (2005) do more than stress the connection between posture and respiration, they advocate complete and systematic courses of study, such as the practice of the Alexander Technique, the Feldenkrais and Yoga.

Probably the most famous and adhered to systems of body mind alignment are the Alexander Technique'and the Feldenkrais Method. I believe that given the popularity of these Techniques in singing circles, they are worth exploring further, even though I readily admit that this book does not directly set out to discuss and evaluate such techniques.Nonetheless, a sampler that may lead those who are more interested into a deeper exploration will do no harm and may serve as a catalyst for some students and even established singers. Indeed, there are many fine books in the market that specialise in this area that may serve as further stimulus to the exploration of these methods. With that in mind, let us say a few words about the Alexander Technique, followed by an introduction to Feldenkrais.

The Alexander Technique is based on the experience of Frederick Alexander, an Australian actor who developed problems with dysphonia. In an effort to comprehend and rectify the problem, Alexander began an analysis of the living body, which rapidly led him to understand the causal relationship between the symptoms and the correct physical habit. This was not only a phonatory phenomenon, but also contains a postural and motor component.This experience led him to the re-education of his postural habits, and the formulation of an original method in which he elaborates the technique he used to accomplish his personal rehabilitation. He defined his new method as 'a method of psycho/physical re-education'.

In his method, Alexander advocated the power of the mind to consciously release muscular tension. The method possesses rehabilitative, preventative and therapeutic value.

Moshe Feldenkrais developed his own method in the 1970s, which in many respects complements Alexander's. The Feldenkrais method can be practiced in either individual or class situation.

One of the first lessons introduced in the Feldenkrais method is the modality referred as 'Functional Integration', which is achieved through the criteria of direct manipulation. In this modality, the teacher's hands become the instrument through which the student learns about the organisation of his body and his personal way of moving. This guides the student towards a rediscovery of forgotten movement and an exploration of other modalities of functional movement.

On the other hand, group lessons referred to as 'Awareness Through Movement' formal course of action, through which the student through the teachers verbal exhortation explore the inherent movement in the more functional daily movement in sitting, raising, walking and opening and closing the mouth.

Daily routine reveals a delicate exploration of the possibilities that movement allows the process of learning and reproduction which is similar to that confronted by a child learning to move in a gravitational camp. Together these modalities offer an alternative way of moving, which in the end enriches the planned movement already in place and which is characterised by repetitive mechanisation, which may in time become incapable of responding to the daily requirements.

Fussi and Magnani quote at length the director of the Feldenkrais Institute of Milan, Mara Della Pergola. I believe that her commentary is so valuable that I am inclined to do the same. Della Pergola contends that:

> One of the concepts at the base of such a method is that everyone acts in accordance with the image they have of themselves, and that image is complete, but can always be improved. Usually we have the impression that our way of speaking, walking, behaving, holding the shoulders and the pelvis is the only way possible. Our appearance, our voice our way of thinking, our relationship with time and space appear to be a given, acquired from time immemorial, the image we have of ourselves is the result of our biological inheritance and of our experience. The movement, according to Feldenkrais,

is the easiest way to access a person. Every action is in fact the result of muscular activity: even seeing, speaking and listening demands muscular action. Movement is the concretization of nervous impulses, and a change in our action implies a preceding change in our central control, that is, in our nervous system. We may become aware of that which is happening, of our sensations and our sentiments only when they are expressed in the mobilization of the body. There is no thought or sensation without a corresponding physical reaction [Della Pergola, in Fussi and Magnani 2003: 133].

If our knowledge of the body and our posture has increased markedly, and it clearly has, then our knowledge of diaphragmatic and thoracic physiology, not to mention the breathing process is no less spectacular. Meano (1967), Mori (1970), Fussi and Magnani (1994, 2014) Mari and Schindler (1986), Juvarra (1987), Bruno and Paperi (1999), Battaglia Damiani (2003), and Sanchez Carbone (2005), all give an excellent account of the physiology and process of respiration.

Anatomy of Respiration

Inspiratory Muscles: The Diaphragm and External Intercostal Muscles

The breathing paradigm that we immediately recognised as the most efficient model for elite singing is based on the double support system in which the diaphragm and abdominal muscles oppose each other, as do the external and internal intercostal muscles (thoracic elevators and depressors respectively). These combined antagonistic forces provide the singer with a considerable support system and good control over the respiratory process.

In the following pages, we will examine in some depth each of the contributing group of muscles, such as the diaphragm, the abdominals, and the intercostals, but perhaps even before doing that we should examine the thorax which houses all the important organs and is activated by the essential muscles just mentioned. We will see how their actions influence the elevation, depression and expansion of the thoracic cage.

Let us therefore examine the thorax, which houses the trachea, the lungs, the heart and the various muscles that control respiration.

The Thorax

The thorax is shaped similar to a pyramidal quadrangular trunk. The thoracic cage is comprised of a skeletal part (dorsal vertebrae, sternum and ribs), and a muscular part that includes the diaphragm. The diaphragm is the muscle that separates the thoracic cavity from the abdominal cavity.

There are 12 dorsal vertebrae and each takes the form of a cylindrical body. They are comprised of two distinct parts, the vertebral body and the neural arc. The circumference that we create between the neural arc and the posterior part of the vertebral body forms the foreman of the vertebrae.

These 12 vertebrae are characterised by the presence on the body, in proximity to the lateral face, of four articulatory facets, which form the costo-vertebral articulators.

The Sternum

The sternum is an unequal osseous body situated on the anterior or median part of the thorax. In the adult, it is composed in three parts: the manubrium, or the superior part, the central body, and the terminal appendix, called the xiphoid process. The first two parts are separated a by a cartilaginous tract in a horizontal direction, forming an angle which varies with respiration. This is known as the angle of Louis.

Along the manubrium we find the facets that articulate the clavicles and the first costal cartilages, whilst along the body we find the articulatory facets for the other costal cartilages (ribs).

There are 12 costal cartilages and they may be subdivided into three groups. These groups are:

- seven (7) real costal cartilages, sometimes called sternal costals, of which the cartilaginous prolongation is united into a singular attachment to the sternum
- three (3) false costals, of which the cartilaginous prolongation is united at the sternum via the costal cartilages immediately above, until they arrive at the seventh costal cartilage
- two (2) floating costals, in which the cartilaginous prolongation remains free.

The above is a summary extracted from the anatomy chapter, written by Bossi, Ghio, and Gilardone in Fussi and Gilardone's book *Clinica della Voce* (2009: 3–4).

Castellani concurs with the above and adds her own valid functional description. She states that thoracic cage forms the superior part of the trunk, and its function is to protect the vital organ, including the heart and lungs. The thorax is sustained by the vertebral column, a flexible structure comprised of 33 vertebrae that act as origin and attachment for many respiratory muscles. The thorax, according to Castellani, forms the bases of the curvature generated by the vertebral column which are then subdivided into five groups: 7 cervical, 12 thoracic, 5 lumber, 5 sacral and 3 coccyx. The 12 thoracic vertebrae act as a point of attachment for the 12 pairs of costal cartilages that constitute the thoracic cage. The ensuing cartilaginous arches are comprised of an osseous part and a cartilaginous part: the posterior part is grafted to the thoracic vertebrae and its arched shape closes anteriorly on the sternum, an oddly shaped bone situated in the middle part of the thorax. Theses cartilaginous costals are subdivided into three groups: 7 real or sternal cartilages which are united anteriorly directly into a single unit on the sternum; 3 false ribs which are united at the sternum via their own cartilaginous extension which connects each rib to the rib immediately above; and finally, 2 floating ribs that do not unite at the sternum at all, and are only attached to the thoracic vertebrae [Damiani (2001), Fussi and Gilardone (2009), and Castellani, 2012: 31–32].

The thorax is the highly mobile casing that accommodates the lungs the heart, the trachea and various other critical organs. The mobility of the thorax is a function of the singer's ability to move virtuosically all the thoracic levers comprised of the cartilaginous costals and numerous muscles, the most important of which are the diaphragm, the intercostals, and the abdominals.

Let us examine each contributing element of our respiratory model in more detail, discussing the musculature, its function and its effect on vocal quality. The first and possibly most famous muscle in the body is the diaphragm and consequently we begin our exploration of the respiratory system by examining it first.

The Diaphragm

As already stated the diaphragm is not only one of the most famous muscles in the body but also one of the most powerful. The diaphragm is shaped like a cupola, which is constituted by a central tendon that is definitely not contractible or inextensible. Fortunately, however, the surrounding muscles fibres of the diaphragm are both contractible and elastic, and it is through we can attain considerable control over both elevation and depression of the diaphragm.

The diaphragm is attached to the sternum, the thoracic cage or costal cartilages, and posteriorly to the vertebral column via two muscular pillars that are attached to the second and third lumbar vertebrae.

The upper surface of the diaphragm constitutes the floor of the thoracic cavity and is in contact with the pleurae (serous membrane covering the lungs and the pericardium).On the other hand, the abdominal surface of the diaphragm is covered in part by the peritoneal membrane.

Meano (1967), Sanchez Carbone (2005), Fussi and Gilardone (2009), and Castellani (2012) all describe the diaphragm as resembling a cupola that is structured by an inelastic central tendon and a surrounding contractile musculature, which separates the thoracic cavity from the abdominal cavity.

Castellani (2012) confirms the above reflections on the diaphragm and elaborates further. She contends that the diaphragm is an inspiratory and involuntary muscle whose principal purpose is to separate the abdomen from the thorax. The diaphragm presents as a cupola that has anterior insertions into the sternum and the lower part of the thoracic cage, that is, costal cartilages; and posteriorly to the vertebral column, more specifically the vertebral lumbar region through the agency of two muscular pillars. Three separate parts form the superior surface of the diaphragm: the inelastic central tendon, which as the name implies 'is of a tendinous nature, and the two lateral parts (left and right), which are comprised of muscular tissue' [Castellani, 2012: 34].

Meano, Fussi and Magnani, Sanchez Carbone, and Castellani inform us that the tendinous fibres of the diaphragm do not possess elasticity, but on the other hand the lateral muscles surrounding the diaphragm possess considerable elasticity [Fussi and Magnani (1994), Damiani (2003), and Castellani [2012: 34]. Juvarra confirms that contraction of the muscle fibres surrounding of the diaphragm flatten the diaphragmatic cupola and causes the abdomen to protrude.

The muscular fascia that have origin in the central tendon are inserted into the second and third lumbar vertebrae through two robust formations called the internal diaphragmatic pillars situated on the left and right of the median line respectively, to the internal surface of the sternum and the internal surface of the last two costal cartilages. Sanchez Carbone contends that:

> The diaphragm regulates the respiratory function and remains one of the most powerful muscles in the body. As with the heart, the activity of the diaphragm is involuntary and continuous throughout one's life. It represents the most important element with respect to thoracic capacity, which represents between 60 to 80 per cent of capacity increase during deep inspiration [Sanchez Carbone, 2005: 56].

Mori (1970) Juvarra (1987) and Sanchez Carbone (2005) all adopt the same position with respect to the diaphragm and the heart, which is, that they are involuntary and continuously functioning organs. Mori, however, goes further, regarding them 'as organs of life for the nutrition of the individual; they are also the most mobile and reactive to every vibration of the human being, reflecting the emotions and influencing the respiratory rhythm' [Mori, 1970: 27].

With respect to the diaphragm, there is now good agreement that the central tendon of the diaphragm cannot itself be controlled. However, Meano (1967) informs us that 'the central tendons of the diaphragm unite the muscular fibres which radiate from this 'centre' to the periphery. It is the contraction of these fibres which provide the agility of movement necessary to raise and lower the muscle during respiration' [Meano, 1967: 26].

Bruno and Paperi (2001) concur with the above assessment of the central tendon and surrounding muscles. Here are their conclusions:

> The diaphragm in particular, whose primary action is that of stretching and lowering itself in the inspiratory phase, pressing down a little on the upper part of the abdomen and laterally on the lower part of the costals, including the back ribs, must transfer its daily emotional function to that expressive energy required for vocal interpretation, especially with respect to great sentiments and certain styles. In reality the diaphragm, which inserts into the sternum and the vertebral column, would not be controllable during phonation, but may be educated through the proper training of surrounding muscles, to finally arrive at the role of air dosing muscle [Bruno & Paperi, 2001: 89].

With the above in mind, I think it fair to conclude two principle facts: the first is that we can attain considerable control over the diaphragm; and the second is that if anyone could learn how to control and activate the muscle fibres emanating from the central tendon, I have no doubt it would a talented artist full of determination and perseverance.

Antonio Juvarra (1987) not only agrees with the above but also actually goes further. In a passage that could have been lifted out of Sundberg and Leanderson (1987), Juvarra also subscribes to diaphragmatic co-contraction. We will elaborate on this further, but for now it behoves us to stay with the diaphragm, and with respect to this inspiratory organ Juvarra contends that 'in almost every school of singing when we speak of the diaphragm we do so in a manner that betrays a high level of ignorance with respect to the true function of this famous muscle' [Juvarra, 1987: 38].

Juvarra declares that when a teacher invites a student to sustain a certain note with the diaphragm, and then visually tries to assess its effectiveness on the basis of the external movement of the abdomen as it withdraws, he may find that this is not an accurate reflection of what is really happening. Simply because the abdomen may be pushing up a relaxed diaphragm; that is, a diaphragm that offers no resistance to what should be an antagonistic action of the abdomen.

Juvarra explains a second and better strategy of producing this much-needed antagonistic tension:

> When we contract the diaphragm, it tends to descend, pushing out the abdomen, whilst at the same time offering its descending force as opposition to the superior ascending force provided by the contraction of the abdominal muscles. In both cases the external visible results are the same, but the antagonistic force of the second method is the only one that is capable of realizing sufficient abdominal tension [Juvarra, 1987: 38].

And that is the major problem with those teachers and scientists who insist that because the central tendon does not possess elastic contractile fibres it cannot be contracted. We agree with this proposition with respect to the central tendon, but that is not the same as saying that the diaphragm through the contraction of its lateral muscles cannot offer a powerful and genuine resistance to the ascending force exerted by the abdominal girdle, creating an antagonistic force Lamperti's lotta vocale (vocal Struggle), and therefore exert considerable respiratory control over both breath pressure and breath airflow.

Let's be honest, if we don't concede the possibility of considerable control over the diaphragm, albeit, by contracting the muscle fibres surrounding the diaphragm in combination with the lateral muscles and posterior muscles, such as quadratus lamborum, then we are intimating that there can be no true 'lotta vocale'. This is an idea that would be resisted by any singing teacher worthy of the name, because they all know that whilst the singer can achieve greater voluntary control and quicker, the exclusive use of the intercostal muscles would prove inadequate for elite singing. Elite singing requires control over combined complex constituted by the external intercostal muscles and the diaphragm for inspiration and the internal intercostal/abdominal girdle complex for expiration. I have no doubt that elite singers train the lateral muscle and posterior muscles to balance the antagonistic forces between the diaphragm, and the abdominal muscle complex and the external/internal intercostals to the degree required to obtain complete control over the dosing of the breath, depending on pitch and intensity.

It is clear that the central tendon does not possess elasticity and therefore has no contractile capacity; consequently, it can only be acted upon and its role therefore is strictly passive, that is, it relies on the contraction of the abdominals to push it back to its original position within the thoracic cage, relying on the contraction of the surrounding lateral muscles attached to the central tendon in order to maintain a downward thrust in opposition to the ascending force of the abdominal girdle. If this were the complete story, we may say that the abdominals assumed the responsibility of dosing the expiratory air, a proposition that has few subscribers in the Italian literature. The lack of devotees to this idea is evidence that authorities believe that in a system that is entirely based on the clash of antagonistic forces, it makes no sense for the abdominal muscles to push the passive diaphragm into the thorax cavity without inducing a reciprocal antagonistic resistance. Absent this antagonistic force, how do we affect a support system?

The answer is that just as the abdominal muscles can act on the passive central tendon to push the diaphragm back into the thoracic cavity, so too can the lateral muscles surrounding the central tendon be trained to maintain a lowered diaphragm, thereby offering resistance and a balancing force to the upward push from the abdominals.

In this matter, I agree with Antonio Juvarra's assertion that when the diaphragm is contracted (that is, when the surrounding muscular fibres are activated), it can only descend because it does not possess the musculature required to raise it [Juvarra, 1987: 38].

In my view, there has been far too much fuss about the passivity of the central tendon. Too often scientists and some knowledgeable singing teachers make the mistake of acting like they have discovered America and the poor ignorant singer is mired in this quagmire of ignorance.

This is not only untrue, but also unfair. Most great singers have very hectic careers: far too busy to play around with these types of physiological distinctions. Distinctions that may be quite significant for those of us who are pursuing research, but not of such moment to those pursuing an international career, and who are constantly learning new roles and new productions of the ones they have already performed. Not to mention that the very best artists are constantly engaged in the struggle to keep up standards and if possible improve on them. What these artists want to know is this: are we able to train the diaphragm to resist the ascending force exerted by the abdominal muscles, and thereby enact the 'lotta vocale' prescribed by the international Italian school? The answer according to the Italian literature is an unequivocal, yes.

The Intercostal Muscles

Internal and External Intercostals

Before discussing the thoracic and abdominal muscles, let us summarise what we have learned in the previous pages. We learned that that the diaphragm is shaped like a cupola, which even though it is possessed of an incontractible central tendon, fortunately can still be contracted via the contractile muscles surrounding the diaphragm. This has the effect of lowering and flattening the diaphragm, which is displaced down pushing the viscera down and out, and laterally expanding the lower intercostals at the level of the floating ribs. At this point the resistance presented by the abdominal muscles comes into play. At this point it is worth recalling Sanchez Carbone's elegant synthesis, 'the compression of the abdominal viscera, which is utilised alternatively by the diaphragm in inspiration and the abdominal wall in expiration, repeats with periodic regularity through the autonomic nervous system [Sanchez Carbone, 2005: 63].

In order to complete our respiratory model, we need to briefly examine the function of the abdominals. These will be elaborated on shortly, but for now let us state that when the abdominals are in a relaxed state they will easily accommodate the forward thrust of the viscera as it is pressed down and out. On the other hand, when the abdominal muscles contract, they can prevent the complete descent of the diaphragm producing negative results on respiration in general and the inspiratory phase in particular. However, compression of the abdominal muscles after a complete inspiration will result in a displacement of the viscera posteriorly towards the vertebral column, and superiorly against a relatively relaxed diaphragm, which is subsequently pushed upward into the thorax, raising the diaphragm and compressing the breath out of the lungs that are attached to the floor of the diaphragm via a double-pleurae.

Now that we have covered the physiological function of the diaphragm at some length, and cast a cursory glance at its antagonistic relationship with the abdominals, let us turn to our physiological knowledge of the thorax in its double inspiratory, expiratory function, before finally examining the relationship between the interactive thorax, the abdominal girdle, and the diaphragm.

Let us begin by recognising that there is still some controversy over the function of the intercostal muscles that elevate and expand the thorax and those that depress and constrict its actions. Given this controversy, it is appropriate that Castellani treats the intercostals as one muscular unit constituted by the external, and internal intercostal muscles. Nonetheless, it is important not to exaggerate this uncertainty. The truth is that there is a very widely accepted theory that has gained considerable legitimacy over the last twenty or so years.

This most notable and credible theory posits that the external intercostals in combination with the cartilaginous portion of the internal intercostals elevate the thorax in a 'bucket handle style', which elevates but also expands the thorax in an anterior/posterior and lateral dimension. This constitutes the universally recommended thoracic position with respect to the Italian school of the 21st century. Further, the theory, states that the remaining osseous portion of the internal intercostals is utilised in expiration to depress and constrict the thorax.

This theory, in which the internal intercostals are regarded as thoracic depressors and the external intercostals are thoracic elevators, is universally accepted in the Italian literature and is therefore the one that will be explored in this book.

Let us continue our journey of exploration. Castellani's theory (2012), is in line with, Mari (1975), Fussi and Magnani (1994), Bruno and Paperi (2001) and Sanchez Carbone (2005), who all agree that the intercostals occupy the space between the ribs, where they find an insertion on the inferior costal margins extending vertically and obliquely to the internal surface of the first to the eleventh rib. More specifically both the internal and external intercostals have origin on the surface of the upper costal cartilage and attachment to the upper border of the next lower rib. However, their muscular fibres run in opposite directions. And as we saw above, contraction of the internal intercostal depresses the thorax, reducing thoracic volume, whilst contraction of the external intercostal raises and expands the thorax. The external intercostals muscles also contribute to an increase in the antero/posterior and transverse thoracic volume.

Damiani (2003) concurs, and following a short commentary on the controversial nature of intercostal function, proceeds to describe the anatomy of the intercostal muscles. According to Damiani, in general the intercostal muscles are all relatively short, thick, and reinforced by powerful connective fibres. According to Damiani, the eleven (11) external intercostal muscles are constituted by slim layers of tissue, which totally occupy the intercostal spaces. The internal intercostal muscles run obliquely from the lower border of the costal cartilage above, to the upper border of the cartilage below. The external intercostals, on the other hand, also are oblique muscles that originate in the lower border of the costal above, traversing obliquely down to the upper border of the rib immediately below. The difference is that external intercostals are larger than the internal intercostals, and they run obliquely in the opposite direction [Damiani, 2003: 28; Sanchez Carbone, 2005; Castellani, 2012].

Battaglia Damiani (2003) believes that in the entire intercostal complex clearly constitutes the static suspensory muscular system, whose principal function is to guarantee the integrity of the intercostal space. Battaglia Damiani concludes that the intercostals behave like active ligaments. She continues:

> The intercostals are inversely oblique. At every inclination or rotation, at every movement of the cervical scapula, the thorax endures a number of contractions, twisting in one way or another. The ideal intercostal space could not be guaranteed without the inverse obliqueness of these muscles, whose fibres are always correctly orientated in a manner that transmits or arrests movement and impedes any overlap such as appears in the respiratory phase [Battaglia Damiani, 2003: 29].

To the degree that the intercostals find a balanced equilibrium over antagonistic 'vocal struggle', they provide the singer with a vocal support system. Although, it must be said, not as complete a support system as when the external intercostals combine with the diaphragm to effect inspiration, and the internals intercostal combine with the abdominals to effect expiration. When these two competing inspiratory/expiratory forces oppose each other, they create an antagonistic tension, which the Italians refer to as the 'lotta vocale', or 'vocal struggle', also known as the '*appoggio* system' of breath management.

I will elaborate at length on the '*appoggio* system' in the following pages, but for now let us concentrate the contribution of this antagonistic muscular pairing to the '*appoggio* system'. The first pairing to be addressed is the inspiratory contribution as represented by the diaphragm and external intercostals.

The Diaphragm and External Intercostals: Inspiratory Muscles

As we have already discussed, inspiration is the combined responsibility of the diaphragm and the simultaneous elevation and expansion of the thorax cavity, which consists of raising the sternum and expanding the floating ribs laterally. The elevation and expansion of the thorax, we concluded, was the function of the internal intercostals whose contraction raises the thoracic cage in a 'bucket handle style' that is, antero/posterior and transversally.

We recall that the diaphragm, which separates the thoracic cavity from the abdominal cavity, is the inspiratory muscle 'par excellence'.

The diaphragm can move up or down altering both cavities as it does: an increase in the thorax cavity is the result of lowering the diaphragm so that it can press against the abdominal wall, pushing the viscera forward and down (known as abdominal respiration). On the other hand, as the abdominal muscles push the viscera and diaphragm back into the thorax, we see an increase in the space of the abdominal cavity, and a decrease in the space of the thoracic cavity.

The Abdominals and Internal Intercostals: Expiratory Muscles

The opposite is true during the expiratory phase. Expiration is the second phase of the respiratory cycle and in everyday life, this calm normal expiration is a purely passive phenomenon, which is essentially effected by the diaphragm. On the other hand, there is broad agreement amongst eminent authors that artistic respiration requires breathing that is willed, active and voluntary. Mori (1970), Juvarra (1987), and Sanchez Carbone (2005) all believe that 'In singing, however, expiration must be active'.

In order to achieve this active, voluntary control, Mori contends that we must gain control over the main expiratory muscles, which are: the internal intercostal muscles, abdominals (internal and external oblique, and transverse and rectus abdominus).

Consequently, we conclude that expiration remains the domain of the internal intercostal and the abdominal girdle; the latter acts against the contracting diaphragm eventually overcoming its resistance. In doing so, it pushes the diaphragm back into the thorax, pressing the air out of the lungs.

A long expiration demands a great deal of care because it must be accomplished with a graduated continuity and contraction of the muscles during the emission of sound; it is this process that yields a free, resonant voice which is in equilibrium in each of its parts. If during the emission the breath pressure is either augmented or diminished or the muscular contraction is too accentuated, the sound will either sharpen or flatten. Sanchez Carbone agrees that 'the art of active expiration is the most important to the act of singing ... the control of expiration constitutes an important element in the formation of the voice' [Sanchez Carbone, 2005: 121].

We have discovered that the internal intercostal (expiratory muscles), contribute to expiration by depressing and constricting the thoracic cage. Generally, the quicker the thorax is depressed the quicker the diaphragm is drawn into the medium part of the abdomen. Consequently, we can say that neither a particularly fast diaphragmatic ascension of the diaphragm nor the uncontrolled depression of the thorax are desirable elements with respect to good singing.In fact, the opposite is true: a good support or '*appoggio* system' is characterised by the ability of the opposing forces of the diaphragm and external intercostal to act antagonistically against the combined force of the abdominals and internal intercostal muscles, keeping them balanced for an unusually long period of time.

The Abdominal Girdle

The dilation of thorax is actuated through the movement of the ribs, which constitute the thoracic cage. Juvarra states that the raising of the superior costals cartilages in the 'pump lever manner' gives way to the so called costal-clavicular respiration which is universally condemned as being harmful to singing; On the other hand, the lateral movement of the inferior false or floating ribs resulting in the so called costo-diaphragmatic breathing is universally applauded. This second type of respiration is essential to the production of the singing voice and the development of its most important elements such as the diaphragm, the inferior costals, the internal and external intercostal, and the muscle complex that constitutes the abdominal girdle.

In their combined action the abdominal muscles constitute the abdominal girdle that connects the lower margins of the thorax and the superior margin of the base, its function being the protection of the abdomen and to sustain the various organs. Amongst them we distinguish:

1. the transversus abdominus, which is constituted by bundles of muscular fibres running horizontally, and which are attached posteriorly to the vertebral column and anteriorly to the cartilages of the lower ribs (the costal)

2. the internal oblique, that radiates fanlike, originates in the thoracic lumber fascia posteriorly and radiates anteriorly towards the centre of

the inguinal ligament

3. the rectus abdominus that combines the two sides of the linea alba (median line), the base and the thoracic cage

4. the external oblique that crosses perpendicularly the fibres of the internal oblique is involve in the breathing mechanism those muscles constitute the intercostal muscles: these occupy the spaces between the ribs of the thoracic cage and protect it in the case of excessive pressure; their action concurs with the raise and lowering of the ribs.

A muscular scheme of this type can contribute to the clarity of ideas with respect to the breathing mechanism, but only if we keep in mind that in singing nothing works in isolation. On the contrary, every muscle group acts in a holistic equilibrated interplay of tensions designed to balance the opposite function of what Arnold Rose calls a 'balanced antagonism'. This occurs above all in the antagonism between the diaphragm and the abdominal muscles, which are of fundamental importance to the breathing for singing and what Lamperti calls the *lotta vocale*.

> These opposing tensions essentially represent the 'appoggio' or 'sostegno' breath management system already mentioned, whilst the frequent reference to the 'appoggio in maschera' is associated with the mechanisms that control the resonance. This last point is realized with the continuous and extremely malleable moulding of the internal spaces (essentially mouth and pharynx), for which the recourse to tension becomes indispensable (voluntarily and gradual in accordance with the desired effect) predetermined by the facial muscles: the orbicularis that pushes forward the lips, the zygomatic that facilitates indirectly the raising of the soft palate) and the dilating muscles of the narice (which use is implicit in every internal smile, or guiding the sound 'with the nose' or to open the face [Juvarra, 1987: 30].

The Lungs

Juvarra also makes a substantial contribution to the study of respiration. According to him, the lungs, which are suspended at the interior of thoracic cavity, are Indispensable to respiration (for phonation). Their shape and size remain necessarily in close relationship to those of the thorax: the raising of the ribs and opening of the chest correspond to the increase in pulmonary area, resulting from the elastic properties.

The lungs are found within the thoracic cavity; these two conically shaped organs are constituted by elastic fibres and porous tissues and are the site of gaseous exchange between the air and blood. Meano reminds us that during respiration a gaseous exchange takes place, which permits 'the blood to absorb oxygen from the air, eliminating the carbon dioxide which is formed in the cells of our body' [Meano, 1967: 30].

The external surface of the lungs is delineated by small fissures, which separate the lungs into different regions called lobes. The right lung is comprised of three lobes (superior, medium, and inferior), whilst the left lung is constituted by two lobes (superior and inferior). This difference is mainly due to the fact that the space occupied by the left lung has to also accommodate the heart. The lungs are contained within an airtight sac constituted by a double membrane comprised of the visceral and parietal pleura. In combination, these membranes form a double walled airtight enclosure. This double membrane covers the thoracic wall, completely encasing the lungs [Angela Castallani, 2012: 32–33].

The visceral pleurae follow closely the contours and movement of the lungs. The right and left pleurae membranes are completely separate, acting as a protective lining for each lung.

Sanchez Carbone (2005), Fussi and Gilardone (2009) and Castellani (2012) inform us that between the pleura there exists a very slim space called the intrapleural space in which is contained a lubricating fluid, which allows the two membranes to slip and slither against each other during inspiration. In addition, the presence of a negative pressure within the intrapleural space allows the two pleurae to remain connected to each other forming the double wall enclosure mentioned above and contributing to the mechanical expansion of the thorax during respiration.

In between the lungs we find the trachea, a flexible tube connected to the cricoid cartilage via the cricotracheal ligament, and which function it is to facilitate the exchange of air in and out of the lungs during respiration. The trachea splits into two parts, the left and right, and even though they are asymmetric between them, the two bronchial branches are constituted by incomplete cartilaginous rings that give it the elasticity and flexibility that. The asymmetry is due to the fact that the right lung has a major respiratory capacity with respect to the left, resulting in the right bronchi being demonstrably shorter than the left. The bronchi are further subdivided into small branches called bronchiole, which again subdivide into miniscule structures known as alveoli. The latter are covered with a thick network of capillaries, inside which occurs the effective gas exchange that takes place during a respiratory cycle [Castellani, 2012: 33].

However, and notwithstanding lingering controversy, there is now universal agreement that the above anatomical and physiological description constitutes a sketch upon which the predominant Italian model of the *appoggio* system will be further developed in these pages. It is also the model through which we will explore, analyse and elaborate the respiratory system taught by the great contemporary Italian masters of the 21st century.

Contemporary Italian literature is full of great exhortations to develop the diaphragmatic musculature in order to control the upward thrust of the abdominal muscles and which would then turn it into the air dosing muscle par excellence. All of the above authors recommend breathing exercises separate to the act of singing. These exercises are designed to achieve muscular control, and all of them have their genesis in good posture.

It is important that whilst Battaglia Damiani has delved into the Alexander Technique, Sanchez Carbone has studied Yoga breathing, and Fussi and Magnani explore both the Alexander Technique and Feldenkrais Method, all of them also refer back to the noble posture advocated by the old masters.

Bruno and Paperi's contribution is most interesting and highly representative of the argument espoused above. Specifically, they suggest that it can be beneficial to muscularly tone the lower abdominal–pelvic area, whilst maintaining the stretched muscles of the abdominal region as well as those of the mid-lower costals, which in good singing are combined with the diaphragm.

We must also pay particular attention to the musculature at the back of the stomach so that it may provide us with a favourable response; the dorsal muscles must also remain elastic in order to render the whole inspiratory area ready for dilation. Bruno and Paperi realise that the singer must develop the respiratory musculature through physical exercise. They continue:

> One must strike a relationship with ones own body in the form of a personalized postural gymnastic regime, and appropriate motor activity. The synergistic elasticity of the antagonistic muscles that stabilize the postural movement must be tied to cerebral control, vestibular (control of the egress of the voice), and visible environment. This will make it easier for the singer to coordinate and harmonize respiration, voice, sentiments and theatrical action. It also aids the diaphragm, which needs to expand during inspiration without the danger of tension that creates difficulties during the diaphragm's measured return to its original position, as well as its emotional participation which is dependent upon that which is been sung; consequently, it is necessary to create a sharp interaction amongst the relevant respiratory elements associated with efficient expiration [Bruno and Paperi, 2001: 89].

Whilst we are anxious to further explore the above issues, it must be obvious that we already have a great deal of knowledge with respect to breathing, all of which leads to one question. If we have all this knowledge available and almost universal agreement that the 'art of breathing is essential to the art of singing', then why do we still produce so many singers, even very gifted ones, who are incapable of conquering breath management? Sanchez Carbone has some perspicacious insights into this question. She contends that many singing teachers address the issue of breathing with their students, and certainly:

> Most of them understand the importance of breathing and therefore make an effort to deal with it. The problem is that most of them don't know how to teach it or whether the student is accidentally stumbling on the right formula. Even in books, the chapters

that deal with breathing are often underdeveloped. Evidently, the author or the teacher has not been able to conquer the principles of good breathing for singing. Consequently, without knowing the essential principles of breathing, they find it difficult to either teach or write about it [Sanchez Carbone, 2005: 46].

With the above in mind, it is easy to understand the importance of elaborating on the 'art of breathing', which the great masters of the past believed was synonymous with to as 'art of singing'.

The Importance of Respiration in The Italian School of Singing

Rachele Maragliano Mori on Breathing

Mori contends that both voice production and singing are complex phenomenon that depend not only on the psychic and physical disposition of the individual, but also on the chain of cause and effect of the physiological, psychological and aesthetical components that influence modern didactic criteria aimed at realising optimum outcomes which often occur naturally [Mori, 1970: 26]. Sanchez Carbone concurs, believing that good singing requires both 'psyche and suma' to fulfill its true potential [Sanchez Carbone, 2005: 15].

Before examining the different types of breathing and the concomitant effect each has on vocal sound. Mori asks us to remember that respiration comprises of two distinct phases, the first is inspiration and the second is expiration, whilst both of these phases are natural for everyday life, they are much more complex for the fulfilment of artistic objectives [Mori, 1970: 26]. Sanchez Carbone agrees with Mori (1970) and Juvarra (1987), in believing that breathing can be divided into two categories: the first category is an automatic and habitual style of breathing designed to preserve life; the second category refers to a more conscious and aware method, which is guided by will as opposed to instinct or habit.

The latter, more conscious and voluntary method is the one subscribed to by most elite singers, and its conquest demands extensive and exact knowledge of the breathing mechanism and its relationship to glottal regulation. Even though *appoggio* is generally acknowledged to be primarily connected to breath management, it is clear that there can be no true '*appoggio* system' without proper consideration of glottal settings: that is, glottal resistance, and resonance balancing. This complex, which is constituted by breath *appoggio*, 'glottal resistance', and the resonance balancing, which the Italians refer as '*appoggio* in maschera', is probably the most concise, yet profound formula in singing. Mori (1970), Juvarra (1987), Bruno and Paperi (2001), Damiani (2003) and Sanchecz Carbone (2005) all subscribe to this theory. In fact, it is not an exaggeration to say that this complex theory is one of the most complete and often referred to theories in the entire Italian vocal literature.

In pursuit of greater clarification and elaboration, let us return to Mori. In her priceless (1970) contribution, Mori is not only eloquent with respect to vocal technique, but also elegant through her indispensable and evocative depiction of a vocal era that was in the process of vanishing even as she was writing about it.

Mori depicts a vivid, dynamic, creative and yet colourful Italian musical scene in which scientists such as Baglioni, and Wicart would arrange conferences that were nothing less than a contest of ideas from which all singers young and old would gain enlightenment and encouragement.

Mori portrays a world of open and lively discussion in which topics such as:

> The type of respiration, the direction we imparted on the soundwaves in the resonating cavity (impostazione), pronunciation, articulation, as well as interpretation. These dialogues would sustain the interest of artists, teachers and amateurs alike all of whom addressed the question of vocal technique that eventually became the mortar that bound together the interpreters, the teachers, the public [Mori, 1970: 7].

Mori explains how addressing these technical elements, finally focused these studies towards the means of expression which was essentially regarded as the high aim of vocal technique [Mori, 1970: 7].

With respect to breathing, Mori remains not only eloquent but also relevant. In a description of the respiratory process that recalls Manuel García, Mori suggests that during inspiration the diaphragm lowers itself and the stomach protrudes slightly forward (mezzo respiro).

It is only after the diaphragm is lowered that the costals are dilated and the stomach retreats slightly. For a full breath, however, the diaphragm must lower completely and only then will the abdomen retreat slightly and the costals dilate [Mori, 1970: 28]. Mori makes a distinction between the passive half breath and the active voluntary full breath.

She continues by suggesting that there are two phases to respiration:

In the first phase, that is, the preparation for the attacking the sound or during a musical pause, the singer can take advantage of it by taking a slow deep breath through the nose. This slow, deep breath will fill the lungs right up to the apex but without exaggerating. This type of breathing requires that the narice remain completely open; it also demands a high soft palate, an open throat and an open chest but without undue muscular tension. However, following the adoption of the singing posture (the noble position) and the initial slow filling of the lungs, subsequent breath renewal should be through the mouth, with a rapid and light movement, but without dropping the chest or displacing the original posture. The above system 'represents the so-called secret of the classical singers of the past, who in the course of executing the sound gave the impression of not breathing at all' [Mori, 1970: 28].

We sense from the above that Mori retains her roots in the distant past of the García, Lamperti schools and the classical singers of that era, whilst utilising the contemporary science available to her generation.

Consequently, we will see that much of what Mori writes about is still relevant today, and that there are some vocal truths that never change.

Normal Respiration

For instance, there is still overwhelming agreement that normal tranquil respiration is comprised of active inspiration and passive expiration. For instance, Meano (1967) Mari (1975), Juvarra (1987), and Bruno and Paperi (2001) all agree with Mori when she states that in quiet respiration 'above all normal respiration consists of active inspiration and passive expiration, with expiration being much longer than inspiration' [Mori, 1970: 26]. Fussi and Magnani (1994; 2003) Mari and Schindler (1986), and Battaglia Damiani (2003) agree with Sanchez Carbone, 'that in the normal at rest position the inspiratory–expiratory cycle is relatively brief, about four seconds. The inspiratory phase is about one second or a little more, whilst the expiratory phase occupies the rest of the cycle time' [Sanchez Carbone, 2005: 26].

Fussi and Magnani agree, and add that in quiet respiration, muscular contraction is required only in the inspiratory phase, whilst the expiratory phase exploits the potential energy stored in the elasticity of the osteo/cartilaginous structures. In this manner, the expansion of the thoracic cavity is followed by a spontaneous return to the so-called equilibrium position with the minimum expenditure of energy.

Fussi and Magnani continue by elaborating further on the physiology as well as the physics of respiration. The physics involve the implementation of Boyle's Law which states that as the volume of a gas chamber increases, the pressure within the chamber will decrease, creating an under-pressure relative to atmospheric pressure, causing the ait to rush into the dilated lungs. They state that:

> The activation of these muscles at every respiratory cycle, causes a simultaneous increase in the volume of the thoracic cavity, and a reduction of intra-thoracic pressure, which are responsible for the dilation of the lungs (creating an under-pressure) which is physiologically filled when the external air (overpressure) rushes into the lungs. The descent of the diaphragm compresses the viscera contained within the abdominal cavity, causing a dislocation towards the only region that possesses the flexibility to yield: the anterior abdominal wall. When muscular contraction of the inspiratory mechanism is terminated, the volume of the thoracic cavity returns to its preceding level, by virtue of the elastic recoil force [Fussi and Magnani, 1994: 30].

The above is only partly right, because it is only true in significantly shallow and artificial breathing, because in truth Agostini found that there are at least two seconds between the end of inspiration and the yielding of the inspiratory muscles (external intercostals and diaphragm) to the expiratory muscles (internal intercostals and abdominals). This is a really significant and often overlooked finding, because it means that for at least 2 seconds man's physiological nature sets up a natural and instinctive antagonistic contest between the inspiratory and expiratory muscles, which prolongation acts to control the considerable natural recoil force. This is the very muscular configuration, which a prolonged manner constitutes the '*lotta vocale*', which as we have discussed remains the basis of the Italian '*appoggio* system'. The implication for the singer and to a lesser extent the public speaker, are enormous; it literally means that respiration is not, and cannot be strictly sequential for three reasons:

1. Because of this natural suspension phase discovered by singers and singing teachers centuries ago and now confirmed scientifically by Agostini.

2. Because the natural recoil force associated with deep breathing can obtain considerable values, and if allowed to flow unopposed would act as the uncontrolled air flowing out of a balloon.

3. There is no way that we can adequately control airflow and subglottal pressure if we wait for the breathing mechanism to stall before recruiting the expiratory muscles.

The truth is that for a smooth transition we have to engage both the inspiratory and expiratory muscles simultaneously: it then becomes a question of which set of muscles dominate in order to check and control the airflow at every point of the scale, at every intensity level and for as long as it is necessary. At the beginning, in order to maintain breath pressure and control and retard airflow, the process inspiratory muscles must dominate to restore balance, and then as the air supply diminishes the expiratory muscles dominate to ensure breath flow to the end. In essence, there is never a time when respiration is sequential, it is always conditioned by a dichotomous push and pull force which is adjusted automatically depending on the stage of the cycle, and the demands of the antagonistic forces pressing against each other, causing the formulation and diffusion of two apparently contrasting versions of the '*appoggio* system', each based on the limited knowledge of only one of the two opposing forces.

Sanchez Carbone (2005) largely agrees with Mori, but is even more specific. She states that the respiratory mechanism can be used either in a habitual and automatic manner, which is designed to preserve life, or it can be used in a conscious and knowledge based manner which is guided by the human will. To accomplish this latter and more voluntary breathing technique, the singer must necessarily attain extensive and exact knowledge of the breathing apparatus.Sanchez Carbone continues, 'the act of respiration is subject to two muscle groups, which when their contract or expand compress the lungs: one muscle group is constituted by the diaphragm and abdominals whilst the other is comprised of the intercostal inspiratory and expiratory muscles' [Sanchez Carbone, 2005: 46].

The heart and diaphragm, according to Juvarra (1987) and Sanchez Carbone (2005), constitute life's organs of nourishment for the individual; they are also the most mobile and reactive to every vibration of the human being, reflecting the emotions, and influencing the respiratory process. Sanchez Carbone agrees on the importance of the diaphragm. She writes that 'during singing, the major dynamic activity emanates from the diaphragm, whilst the auxiliary breathing muscles are engaged in the maintenance of the dilated thorax position. This objective must be accomplished in a manner that is commensurate with maintaining the maximum expansion of the thorax and the most open position of the diaphragm' [Sanchez Carbone, 2005: 48].

In conclusion then, we might say that vocal respiratory mechanism is constituted by a double support system, the first is the 'inspiratory mechanism', which is comprises of the diaphragm and external intercostal, the second is represented by the antagonistic 'expiratory muscles' which is comprised of the internal intercostal and the abdominals.

The foundation of the respiratory mechanism is constituted by the diaphragm, which encompasses the central tendon and its surrounding muscles. We have established that the central tendon does not possess any contractile elastic fibres and is therefore inextensible, consequently it cannot of itself move. However, the muscles surrounding the diaphragm are completely contractile and extensible and are capable of considerable contraction, which in the process lower and flatten the diaphragm. Even more importantly, such contraction creates a resistance to the upward thrust created by contraction of the abdominal muscles.

The external intercostals are engaged in elevating the thoracic cage in a 'bucket handle style', and when combined with diaphragmatic contraction, they also expand the thorax and the lower ribs in an antero/posterior and lateral dimension.

Contraction of the internal intercostals, on the other hand, causes the depression of the rib cage, and compression of the breath contained in the lungs, but even more importantly, it can cause the premature raise of the diaphragm. In what may appear to be a paradox the elevation of the thoracic cage helps to maintain a lowered diaphragm and expanded lateral position.

The combined action of the internal intercostals and the abdominals has the effect of squeezing the lungs both from below through the contraction of the abdominal muscles and from above through the depression of the thoracic cage. Given these powerful expiratory forces, there is only one way to create equilibrium, and that is by generating an opposite but equally powerful force. This antagonistic force is provided by the contraction of the diaphragmatic musculature and the retention of the inspiratory position through the external intercostals.

The lungs follow the contours of the thoracic cage and are essentially a centre for gas exchange in which the blood absorbs the oxygen of the air, and expels the carbon dioxide produced by the body cells.

In addition, the contemporary Italian teacher asks us to approach singing in a holistic manner. In order to obtain the best results for singing, the Italian master asks us to harmonise the physical aspects of singing with the mental, psychological and emotional.

According to Mori, the most compelling reason for educating the respiratory mechanism is the requirement to exercise the muscles involved in the control and guidance of the respiratory function (that is, abdominal girdle, diaphragm and thorax), and that should happen even before beginning the education of the voice proper.Mori contends that 'we must learn the significant movements of the respiratory mechanism, so that we may voluntarily reduce all extraneous muscle contraction to a minimum. Refining these muscular movements results in an economy of action and the correct distribution of energy' [Mori, 1970: 29].

Mori continues her argument on the rational education of respiration by citing the model manifested in the natural singer. She suggests that there are people who believe that breathing is an instinctive action, requiring only a gross indication from the teacher to send the student in the right direction towards regulating the breath.With respect to vocal technique, Mori contends that it is undeniable that there are some genuinely natural singers, embodying certain vocal truths that are worth observing.The rest of us should avail ourselves of their naturalness without exaggerating breathing exercises. It is in fact a wise thing to breathe naturally, because natural breathing is the most appropriate. Therefore, the ideal of anyone who wishes to become a good singer should be that of eliminating any obvious effort. It should be that of knowing how to adapt the physiological and musical rhythm. The objective of every teacher wishing to serve the art should be to guide the student towards a better understanding of his nature, and of his instrument. This renders the control necessary in order to place the instrument at the service of the art.

A good place to start this cohesive and holistic technique is by initiating a regime of light physical exercises to keep the body in shape and responsive, a process that, according to Sanchez Carbone, has the effect of alerting the mind and mental faculties, so that physical exercises has instinctive and unconscious respiration.

Respiration has the effect of energising the mind as well as the body. Sanchez Carbone also warns against overdoing physical exercises because overworked muscles tend to be unresponsive and rather rigid. Whereas in singing, the opposite response is required. Mori (1970), Juvarra (1987), Bruno and Paperi (2001) all agree with Sanchez Carbone (2005), exhorting the singer to strengthen her breathing through systematic exercises to develop the thorax, strengthen the abdominal muscles, and gain control over the diaphragm.

Having examined the nature of passive, natural breathing, Mori concludes that breathing for singing makes different and greater demands.

Mori argues that 'the nature of breathing required for singing is very different to the instinctive breathing we employ in everyday life, or even the type of breathing we use purely for speaking: breathing for life can be quite instinctive whilst breathing for art has to be acquired through study and art' [Mori, 1970: 26].

Mori contends that when we practice deep breathing, we activate both the inspiratory and expiratory muscles, each phase demanding the contraction of a predetermined group of muscles [Mori, 1970: 26].

Even during speaking, let alone elite singing, breathing begins to adopt a more physically demanding and more sophisticated type of expiration, depending on the length or brevity of the phrase and significance of the expression. By comparison, however, the demands made on the respiratory mechanism during the act of speaking fade into insignificance relative to those made on the mechanism during the act of elite singing. Mori contends and I agree with her that 'respiration for artistic singing is voluntary and conscious and it is therefore necessary to progressively educate both the inspiratory and expiratory phases of the breathing cycle' [Mori, 1970: 27].

In Mori's scenario expiration becomes not only more productive, but also and always more complex, depending on the expressive demands of the piece, and the emotional maturity of the singer [Mori, 1970: 27].

Juvarra (1987) concurs but is even more specific arguing cogently that the diaphragm and the abdominal muscles act in an antagonistic manner: the first (the diaphragm) is essentially an inspiratory muscle whilst the second (the abdominal girdle) is expiratory. He insists that it is 'Only when this knowledge becomes our point of reference can we independently control these two separate forces, which are indispensable to the high register where muscular coordination is necessary to the development of an adequate *sostegno*, and which is quite different from to the automatic and instinctive respiration regarded as normal breathing' [Juvarra, 1987: 38].

Juvarra emphasises the differences between *sostegno* and normal instinctive respiration associated with everyday breathing. He reinforces the widely accepted idea that *sostegno* breathing is a more conscious and voluntary system of respiration. Unfortunately, according to Juvarra, we do not possess a clear idea of the diverse functionality and possibilities of these muscles. In fact, according to Juvarra, most singing schools begin by speaking exclusively about the diaphragm in a manner that highlights functional ignorance.

For instance, Juvarra informs us that when a student sustains a certain note with the diaphragm, and in the process, notices the abdomen pushing the diaphragm back into the thorax, it does not necessarily mean that the diaphragm is contracted and offering resistance, it may actually be quite relaxed [Juvarra, 1987: 38].

According to Juvarra, the contracting diaphragm can only descend because contractile fibres surrounding it shorten upon contraction, and in so doing pull the diaphragm down leaning it against the abdominal viscera. It is therefore not possible to raise the diaphragm by contracting its surrounding muscles. Consequently, we conclude that raising the diaphragm must be the result of utilising a different mechanism. This knowledge allows only two conclusions:

When the abdominal muscles contract and recoil, they push the diaphragm upward, but in reality, it is only the abdominal muscles that are contracting and providing indirectly the force that raises the diaphragm.

There are two means of raising the diaphragm when the abdomen is retreating:

- The first is the exclusive contraction of the abdominal muscles, leaving the diaphragm in a relaxed state;

- The second relies on the contraction of the diaphragm, which tends to descend, pressing out the abdomen, which at the same time opposes this descending force with a superior ascending force, provided by the contraction of the abdominal muscles. In both cases the visible and external results are the same, but the second method is the only one in a position to raise sufficient abdominal tension.

This explains the paradox, in which so many schools of singing teach that in the high register (in which we require greater muscular involvement and greater subglottal pressure), we should raise the diaphragm, whilst in other schools they teach that you sustain this register by lowering the diaphragm. The consistent ignorance of these two opposite forces pressing against each other has caused the formulation and diffusion of two apparently contrasting versions of the *appoggio*, each based on the limited knowledge of only one of the two opposing forces. *Appoggio* is based on the singer's ability to stimulate and put into motion the correct antagonistic forces [Juvarra, 1987: 38].

For instance, normal and quiet expiration does not require the contraction of the abdominal muscles, because, tranquil expiration is essentially produced by the elastic recoil force of the lungs. There is no appreciable intervention of the abdominal muscles and therefore no possibility of efficiently controlling the expiratory phase of the breath cycle [Juvarra, 1987: 38].

With respect to the two breathing categories discussed above, Sanchez Carbone goes even further, believing that instinctive breathing is only just adequate for life, but definitely lacks the level of brain cell stimulation required to produce the physical and mental energy associated with good singing. She believes that:

> Any obstacle to respiration will cause an acute indisposition, and a lack of oxygen certainly reduces not only physical vitality, but since respiration influences both body and mind, it may also interfere with mental processes. Consequently, we may conclude, as demonstrated by science and good sense, that every improvement in the way we breathe may revitalize both mind and body [Sanchez Carbone, 2005: 24].

To achieve this body/mind revitalisation and the physical and mental energy required for elite singing, and high-level athletic, intellectual and artistic endeavour, Sanchez Carbone recommends 20 minutes of breathing exercises at least once a day, separate to the singing exercises one must perform daily. These breathing exercises should be combined with light general exercise, but most importantly, with a regime of yoga, which is designed to achieve this mind/body harmonisation required for elite performance.

According to Sanchez Carbone, in everyday life, we utilise only the bare minimum of our vital capacity. In fact, the majority of people breathe in a mechanical, unconscious manner, utilising only a small part of their lungs, and entrusting their very existence to nature and involuntary muscular action. She maintains that in quiet respiration, which is passive and involuntary, the lungs utilise only a tenth of their capacity, depending on the individual's, age, gender, activity, thoracic development, and stress.

Consequently, we can say that for those of us who wishing to live an active and intelligent life, it is necessary to pay attention to our respiratory strategy, which conditions us and is in turn determined by our lifestyle, much of which is based on habitual behaviour.

The streets of every city are full of people with an oxygen deficiency, leading to clouded minds and physical fatigue: the unfortunate result of incorrect breathing. The majority of people inspire incorrectly, even that small minority who manages to breath more deeply fail to exhale vigorously. Unaware of their oxygen deficiency, they erroneously believe that their minds are firing on all cylinders, capable flashes of brilliance, but Sanchez Carbone contends 'that men who only half breathe, only half live'. Sanchez Carbone argues that:

> Since respiration remains an indispensable physiological act, it follows that the respiratory apparatus plays a major role that allows us to furnish the cells of the organs with a quantity of Oxygen necessary for their existence. This occurs in an osmotic process in which the air loads the red cells with oxygen and in an equal but inverse process, the red cells expel the carbon dioxide produced by the combustion of the cells residing in the organs. The air used in the homeostasis constitutes the source of energy employed to excite the vocal folds and produce sound. If the blood passing through the capillaries of the alveoli in the lungs is entirely purified by the oxygen, the body will receive more energy and the mind will become more active [Sanchez Carbone, 2005: 22].

She argues that the best way to ensure maximum oxygenation and therefore optimum energy levels is through a regime of physical exercises, breathing exercises and yoga.

Sanchez Carbone contends that yoga teachers have known for thousands of years the fundamental benefits attained by meditation and respiration, including a calm and serene mental attitude. Sanchez Carbone confirms that the state of mind we strive for in singing is very close to that practiced in yoga, and this above all represents the beginning of controlled respiration [Sanchez Carbone, 2005: 37].

The dynamic respiration evoked by yoga can be of great help to the singer, simply because it induces deep breathing, which in turn improves breath renewal and oxygen refurbishment, creating more energy than is possible with normal respiration. Sanchez Carbone continues:

> We must think of body and mind not as two distinct and separate entities, but rather as two parts of a single unit which are totally dependent, and complementary to each other: an active healthy body can reawaken the whole being, including the mind, rendering it much more energetic and alert which in turn has an effect on physical well-being [Sanchez Carbone, 2005: 38].

To attain the best results in both spheres, it is necessary to undergo a prolonged and completely balanced education, with respect to singing, the awareness that voice transcends the constraints of its origin in the throat.

By giving the responsibility for inspiration and expiration to the whole body instead of just the local respiratory muscles, whilst allowing the inhaled air to reach all the nerve centres and all the chakras associated with the philosophy and practice of yoga, which awaken all psychic sensibilities by concentrating on the solar plexus. When we do this, we finally realise that the connection with the body, which begins with a holistic respiration, forms the basis of correct vocal emission. We refer to that internal perception that speaks of the voice not strictly as a local phenomenon (in the throat), but rather as an expanding one, involving in various ways the whole body, generally not associated with vocalising.

Following this most interesting deviation, let us return to Mori, who is 'astonished that supporters of natural breathing seem to miss the fact that breathing for singing occurs at a different level than common everyday breathing'. This is mainly because the musical period is longer, over much wider vocal range, with greater levels of intensity.

Sanchez Carbone agrees, believing that in singing, respiration is influenced by a number of elements, including: 'the duration of notes, the musical rhythm of the sung phrase, the intensity of the voice, the melodic line, the frequency and correct function of the vibrator and resonator: all of which have consequences on breath pressure and lung capacity' [Sanchez Carbone, 2005: 35].

Consequently, Mori concludes that breathing for singing demands a major reserve of energy for an exceptional functional and productive result.

Instinctive and Volitional Respiration

In these pages, we have discussed at length the need for active and volitional muscular contraction for the purpose of achieving the high level of control over the instrument as is required for artistic endeavour.

Arriving at the level of volitional muscular contraction required for elite singing requires an intensive period of muscular education designed to provide the singer with an understanding and a conviction that the abdominal muscles are the instinctive force relating to the act of expiration. We conclude from the above that the importance of activating the abdominal wall during vocal emission (singing) is self-evident.

Mori confirms this, informing us that many excellent classical singers have often used an elastic belt to sustain the abdominal muscles [Mori, 1970: 27]. Meano (1967) challenges this notion. He does not believe that the elastic belt invented by Sbriglia is necessary. In fact, he contends that 'the abdominal muscles constitute a true elastic belt of notable strength in contraction and great agility in movement. They mobility is as important as the diaphragm in the production of sound [Meano, 1967: 28].

In line with Meano, Juvarra (1987) remains convinced that the abdominal girdle was an excellent inbuilt and natural substitute for the material belt often used by singers. Sanchez Carbone (2005) concurs, but goes further, stating that elastic belts are not only unnecessary, but they may yet prove harmful to the whole act of breathing.

Even though Mori subscribes totally to the importance of the abdominal muscles, believing that their natural action remains the instinctive and unconscious expiratory force, she does not believe this to be the main issue. She contends that the really important and intelligent regulating force with respect to the study of breathing is that of educating and training the thoracic muscles. According to Mori, in contrast to the instinctive action of the abdominals, thoracic muscular 'action is willed and voluntary'. Consequently, we conclude that the thoracic force is generally the one entrusted with the task of restraining the instinctive force applied by the abdominal muscles. In fact, Mori reminds us, that the old masters 'recommended tirelessly the action of sustaining the chest'. Whilst also recognising that 'the costal aspects of breathing are also very important'.

Baglioni contends that the air required for the act of singing is provided primarily by the thoracic and intercostal muscles, and only complimented secondarily by the abdominal muscles. Meano (1967) confirms Baglioni with respect of the primacy of the thoracic and costal muscles over the abdominals, during phonation.

Mori utilises the research conducted by Baglioni and Meano to extrapolate that the action of the abdominals is critical to the maintenance of the instinctive and natural movement intended to free the superior thoracic region from excessive effort, whilst also equipping the thorax as an elastic resonance cavity that facilitates the movement of the larynx. If we wish to achieve all of this in the most natural manner, then the abdominals must provide an antagonistic support system. This scenario does not exclude the fact that during phonation the combined action of the thoracic and the abdominal muscles constitute a muscular complex of fundamental importance. It is the characteristic interplay between the thorax and diaphragm that provides the sustained accent that gives life to both sound and word [Mori, 1970: 27].From the above, Mori concludes that 'the production of sound is easier to voluntarily control through the thoracic region [Mori, 1970: 27].

Mori, like Juvarra (1987), Fussi and Magnani (1994) and Bruno and Paperi (2001), Damiani (2003) and Sanchez Carbone (2005) considers three primary types of breathing strategies:

1. The first is the abdominal breathing system.

2. The second is the clavicular system — which is believed to be highly damaging;

3. The third is the costo/diaphragmatic system — considered to be the classical breathing style for singers.

The third category can be further subdivided into costo/thoracic or costo/abdominal: better known as *sostegno* or *appoggio*. Very briefly:

- The first type of respiration refers to the abdominal breathing model, which is regarded as potentially harmful unless it is combined with the use of intercostal muscles.

- The second type of respiration is also regarded as potentially harmful, because it invariably raises the upper thorax excessively (too high), an action which transforms it into clavicular breathing, a style of breathing that is universally condemned by all authorities.

- The third type of respiration, that is, the balanced costo/diaphragmatic respiratory model is highly regarded and the one that is recommended by most authorities. In the following pages, we will elaborate further on all the advantages and disadvantages of each respiratory strategy.

Following in Meano's footsteps (1967: 48), Mori contends that respiration is accomplished in two phases: in the first phase, that is, the preparation for vocal onset or during a musical pause, the singer adopts the singing posture (the noble position), taking a slow deep breath through the nose, and filling the lungs right up to the apex, but without exaggerating. This type of breathing demands a completely open narice, a high soft palate, an open throat, and an open chest, but without undue muscular tension. However, following the initial slow inspiration, each subsequent breath renewal should be through the mouth, with a rapid and light movement, but without dropping the chest or displacing the original posture. The above description, according to Mori, 'represents the so-called secret of the classical singers of the past, who in the course of executing the sound gave the impression of not breathing at all' [Mori, 1970: 28].

Mori warns that whilst the above belcantist respiratory model is an exemplary and proven paradigm, it is important to maintain balance and equilibrium and not to exaggerate any particular aspect of it. This equilibrium is indispensable, because if the singer inhales too much breath, storing the excess air within his lungs, the pressure will become too strong, and can harm the lungs. On the other hand, if expiration is prolonged beyond thirty seconds, the vocal organs will generally become congested. Good expiration, according to Mori, 'must be prepared by a perfect execution of the 'apnea' principal. 'Apnea' is best defined as that split second of 'suspension' or of 'expectant attention' that precedes every attack conceived with concentration and measure'. Mori concedes that we actually do many of these things instinctively, but she considers, and I agree with her, that these actions must also be systematised, studied and reproducible [Mori, 1970: 29].

In her quest for a more systematic respiratory model, Mori has found a fellow traveller in her distinguished contemporary Nanda Mari. Mari laments the fact that the study of singing today is generally too short and too lacking in system. She believes that there should be more formal courses in anatomy in physiology as part of vocal degrees, and that singing students should adjust their expectations in terms of the number of years of study required before a credible stage debut is possible. Finally, Nanda Mari compares the 10 years of study typically required by a concert pianist before attempting a debut to the much shorter study time allowed by singers before a debut [Mari, 1975: 30].

In a similar and perspicacious vein, Rachelle Maragliano Mori asks us to consider the violinist whose quest to dominate her bow has great affinity with a singer's desire to dominate her breath. Mori informs us that in order to achieve her objective 'the violinist practices that function separately for years with maximum discipline, in order to gain control to the point of becoming automatic'. Mori then asks 'why should the singer not do the same'? [Mori, 1970: 29].

Mori also acknowledges the greater difficulties confronted by opera singers relative to other singers. This is simply because opera singers must subordinate their talent to the ideas of the composer who seriously predetermines the limits of their performance.Even allowing for the fact that the singer may choose the type of music that is better suited to her voice and temperament, ultimately, singers are still required to subordinate they will and talent to the expressive intentions and creativity of the composer, something that neither the amateur nor pop singer is required to do.

About Appoggio

I personally don't think that the natural elasticity of the muscles is in itself sufficient to satisfy the requirements of elite singing. This is especially so with respect to the dramatic repertoire, which demands require a much more controlled and voluntary respiratory style than does the lyric repertoire. These antagonistic muscular requirements can only be achieved by involving a heightened equilibrium of the antagonistic muscles to better manage tension, pressure and dynamic breath consumption.

Appoggio and Sostegno

Having examined the mechanism of respiration and extolled its significance, we then turn to the importance of posture as an instrument for coordinating the respiratory mechanism. Consequently, we are now in a position to explore the 'how' this type of higher purpose respiration required for singing is achieved.

But first let us recall one or two important findings:

1. The first: the Italians see singing in general and breathing in particular as a whole-body experience, rather than a localised muscular sensation.

2. The second: let us recall that the Italians are very strong in advocating an active, muscular and volitional breathing system for elite singing and athletic endeavour, a type of respiration which they differentiate emphatically from the passive, instinctive and natural breathing employed in everyday life.

Italian authors are emphatic in their belief that body and mind are two parts of a single unit. To achieve this body/mind revitalisation and the physical and mental energy required for elite singing, and high-level athletics, intellectual and artistic endeavour, through daily breathing and physical exercises.

In general, Italian authors believe that the level of respiratory proficiency required for elite singing is very rarely found in nature. However, they also believe that respiratory dexterity can be attained through rigorous and systematic training not only of the respiratory muscles, but also by training the extrinsic suspensory muscles that coordinate respiration with laryngeal position, and influence glottal shape, and adduction, and subglottal pressure.

The Italians believe in the validity of more than one respiratory strategy, such as *sostegno*, *appoggio* and *affondo*. There are, however, two strategies that they don't adhere to, and these are the clavicular, and exclusively abdominal respiratory strategies. The Italians appreciate that each of these strategies yields a distinctive vocal quality.

From the above we may conclude that artists are not just interested in respiration for the mere purpose of survival, which requires only the exchange of gases, but rather as to how it applies to elite singing.

We recall Mori's statement to the effect that respiration for artistic singing has to be 'voluntary and conscious' and that both the inspiratory and expiratory phases of the breathing cycle need to be educated [Mori, 1970: 27].

Fussi and Magnani subscribe to Mori's proposition and further suggest that artistic phonation is a highly specialised activity, requiring serious muscular training, all of which is ultimately aimed at the 'aesthetic enjoyment and spectacular communication' that not only relies on important inspiratory function, but also controls it and directs it towards its eventual success. For this reason, we may speak of a number of levels of respiratory management, the most basic of which is breathing for living, the others are as follows.

Exchange of Gases Guaranteeing Life

Carlo Meano (1967) confirms that the lungs are an exchange system that allows 'the blood to absorb oxygen from the air, whilst eliminating the carbon dioxide which is formed in the cells of our body [Meano, 1967: 30].

The second relates to harvesting the breath for communication, which I take to mean mainly everyday verbal communication. The following is an elaboration of the important relationship between respiration and communication. According to Fussi and Magnani:

> Amongst the various modes of communication, voice is without doubt the most economic and effective. However, in order to realize its potential, it must partake of something that would in any case be produced involuntarily: the expiratory airflow. Distortion of such airflow, even if it does not prove harmful to the vocal mechanism, may nonetheless weigh heavily upon the vocal function designed to give substance to the physiological conditions in which functional optimization may be realized [Fussi and Magnani, 1994: 29].

If we agree that the above description is an example of what occurs in the daily application of vocal function, then it must follow that the relationship between voice and breath is even more complex in the pursuit of professional artistic endeavour, wherein, in large part, the singer's training consists of learning to correlate respiration with the vibratory function through the proprioceptive sensations provided by the proprioceptive receptors located throughout the vocal mechanism (joints and ligaments). This includes the reflexes generated by the breathing apparatus acting directly upon the larynx.

Nanda Mori (1970) concurs with the above, suggesting that:

> Even during speaking, let alone elite singing, breathing begins to adopt a more physically demanding and more sophisticated type of expiration, depending on the length or brevity of the phrase and significance of the expression [Mori, 1970: 27].

In Mori's scenario expiration becomes not only more productive, but also and always more complex, depending on the expressive demands of the musical piece being performed, and the emotional maturity of the singer [Mori, 1970: 27].

Fussi and Magnani next discuss not only the idea of transmitting one's thoughts but also of respecting aesthetic and artistic choices;

Mori is also eloquent with respect to this third point. She contends that 'respiration for artistic singing is voluntary and conscious and it is therefore necessary to progressively educate both the inspiratory and expiratory phases of the breathing cycle' [Mori, 1970: 27].

Fussi and Magnani reinforce Mori, but also elaborate on the original idea. They state that 'Artistic' vocalising requires not only an airflow, which can be qualitatively, and quantitatively measured, but also an original modality of control, which forms the foundation of the *appoggio* method. Let us recall that for the Italians *appoggio* means much more than just leaning on the breath, it also partakes of such issues as 'glottal resistance', without which, *appoggio* cannot exist, as well as issues of supraglottal or 'acoustic reactance', which facilitate the vibration of the vocal folds.

They continue:

> If the airflow meets with a glottis that has been voluntarily adducted at the midline, it will naturally apply a positive pressure against the inferior surface of the vocal folds. The value of this pressure will be proportional to the force of expiration and the area upon which the force is exercised. If the glottis is not completely closed, which is the normal case during speaking and singing, the subglottal pressure depends also on the resistance encountered by the airflow traversing the glottis…The regulation of subglottal pressure is due to the coordination of many factors; the most important of which are the expiratory force, the activity of the intrinsic muscles with respect to tension and adduction, and the state of tension in the extrinsic muscles [Fussi & Magnani, 1994: 33].

In conclusion then, Mori (1970), Juvarra (1987), and Bruno and Paperi (2001) and Sanchez Carbone (2005) all agree with Fussi and Magnani (1994) that air consumption is not just a function of the respiratory muscles but also the muscles of adduction. They maintain that the regulation of subglottal pressure is due to the coordination of a number of factors, the most important of which are the expiratory forces combined with the activity of the intrinsic muscles which determine the shape, tension and level of adduction of the vocal folds, not to mention the level of contraction of the extrinsic muscles [Fussi & Magnani, 1994: 33].

In the process of applying vocal principles, and elaborating on vocal function we find ourselves confronting two elements:

The first refers to the air pressure that is applied against the vocal folds; and the second refers to the resistance with which the vocal folds oppose the airflow. When the resistance at the glottis has been conquered, the vibratory cycle begins to be self-sustaining, with a continuous readjustment of the delicate equilibrium until the airflow is terminated by the inspiratory abduction. With every breath renewal, the vocal folds resume their adducted posture and the event repeats itself. (It is important to recall that the continuous vibrations can only become self- sustaining through the asymmetric opening and closing of the vocal folds, beginning with the opening of the inferior edge, or the activity of the mucosal-wave).

The principle expiratory force is provided by the elastic recoil force, which builds as a result of the contraction of the inspiratory muscles. This expansion of the thoracic cavity, and therefore the lungs, is mainly due to the contraction of the external intercostals, which once having expanded the thorax create a momentary phenomenon which the Italians refer as 'apnea', or an instant of suspension before finally surrendering to the expiratory phase (contraction of the internal intercostals and abdominal). The function of this inspiratory phase is simultaneously complemented by a gradual relaxation of the inspiratory muscles (external intercostals and diaphragm). It then follows that the greater the displacement from equilibrium position produced by the contraction of the inspiratory muscles, the greater the rebounding muscular recoil force. We conclude from the above that the force of retraction is related to lung volume and depth of inspiration. This situation spawns two major consequences:

- Artistic vocalisation requires an airflow that is capable of generating adequate levels of subglottal pressure. In the professional singer, inspiration, even when allowed spontaneous activation, must be optimised with physiological potential;

- The possibilities of voluntary control over the elastic recoil force are evidently quite modest. Consequently, we must find a method that makes a certain amount of intervention possible.

As stated at the beginning of the chapter, the descent of the diaphragm during inspiration, which at first is instinctive, can be trained and 'voluntarily controlled', producing a down and out displacement of the abdominal wall (the laterals are also involved). This is the result of the diaphragm leaning on the viscera below, creating a protrusion of the abdominal wall. Only with the rise of the diaphragm, resulting from an 'involuntary contraction of the abdominal expiratory muscles', does the compressed viscera recover its original position. This recovery is facilitated yet again by the elastic recoil forces from the abdominal wall. On the other hand, if the abdominal wall were allowed to become flaccid and distended, it would also become progressively dilated [Fussi & Magnani, 1994: 34].

I find Mari and Schindler's description very similar to Fussi and Magnani's, which should not be surprising since the latter both studied with Oskar Schindler.

These authors believe that during its normal descent, the diaphragm tends to compress the viscera which, being inelastic, permits the lowering of the diaphragm but only if the viscera can shift elsewhere. According to Mari and Schindler:

> Since the posterior abdominal wall, and the pelvic floor are both rigid, the viscera can only move forward and laterally, but this can only occur if the abdominal muscles are maximally relaxed. Naturally, the abdominal muscles (in particular the recti and obliques) are completely relaxed during inspiration but must contract during expiration (*sostegno*), only to once again press the abdominal viscera inward which, as a result of visceral inelasticity, passively raise the diaphragm towards the thorax and in so doing increase the air lung pressure (subglottic pressure). On the other hand, in

resuming the inspiratory position, the diaphragm and inspiratory muscles (external intercostals) assume their active (contracted) function, whilst the abdominal wall assumes its passive (relaxed) position [Mari & Schindler, 1986: 70–71].

I here remind my reader that the abdominal wall is constituted by a muscular complex which includes the internal and external oblique muscles, and the transverses and rectus abdominus muscles. Of great interest to the singer is the significant fact that these abdominal muscles are comprised of striated muscle fibres, which are under the direct (voluntary) control of the cortex. It is by means of these muscle fibres that during the expiratory phase the singer can voluntarily vary abdominal pressure, meaning that we can regulate and modulate the rise of the diaphragm and the consequent subglottal pressure.

These expiratory forces are the means by which the professional artist regulates subglottal pressure and airflow. In fact, we base the technique of 'vocal *appoggio*' on the management of these elements. Consequently, the professional artist must acquire systematic control over subglottal pressure, not by forcing, but through an intimate knowledge of regulating the abdominal wall.

In general, there is broad agreement amongst Italian authors that the voluntary and active control of the respiratory process is the only strategy that is appropriate for elite singing. However, the choice of a conscious and voluntary respiratory strategy does not complete the equation; the singer is also required to choose a physiological strategy that is appropriate for the style of music she is singing. This can be predominantly *sostegno, appoggio* or *affondo*, although too often in lesser knowledgeable and aware singers, *sostegno* becomes 'clavicular, and 'affondo' deteriorates towards 'abdominal', both are inimical to good singing.

From the three acceptable models, *sostegno, appoggio* and *affondo*, the Italians argue that the choice of breathing strategy is very closely connected to the type of repertoire, but is also mediated by the singer's physiology and physiognomy. However, in the final analysis we conclude that the link between repertoire and an appropriate respiratory strategy is mainly governed by repertoire and not, according to the Italian literature, the physiognomy of a particular singer which is of secondary consideration.

Let us proceed by examining the various and competing strategies, beginning with the 'Belly in' and 'Belly out' models, and we compare these in a broad sense with the *sostegno* and *appoggio* model of the international Italian school. Although, it must be said that the Italian models are far more complete in as much as they both maintain a significant, in fact, a defining lumbar/lateral orientation, which is absent from both the 'Belly in' and 'Belly out' models. The Italians have understood intuitively over centuries that the vertical aspects of respiratory strategy are not sufficient for elite singing. The above notwithstanding, let us examine the advantages and disadvantages of the latter strategies.

The 'Belly In' and 'Belly Out' Strategies

The 'belly in' and 'belly out' strategies are based on research performed by Hixon and Hoffman (1979). Utilising this research, Sanchez Carbone underlines the advantages and disadvantages of both methods of respiration, thereby explaining the fact that muscular contraction is more effective when acting upon muscles which are distended (relaxed muscles), rather than an already contracted muscles (recalling that muscles shorten when contracted).

Sanchez Carbone agrees with these conclusions and emphasises that in the 'belly in' strategy the diaphragm and the internal intercostal (expiratory) muscles are both relaxed and can therefore be recruited (contracted), to thereby increase subglottal pressure; on the other hand, when the abdominal muscles are contracted, a condition that reduces their efficiency with respect to the expiratory force.

On the other hand, the 'belly out' position is generally associated with a high and protruding position of the thoracic cage, offering similar advantages to the other method, that is, the result of extended and relaxed intercostal and abdominal muscles. The disadvantage with this strategy is represented by the contraction of the diaphragm, which withstands a notable pressure from the abdominals pressing it back into the thoracic region, diminishing lung volume. The diaphragm will eventually return to its relaxed state, but only when the lung volume has been sufficiently reduced and the instrument is ready to switch to the inspiratory phase of the cycle [Sanchez Carbone, 2005: 82–83].

Sanchez Carbone concludes that whilst both strategies have advantages and disadvantages neither can be declared superior to the other.

It must be said that most Italian authors refer to the *sostegno* of the classical period and the *appoggio* of the post Mozart, Rossini period partake of a broad lateral/lumbar-dorsal orientation, which the 'up and in' and 'down and out' strategies do not.

In an effort to avoid the confusion ensuing from these different transmutations of the *sostegno* and *appoggio* systems, the Italians developed an elegant respiratory strategy that emphasises muscular elasticity and flexibility, which is embodied in the common terrain between *sostegno* and *appoggio*.

Fussi and Magnani (1994), Bruno and Paperi (2001) and Sanchez Carbone (2005), all make use of this paradigm. For convenience, I have chosen the Fussi and Magnani description, but any of the others would have been just as appropriate.

Fussi and Magnani on Sostegno and Appoggio

According to Fussi and Magnani (2003), *appoggio* is that component of respiratory control through which the subject, by maintaining the contraction of the external intercostals and the serratus posterior superior, work to retard the resultant rise of the diaphragm. This has repercussions for the economy of air consumption and control of subglottal pressure exerted over the first phase of expiration.

Sostegno, on the other hand, represents the level of control over the expiratory phase of the cycle through which the subject, by contracting the musculature of the abdominal wall, produces an increased abdominal pressure that facilitates the rise of the diaphragm: this increases the singer's ability to regulate subglottal pressure throughout the expiratory phase, but in particular at the end of the phase, when the natural recoil force is diminished [Fussi & Magnani, 2003: 172–173].

Sostegno is also the subject of Luigi Cocchi's inspired commentary on the (1803) Method of the Paris Conservatoire. In it, Cocchi maintains that, notwithstanding the fact that the '*sostegno* system' of breath management has a long and noble history of majestic results, it was nonetheless, furiously opposed by many detractors.

In his excellent (1952) book, Cocchi underlines the differences between respiration for singing and respiration for talking: the latter primarily involves inspiration for breath renewal and begins when the abdomen swells and protrudes in its superior part; only then and as a second movement does the abdomen descend, transforming itself into an expiratory mechanism. On the other hand, with respect to breathing for singing, Cocchi is completely in line with Mengozzi whom he cites liberally:

> Inspiration for singing requires a flattening of the stomach, followed by its immediate and prompt elevation, and a swelling and protruding the chest. During expiration then the stomach slowly returns to its natural state and the chest lowers proportionally, charged with the responsibility of preserving as long as possible the air introduced into the lungs. This must not be allowed to escape except a little at the time without shock; in other words, it is necessary that it flows with fluidity [Cocchi 1952 in Damiani 2003: 83].

Delfo Menicucci (2011) provides a more contemporary interpretation of the '*sostegno* system' of breath management, which he mistakenly refers to as *appoggio*. Menicucci contends that:

> There is no doubt that in reading the treatises of the sixteenth and seventeenth centuries we may hypothesize that the prevalent system of appoggio pertaining to the period was based on the maximum withdrawal of the abdomen, and sustaining the chest in a high militaristic position, giving prominence to the manoeuvre intended to take the sound away from the throat. These methods were theorized by the great masters of the past, who were concurrently acclaimed composers and distinguished singers. Their accounts and chronicles

of the times illustrate a hyper-expanded thorax of the castrati, describing their ample and incredibly powerful sounds, they regaled us with stories of singers capable of decorating precious melodies, executing unthinkable agility, telling us stories of sopranos with a four-octave range and other fascinating things. No is there any reason to doubt the chroniclers of this period, nor the teachers that founded the vocal tradition with such attention and ingenuity over so many centuries [Menicucci, 2011: 64].

Menicucci believes that even today we can still validate the beauty and flexibility of voices that are considered *appoggiati* through abdominal withdrawal by comparing them with other forms of *appoggio*. Such comparisons, according to Menicucci, will demonstrate that these voices possess maximum agility, optimum power and maximum propensity to satisfy.

Bruno and Paperi confirm that:

> In the middle of the eighteen hundreds, we were right in the midst of the Verdian revolution and, with respect to the Italian scene, and those that were writing treatises at the time, and should have had their finger on the pulse, still seem to prefer the Rossinian school, or perhaps Bellini and Donizetti, but certainly not the actual contemporary school [Bruno & Paperi, 2001: 79].

It was the dramatic revolution inspired by Verdi, and Wagner that stimulated the artistic imagination, creating a completely new, more dramatic and more voluptuous sound-world that began competing with the established Mozart, Rossini, paradigm. These composers had been so well served by the '*sostegno* system' of breath management, which was essentially an 'up and in' system.

In general, Italian authors believe that the music of composers of the classical period and early *bel canto* composers as exemplified by Mozart and Rossini are better served by the 'up and in' or *sostegno* respiratory strategy, whilst those of the following period, as exemplified by Verdi, Wagner and Puccini and the verismo composers are better served by the 'down and out' or *appoggio* respiratory strategy.

This Verdian revolution had tremendous repercussions for vocal technique. Mori (1970), Juvarra (1987), Bruno and Paperi (2001), and Damiani Battaglia (2003) all believe that the transition in musical style was the catalyst for a new and more relevant vocal paradigm, which in large part was driven by a lower respiratory strategy, utilised in a more vigorous manner.In truth, the problems relating to respiration had been brewing for some time, many of them had been conveniently blamed on the female corset, but no one bothered to ask why men were also suffering with a similar problem, which today is readily recognised as clavicular breathing (an elaboration of this excessively high breathing will soon follow). For now, let us content ourselves that the numerous problems experienced by the mid 1800s can be traced directly to the change of vocal literature from the late Baroque, and *bel canto* period to the new dramatic repertoire.The problems were fuelled by unprecedented development of the orchestra and performing spaces, that is, orchestras were much larger, orchestration was richer and more intense, auditoriums were much larger, and then there was the unrelenting rise in orchestral pitch.

The situation was further and unintentionally aggravated by Bernardo Mengozzi, who wrote the original *Method du Chant* for the Paris Conservatoire. Mengozzi was a tenor of considerable mark, and a learned member of the famous Bolognese, or Bernacchi School, which with Porpora's Neapolitan school, was arguably the most successful school of singing in the high Baroque. Mengozzi had intended to record a systematic description of this illustrious school, not only for the immediate benefit of the Paris conservatoire, but also for posterity. There is no doubting his noble intent, but whilst the objective of the exercise remained lofty the execution was rather clumsy, embodying muscular rigidities that were never part of the original, organic '*sostegno* system' as taught him by the Bernacchi school. I am not chastising Mengozzi, because it is obvious that in the absence of objective scientific knowledge, which we know was scarce at the time, authors only had recourse to words, which are often painfully inadequate to explain vocal processes and especially sensations relating to singing.

(Although, it is appropriate to remind my reader that since Mengozzi was working in Paris, he would have had access to Jean Baptiste Berard's work. Berard provided a description of the breathing system that was light-years ahead of its time. Unfortunately, it was not widely adopted by either by the Italian or the French school for many generations.)

Nonetheless, historically, I am thinking of the problems created by inadequate and intemperate language for the great Manuel García whose designation of the *coup de glotte* for vocal onset unleashed a torrent of venomous criticism not only by his contemporaries but also future generations. Contemporary authors now agreed that the 'caress of the glottis' would have been more appropriate and saved him a great deal of pain. Another great idea that met with an unhappy outcome, again, mainly because of language, was Jean de Reske's notion of singing in the mask or as he referred to it *chanter dans le masque*. The problems experienced by Mengozzi, García and de Reszke should be enough to convince us of the difficulties that may ensue from loose language.

If we, the singing fraternity of the 21st century are expressing ourselves better than our predecessors, it is for two reasons: the first is that the twentieth century has emphasised the importance of language, and the second is that we have excess to more tangible and objective knowledge than we have ever had before and our reliance on esoteric description and intangible, subjective vocal ideals have substantially subsided. This transition from empirical to objective knowledge occurred as a result of greater proliferation of new scientific, physiological and anatomical knowledge, but it has also provided us with a common vocabulary and sharpened our descriptive focus and intent.

These developments notwithstanding, loose language remains a problem even today. For instance, we see above that Menicucci refers to what is a clearly a description of the old schools 'sostegno system' of breath management, as the *appoggio* of abdominal withdrawal'.By its very nature withdrawal and the 'up and in' technique cannot be called *appoggio*. I am of the opinion, which I share with Antonio Juvarra and Sanchez Carbone, that whilst *sostegno* is characterised by an ascending orientation, *appoggio*, which means to 'lean on', or 'lean against' has a decidedly downward orientation.

I like Juvarra's narration with respect to what I believe to be one of the two defining characteristics of the '*appoggio* system' of breath management: that is, the first is a downward orientation, whilst the second, pertains to the leaning out against the lateral/lumbar-dorsal region and therefore partaking of both the down and out orientation and lateral/lumbar/dorsal aspects. Nanda Mari encapsulates the pictorial image with wonderful incisiveness when she suggests that it is like 'wearing a life buoy around your waist' Nanda Mari (1975). Juvarra (1987) confirms the downward orientation associated with *appoggio*, and then gives the big warning on the dangers of focusing on the upward movement of the abdominal muscles. In the following passage, Juvarra describes this process eloquently:

> Embodied in the idea of 'appoggio' is the notion of downward movement, which can be formalized in a specific activity to control the diaphragm (above all, during vocal onset or for the upper register) or it may be translated into generic suggestions of imagining the sound from above, in a way as to indirectly elicit the correct muscular coordination without excessive rigidity or equilibrium. On the contrary, by focusing on the upward movement of the abdominal muscles, utilizing it as an element of control (as it happens in certain schools that teach sustaining the high notes by raising the diaphragm), we elicit the hyper-activation of the expiratory elements, which are already functioning automatically, and which hyper activation only serves to unbalance the mechanism [Juvarra, 1987: 33].

Juvarra reminds us that the level of muscular antagonism varies, depending on the effect to be achieved. He also believes that the developmental phase of this antagonistic mechanism must correspond with an elastic and flexible use of the musculature. To that end, he recommends exercising it with 'vocalizzi' that 'set the diaphragm into dancing', whilst the abdominal muscles create a firm wall: the danger with the latter is that it risks becoming a rigid block.

Sanchez Carbone agrees with Juvarra, and also exhorts the singer to avoid activating the diaphragm only to oppose to the wall-like resistance generated by the excessively contracted musculature of the abdominal wall, which frequently leads to rigidity. In common with Juvarra, Sanchez Carbone warns the singer against blocking the breathing mechanism, which creates tension around the neck and throat.

Her remedy is identical to Juvarra's, in as much as they both recommend staccato exercises, complemented by 'staccato vocalizzi' designed to build flexibility and mobility into the diaphragm [Sanchez Carbone, 2005: 115].

Interaction Between Sostegno and Appoggio

In analysing the different breath management strategies, Italian authors have become aware of the controversies and inconsistencies pertaining to respiratory strategies, especially those controversies that are elicited by incorrect or loose language. Consequently, some of authors have developed an elegant model in which the lowering of the diaphragm in a decidedly down and out orientation represents the *appoggio* part of the equation, whilst the contraction of the abdominal muscles with its ascending orientation fulfils the *sostegno* part of the equation.

Bruno and Paperi (2001) agree and contend that the quest for antagonism leads to the simultaneous contraction of a stretched diaphragm leaning against the pelvic/abdominal muscles. It is the interaction of the 'sostegno' and *appoggio* systems that cause the alterations in subglottal pressure and the stable expansion of the diaphragm which is ready to respond to our musical intentions.

Bruno and Paperi continue by suggesting that with this strategy:

> We gain the sensation that the 'appoggio' senses the 'sostegno' and the 'sostegno' senses the 'appoggio'. This occurs from the time we first inspire the breath without excessive tension, through to the slow alteration of the musculature throughout the act of expiration, that contracts the diaphragm, ribs and the superior abdominal region, providing us with reassurance and vital energy, not force [Bruno & Paperi, 2001: 97].

Fussi and Magnani authoritatively take up the same theme, suggesting that:

> That which is generally defined as 'appoggio' can be understood as a complex technique in which two muscular components are functionally distinctive. The appropriately named 'appoggio' represents that condition experienced at the end of inspiration, which allows the control of the diaphragm by retaining its lowered and stretched position through the action of the external intercostal muscles that maintain the amplitude of their parameter (like the skin of a well-stretched drum). They control the spontaneous diaphragmatic tendency to rise, ensuring that the return of the diaphragm to its original position is not erratic but rather connected to the dynamic requirements of vocal emission (piano, forte, high and low).

Fussi and Magnani continue:

> This method of control is the one represented by the pedagogical dictum such as 'push down and out' or 'sit on the breath'. However, it is a question of definition that if we lean down on something there must be something there to sustain us, and the more

used we become to being sustained the more comfortable we become about remaining 'appoggiati' [Fussi & Magnani, 2003: 173].

Further, Fussi and Magnani believe that during 'onset', and the ensuing sostenuto, the dominant feeling should be and generally is one of *appoggio*. However, in agreement with Bruno and Paperi's statement above, they also contend that the singer should feel the presence of a certain minimum level of *sostegno* (the ascending force of the abdomen), that allows us to experience the comfortable but antagonistic sensations of *appoggio*.

In returning to Bruno and Paperi, we find that they have developed a similar respiratory strategy, but with an interesting difference.

They actually contract the lower abdominals at the beginning of inspiration because they believe that there are singing schools that:

> Concentrate on the inspiratory movement first and then oppose it with the (upward flow) of the 'sostegno' in two separate phases, before the beginning of a phrase; we are of the opinion that it is more useful to introduce a little muscle tone on the part of the lower pelvic/ abdominal muscles almost from the beginning of inspiration, thereby helping with the synergistic movement involved in opening the ribs without causing negative tensions in the superior regions of the thorax. This will bring about a slight retraction of the pelvic/ abdominal region at the moment we dilate the lower costo/diaphragmatic region, which should be treated with extreme relaxation, and the easy and light downward action of the diaphragm [Bruno & Paperi, 2001: 92–93].

What is different about this strategy is that Bruno and Paperi concentrate on bringing the abdominals up to meet the diaphragm as it descends towards the abdominals. This strategy has the added advantage of building a foundation for the diaphragm to sit upon, but it also ensures that the diaphragm cannot lower beyond a certain predetermined level, which is a criticism often levelled at the 'down and out' and the 'affondo models'. Generally, it has the added benefit of ensuring that the lower floating ribs expand laterally. The only danger with this model is that often the singer does not relax the abdominal girdle, which allows the diaphragm to lower sufficiently, ensuring a down and out and lateral/lumbar/ dorsal expansion, the absence of which results in a high and shallow respiration.

Nonetheless, there is a historical precedent for this strategy and its provenance can be traced back to the Porpora Neapolitan School through the García's and Luigi Lablache, both of them students of Giovanni Ansani. We recall that Manuel García recommended the return of the 'gastric fontanella', that is, the abdominal wall of the epigastrium, which is the physiological component that retreats into an inward and upward position (in an almost imperceptible manner prior to vocal onset). This has the effect of sustaining the contracting diaphragm as it lowers at the end of inspiration. According to Fussi and Magnani, if the equilibrium between these two elements is unbalanced by an excessive and constant *appoggio* during the entire musical phrase (emphasising the 'down and out' mode), the singer experience thoracic depression. Fussi and Magnani continue:

> This kind of sensation is tied to the fact that during the emission of a musical phrase, utilizing only the 'appoggio' component, the diaphragm is forced down and is therefore no longer in a position to control either subglottic pressure or airflow, which function is consequently substituted by the collapse of the sternum and the thorax (a stance which some have called the Gorilla posture) [Fussi & Magnani, 1994: 174].

These authors also assert that this unbalanced physiological stance, with its excessively plunging diaphragm and a lower than recommended larynx, gives the voice a thunderous, heavy character, which often results in flat intonation, and a wide vibrato approaching a wobble [Fussi & Magnani, 1994: 174].

Sanchez Carbone concurs with the above, suggesting that abdominal breathing, absent the lateral movement of the lower floating ribs, is decidedly unbalanced and could prove detrimental to the vocal instrument.

On the other hand, a very different and diametrically opposite vocal quality is elicited from the *sostegno* system. Recalling that *sostegno* is characterised by an 'up and in' movement of the abdominal, we can surmise that in certain circumstances the diaphragm rises very quickly. This creates an excess pressure, which forces the singer to employ the extrinsic laryngeal muscles, unbalancing laryngeal posture and constricting the throat. This respiratory strategy frequently produces sharp intonation and a vibrato that is narrow and 'goaty' [Fussi & Magnani, 1994: 174].

According to Juvarra (1987), Fussi and Magnani (1994) and (Sanchez Carbone (2005) contend that 'singing on the breath', means nothing more than finding the equilibrium between these two antagonistic elements, *appoggio* and *sostegno*.

There is also good agreement in the literature that some singers are more sensitive to the '*appoggio* element', whilst others are more aware of the 'sostegno element' (sometimes certain different perceptions are tied to vocal category and repertoire). Needless to say, both elements are extremely important and should be in balance and properly understood by the singer [Fussi & Magnani, 1994: 174].

Appoggio or Sostegno

Bruno and Paperi add their considerable voice to this argument, by suggesting that we should acquire the right sensations, and the right feel for this technique. They contend that in a supine position (laying on one's back), with legs quite relaxed, the singer should experience a modest expansion of the lower thoracic cage, followed by a light suspension (apnea). If, at this point, we place the thumb on the lowest rib and the medium finger against the abdomen, and expire lightly, we become aware of the double antagonistic action of the muscles involved in expiration, even through the demands made by artistic singing. Bruno and Paperi maintain that there are a number of professional singers who use the above system, which is generally associated with certain didactic schools:

> In which the superior abdominal region, having attained a certain expansion, marginally retreats just prior to the 'onset' of sound. The maturing of this technique will better instruct the singer as to the best way of establishing equilibrium between opposing forces. Once having discovered this double mechanism of simultaneous activity of 'sostegno' and 'appoggio', we need to use this knowledge to guide the raising of the diaphragm without substantially altering the position of the larynx, just above the subglottal pressure, in a manner that preserves both the colour and the musical line. The lower abdominal/pelvic region will be educated to react spontaneously during expiration, producing an appropriate and steady rising of the diaphragm. The diaphragm, combined with other elements involved in respiration, such as the lungs and the ribs, must learn to manage the 'braking' or (checking) action of the inspiratory muscles in a manner that provokes its function as a foundation of variable levels which can be graduated and controlled by the muscles below which remain in close contact [Bruno & Paperi, 2001: 94-95].

Bruno and Paperi suggest that if, as a result of engaging in this double and synergistic action of the *appoggio* and *sostegno*, a student feels an element of light rigidity, she should resort to a respiratory technique involving two distinctive actions before the onset of sound, rather than the co-contraction which is a more arduous technique, at least in the early days until it becomes second nature. They also remind us that the stretched diaphragm associated with *appoggio*, when opposed by the lower pelvic/abdominal muscles, should not overcompensate by engaging in the 'stroke of the chest technique', which even García condemned 160 years ago. The detrimental effects associated with this technique include a shifting of the air column and a high laryngeal position [Bruno & Paperi, 2001: 94].

In summary, we have discussed the *appoggio* and *sostegno* system of breath management, the 'belly in' and 'belly out' model, and the elegant combination of these two created by the Italians as an accommodation designed to avoid the controversy ensuing from these distinct and different paradigms. We also looked at the double action of *sostegno* and *appoggio* advocated by Bruno and Paperi, which is really nothing other than the co-contraction already expounded by Juvarra, and Sanchez Carbone, and adds to the weight of their thinking. Through it all, Italian masters have found a way to reconcile many of these models and support systems: for instance, they advocate *sostegno* for the *bel canto* style and *appoggio* for Verdi, Wagner and Verismo style.

Nonetheless, there are two models that even the ingenuity and good will of the Italians could never reconcile with good or *bel canto* singing and these are the 'clavicular' and 'abdominal' paradigms, the latter is sometimes referred to as the 'affondo' system of breath management.

These are the models we are going to examine now, if only to discover how to identify and avoid them.

Clavicular Respiration

According to Fussi and Magnani, 'clavicular' or superior thoracic respiration is not a respiratory strategy generally advocated by too many voice rofessionals. Nonetheless, there is no getting around the fact that a number of students suffer with this affliction, especially, at the beginning of their study [Fussi & Magnani 1994, 174–177].

This type of 'clavicular' respiration cannot be regarded as a viable strategy because as a function of incorrect respiration it is generally undesirable. This strategy it is not planned, it is not consciously chosen, and its inherent tensions and rigidities should be eschewed.

These rigidities, which are rarely detected when the singer is at rest become very obvious when she is at work: the major indicator is a rising of the shoulders and clavicles, a contraction of the sternocleidomastoid, and a swelling of the jugular. This muscular configuration limits the descent of the diaphragm, creating muscular tension, which is frequently transmitted from the chest, shoulders, and neck to the vocal mechanism itself. It is worth reiterating that this type of muscular tension is very rarely isolated; more often than not it involves not only the thoracic cage and larynx, but also the vocal tract, which hinders vocal efficiency and quality [Fussi & Magnani, 1994: 176].

Mori (1970), Mari (1975), Juvarra (1987), and Sanchez Carbone (2005), all condemn clavicular respiration. Sanchez Carbone's maintains that in large part the problems relating to 'clavicular' respiration occur because of misconception. Her views are representative of other Italian authors, who believe that, 'clavicular' respiration may be perceived by the inexperienced singer as filling the lungs with air when in reality there is very little lung dilation, what the singer actually experiences' is muscular tension, and rigidity which gives the impression of lung dilation.

This type of respiration disrupts not only the '*appoggio* mechanism', but also, correct vocal function. Sanchez Carbone believes that the best strategy to counter this insidious problem is that:

> In order to avoid high thoracic (clavicular) respiration, the singer must maintain a relatively high position of the chest and sternum, so that the thoracic muscles may move forward externally. The singer must avoid an expansion of the pectorals during emission: these are already in a relatively high position and should not require further inspiratory dilation. In the final analysis, a calm, complete, and physiological ample respiration, which is neither forced nor excessive, is not only appropriate, but also constitutes the very essence of singing [Sanchez Carbone, 2005: 120].

I have no doubt that Sanchez Carbone's remedy is very effective. It, nonetheless, remains a fact that many students suffer with this problem at the beginning of their vocal studies. It is also true that singing teachers encounter considerable resistance from students who find it difficult to accept that this low respiratory strategy is correct.

The fact that there is not a single authority in the literature that lauds 'clavicular' respiration, or doubts the correctness and importance of low diaphragmatic/costal respiration, does not seem to penetrate the consciousness of a student infected with this disease.

Sanchez Carbone again has an illuminating theory as to why it has proven difficult to penetrate the student's consciousness with respect to vocal technique in general and respiratory technique in particular.

Sanchez Carbone's compelling theory is related to the fact that singers manage their voices on the basis of 'sensations' and 'perceptions', which are not always reliable. This is especially true of a young singer who is not used to transferring the 'sensation of deep breathing' from the thoracic area (clavicular muscular tension), to the 'reality of a deeper and much lower' (costo/diaphragmatic) respiration. The difficulty is not so much in rectifying the muscular realignment required to achieve a deeper respiration, but rather convincing the student that her perceptions need re-educating, simply because these perceptions are the product of incorrectly interpreted sensations. The misunderstanding is the result of muscular contraction, which gives the singer the impression of a full breath, but which is in reality muscular tension. In effect, correct deep breathing is a function of an expansion around the tenth rib, which is the only physiologically correct strategy. (This is true irrespective of whether the singer favours the *appoggio* or '*sostegno* system' of breath management) [Sanchez Carbone, 2005: 104–105].

I sometimes think that singing teachers, myself included, spend too much time trying to save students from themselves, only because we see the artist they could become and it is human to want to close the gap between what might have been and the reality. In our eagerness to help, we often forget that most people are not destined to become the person or the artist they may have been and perhaps should have become. So that statistically we are fighting a losing battle before we even start. I think sometimes we should accept defeat gracefully and cut our losses rather than waste so much time and energy on people who although talented, are for other relevant reasons destined to fail.Our predecessors were much harsher but also much wiser than we are today. They understood in an instinctive manner, and in a way that our more intellectually sophisticated generation, with its obsession to save everyone from themselves, ever could, that if a student places enough obstacles between themselves and they career goals, one of those obstacles is going to trip them over.

Abdominal Respiration or Affondo

The technique of inferior 'abdominal' respiration, associated with sternal collapse, and typically inspired by Germanic Schools, is in fact the complete opposite to the 'clavicular' respiration discussed above. This abdominal strategy, which is characterised by an unimpeded diaphragmatic descent during inspiration, creates considerable obstacles to diaphragmatic ascent during expiration.

This type of exclusively abdominal respiratory strategy is characterised by a didactic terminology based on the notion of the diaphragm 'pushing down and out', forcing the inspiratory muscles to remain excessively contracted, resulting in considerable interference of the natural and gradual ascent of the diaphragm during vocal emission. Excessive contraction of the inspiratory muscles, which prevents the natural raise of the diaphragm, results necessarily in the collapse of the thorax, and sternum, which is the only other technique, albeit inferior, of raising subglottal pressure. This extreme downward thrust tends to block the abdominal muscles, preventing them from fulfilling their natural function: muscular contraction resulting in a simultaneous abdominal withdrawal, raising the diaphragm, and a consequent rise in subglottal pressure.

This muscle configuration facilitates the *sostegno* component of the respiratory cycle, which influences vocal quality and vibrato, and the high register.

The main corrective procedure for excessive inferior abdominal respiration is characterised by the unrelenting quest for a balanced equilibrium, which is designed to counter the excessive downward push of the diaphragm during the *sostegno* phase of the respiratory cycle. Inherent in this quest is the understanding that during the *sostegno* (expiratory) phase of respiration, the diaphragm should be allowed to gradually relax and return to its original resting position. This muscular realignment involves both the postural and abdominal musculature. Failure to allow the natural and gradual relaxation of the muscle fibres surrounding the central tendon of the diaphragm, with a concomitant contraction of the abdominal muscles will have a detrimental effect on the sound. With respect to vocal quality, Fussi and Magnani believe that:

> The most common vocal characteristic of this respiratory strategy can best be defined as 'heavy' quality. The singers who subscribe to this strategy generally end by excessively plunging both the diaphragm and larynx; this imbues the voice with a thunderous character frequently associated with bad intonation (typically flat). Invariably, the singer attacks the sound with a 'portamento' from a third below, resulting in a vocal

quality characterized by a wide vibrato approaching a wobble. On the other hand, the singer who exceeds only to the demands of 'sostegno', that is, 'pushing up and in' which has the effect of raising the diaphragm very quickly, produces a 'goaty' vibrato [Fussi & Magnani, 1994: 175].

The above description of abdominal respiration appears, on the surface, to be almost identical to Menicucci's description of the Italian 'affondo system' as taught by the famous Italian teacher, Arturo Melocchi. Melocchi has long professed to have learnt the 'affondo' respiratory system from a teacher in Russia, and that his only credit was to have had the good sense to transport it to Italy. Be that as it may, nobody did more to lend the system legitimacy and also controversial notoriety. The 'affondo system' of breath management is most vividly embodied in the singing of the legendary tenors Mario del Monaco, and in a moderate manner, in the singing of the great Franco Corelli.

According to Menicucci:

> The 'affondo' system utilizes a radically and exclusively low abdominal inspiration that does not even attempt to involve the floating ribs. It is not only one of the laws of the 'affondo' technique, but also the conclusion of many phoneticians, that a student at the beginning of his studies can derive major advantages, shortening by a considerable time the term required to conquer vocal technique but also to attain the power of articulating the lower region of the abdomen, which is later complimented by the action of the lower floating ribs. The reason for this is obvious: the articulation of the lower abdominal muscles can also include those of the ribs, whereas, the opposite is not at all assured [Menicucci, 2011: 44].

As I suggested above, at first, there appears to be little difference between the extreme form of abdominal breathing and the '*affondo* system' of breath management. However, a closer analysis reveals significant differences, such as:

- The *affondo* system of breath management is predicated on the early development of the abdominal area, it does not advocate an extreme and rigid form of abdominal respiration.

- The *affondo* system of breath management allows, as a second phase, for the lateral and balancing expansion of the lower floating ribs.

- The logic of the *affondo* system is based on the notion that gaining control of abdominal respiration in the first phase does not exclude the inclusion of the lateral component in the second phase, whereas, aiming for the lateral component can and often does exclude the abdominal component.

I personally do not agree with this logic, because my experience is that the abdominal and costal components cannot only coexist, but can and should be developed simultaneously. The difference is that the simultaneous model eliminates the danger of the excessively plunging diaphragm and larynx in the hands of lesser teachers or reckless students. I think as teachers we have two responsibilities:

- The first is to develop the student's gifts to the full extent.
- The second is to foresee what may go wrong when operating so closely to maximum capacity, and one of the things that may go wrong in this instance is the excessively plunging diaphragm and blocking of the abdominal muscles.

According to Fussi and Magnani, since singing and phonation generally manifest themselves in the expiratory phase, and given that the diaphragm is totally inactive in this phase, and its rise is regulated by the expiratory muscles (abdominal, and intercostal muscles), we conclude that all didactic terminologies that advocate direct action such as 'push the diaphragm up', 'keep the diaphragm low', or 'push the diaphragm in', are all inappropriate, even if metaphorically useful in eliciting the correct muscular coordination.

I feel compelled to point out that whilst I agree with Fussi and Magnani that most of these didactic designations are inappropriate, I don't agree with the contention that the diaphragm is totally inactive during expiration. This notion does not conform with the prevailing view amongst Italian authors who overwhelmingly adhere to diaphragmatic co-contraction, nor does it conform with research findings from Von Euler, Leanderson and Sundberg (1987, 1988, 1990, 1992), which found that there is definite co-contraction of the diaphragm in many cases during singing. Italian authors understand very well that the central tendon is inextensible, but they also believe that the use of the surrounding muscle fibres can control the diaphragm sufficiently to turn it into a dosing muscle by offering some resistance to the upward and dominant thrust of the abdominal contraction. Consequently, I feel that asking the student to keep the 'diaphragm steady' as opposed to low whilst emphasising the importance of not blocking the natural abdominal function that pushes it back into the thorax, not only appropriate but rather efficacious).

Elastic Recoil Force

So far, we have discussed the most important and relevant muscles involved in the act respiration in both the *sostegno* and *appoggio* respiratory technique; it is now time to discuss the inherent elastic recoil force provided by the lungs at varying levels of volume.

At full lung volume, the elastic recoil force provided by the elasticity of the lungs, and the over 300,000,000 alveoli contained therein, combine with the recoil force of the expiratory muscles, to produce an excessively high level of subglottal pressure. Certainly, a higher pressure than is either required or desired relative to the intensity of the sound emitted; especially, for the early part of the singing cycle. The singer is then required to produce an antagonistic muscular force designed to reduce subglottal pressure to an acceptable level at the moment of vocal onset. And this is what the old masters referred to as holding back, and contemporary singers refer to as 'checking' the breath. We achieve this by maintaining the contraction of the inspiratory muscles, which retard the rise of the diaphragm, and maintaining the expanded position of the inspiratory muscles (external intercostal). Consequently, the thorax will maintain its moderately high position through the continued contraction of the external intercostals, whilst contraction of the abdominal wall supports their action.

Fussi and Magnani explain:

> In the course of a musical phrase, the air pressure diminishes in direct proportion to the breath consumption required for singing. It therefore remains a fact that to maintain the pressure levels required in the following phase of expiration, the diaphragm begins to rise and is accompanied in its ascension by the abdominal muscles. In the latter part of a musical phrase, the abdominals intensify their action of sustaining the sound, resulting in the progressive reduction of pulmonary volume. Whilst we begin with dominant sensation of 'appoggio' at the beginning of the musical phrase we gradually substitute this with an increasing value of 'sostegno' by the end. [Fussi and Magnani, 1994: 176–177].

Conclusions

All the talk about the *appoggio* interacting antagonistically with the *sostegno* may give the impression that the Italian authors are apt to emphasise the vertical elements of the respiratory strategy, nothing could be further from the truth. In fact, the Italians are totally committed to the costo/diaphragmatic model, with many authors also citing the importance of the lateral/lumbar/dorsal region. The Italian respiratory paradigm is inclined to explore a greater level of diversity, and is generally broader and more organic than many other paradigms.

Although, the Italians are determined to remain loyal to the two mainstream paradigms, which they refer to as the *sostegno* of the old *bel canto* school and the *appoggio* of the more modern, dramatic Italian school, they are equally determined to accommodate a moderate diversity and even small variations within mainstream paradigms.

For all their willingness to accommodate diversity, the Italians have not been able to support 'clavicular' nor 'abdominal' respiration, which is rejected universally amongst the most reputable schools. The reasons for the wholesale rejection are many and powerful. Probably, the first and foremost is related to the incorrect use and extreme contraction of the neck muscles, the shoulder girdle, and the pectorals. This excessive tension applied to the shoulder and neck muscles, creates the perception of fullness, but in fact has little to do with thoracic/lung dilation and everything to do with excessive muscular tension: a tension that is difficult to isolate and is typically transmitted to the laryngeal and pharyngeal muscles.

Abdominal respiration has the opposite effect, the diaphragm is retained in such an excessively low position that it tends to block the natural function of the abdominal muscles responsible for pushing the diaphragm back into the thorax.

Definition of Appoggio

We have argued in these pages that even though the *appoggio* and '*sostegno* systems' represent two opposing muscular systems, in effect, Italian contemporary pedagogy regards them as two sides of the same coin. They certainly share the same overarching objectives: the regulation and management of subglottal pressure, and control of the ensuing airflow. Mari and Schindler confirm the above statement. They contend that:

> For a singer, the final aim of respiration is the accumulation of a considerable quantity of air in the lungs which is then used to produce a steady flow of air and a constant subglottal pressure, both of which a controllable and controlled. The air can accumulate in the thorax through the expansion of the anterior -lateral wall of the costorsternal cavity, and the downward movement of the diaphragm, whilst the posterior costovertebral wall remains practically immobile [Mari & Schindler, 1986: 68].

The mechanism for achieving this balanced equilibrium is represented by the retention of the inspiratory phase for an unusually long period of time; that is, the balance between the double support mechanism, constituted vertically by diaphragm and the abdominal girdle and laterally by the external and internal intercostals. The mechanism for the application of the *appoggio* strategy is primarily comprised of the 'noble posture' as represented by the double support system and preserved for an indefinite period of time. The combination of the double support system, and the retention of the inspiratory position for an extended period of time remain the major characteristics of *appoggio*.

Juvarra and Sanchez Carbone elaborate on the *appoggio* technique and its provenance. Juvarra argues that in the art of vocal pedagogy, the term *appoggio* or *sostegno* refers to that particular technique in which the antagonistic action of the internal and external muscles is responsible for the production of particular sounds frequently referred to as 'canto sul fiato' by some authors, and as '*voce appoggiata*' by others, both spring from the '*appoggio* system' of breath management.

An elegant definition of the '*appoggio* system' of breath management is to be found in the Enciclopidia Garzanti della Musica (1974). This definition confirms that the Italian view of '*appoggio* system' is much broader and holistic than is sometimes understood. Specifically, there are two conflated but different levels of *appoggio*: the first deals with respiration and its focal points are concentrated around the abdominal, thoracic and diaphragmatic muscles, and the second focal points are concentrated around the proprioceptive sensations impinging on the face, the teeth, the neck and other focal points. The following is my translation of that the Enciclopidia Garzanti's definition:

> In the terminology of vocal technique, we refer to the region in which we experience maximal muscular tension during singing as the point of 'appoggio': this may occur in the abdominal/diaphragmatic or thoracic region (that is, 'appoggio' at the abdomen, diaphragm, thorax, or chest), or in that part of the facial cavity where the cervical resonances of the sound are perceived (appoggio at the teeth, 'appoggio' at the palate, 'appoggio' at the nape of the neck, and so forth). The point of 'appoggio' varies depending on the type of emission we adopt [Enciclopidia Garzanti, 1974: 35].

At this point, it is worth adding that every Italian author of substance has addressed the concept of *appoggio*. Sanchez Carbone's contribution is particularly memorable with respect to this vocal strategy. She confirms that,

The term *appoggio* coined by the Old Italian school of singing, does not simply mean controlling and sustaining the breath, but also includes factors of resonance, and controlling the emission of the voice.

Further, Sanchez Carbone contends that the old Italian school of singing has never separated the two fundamental components of singing, that is, the production of sound and its resonance, such as has occurred with other pedagogical directions. According to her, *appoggio* is a system of uniting and equilibrating the actions of the muscles and organs located between the thoracic cavity and the neck, actions that control the relationship between the thorax and supraglottic resonances.

The conventional expression of the belcantists 'singing on the breath' resulting from the *appoggio* mechanism, is the point of arrival of a correct vocal education, considered indispensable by the *bel canto* school. Sanchez Carbone rightly declares that 'singing on the breath' to manifest itself as the opposite of a forced or pushed emission. She continues as follows:

> The emission 'on the breath' is also the foundation of that particular technique of producing the sound that acts upon the intention of amplitude, and amplifying the sound naturally, levelling the vocal line, the emission of the voice in all its extension, and in the meanwhile displaying the qualities required for good singing, such as ring, smoothness, and brilliance of the sound. It activates an action that safeguards the health and integrity of the phonatory organ [Sanchez Carbone, 2005: 102].

Juvarra (1987) and Sanchez Carbone (2005), both believe that the *appoggio* system of breath management is associated with certain physiological postures and antagonistic muscular configurations, which Juvarra contends 'can be regarded as the engine of the voice, and which are mainly concentrated around the abdominal lumbar girdle'.

Sanchez Carbone agrees with Juvarra, and provides the provenance of this historical and legendary pedagogical technique dedicated to managing the dosing of the airflow required for artistic singing. She contends that *appoggio* has its roots in the literature of the Italian school of the 18th and 19th century.

Juvarra (1987), Mori (1970), Mari (1975), and Bruno and Paperi (2001) and Damiani (2003), and Sanchez Carbone (2005) all believe that the coordination of this technique relies primarily on the 'noble posture' of the singer which is not only responsible for inducing the correct muscular balance but also for the retention of the inspiratory position for as long as possible.

The historical pedagogical approach to obtain the necessary coordination demanded by artistic singing is that technique associated with the dosing of the air known as *appoggio*. This has its roots in the literature of the Italian school of the eighteenth and nineteenth centuries. According to the technique of *appoggio*, the breath should retain the inspiratory position as long as possible (contraction of the external intercostals), retarding the expiratory action of the internal intercostal muscles. This balanced and dynamic muscular equilibrium will develop into what is known as the *lotta vocale* (vocal struggle).

The position of the abdominal muscles during singing remains in the inspiratory position for a longer period than that which occurs during normal phonatory behaviour. *Appoggio* is a system of governing the breath based on prolonging the inspiratory posture and on slowing down the expiratory phase.

The *appoggio* technique can be systematically developed with repetitions of 'onset' exercises, which consists of deep inspiration, tranquil adduction of the vocal folds, followed by a rapid, decisive and vibrant onset (abduction of the vocal folds to execute staccato) [Sanchez Carbone, 2005: 103].

Emission is terminated with the release of the sound (abduction of the vocal folds), with immediate and silent breath renewal; the release of the sound coincides with the renewal of the breath. We must proceed by gradually prolonging the emission in these exercises [Sanchez Carbone, 2005: 103].

The best way to achieve this is through the systematic exercise of the relevant muscles. For instance, the systematic repetition of onset produces the muscular antagonism of the antero/lateral abdominal wall, which encourages the muscles of this region to acquire a certain level of strength and brevity as is required by the singer/athlete.

In the *appoggio* technique, the diaphragm, the intercostal muscles, the thoracic cavity and all the muscles of the thorax (antero/lateral and posterior) are conditioned in such a dynamic way as to allow the dosing of the breath to respond to the great variety of demands made by the singer.

Knowledge of diaphragmatic function during the inspiratory cycle, as well as phonation, can save the teacher and the student a lot of time, eliminating systems of respiration founded on erroneous principles with respect to the respiratory cycle [Sanchez Carbone, 2005:103].

At this point, I think it would be useful to take a short detour from our text just to elaborate on the development of the '*appoggio* system' of breath management.

Chapter 12

The Development of the Appoggio System

Inveighing against the high breathing system that had visited a myriad of problems on so many singers in France, Britain and even Italy, Dr. Louis Mandl of Paris proposed a method of breathing for singing predicated on the exclusive activation of the lower abdominal muscles.

This system of breath management, best described as Hixon and Hoffman and treated in this text by Sanchez Carbone is closely related to the 'down and out' strategy that originated with Dr. Louis Mandl of Paris in 1853. However, one may argue that had the concept not been embraced and popularised a decade later by Francesco Lamperti, the method could well have been stillborn. It was Lamperti, an international authority on voice of genius proportions, who adapted and implemented Mandl's work in the early 1860s, thereby legitimising it, and popularising it with other teachers. What most of these teachers didn't realise was that Lamperti had adapted Mandl's original method and in the process, had created a more balanced model which was all his own. This system came to be known as Lamperti's '*appoggio* system', which was characterised not only by a combination of costo/diaphragmatic breathing as opposed to Mandl's original diaphragmatic/abdominal model, but he also included elements of vertical laryngeal position and resonance focal points, transforming Mandl's ideas into a more sophisticated and balanced model. One important element he retained from Mandl was the notion of the 'lotta vocale' or vocal struggle.

With respect to the '*appoggio* system', Lamperti had such a monumental success with his adaptation of the *appoggio* principles that other teachers were enticed to adopt it. Consequently, Mandl who was seeing as the originator, became a famous physician, who was asked to contribute a chapter on breathing for several international publications, including Delle Sedie's in Paris, Alberto Randeggar's book in London and even Giovanni Battista Lamperti in Berlin. In Britain, Behnke and Browne more than anyone else were responsible for the legitimisation and popularisation of Mandl's work, which was acknowledged as the force behind Francesco Lamperti's famous lotta vocale, or vocal struggle. But let us be very clear, Mandl's emphasis on the vertical aspects of breathing was seriously compromised and incomplete, it took a genius of stature, such as Francesco Lamperti, to realise that without the inclusions of the laterals and the lumbar dorsal region, the costals and the posterior pillars, a true '*appoggio* system' could not be achieved.

This fermentation created an atmosphere of experimentation, in which many different variations of these two strategies appeared. For the moment, however, let us accept that all three of these systems remain very influential.

For a time, the 'up and in' and 'down and out' models, discussed in these pages by Sanchez Carbone, competed with *appoggio*, but some point it was understood that both of these systems were flawed. According to Miller, both of these systems are based on misconception of vocal mechanics with respect to breath management. I agree with Miller, but also accept that there are certain singers who will never shift their position. To those singers, I would say: It's all in the way you arrive in the 'up and in' that makes all the difference. It's true that the Old Italian masters used the '*sostegno* system', which was essentially an 'up and in' system, but they also complemented this with costal breathing. They also raised substantial breath pressure by placing downward pressure at the sternum. This also has the effect of preventing the breath from becoming clavicular. All of which informs us that you can't just tuck your stomach in and lift your chest and call this a support system in the sense that the Old Italians referred to the system known as '*sostegno* system', because that is most certainly not what the great masters taught.

The Mechanics of Appoggio

With respect to the '*appoggio* system', Callaghan, following in Richard Miller's footsteps, is most eloquent. Having followed the debate closely, Callaghan forms the view that neither the 'up and in' nor the 'down and out' model are sufficiently complete and consequently comes down in favour of the '*appoggio* system'. Callaghan privileges the '*appoggio* system' propagated by Lamperti because she believes that: 'the flexible approach of *appoggio* seems to answer the need for dynamic breath management strategies to meet different musical demands and to suit different body types' [Callaghan, 2000: 39]. This flexibility, I believe, encapsulates the reason why the *appoggio* system dating back to the 1860s, has become so dominant.

It was also during the 1880s, with the support of Delle Sedie, Randeggar, Stockhausen, Mackenzie, and Behnke and Brown that the new Mandl/Lamperti '*appoggio* system' became the dominant paradigm.

Mori (1970) believes that in order to acquire an adequate respiratory technique, the abdominal, thoracic and the auxiliary muscles, and the muscles surrounding the diaphragm must be properly educated. The effective work of respiration, according to Mori, depends on two antagonistic forces, those that provide the expanding movement of the thoracic wall, the diaphragm and the lungs and those that retard that movement. Retardation is a function of the elasticity of the muscle tissue and the resistance of the air passage.

Juvarra (1987) elaborates on Mori's statement above. He believes that is important to recognise that the maintenance of the inspiratory position is not only part of the antagonistic relationship between inspiratory and expiratory muscles, but it also coordinates the activity of the entire muscle complex, including the epigastric/costal/ umbilical area, which combines with diaphragmatic /abdominal contraction and lateral/ lumbar region, all of which allows for a controlled retraction of the thoracic cage and the lungs.

Juvarra (1987) and Menicucci (2011) and Sanchez Carbone (2005) confirm that the particular muscular settings associated with *appoggio* have an effect on sound quality. Juvarra believes that the *appoggio* technique is designed to not only amplify the natural voice, depending on the acoustic requirements of the opera, but also to impart amplitude and a uniform (homogenous) quality throughout the vocal range, whilst also fulfilling the aesthetic demands of '*smalto*' (ring) and '*morbidezza*' (smoothness) of the sound, qualities that safeguard the wellbeing of the instrument. Sanchez Carbone (2005) uses almost identical language to describe this phenomenon. Menicucci (2011) reminds us that we can validate the quality of '*voce appoggiata*' even today, simply by employing the '*sostegno* system' of the old school with its resulting characteristic quality, which he believes is still valid, especially in the *bel canto* repertoire.

Following an analysis of the above, Juvarra concludes that the, *appoggio* system is designed to govern the airflow through the two simultaneous and antagonistic muscular objectives: the first objective is meant to prolong the inspiratory posture, whilst the second, which is closely connected, is designed to slow down the expiratory phase.

These objectives are achieved through the simultaneous contraction of the external intercostals and diaphragm, which retard the expiratory action provided by the internal intercostal and the abdominal muscles, striving to return to their original relaxed state; whilst the second, the slowing down phase, requires the co-contraction of the diaphragm and the abdominal muscles and that of the external intercostals.

These muscular forces provide, in large part, the necessary natural recoil, which is also aided by the automatic retreat the abdominal muscles in an 'up and in' direction, an action that raises the diaphragm and elicits the natural recoil force of the alveoli within the lungs.

This might suggest a one-way action, which is not true, because the diaphragm can also be co-contracted to retard and regulate the retreat of the abdominal musculature, without either blocking the abdominal muscles, or preventing them from fulfilling their function. We are also reminded by Juvarra that co-contraction can occurs at different levels of intensity, but it doesn't have to be extreme, it just has to balanced depending on the repertoire to be performed and the effect to be achieved.

From the above narration, we may conclude that in the very best schools, those dedicated to the management of the various firm but flexible levels of co-contraction, the diaphragm also remains active, retarding the rise of the abdominal muscles whilst never blocking. Juvarra reminds us that this manoeuvre also involves not only the diaphragm, but also the lumbar/abdominal region and the costals, all of which correspond with the breathing adopted by the classic masters of singing.Juvarra is very clear on the need for co-contraction and he has considerable support in this important respiratory principle, not only by Sundberg and Von Euler, who proved conclusively that co-contraction occurs regularly, but also many other major Italian authors such as Mori (1970) Bruno and Paperi (2001) and Sanchez Carbone (2005).

Juvarra argues convincingly that the role of the diaphragm in the expiratory phase is not to block the rise of the abdominal muscles but only to retard them. He contends that given that vocal emission is closely correlated to some form of expiration, the movement of the abdominals withdrawing under their own muscular contraction is generally clearly observable. This slowly retreating action becomes even more obvious during longer phrases.

According to Juvarra:

> The task of the diaphragm is not to impede or block this naturally retreating (abdominal) movement, but rather to control and graduate its withdrawal. In reality, there are two different active muscular tensions, but in practice the conscious control is limited to one, that of the diaphragm, because the abdominal muscles, which are responsible for expiration, function automatically if inspiration has been executed correctly. The level of muscular antagonism is variable, depending on the relationship between the effects to be achieved, and the means required to achieve it, but it is as well to confirm that the initial developmental phase of this mechanism must correspond with an elastic and flexible use of the musculature, exercising it with 'vocalizzi' that set the diaphragm into dancing, whilst using the abdominal musculature to create a firm wall, which brings with it the risk of blocking and creating noxious rigidity.
>
> The conscious control over the lowering of the diaphragm gives the perception of working as a piston or an inspiratory air pump, giving origin to the sensation of reversing the direction of the vital force of either inspiration or expiration of the sound, such as singing the high notes whilst thinking low [Juvarra, 1987: 33].

With respect to muscular antagonism, Juvarra believes that it is variable, depending on qualitative requirements, including sound quality, intensity and pitch. However, within these constraints, the region of the epigastrium (Mancini's power of the chest), remains the most important focal point for the concentration of localised muscular antagonism. To obtain the complete efficiency of the *appoggio*, the lower costals must remain expanded, but not at the expense of curving the back, hunching the shoulders, or collapsing the thorax. The body must remain properly aligned and muscularly coordinated, and Juvarra is aware that this level of muscular coordination cannot be achieved quickly; it takes time. Consequently, he warns against the premature implementation of certain arduous techniques.

Finally, he expresses the ideas of many Italian authors when he maintains that umbilical protrusion, which reduces the act of supporting the chest, is completely foreign to the Italian classical tradition whether it be *sostegno* or *appoggio*. Juvarra maintains that:

> To arrive prematurely at this phase in which notable muscular tensions occur and animate the functional aspects of the vocal instrument without before learning to master it, and to graduate its intensity without involving the throat, is one of the most dangerous temptations for beginning voice students. Many students fall into the trap of trying to conquer methods, which are theoretically correct, such as the 'affondo', prematurely, leading to muscular rigidity [Juvarra, 1987: 32].

Juvarra (1987), Bruno and Paperi (2001) and Sanchez Carbone (2005), all agree that during the inspiratory phase of the cycle, the singer perceives an expansion of the anterior and lateral abdominal wall, around the tenth rib just below the thoracic cage. According to Sanchez Carbone, the degree of expansion depends not only on the development and coordination of the musculature, but also on individual morphology.

The vocal function must be understood as a phenomenon of global sensation, perceived principally as a sensation of resistance, and of a firm but flexible *sostegno* at the level of the abdominal girdle, including the rectus abdominus, and the inferior wall of the thorax, and also the paravertebral region. Sanchez Carbone suggests that,

> This sensation of muscular tonicity, informs the singer not only of the activity and position of the organs, but also their level of flexibility and efficacy. For the singer, it is a question of achieving a gradual and controlled return of the diaphragm to its original position during vocal emission. The singer controls expiration by maintaining the inspiratory muscular position, which largely neutralized the natural antagonistic expiratory action caused not only by the natural recoil force but also by musculature contraction [Sanchez Carbone, 1987: 32–33].

In line with Juvarra (1987), Bruno and Paperi (2001) and Sanchez Carbone (2005) also believe in the co-contraction of the respiratory muscles. In fact, there is hardly an author of any stature who does not believe in the co-contraction of the internal and external intercostals, that is not a question up for debate. The difference between the adherents of co-contraction generally is not that they believe in the antagonism between the internal and external intercostal muscles, but rather they believe in the co-contraction between the muscles fibres surrounding the diaphragm and the abdominals. More and more authors today, including Sundberg and Von Euler, James Stark, Juvarra, Bruno and Paperi and Sanchez Carbone are all convinced that diaphragmatic/abdominal co-contraction takes place. I personally adhere to the following Sanchez Carbone narrative and cite it at length:

> The inspiratory muscles then act as a 'brake', by maintaining the inspiratory position for a considerable time, although these muscles should not become rigid and in fact they de-contract (relax) slowly and gradually during the act of expiration. The rate of de-contraction of the inspiratory muscles is dependent on the artistic requirements of the piece, with the air leaving the body slowly and by the gradual squeezing of the thoracic cavity. The 'inspiratory brake' can therefore be either costal or diaphragmatic: the first is constituted by the muscles that dilate the thoracic cage and that, by maintaining their contraction during the expiratory cycle, impede the exceedingly rapid collapse of the thorax; the second is constituted by the diaphragm which by contracting even during expiration, maintains its lowered position, impeding the abdominal viscera, which are compressed by the abdominal girdle, from pushing into the thoracic cavity too rapidly, or violently, or uncontrolled, provoking a rapid reduction of the thorax [Sanchez Carbone, 2005: 105].

Sanchez Carbone contends that the more tenaciously the singer clings to the inspiratory position (the expanded thoracic cavity), the slower and more gradual the relaxation of the diaphragm and the expiratory costal muscles transpires, provoking a greater contraction of the thoracic/ abdominal girdle which creates the expiratory required force [105].

Sanchez Carbone concludes from the above:

> Every expiratory emission partakes of the 'lotta vocale', the struggle between the inspiratory and expiratory muscles: that is, the first aims to keep the thorax dilated and operates as a 'brake' to the airflow; whilst the second constricts the thorax and 'accelerates' the airflow. The expiratory tension must be in perfect equilibrium with the inspiratory tension during vocal emission. Such equilibrium allows for a precise vocal onset, that is, an instantaneous emission of a vocal sound that is of well-defined intensity, and of good quality that would otherwise be impossible. Any impurity, such as breathiness or turbulence in the emission will be eliminated instantaneously. And it is as the result of this voluntary and conscious muscular antagonism that the expiratory current is formed, incessantly controlled, modelled, forged and elaborated for the purpose of acquiring all the gradations of intensity and duration, corresponding to the demands of the art of singing [Sanchez Carbone. 2005: 106].

Sanchez Carbone is absolutely right! There is no question that these antagonistic forces were exactly what both Mandl and Lamperti referred to as the 'lotta vocale'. Just as a matter of interest, the designation was originally assigned to the co-contraction between the diaphragm and abdominal musculature; it was only later that Lamperti realised that even though this vertical model was a considerable advance on the 'clavicular' breathing that preceded it, the paradigm remained incomplete. It was at this point that he decided to add the lateral movement of the lower floating ribs to the strategy. Notwithstanding the above historical elaboration, Sanchez Carbone has provided us with a compelling description of the Lamperti/Mandl 'lotta vocale'. She describes not only the contribution of the antagonistic 'vocal struggle' towards a steady stream of 'subglottal pressure', but she also describes its effect on 'airflow' and steadiness and firmness of tone.

Bruno and Paperi concur with the principle of co-contraction and the 'lotta vocale'. They too believe that:

> The primary function of the diaphragm, particularly in the inspiratory phase, is to expand and lower itself, pressing down anteriorly against the abdomen and laterally against the lower costal ribs all the way back to the spine, where it transfers the daily emotional function to that of interpretative expressive energy, especially with the respect to the big sentiments associated with certain styles.

Bruno and Paperi elaborate not only the physiology of the diaphragm but also its educational capabilities. They contend that:

> In reality, the diaphragm, which is inserted to the sternum and vertebral column, is not normally controllable during phonation; however, by implementing a considerable training regime of the surrounding muscles of the central tendon, the diaphragm can be educated to assume the role of dosing the airflow [Bruno & Paperi, 2001: 89].

The views expressed by Bruno and Paperi represent in a general way, those of the most authoritative Italian authors, all of whom adhere to the notion that although the central tendon does not possess extensible and contractile fibres, the surrounding muscles do, and these muscles can be educated to maintain a lowered and antagonistic position not only against the abdominal viscera, but also against the lateral/lumbar region [Bruno & Paperi, 2001: 89].

Fussi and Magnani concur with the principle of co-contraction, but with considerable variations from that described above: variations that I believe disadvantage the singer. In essence, they believe in a more limited co-contraction' involving the internal/external intercostals, but this is only one element of the double support system required for elite singing, the other, as we have argued above, being the co-contraction of the diaphragm/abdominal complex.

That which is generally defined as *appoggio* can be understood as a complex technique.

By failing to establish the co-contraction between the diaphragm and the abdominals, Fussi and Magnani relegate the responsibility for maintaining a low diaphragmatic position to the expanded thoracic region supported by the contraction of the abdominal girdle. In so doing, they disregard the possibility of educating the muscles fibres surrounding the diaphragm in a voluntary and conscious manner which, other Italian authors believe, produces a more direct control over the lowered diaphragmatic position.I don't believe that the position adopted by Fussi and Magnani's is sustainable in the 21st century, when the overwhelming evidence points to the importance of co-contraction of the double support system, that is the internal/ external intercostals and the diaphragmatic/abdominal muscles, which together form the foundation of elite singing.

I don't deny, that at first glance, and because of its concentration on the thoracic region, their strategy may appear to be more viable with respect to the *sostegno* system of breath management, because the diaphragm and the abdominals meet at a higher level within the thoracic cavity, but really that misses the point, which is not, at what level of thoracic cavity these two antagonistic elements interact, but whether they co-contract simultaneously or sequentially.

I understand that this issue, the physiological level of encounter within the thoracic cage, that is, the level at which the diaphragm and abdominals actually meet is important, and we have already discussed the almost universal rejection by the Italians of both the 'clavicular' and 'abdominal' strategy, but the issue of sequential contraction or co-contraction is if anything even more important to elite singing.Let us deal with both issues separately.

The issue of 'abdominal' breathing is of concern to many Italian authors who are genuinely concerned about the diaphragm plunging too deeply, blocking of the abdominals from pushing the diaphragm back into the thorax. This concern was the stated reason for Bruno and Paperi's alternative paradigm, advocating a moderate contraction of the abdominals even before the diaphragm begins to lower. This strategy is designed to build a pavement under the diaphragm, establishing limits to its downward thrust.

This is a very valid strategy for ensuring a more balanced lowering of the diaphragm. However, it is not the only strategy, and in fact, I believe that a better and more organic strategy is one of ensuring the instantaneous activation of both diaphragm and lower costals (floating ribs). The simultaneous and spontaneous movement of the diaphragm and laterals ensures a more organic, fluid and balanced activation of the diaphragm and lower costals. It is also appropriate to recall that the final lateral movement of the floating ribs has the effect of automatically withdrawing the abdominals. This results with a similar outcome and effect as the Bruno and Paperi strategy, but it is achieved a much more natural and spontaneous way, requiring much less vertical calculation, which I believe is important. Either way, these two strategies will provide the singer with two different strategies both of which end in a balanced equilibrium.

In contrast to Fussi and Magnani's thoracic strategy of *appoggio*, Juvarra contends that *appoggio* is characterised by a downward and outward orientation. Consequently, we conclude that Fussi and Magnani's exclusively thoracic strategy, with its lack of diaphragmatic foundation, is inadequate for *appoggio* nor is it the best strategy for optimising control over a constant subglottal pressure and airflow, both elements are critical to the spinto and dramatic repertoire.

The second issue, that is, co-contraction is also of great importance whether the muscles contract sequentially, or co-contract ranging from too much recoil force at the beginning of vocal emission, which needs to be retarded and converted to a more moderate and balanced force, through to the undernourished force that needs to be reinforced towards the end of a phrase.

Fussi and Magnani, treat this particular topic of breath consumption and the muscular activation required most elegantly. They suggest that:

> In the course of a musical phrase the air pressure diminishes as a result of breath consumption during singing. It remains a fact therefore that to maintain the pressure required in the following phase of expiration, the diaphragm begins rising and is accompanied in its ascension by the abdominal muscles.
>
> These (forces) intensify their action of sustaining the sound towards the end of a musical phrase, which is accompanied by the progressive reduction of pulmonary volume. Whilst we begin with dominant sensation of 'appoggio' at the beginning of the musical phrase we gradually substitute this with an increasing value of 'sostegno' by the end [Fussi & Magnani, 2003: 175].

On the other hand:

> In the expiratory phase that follows, it is imperative that the active contraction of the abdominal musculature exerts a steady control over the retreating force of the abdominal wall, repositioning the viscera and guiding the ascending excursion of the diaphragm, which allows the voluntary management of subglottal pressure without external shocks or jerks [Fussi & Magnani, 2003: 176].

Sanchez Carbone (2005) agrees with Fussi and Magnani but sounds a note of caution when she suggests that:

> Sustaining the breath does not mean retarding the column of air to the degree that will inevitably cause the closure of the glottis and hardening of the muscles. On the contrary, it means the exercising of the abdominal and intercostal muscles in such a way as to sustain a gentle, uniform, constant, harmonious, and smooth expiration without shocks, tensions, and undue muscular hardening, which will result in maximum control over airflow, and sustained subglottal pressure [Sanchez Carbone, 2005: 103].

Sanchez Carbone maintains that, the *appoggio* technique coordinates the whole instrument, manifesting visually through the postural alignment (noble posture) of the singer; that is, the absence of the raised chest during singing or breath renewal, and the correct muscular action designed to retard the inward movement of the abdominal wall in close relation to the phrase being sung [Sanchez Carbone, 2005: 103].

Fussi and Magnani concur, adding that once the singer recognises the need to hold back the breath they will also realise that the best way to achieve this is to maintain the contraction of the expiratory muscles, which retard the rise of the diaphragm to its original position. The thorax will then maintain its position through the contraction of the external intercostals whilst the abdominal wall supports their action.

At this point, my reader could be forgiven for thinking that notwithstanding our earlier concentration not only the vertical aspects of breathing (Abdominal/diaphragmatic) but also on the lateral and posterior/anterior characteristics are of secondary importance. That is not the case, because although the lowering of the diaphragm and the its interrelationship with the abdominal wall remains fundamental, there no doubt that for elite singing, the lateral and lumbar/abdominal region is of fundamental importance.

The above is reflected in the Italian literature as demonstrated in these pages. We recall that authors as diverse as Mori (1970) Mari and Schindler (1986), Juvarra (1987), Fussi and Magnani (1994 & 2003), Bruno and Paperi (2003), Sanchez Carbone (2005) Menicucci (2011), all strongly advocate for the use of what some refer as a mixed respiratory strategy, and others call costo/abdominal or costo/ diaphragmatic. Notwithstanding the small variations in name they all advocate the use of the lateral lumbar region, and many of the most prominent promote the simultaneous contraction to the two posterior muscular pillars which activation anchors the diaphragm down, and which have been treated at length earlier in this chapter.

Menicucci reminds us that this type of abdominal breathing is universally valid whether it is employed in everyday life, during sporting activity, or playing a woodwind instrument, and other psychophysical energies.

In singing, it is possible to perfect the inspiratory act by encouraging the contribution of thorax through the sensible dilation of the floating ribs, whereupon we may utilise all the pulmonary capacity. In this way, we can arrive at the best inspiratory performance. The manoeuvre so achieved is known as mixed respiration or costo/diaphragmatic.

In examining the Italian literature at some depth, there is no question that the Italians are very holistic with respect to breathing. Nanda Mari refers to the sensation of having a life buoy all around the circumference of your waist. Amongst those advocating the mixed model, I like Bruno and Paperi's description best. They believe that,

> Amongst the various and competing models of respiration, they prefer:
>> Once we discover the double mechanism which simultaneously activates both sostegno and appoggio, there is a need to skilfully guide the rise of the diaphragm, without sub-

stantially modifying the vertical position of the larynx above the subglottal pressure, in a manner that does not impact deleteriously in either vocal colour or musical line. The lower abdominal/pelvic zone needs to be educated, in experience, to act almost spontaneously so as to induce a smooth rising of the diaphragm [Bruno & Paperi, 2001: 95].

The lower costal diaphragmatic model, which is the 'mixed model' of respiration that demands an ample and flexible inspiration that avails itself of the 'sostegno' provided by the balanced tensions of the lower abdominals, as well as the pelvic and sacral region Bruno & Paperi, 2001: 95].

Summary

There is broad agreement in the Italian literature that, since the *appoggio* technique is a more onerous paradigm than that required in everyday life, it is not naturally present in most cases. However, the literature is just as adamant, that this technique can be systematically developed with repetitions of 'onset exercises', consisting of deep inspiration, tranquil adduction of the vocal folds, followed by a rapid, decisive and vibrant onset. Physiologically, the systematic repetition of onset produces the muscular antagonism of the antero/lateral abdominal wall, which encourages the muscles of this region to acquire a certain level of strength and brevity as is required by the singer/athlete.

Sanchez Carbone informs us that whilst emission initiates with 'vocal onset' which should always be associated with a concomitant airflow, the release of Emission is terminated with the release of the sound (abduction of the vocal folds), with immediate and silent breath renewal: the release of the sound coincides with the renewal of the breath. 'We must proceed by gradually prolonging the emission in these exercises' [p. 103].

In many respects *appoggio* is really about understanding and exercising the muscular function that slowly, and patiently strengthens the musculature, involved in the extraordinary work of educating the vocal instrument.

Conclusions

The following paradigm is one derived from extensive analysis of respiration in the Italian literature over the last fifty years. The following is based on a synthesis of the respiratory model, which I believe best represents the most prevalent model in the Italian literature: The abdominal/costo/diaphragmatic model.

The paradigm elaborated by contemporary Italian master is a multifaceted, sophisticated and complete costo/abdominal diaphragmatic model, which in my opinion is worth the effort of a closer and in-depth analysis. There are several features to this respiratory model, of which the following are the most important:

It is widely accepted that the diaphragm is the major inspiratory muscle, and that the central tendon of the diaphragm does not possess contractile muscle fibres and therefore cannot be itself directly controlled. However, there is wide acceptance within the contemporary Italian school that contraction of the muscle fibres surrounding the central tendon provide good control over the diaphragm, creating an adequate antagonistic force that opposes the force exerted by the contraction of the abdominal wall (abdominal girdle). This antagonism is referred to as the 'lotta vocale' forms the bases of the Italian '*appoggio* system' of support

As a result of this antagonism, Italians believe that the diaphragm is not only the inspiratory muscle par excellence, but they also regard it as the major breath dosing muscle. The latter is only true when the diaphragm offers its resistance to the ascending force of the abdominal girdle (this is comprised of internal and external oblique, transversus, and rectus abdominis).

The Italian masters are aware that this antagonistic stance can only take place as long as the external intercostals (inspiratory muscles) maintain their moderately high position. By moderately high, the Italians mean the 'bucket handle model', which raises and expands the thorax transversally and not the 'pump lever model', which is essentially seen as too high and expanding the thorax in a dangerously vertical direction associated generally associated with clavicular breathing.

The Italians also acknowledged that the diaphragm is the foundation of the thorax and it acts to divide the thoracic cage from the abdominal cavity. Consequently, diaphragmatic contraction increases the longitudinal diameter of the thoracic cavity.

Italian masters of the 21st century are very aware of the controversial and antagonistic nature of the intercostal muscles. The external intercostals dilate and elevate the thorax whilst in expiration the internal intercostals depress and constrict the thorax.

I believe that it is absolutely critical for those of us who do this work to examine everything in fine detail, conquer that detail and share it with our students to the degree that they can cope with it or prepared to accept its importance. For the truth is that for some of these exciting stage animals such as Sutherland, Freni, Caballe, Netrebko, Pavarotti or Domingo, Alagna or Kaufmann the doing is the thing. They couldn't care less about this kind of descriptive detail. All they know is that they have found a way to use the diaphragm as an antagonistic force against the ascending force generated by the contraction of the abdominal muscles. If you said to them 'you do know that you can only lower the diaphragm through the agency of the surrounding muscles of the central tendon', they would probably accept it. On the other hand, if you start the conversation by saying, 'you do know that you can't really lower the diaphragm because the central tendon does not possess elastic contractile fibres', then I suggest that you would have lost them before the end of the sentence.

Someone like Domingo would probably think, even though he would be too polite to say it, 'this is the reason I never graduated from the conservatorium because I couldn't wait to get away from those 'Conservatorium Rats', the phrase he uses in his book 1985 book, '*My First Forty Years*'. Sutherland would probably think something like, 'that may well be the true, but somehow I learned how to control it and 'It took me a long way'.

Tetrazzini would probably respond with one of her famous phrases such as you are probably right, and 'some people say that they can't see me breathe, but they certainly can't say that I ever run out of breath'.

I believe that it is imperative that scientists, teachers and researchers maintain their quest for truth and excellence. However, I don't believe that it is necessary to present our findings in a manner that may be interpreted as demeaning, petty or pedantic. We should at all times keep in mind that great artists are the ones who are doing it, we, for all our good intentions and valuable advice just talk about it. Having said that, I know many great artists who are genuine in the quest for knowledge, they really want to know not only how things work but also how this knowledge may improve their performance. So, we have an attentive audience, we just need to treat them with respect. Failure to do so may engender an element of animosity and even derision.

Chapter 13

Laryngeal Physiology and the Vibratory System

Sanchez Carbone contends that it is relatively easy to emit a vocal sound, but much more difficult to explain the considerably onerous and hidden work behind its emission. The mechanism responsible for voice production is determined by a muscular system in which the vocal folds remain the central focal point, and in which the final product is the result of a functional process that imbues the voice with its unique character and quality. She reminds us that vocal characteristics are essentially determined by laryngeal efficiency.

Based on this premise, it is clear that voice production is much more a matter of educating the muscular system that produces the vocal vibrations and which is itself a system that is subject to specific functional laws, rather than educating the voice itself.

Vocal emission, according to Sanchez Carbone, entails the coordinated and balanced action of many muscles and not just those that constitute an integral part of the larynx, but also a number of separate structures in many regions of our body that carry out independent functions. These are adapted in a synergistic manner to produce that unique human characteristic, the production of speech and song.

In the process of vocal emission, the muscular complex involved in phonation must find the correct equilibrium between the various muscular groups responsible form voice production. To fulfil this function with efficiency and grace, it is necessary that all the inspiratory and expiratory muscles must be placed at the disposal of the respiratory function; the same applies to the muscles responsible for shortening, lengthening and tensing the vocal folds, and all the muscles responsible for adapting the vocal tract for its resonatory function.

Significantly, Sanchez Carbone suggests that sound quality is not only influenced by vocal acoustics but also the imagination, i.e., the mind's ability to vividly imagine the sound before it is emitted. These are the elements that elicit the correct physical reaction. Even so, the sound emitted does not represent the intrinsic quality of the voice, nor the precision of the mental concept and image of the sound, but rather the condition of the voice and its reactive muscular coordination. Consequently, there may be a discrepancy between the clarity with which the singer conceives the image of the sound and the physical capacity to transform that concept into reality. The manner in which the vocal organs react depends on the clarity and precision of the mental concept as well as the efficiency with which the respiratory muscles respond to the mental image of the sound, and the manner in which the psychological aspects of voice production can either help or hinder muscular action.

If the vocal organs are capable of functioning as requested and the mechanism is capable to reacting and exercising any type of voluntary control over the function of the laryngeal mechanism, it would be reasonable to affirm our capacity to intentionally control the regulation of such laryngeal action. In truth, no such voluntary control is possible. Mainly because the vocal organs respond to external stimulus, in the form of nervous impulses communicated to the brain.

Sanchez Carbone concludes that in effect all of the human body influences vocal sound, either directly or indirectly. She contends that to emit a vowel requires a considerable amount of work, not so much for the amount of force generated but rather for the number of muscles activated. Humans do not enjoy conscious control over the action of the intrinsic muscles of the larynx, and consequently have no control over the vocal folds. Nor do they have control over the various positions assumed by the larynx in the production of the spoken word or for that matter that of the singing voice. The voice is the result of activating a number of mechanical and physical factors. In short, it is the final synthesis of a complex that remains unique and indivisible, the product of simultaneous and harmonious actions on the part of multiple organs that both support and are guided by nervous impulses [Sanchez Carbone, 2005: 143].

Sanchez Carbone cites Claire Dinville in a passage that I liked so much that I quote her under: Dinville believes that:

> Vocal function is a muscular activity that cannot develop and acquire emotional and expressive qualities without pursuing a complex of proprioceptive, and kinaesthetic sensations that take into considerations the laws of physics, acoustics, phonetics and the physiological function of the organs. It is lived as a vibratory phenomenon, a global sensation of movement and muscular action [Dinville in Sanchez Carbone, 2005: 143].

In general, I concur with Sanchez Carbone with respect to educating the physiological aspects of the instrument through the training of the relevant musculature. I also believe that the musculature involved in voice production goes far beyond the intrinsic and extrinsic laryngeal muscles, but I also believe in the power of the educated mind and its ability to give the right orders and attain corresponding physiological response. Consequently, we can assume that when we transfer the responsibility for the authentic, unique and personal sound quality to the vocal instrument itself, we automatically undermine the personal prejudices associated with the sound world of both the student and the teacher. The only way to really attain the natural and unique sound of each individual singer is to educate the physiological instrument and refrain from either interfering or making particular sounds that we believe are good or desirable, but which may not be genuine or natural sounds to that particular voice. By putting the onus back in the naturalness and creativity of the vocal instrument whilst paying attention to the results it yields and the type of sound it produces, we are likely to discover our natural sound.

I also agree with Sanchez Carbone that we cannot directly and consciously control the laryngeal muscles, but I do believe that we can indirectly but consciously control laryngeal movement. Nonetheless, on balance, I conclude that where possible we should allow muscular action and reaction to occur without conscious interference. The complication of course is that this only applies when the wisdom of the instrument is already on the right track. If in fact we are trying to reprogram the instrument, then the assistance of a master teacher is indispensable.

Simply because it is only when we know in great detail and with great precision how the instrument works that we can consciously guide it in a gross way whilst allowing the subconscious to assist nature in the fine and continuously altering adjustments.Singing can and I believe should be set in motion and guided more consciously and to a much greater degree than many teachers and singers are prepared to concede.The confusion arises because singers and singing teachers tend to forget that just because on a good day everything seems to be working smoothly and in accordance with natural laws now, it doesn't mean that in the early years of training we didn't spend many hundreds of agonising hours building a solid technique and consciously programming our minds to unconsciously reproduce the very best of vocal technique.

In large part, the art of great teaching is to program and reprogram the vocal instrument in accordance with its natural inclination so that most days it works with little thought or intervention.And then, being a human and vulnerable instrument, there are always days when the voice doesn't respond in the usual manner no matter what we do or how hard we try.And on those days, it is not going to be as easy, nor as fluid, nor as natural no matter what technique we adopt. However, if you have an intimate knowledge of how the instrument works, you may still give a respectable performance. The sad thing is that in the aging voice these events tend to occur more frequently.

The great castrato, Gaspare Pacchierotti provides the evidence that the aging process is a difficult one. It is widely accepted that historically, Pacchierotti was the greatest castrato after Farinelli, and these are his poignant insights at the end of his illustrious career. Pacchierotti remarked that 'when you are young you have the voice but you do not have the knowledge and when you are old you have all the knowledge, but you no longer have the voice'. The young should remember that there is a price to be paid for an overinflated ego, and too much independence, and that price is that by the time you have reinvented the wheel, your career is almost over, and even then, there is no guarantee that you have been able to put it together to the same degree as the geniuses that have gone before us. So, the price for stupidity is that of remaining a mediocre artist for at least the first half of your career, and the possibility that the process will shorten an already inferior career. These are the very people who then spend the rest of their lives looking for scapegoats, or worse still, looking for ways to kill the messenger. Well, they can do all of that, but in the end, they will be forced to confront the truth, and that is, that they are responsible for the life and career they have created for themselves.

I adhere very strongly to the above credo, which I also believe both reflects and compliments much of the Italian literature as exemplified by Sanchez Carbone's cogent argument above.

With the above in mind, it is time to resume our discussion on the anatomy, physiology and science of the vocal source. And the first author we are going to discuss is the Italian vocal scientist and physician, Carlo Meano. His research dominated the field in Italy from the later forties to the late sixties, and is still highly regarded today. His book was published in Italy in 1964 and the English translation appeared in 1967, the very year that marks the beginning of the fifty years that we address in this particular history of Italian Vocal Pedagogy (1967–2017).

Carlo Meano

Carlo Meano was the first Italian author to delineate the anatomy, and explain how the laws of physiology and acoustics impact on the various techniques, and even more importantly, can predict the consequences of particular physiological adjustments on both technique and aesthetic outcomes. Meano was an ear, nose and throat specialist who treated and advised many of the great singers and actors of his generation.

Based on his vast knowledge of the vocal instrument, he was able to draw certain conclusions between cause and effect, or in a singer's case between technique and outcome.

Meano informs us that the vocal folds are encased within the larynx, but more towards the anterior part of the neck. The larynx itself is constituted by a group of cartilages which are connected by ligaments and muscles and which are internally covered by a mucous membrane forming thereby an organic solidity that is both mobile and elastic.

In its external skeletal conformation, the larynx sits above the trachea (a series of cartilage rings) that resembles a capital on a small column. The base of the scaffolding resides on the cricoid cartilages, upon which we find the thyroid cartilage. These major cartilages combine to constitute the external scaffolding of the larynx. Connected to the cricoid by an elastic membrane, the thyroid moves up and down, backward and forward. Above the thyroid we find the hyoid bone overhang the thyroid cartilage, whilst projecting upward at its summit we find the epiglottis. The epiglottis is fixed firmly by its stem to the internal wall of the thyroid immediately above the point of attachment of the vocal folds. This attachment, whilst firm is sufficiently mobile to ensure its protective function by folding back automatically, thereby covering the glottis and guiding food and into the oesophagus [Meano, 1967: 30-31].

These structural facts, have been confirmed by a number of authoritative Italian authors over the last fifty and will be elaborated on in these pages by authors such as Galignano, Damiani, Fussi, Juvarra, Magnani, Mori, and Sanchez Carbone to name but a few. Authors such as Meano (1967), Mori (1970), Juvarra (1987), Fussi and Magnani (1994), Damiani (2003), and Sanchez Carbone (2005), and Galignano (2013) have all described laryngeal structure in very similar terms.

Meano wrote his excellent book, *The Human Voice in Speech and Song* in 1967, about the same time as William Vennard was rewriting the second edition of his monumental book *Singing: The Mechanism and the Technique* published in 1967. Consequently, Meano displays certain similarities with both William Vennard and the earlier author Henry Holbrook Curtis. His great contribution is to bring a more European sensibility to the scientific material of his day, he seems to have had a first-hand experience of the development and debate raging over the neurochronaxic theory which was invading the European research agenda in the late forties and the early fifties, but he also places great value on understanding the mental and physiological processes of voice production, not always present in purely mechanistic works. That said, Meano displays many affinities with Vennard in his scientific approach, but by virtue of his profession also displays similarities to Curtis. However, he brings greater scientific rigour than did Henry Holbrook Curtis, and remains much less controversial.

Meano continues by summarising the mental processes undertaken by the brain during voice initiation and production. He follows this with a detailed analysis of the anatomy and physiology of voice. According to Meano,

The human brain sends cerebral impulses via the neurons of the nervous system. It does so through an endplate or battery charge, and this meeting of the nervous impulse and the motor plate causes an excitation of the muscle fibres.

Meano cites Raul Husson, who in 1951 carried a number of experiments at the Sorbonne in Paris, the result of which convinced him that the vocal folds vibrate as a result of a nervous excitation independent of the expiratory air, and that this impulse originates in the cerebral cortex, similar to the excitation of the muscles in the body. Consequently, the mechanical, or more correctly called myoelastic/aerodynamic theory was temporarily substituted by the neurochronaxic theory of voice production. Meano became increasingly aware that this theory, which he had nurtured alongside Husson, was no longer sustainable, but Meano maintains a sentimental fondness for the neurological aspects of voice production.

Having described the external structure of the laryngeal tube, Meano now describes the internal laryngeal vestibule, which according to him, consists of an ascending structure comprised of the following organs:

- the true vocal folds
- the recesses or cavities known as the ventricles of Morgagni
- the two superior folds that are less accentuated, and are also known as the false vocal folds.

In this process both the true and the false vocal folds are spread apart for inspiration, but only the true vocal folds come together (adduct) in firm contact at the inner margins during voice production. They do so in order to resist the pulmonary air-pressure that animates the vocal folds, and indispensable element for the creation of resonant sound.

Before beginning an elaborate dissertation on the nature of the vocal instrument, Meano suggests that physiological knowledge of the instrument 'is indispensable for voice professionals' who are required to protect their instrument and often this knowledge can give a warning to the dangers ensuing from certain techniques [Meano, 1967: 25].

I believe that Meano is right: a deeper understanding of the instrument is indispensable, but not just for passive reasons as he suggests, but rather knowledge is indispensable to maximising performance and maintaining a first rank elite career. The type of passive benefit that Meano is referring to was probably more acceptable during his time when people reading books thought the best you could do was to learn to maintain a healthy singing voice, but that was then. Today with the much deeper knowledge of the voice, singers are not just seeking to maintain physiologically efficient instrument. Today's singers have much more ambitious agendas and one of their major objectives is to maximise performance effectiveness. We need to move beyond that developmental phase if we are to become great singers, and by extension create opportunities to become great artists.

Anatomically, Meano contends that the conformation of the larynx is physically dominated by the thyroid cartilage, which by virtue of its size and position is the largest and most prominent cartilage in the larynx, dominating the laryngeal structure, often referred to as the Adam's apple.

The larynx is suspended from the hyoid bone via the elastic thyrohyoid muscle. The thyroid cartilage hangs from the hyoid bone above, whilst resting on the cricoid cartilage below. The cricoid cartilage is the thickest and strongest cartilage in the larynx and forms the foundation upon which the thyroid cartilage rests. The two arytenoid cartilages are situated on the posterior facets of the cricoid, whilst the cricoid itself is attached to the first tracheal ring below.

The epiglottis is the only other prominent single cartilage. It is shaped like a leaf with its inverted apex and is attached anteriorly to the cricothyroid by the epiglottic ligament, and projects superiorly to a level above the hyoid bone.

Meano describes the importance of the epiglottis as follows:

> The epiglottis is shown protruding above the thyroid, immediately above the point where the vocal folds are attached. The epiglottis is sufficiently mobile and folds over backwards during the act of swallowing, covering and protecting the glottal rim as food passes through the throat to descend behind the trachea into the oesophagus. The epiglottis, in relation to its development and to its elasticity, contributes to the resonance of the lower pitches of the sound [Meano, 1967: 31].

Meano next addresses the paired arytenoid cartilages. These cartilages are situated in the internal space of the larynx, a space that is constituted by the scaffolding created by the connection between the thyroid and cricoid cartilages. Meano regards the arytenoid cartilages as perhaps the most important in the larynx, simply because they are responsible for creating changes in the tension, length and mass of the vocal folds. He informs us that one of the parts of the vocal folds is attached to the margins of the vocal folds themselves (vocalis), whilst the other is attached to the corresponding arytenoid cartilage [Meano, 1967: 32].

He also reminds us that the internal formation of the larynx, with its omnipresent mucous membrane covering, makes the internal aspects of the laryngeal tube far more interesting than the external structure of the larynx. He informs us that the vocal folds are comprised of two protrusions emerging from the mucous membrane on either side of the laryngeal wall. These protuberances, which represent the true vocal folds, are to be found just above the first ring of the trachea. Above them we find the two recesses, or cavities, forming the ventricles of Morgagni, and above these ventricles we find two false vocal folds that are much less accentuated. The true vocal folds come into firm contact at their internal margins in order to resist the passage of air-which must animate the true vocal folds if we are to produce a truly resonant voice:

> The two muscular bands within the thickness of the vocal folds are greatly enlarged, demonstrating the diverse directions of the fibres. It is well to note that the muscular fibres of the two bands are much more complex. The fibres run in diverse directions, crossing diagonally over each other and, in their entirety, resemble a structure similar to that of the lips [Meano, 1967: 75].

Meano teaches that the vocal folds are constituted by two muscular bundles: the fibres of the first bundle run in the natural direction of its fibres, that is, from the marginal bands of the vocal folds to the internal wall of the thyroid. The fibres of the second muscular bundle run in diverse direction, moving from the marginal bands of the vocal folds to the lateral margins of the arytenoid cartilages. The fibres of the two muscular bundles interweave in a criss-cross manner so as to remain independent of their action. The fibres of the first muscle bundle run transversely from the anterior internal wall of the thyroid to the marginal bands of the vocal folds. This bundle is called the thyrovocalis muscle and acts as true muscular tendon. The second muscle bundle is called the aryvocalis muscle and its fibres are attached at one end to the marginal bands of the vocal folds and to the other on the lateral external border of the arytenoid cartilages. It is worth recalling that the arytenoids constitute a part of the internal aspects of the larynx and possess great mobility. The names designated to these muscles bundles are the thyrovocalis and the aryvocalis are derived from their point of insertion. The first bundle, which is attached to the internal part of the anterior facet of the thyroid cartilage and is directed diagonally towards the marginal band of the vocal folds where its posterior half is attached, hence the name thyrovocalis muscle. The second muscle bundle is attached to the anterior part of the arytenoid cartilage and proceeds in a diagonally direction towards the marginal band of the vocal folds to which it connects its entire length and hence the name aryvocalis muscle.

Meano concludes that the names given to the muscle bundles, which are the thyrovocalis and the aryvocalis are derived from their point of origin and attachment or insertion. The first bundle is attached anteriorly to the internal wall of the thyroid cartilage and is directed diagonally towards the marginal band of the vocal folds where its posterior half is attached, and consequently the name, the thyrovocal muscle. The second muscle bundle is attached to the anterior part of the arytenoid cartilage and it runs in a diagonal direction towards the marginal band of the vocal fold to which it connects in its entire length- and therefore the name aryvocalis muscle.

Sanchez Carbone elaborates on the fact that a number of authors have addressed the morphology of the vocal muscle. As early as 1837, Levin Jacobson had acknowledged and examined the complex phonatory problem presented by the complex structure of the vocal muscle and the diverse direction of its fibres. He ascertained two important issues:

> The first was that the name given to the laryngeal muscles expresses very well its point of insertion, the direction of its fibres and the action to fulfil its function.

> The second discovery was that muscular mass is constituted by various fibres that are connected together and running longitudinally from the thyroid cartilage to the arytenoid cartilages, which contraction serves to bring the two cartilages closer together (thyroarytenoid). Such muscle contraction, not only brings these cartilages closer together, but also shortens the glottis in its anterior/posterior dimensions, and thickens the vocal folds, but it also the major determinant of transversal thickness.

In addition, the variable contraction of the vocal folds establishes the limits of the various vibrant parts, and modifies the elastic coefficient of the vibrant mass of the vocal folds.

In the vocal muscles in its entirety, the major activity resides in this muscle bundle, in which as the voice rises towards the higher register, the muscle relaxes and the vocal folds thin out. Another important muscle bundle originates at the vocal processes of the arytenoids and is directed diagonally and therefore is curved towards the free margins of the vocal folds to which they are connected throughout its length (aryvocalis muscle).

The second bundle of muscle fibres runs obliquely, bringing the vocal folds closer together from their marginal points, interacting with their points of insertion to modify fundamental frequency.

Other muscle bundles run in a transversal direction from the internal surface of the thyroid cartilage anteriorly to the rim of the vocal ligament (corresponding to the posterior half of the margin of the vocal folds). These muscles are known as the thyrovocalis muscles that constitute Jacobson's muscle. Its contraction smooths out the mass of the vocal ligament laterally, producing therefore the abduction a vocal fold at the median plane. It enlarges the *rima glottides* and it collaborates in modifying the thickness and tension that contributes to the intonation of tones at various frequencies [Sanchez Carbone, 2005: 180].

These three muscular bundles, which are in fact three discreet muscles, are united into one, allowing the vocal folds to modify their tension, thickness, length and width, in fact, everything necessary to the phonatory function. Their synergistic action is of great importance to the mechanism of registers. They are formed by a large number of fibres, each of which is capable of contracting in isolation upon the particular part of the vocal folds to which it is connected.

When these muscle fibres contract, their action takes place on the part of the vocal folds upon which they are inserted. In other words, their muscular action is limited to that portion of the vocal folds upon which the muscular fibres are inserted.

Finally, we can say that the vocal muscle is largely responsible for determining the level of tension and adduction of the vocal folds during phonation. It is therefore connected to the mechanism of registers. The arytenoid muscles are also responsible for determining the approximation (medial compression) of the vocal folds. The vocal muscle also determines the shape of the glottis during phonation. The adduction (closing) of the glottis is a function of the adductory action of the lateral cricoarytenoid and the transverse and oblique interaytenoid muscles; whilst the posterior cricoarytenoid remains responsible for abduction of the vocal folds, and finally, contraction of the cricothyroid muscle determines vocal fold length.

From the above, Meano concludes that the fibres of the vocal muscles originating from the internal wall of the thyroid extend out to meet the marginal band of the vocal folds. In a state of relaxation, the vocal folds are not taught, they do not approximate, and the glottis opens easily, allowing the inspiratory air to rushes into the lungs. When the fibres of the vocal muscles contract, they shorten and thicken, causing the vocal folds to approximate. At the moment of contraction, the vocal folds thicken, and approximate which has the effect of opposing the expiratory air, an interaction that sets the vocal fold fibres into vibration.

In examining this data, Meano explains that the two muscular bands are formed by innumerable muscle-fibres. Each of these fibres is capable of contracting separately and in so doing acts upon a minute portion of the vocal folds to which it is connected. Consequently, it is possible to obtain an infinite number of modifications in length, width, thickness, and therefore tension of the vocal folds. It is also important to recall that the vocal folds are subject to the laws of physics and these state that any elastic cord stretched between two points, which is excited by an external force will vibrate. The more distance between these two fixed points, which serve as vocal fold attachment, the lower and slower the sound. However, as the distance between these two points of attachment id diminished, so is the vibrating length of the vocal folds, which quickens the vibrations and raises the pitch of the sound.

Meano is right about the law of physics, it is essential that in the course of increasing fundamental frequency we must reduce the length of the vocal band, but this does not explain the relationship between length, thickness and overall mass, and thereby tension created by the vocal folds. Nor does it explain such subtleties as depth of the of the mucosal wave, length of vocal folds closure within the vibratory cycle, and above all it does not explain posterior occlusion which gradually limits the length of the vocal fold that is set into vibration. It is important, however, to stress that it does this only once the vocal folds have been stretched to their full length. This is actually more of a vocal fold adjustment in order to attain very high notes in a vocal healthy manner. As a matter of interest, it is quite possible to reach those same high notes, at least for a time, without the systematic posterior occlusion referred to above. The problems a twofold: the first is that we emit a relatively ugly, uncultured sound; the other is, that in the longer term, it can be ruinous for the vocal instrument [Meano, 1967: 82].

Meano informs us that during clinical examination and even stroboscopic observation, it is possible to perceive that during the production of high sounds, the portion of the vocal folds set into vibration is limited to the anterior portion of the folds. He also stresses that during the production of the lower register of the voice, the portion of vocal fold set into vibration extends to the entire length and mass of the vocal folds.

According to Meano, in the higher register the vocal folds vibrate only in their anterior part, the anterior fibres of the aryvocalis muscles are tautened through the action of the arytenoid cartilages rotating on their central axis. On the other hand, for lower and intermediate sounds, the vocal folds contract in their entirety. It is in this register that the thyrovocalis muscles are recruited and the fibres of the aryvocalis are relaxed and inactive [Meano, 1967: 83–84].

From the above, Meano concludes that the vocal muscles are a true regulatory muscle over all the vibrating mass of the vocal folds. Its action develops naturally in cooperation with other extrinsic muscles of the larynx. These muscles alter their mass, length and position as necessary during the act of phonation. Meano finally reminds us that the vocal instrument, like other musical instruments, is subject to the laws of physics and acoustics [Meano, 1967: 84].

Summary of Meano's Work

Meano does very well with the simple aspects of laryngeal physiology, but let us be honest, Meano was a man of his times and it is obvious that in certain respects he is still feeling his way. A much more contemporary rendition and therefore a more elaborate description of Laryngeal Anatomy and Physiology is given to us by Fussi and Magnani's (1994), Fussi and Gilardone (2009) and Marco Galignano (2013).

Historical Perspective — Oskar Schindler

Schindler confirms that ever since ancient times there have been attempts to explain the function of the organs involved in producing sound. At first, they compared these organs that produce voice to other musical instruments, but eventually through the study of anatomy and physiology.

In the 2nd century Galen compared the vocal organ to a flute whose body was constituted by the trachea. During the renaissance, Frabrizio d'Acquapendente confirmed this this impression, by suggesting that the larynx corresponds to the aperture of the flute, and the bucco-pharyngeal cavity corresponds to the body of the flute. In 1741, Ferrein used cadavers to perform some experiments from which he discovered two formations which he compared to two violin chords vibrating under the pressure produced by the current of air, which acted like a violin bow. Ferrein also discovered that by altering the tension of the vocal chords, we could also alter fundamental frequency, producing both higher and lower tones.

Schindler suggests that notwithstanding the fact that modern science has proven that the vocal folds are more like ribbons which vibrate more like a membrane than vocal cords, the inappropriate nomenclature proposed by Ferrein in 1741 has endured.

In 1814 Luskovius demonstrated that the vibratory motion of the vocal folds occurred primarily on the horizontal plane. The proof of his theory was obtained by an experiment that involved touching the vocal folds during its vibratory cycle, only to discover that the sound produced did not alter substantially.

In 1831 Müller attributed to the vocal folds the function of a vibrating reed. This attribution occasioned a great deal of discussion as to whether it was the vocal fold that was set into vibration or the air within the larynx.

In 1898 Ewald described the myoelastic theory. This theory confirms that during phonation, and due to the expiratory air pressure, the vocal folds open and in so doing allow a small amount of air to escape, and converting it into vibrations. This is followed by a reduction of subglottal pressure, leading to a return of the adductory phase and a repetition of the vocal cycle: every escape of air creates a new pressure wave which in turn projected into the bucco-pharyngeal cavity. The principal flaw in this theory is its inability to explain how the singer can vary intensity of sound without also simultaneously modifying frequency [Schindler, 2010: 68].

The issue of the essential passivity of the vocal folds during the vibratory cycle was addressed and amended by Baglioni. He based his work on histological studies of the thyroarytenoid muscles. These studies have demonstrated three systems of muscular fascicles. These consist of the longitudinal thyroarytenoid muscle, in association with the thyrovocalis muscle and the aryvocalis muscles. These muscle fascicles or muscle strands combine to constitute the thyroarytenoid muscle. The aryvocalis courses obliquely between the arytenoids and the free borders of the vocal folds; on the other hand, the thyrovocalis muscle run from the thyroid cartilage to the free border of the vocal folds. Contraction of the aryvocalis limits the longitudinal segment of the vocal fold that is set into vibration. This is generally the mechanism from which we derive the frequency of pitch within the falsetto register. On the other hand, contraction of the thyrovocalis reduces the vibratory mass of the vocal folds that is set into vibration in the transverse dimension. This mechanism varies the frequency within the chest register. Based on the above, Baglioni theorised that these muscular formations may contract synergistically or singularly producing two diverse modalities, which vary the frequency of tone by limiting the vibrating mass of the vocal folds and in the longitudinal dimensions from which we derive variations of frequency.

This persisted unchallenged until 1950, the year Husson proclaimed the neurochronaxic theory. Interesting as this theory was, its premises were strongly contested by many authorities, leading to a renewal and confirmation of the myoelastic aerodynamic theory, which was given its final and more refined form in 1963 by Van den Berg and valenciennes [Schindler, 2010: 67].

Schindler Next Interprets Raul Husson's Neurochronaxic Theory

This theory postulates that the vibrations of the vocal folds do not depend on the thrust of the expiratory air pressure but rather on the effect of the neuromuscular activity. The vocal muscles respond to a shock on shock of the impulses of the nervous impulses originating at the brain each contraction corresponding to the vibratory frequency of the fundamental being emitted. The frequency of the vibrations would be imposed by the volleys discharged by the recurrent nerve into the neuromuscular plaque controlled by the bulb of the nervous system. The frequency of the sound emitted depends upon the rhythmic discharges of these volleys. In this way, the mechanism that regulates frequency would be independent of the mechanism that regulates intensity. The neurochronaxic theory is based on the analysis of the microscopic anatomy of the vocal muscle. These microscopic muscles were studied histologically by Göttler in 1950; he found that the vocal muscles are comprised of two separate muscle bundles (the aryvocalis and thyrovocalis muscle) which fibres cross each other. Husson's theory was based in the belief that when an action potential originating at the recurrent nerve connects to the vocal folds, the fibres of the arycocalis and the thyrovocalis contract and shorten. The free border of each vocal fold curves towards the outer face for a very brief instance, and the vocal folds themselves are detached from each other. At this point, under the action of the subglottal pressure, a small amount of air escapes the small fissure which is produced at the glottis plane, escaping towards the bucco-pharyngeal cavity above, before the relaxation of the aryvocalis and the thyrovocalis muscles cause the sudden closure of the vocal folds through their approximation [Schindler, 2010: 68].

Such approximation ceases its action a fraction later when a new recurrent action potential reaches the fibres of the vocal muscles. In practice, everytime the vocal folds separate through the force of an action potential originating at the recurrent nerve, a small quantity of air escapes through the glottis, producing an increase in pressure in the vocal tract. The frequency of the variation of pressure (the Fo of the sound produced), is determined by the number of openings at the glottis. This depends in turn on the frequency of the recurrent action potentials. In this way, we create the beginning of a shock upon shock or recurring action upon action.

A theoretical consequence of the theory espoused by Husson, which was of great importance to singing, was the ability to explain the existence of vocal registers. We know that a nervous fibre cannot transport more than 300 impulses per second. Such limits are dictated by the existence of a phase which is physiologically indifferent to the stimulus, during which the nerve is unexcitable. Husson admits that in exceptional cases the recurrent nerve may transport up to 500 impulses per second, in which situation all the fibres of the vocal muscle would vibrate, but without creating 'tetany' (tetany is defined as a spasm of the voice box due to an overactive neurological reflexes). This, according to Husson, is due to the low chronaxic (2 ms).

This therefore would allow for an explanation of the low register which was defined by Husson as the monofascicle register. In fact, 500 Hz is approximately the superior limit of the low register for the counter tenor. In order to explain the high register, however, Husson believed that a phenomenon occurs in which the fibres of the recurrent nerve are divided into different groups that are sensitive to the particular workload, and which Husson refers to as double phase. That is the fibres of the recurrent nerve are divided into two separate groups.

The *passaggio* from the low register to the high register corresponds to the passaggio between the monofascicle modality (low register) and the bifascicle modality (high register), where the simultaneous vibrations of the monofascicle mechanism in combination with the Bernouille effect produces the low registers, whereas when we transition from monofascicle into biofascicle, where the fibres are divided into two separate groups, with only half of the two fascicles, that is, only one fascicle is set into vibration producing the high register. This avoids the possibility of tetany, that is, the spasm of the voice box, and allows the singer to reach notes around the 1000 Hz, corresponding to C5.

The following are the practical consequences of Husson's neurochronaxic theory:

- With respect to voice classification, Husson posited the concept of excitation of the recurrent nerve. In so doing he confirmed the notion that the possibilities of a singer depend uniquely upon the excitability of that nerve.

- In terms of vocal technique, Husson turned everything on its head. He now posited the concept that the mental processes of singing are extremely important, relegating the respiratory aspects to the secondary level. In the study of singing it would be important to cultivate the aspects of mental concentration, from which depends the quality of the recurrent impulses.

- In terms of pathology, the approach would be exclusively neurological.

According to Schindler, the neurochronaxic theory is interesting because it goes beyond an ingenious explanation of vocal registers, by reserving a special place, practically exclusive, to the role played by the nervous system in singing. On the other hand, the theory opens itself to a number of criticisms; above all, it demands the perfect equality in the length of the two recurrent nerves in order to obey the imperatives of synchrony at the level of the vocal folds. Alternatively, it may be considered that the difference in length maybe compensated by a difference in vocal fold thickness. Anatomically speaking, neither of these two hypotheses has been proven correct: the left recurrent nerve is longer than the right nerve, and both are identical in terms of thickness.

As important as the above criticism is, the strongest criticism of the theory is reserved for Husson's failure to address the role of the mucus membrane covering the vocal folds, which has proven to be very important in the creation of human sound. In fact, he concedes that the vocal muscle may be a bit grazed, but fails to observe the evidence suggesting that the most banal form inflammation of the larynx involves the mucus membrane affecting the vocal product [Schindler, 2010: 69].

This all happened in the 1950s, and since this book has declared its intention and objective to concentrate on the development of vocal technique in the second part of the 20th century and the early part of the 21st century, it seems appropriate to analyse and prioritise the theories developed and evolved during this period. Schindler and his colleagues and students including Franco Fussi and Silvia Magnani have done a great deal of work in the area of recording and commenting on these theories, making my work of translating much easier than it would have been. Schindler addresses the Aerodynamic theory of Moore and Von Leden (1958).

These authors contend that the most important element of voice production, or the creation of glottal vibration, maybe attributed to the expiratory airflow traversing the glottis. When this airflow is combined with a constricted laryngeal tube, it induces the Bernoulli effect. This affect contends that a substantial aspiration causes the already partly adducted vocal folds to meet at the midline.In this manner, we can verify the rhythmic compressions and rarefactions at the glottal level which is responsible for the formation of laryngeal sound.

Schindler next addresses the muco-undulatory theory developed by Perillo, and the myoelastic theory brought to completion by Van den Berg and Vallancien.

Schindler inform us that these theories were essentially spawned in the second part of the 20th century as a response and reaction to the failed neurochronaxic theory developed by Husson. According to Schindler, and notwithstanding the fact that Husson's theory was considerably flawed, he managed to single handed reignite the debate on the vexing question of 'what are the compelling elements in the creation of the human voice?', and 'how does the knowledge of anatomy and physiology inform us in this quest for truth and clarity'?

These and other related questions sent vocal scientists on both sides of the debate into a frenzy of research activity, which was perhaps Husson's greatest, if unintended contribution to vocal science. Raul Husson is an almost forgotten figure today, especially, in the English-speaking world with its narrow black and white approach. His contribution to voice science and voice production, however, was very considerable indeed. It is true that Husson's neurochronaxic theory proved to be mechanically incorrect, but his emphasis on the neuromuscular and mental processes of singing, have changed forever the way we view voice production. And the research that both Husson's supporters and adversaries accomplished as a result of the controversy has proven to be invaluable.

Perhaps, it is time to remind my reader that Raul Husson was not a fly by night; he was not the *enfant terrible* of French research, he was in fact a mainstream scientist of considerable stature and gravitas at the Sorbonne in Paris. His research into respiration and resonance was very impressive for its period and is still regularly cited in Italian and European literature. In short, Husson was much more than his failed neurochronaxic theory.

At any rate, Schindler contends, and I agree with him, that Husson created the environment for a furry of research activity, for open discussion, for the exchange of ideas, and the development of new experimental methodology on a scale never seen before. These included not only the intensification of research on anatomy and physiology of singing, but also ultra-rapid cinematography (Vallancien), and laryngeal electromyography (Andersen & Faaborg) and the building of artificial models of the larynx in order to study its function [Schindler, 2010: 69-70].

Perello was the one who put the role of the mucosa in voice production centre stage. He affirmed that the vibration of the vocal folds is nothing more than the setting into vibration of the soft tissue (membrane) that covers the vocal fold muscle by the aspiratory air. Perello's theory is based on certain clinical observations confirming its importance. The theory confirms five important states of being for the mucosa:

1. The laryngeal mucosa is gifted with great (lassita) flexibility that explains the frequent pathologies.

2. The dryness of the vocal fold mucosa, which is the result of climatic changes, including intense heat, air conditioning, or simply oral respiration, producing dysphonia.

3. A discrete inflammation of the vocal folds produces important vocal alterations.

4. Premenstrual dysphonia is the result of a thickening of the superficial layer of the lamina propria, which with the epithelium membrane constitutes the cover of the vocal folds residing at their free border.

5. Stroboscopic analysis often reveals a normal vibration even if the paralysed vocal fold by the (resezione) of the recurrent nerve.

Perello informs us that the element which presents as vocal fold vibration during stroboscopic analysis or ultrafast cinematography appears to be in effect an undulation of the vocal fold mucosa which during phonation is directed from the subglottal zone to the ventricle. Under the influence of the air current, the mucosa seems to agitate, undulating similar to a carpet flapping as it is beaten [Perello in Schindler, 2010: 70]. (I prefer, Vennard's adage of a sail flapping in the breeze).

Glottal closure begins at the inferior part of the glottis propagating to the superior part, and as it closes at the superior part of glottis, the inferior part begins to open. So, both the opening and the closure of the glottis originate at the inferior edge of the vocal folds. According to Bernoulli the moment when a sufficiently first air current traverses the closed glottis, it automatically decreases the pressure at this level.

Marco Galignano

In his 2013 book *Pedagogia e scienza della voce (2013),* Marco Galignano asks the central question pertaining to the production of sound. Galignano asks, 'what is the precise mechanism that sets the vocal folds into oscillation (vibration).

His answer is instructive. He states that as of now we don't know with precision the exact mechanism that sets the folds into vibration. His conclusions, however, are incorrect. Vocal science is in fact united in its belief that the vibratory phenomenon is determined by the encounter and collision between the vocal folds and the subglottal airflow being pressured through the glottis by the antagonistic action of the respiratory muscles. It is true that there was a moment there in 1951 when the scientific community was divided between the neurochronaxic theory and the myoelastic/aerodynamic theory. I must emphasise that science is essentially satisfied with its knowledge of vocal fold anatomy, and physiological function of the laryngeal apparatus. Satisfied in this instance may be defined as being secure in what it knows but still eager for more knowledge and better ways to activate it.

As with Schindler before him, Galignano elaborates on four different theories, and these are the neurochronaxic theory, the muco-undulatory theory, the aerodynamic theory and the myoelastic theory. Let us deal with these theories at some length. Although, I must say, it is difficult to separate the muco-undulatory theory, from the aerodynamic theory. This is mainly because the mucosal wave is essentially a part of the myoelastic/aerodynamic theory. And whilst Galignano separates these for the purpose of a closer examination, I cannot see how in practice they can so be so subdivided. Given the anatomy, I can't imagine an aerodynamic theory without the myoelastic component or the muco-undulatory component. Consequently, I can only consider two distinctive and at the neurological level seriously competing paradigms. These are the neurochronaxic theory and the myoelastic-aerodynamic theory, and I will content myself by examining these two major theories of voice production. A historical examination reveals that after the original flurry of activity and the mounting excitement provoked by the passionate advocacy of the respective proponents of these theories, the neurochronaxic theory was discredited and the myoelastic/aerodynamic theory declared what it always was, the only credible theory of voice production.

The Hypothesis of the Mechanical Workings of the Vocal Folds

With respect to the myoelastic theory, Galignano cites Clemente Napolitano who contends that over the years a number of theories have been advanced but he believes that the most credible one is the myoelastic/aerodynamic theory in which the vibrations characterised by the tonal frequency of the emitted sound are subject to the aperture of the vocal folds caused by the expiratory air pressure. This process entails the passage of a small quantity of air in the supraglottal region, followed by a reduced subglottal air pressure the adduction of the folds and a new repetition of the cycle. (There must be a more contemporary explanation of this process that also incorporates the Bernoulli effect).

Let us elaborate on these two major theories with a view to clarifying the issue.

The Neurochronaxic Theory

Conceived and posited by Raul Husson in 1951, contends that the oscillation of the vocal folds is not a passive mechanical phenomenon, but rather an effect created by the neuromuscular activity. The vocal muscles respond to the voluntary nerve impulses, which are both concentric and rhythmic, and which originate in the brain: depending on the frequency of the nerve impulses we would vary the opening of the glottis, that is, the vibratory frequency of the vocal folds. Even though we should be grateful that the elegance of the neurochronaxic theory rekindled a fiery exchange of ideas with respect to vocal physiology, the theory lost its value because too many affirmations remained in the theoretical realm.

Notwithstanding the elegance of this theory, Meano considered that the air pressure is of fundamental importance in the vibratory cycle, and consequently adopts it an alternative possibility. To review the elementary physiological pressure to the single fibres of the laryngeal muscles, different to the physical tensions together with muscle mass.

The Aerodynamic Theory

This combines the Myoelastic theory and that of the Muco-undulatory theory, leading once again to the laryngeal sound and not to the rhythmic interruption of the expiratory current, but to the rarefaction and compression of air at the level of the glottis.

In their diversity, these theories indicate the importance of two fundamental factors of phonation: the influence of the cerebral cortex and the coordination of the expiratory pressure and the adduction of the vocal folds. Mori (1970), Juvarra (1987), Bruno & Paperi (1999), Damiani (2003), and Sanchez Carbone (2005) all accept the myoelastic/ aerodynamic theory of voice.

The Myoelastic/Aerodynamic

The myoelastic/aerodynamic theory states that voice production is a function of the air pressure coming from the lungs meeting the resistance of the vocal folds, overcoming it and in so doing setting the fibres of the vocal fold muscles into vibration. According to Angela Castellani this process produces what she refers to as no more than a 'raspberry', sometimes also referred to as Bronx cheer. The soundwave from this Bronx cheer contains a complete harmonic series, that is, the fundamental plus a number of harmonics that are multiple integers of the fundamental. This sound has very little carrying power and penetration, nor can it be considered a vocal sound that we would normally associate with international elite singing. In order to achieve that we need to filter this primary sound, which is the product of the voice source, through the vocal tract (resonator) which enhances the original source sound, and which is the subject of the next major chapter in this book. For now, let us deal at length with the most important contemporary theories contributing to the present state of singing in the 21st century Italian bel canto school.

Having dealt with the breathing aspects of voice production, and introduced the laryngeal mechanism and aerodynamic/myoelastic voice theory, we are now ready to examine the contribution of the voice source.

The first thing to say about the voice source is that it is still amazing to me that two elastic bands of muscle which we have come to know as vocal folds can be so instrumental not only in the production of sound, but also in the minutiae of voice production such as pitch, intensity, registers and timbre or voice quality. It is important to remember that the voice quality is essentially determined by the quality of the harmonics issuing from the voice source, this being the result of the interaction between the collision of the vocal folds and the cushioning of provided by the subglottal airflow. The final attribution to vocal quality, however, is a product of vocal tract filtering of these partials, which essentially means matching the harmonic partials issuing from the voice source with the formants of the vocal track, which imbues the sound with its own characteristic timbre. The other thing to remember is that as important as the vocal tract maybe it can only filter the product offered by the vocal folds but it does not produce primary harmonics on its own right.

According to Mori, the vocal folds are the physiological element that, animated by muscular vitality, expiratory air current and the shape and position of the resonating cavities, creates the condition for the phenomenon of voice production.

Mori gives a compelling narrative of the voice source from a singing teachers point of view, we are now going to review the musings of the first physician in the 1960s to write a substantial anatomical and scientific treatise in the Italian language.

I admire Rachele Maragliano Mori's (1970) narrative very much. Consequently, I will present it here at length. Mori contends that with respect to the mode of voice production,

> A number of theories have been developed and debated, but it is the generally accepted opinion final analysis, it is the product of two antagonistic forces. One force is the is the result of the expiratory column of air directed from the base towards the glottis

which is the other force consisting of the resistance of the vocal folds which in their movement of adduction and tension oppose the forces of the expiratory column of air. This is the product of the interplay between the forces and pressures of the breath and the vibratory mass of the vocal folds or vocal lips. The vocal folds in reality two small muscles inserted into the mucous that furnishes the laryngeal wall. These muscles, which are more appropriately called the thyroarytenoids, are connected anteriorly to the thyroid cartilage (Adam's apple) and posteriorly to the arytenoid cartilages [Mori, 1970; 13].

The expiratory airflow is not only 'conditio sine qua non' of a certain vibratory modality of the vocal folds (whichever genesis myoelastic or neurochronaxic we accept) but is also the phonic vehicle, albeit the only means by which it can be stretched out slowly by its laryngeal origin. The sound produced rises from the vestibular tube into the adjoining resonating cavity where it is transformed into voice, enriching all of the characteristic timbres [Mori, 1970: 13].

At this point we should recall that the quality we refer to as vocal timbre is primarily determined by the relative strength of the harmonics produced by the voice source. So that the final product is determined long before the sound waves reach the vocal tract. They are the product of the interrelationship between the various breathing strategies and the contact with the elastic muscle fibres that constitute the vocal folds which in turn determine the type of onset ranging from breathy to firm onset, the type sound we produce ranging from loose to pressed phonation. It achieves all of this through the stretching, lengthening and tensing of the vocal folds. And it is through these techniques that we obtain such a large range of frequency, intensity, timbre or quality.And through the filtering process, the closing rate and skewing of the spectrum, it also offers an infinite range of colours, some that emphasises the energy of the upper harmonics often at the expense of the lower harmonics, which results in a brilliant sound, other singers emphasise the lower harmonics given their voice a round, velvety colour. The thing to remember is that great singing needs a balance of all these qualities. You can produce a balanced sound that emphasises brilliance and carrying power whilst still maintaining roundness, warmth and colour.

Mori continues her narrative by contrasting the myoelastic and neurochronaxic theory. She suggests that the myoelastic theory has its origins in the periodic vibrations of the vocal folds created by the interruption of the equilibrium found between the muscular vocal fold adductors that determine the closure of the glottis and the antagonistic subglottic pressure that opens them. The neurochronaxic theory, on the other hand, is a function of the regulation (pulse by pulse) of the vocal fold vibration by means of the efferent directive originating in the control nervous system.The vocal folds are enclosed within the larynx, and for this reason they are referred to as the phonatory organ. It is found in the anterior part of the neck and is constituted by a group of cartilages that are connect by ligaments and muscles and is internally covered by a mucous membrane, forming thereby an organic solidity that is both mobile and elastic.

According to Mori, the vocal folds are enclosed with in the larynx, which is often referred to as the phonatory organ. It is found in the anterior part of the neck and is constituted by a scaffolding of cartilages which are united by ligaments, and muscles, and which are covered internally by an elastic mucus membrane, forming an organic but solid frame, which is characterised both by mobility and elasticity.

The external skeletal frame of the larynx sits above the trachea which itself is comprised of a series of cartilage rings. This tracheal frame forms the base of the cricoid cartilage which is the base of the laryngeal scaffolding proper, and upon which we insert the thyroid cartilage. The thyroid can move from high to low and back to front and is connected to the cricoid by an elastic membrane (thyrocricoid membrane). Above the thyroid we find the hyoid bone, and the epiglottis that projects vertically upward beyond the frame of the hyoid bone. This is fixed very tightly with its stem on the angle of the internal wall immediately above the point of attachment for the vocal folds. Notwithstanding its firm connection to the inner wall of the thyroid, the epiglottis remains sufficiently mobile so that it can fold backward covering the *rima glottides* like a lid, and guiding food past the trachea and into the oesophagus.

The inner laryngeal vestibule, which is formed by the combined cricoid and thyroid cartilages, also houses the two arytenoid cartilages, which, as a result of being able to move and tense the vocal folds are perhaps the most important cartilages of the larynx. In fact, one of the two muscles bundles that comprise the vocal muscles inserts into the margin of the vocal folds posteriorly and the thyroid cartilage anteriorly.

The two arytenoid cartilages are situated in the well-defined processes on the superior border of the posterior wall of the cricoid cartilage and, in order to fulfil their function, are necessarily very mobile. At this point, Mori informs us, the arytenoids can rotate upon the central processes as if fixed on it by a pivot.

The true vocal folds which should be distinguished from the false vocal folds above them, and which limit superiorly the ventricles of Morgagni; that is, the two lateral cavities or recesses that are situated superiorly above the true vocal folds. These are the elastic bodies, which, when activated by the airflow, with the rapid, delicate, almost imperceptible but decisive action of the various collaborative muscles, produce the primary vibrations of the vocal folds. These are then filtered through the vocal tract where they are transformed into the vocal sound we have become familiar with. It is from such antagonistic muscular action that the vocal sound is born.

Mori's is aware that her depiction of the vocal instrument is a rather rudimentary explanation of the physiology of voice, but she doesn't regard it as her responsibility to go further. But that was 1970 and we are now in 2017 and there is no excuse for any of writing on this subject for not going further. And indeed, a review of the Italian literature clearly reveals a number of authors who have gone much further.

Specifically, Bruno and Paperi (1999), Damiani (2003) and Sanchez Carbone (2005) have all given comprehensive depiction of the anatomical and physiological aspects of voice production. With respect to the voice source, I particularly like Fussi and Magnani (1994), Fussi and Gilardone (2009), and Marco Galignano (2013).

General Description

According to Fussi and Gilardone (2009), anatomically, the larynx extends from the pharynx to the trachea. It is situated below the hyoid bone, and in front of the lower cervical vertebrae. It is formed by a large number of cartilages that articulate upon each other through the agency of ligaments and muscles. The larynx is the organ responsible to sound production, and may be subdivided into three separate anatomical levels: the supraglottic level, which constitutes the laryngeal vestibule, structured in the form of a funnel.

The second glottal level corresponds to the space formed between the vocal folds when they are separated. Above the vocal folds we find the vestibule of the larynx with its recesses called the vestibule of Morgagni and above that we find the false vocal folds that although displaying similarities to the true vocal folds, they generally play no physiological part in the production of vocal sound.

The third posture of the vocal folds refers to the subglottal level which portion widens to give origin to the trachea. The larynx is innervated on every angle by the recurrent nerve and the superior laryngeal nerve.

Galignano compliments the above description with the following:
The larynx extends in the body to as far as the trachea, beginning from the pharynx, the vertical cavity is comprised of muscular-membranous tube that we see when we open our mouth and look beyond the faucial arches. Within the neck, the larynx is situated below the hyoid bone above from which it gets its support and anteriorly to the last cervical ring. It extends vertically from the 3rd or 4th vertical vertebrae to the 6th vertebrae [Galignano, 2013: 65].

The dimensions vary considerably: in the male, it is about 45 mm high with an anterior posterior dimension of about 35 mm in the highest part; whilst in the female the dimensions are, respectively about 35 mm and 25 mm.

The hyoid bone is a floating bone upon which the tongue is connected. It is the only bone in the body that has no connections to other bones. The articulation, indeed the movement of the cartilages described herein, are facilitated by the complex of the muscles, and ligaments that support the structure, until the larynx can be developed into the anatomical organ that produces the vocal sound, as well as having other function.

The larynx is responsible for three fundamental roles:

1. It is involved in respiration.
2. It guarantees the projection of extraneous material (food and liquids).
3. It remains the principal organ of phonation. The sphincteric activity remains the larynx's principal function because, from it we derive, the inherent protection of the airways, certain reflections such as the sneeze, coughing, hiccups, crying and laughing. In addition, the sphincteric activity is an integral part of other physiologic activities such as parturition, defecation, weight lifting, and actions that demand intrathoracic pressure.

The protection of the airways is generally realised through a reflexive spasm of the larynx, which is typically the result of a sudden stimulation of the mucous membranes within the laryngeal vestibule. This is generally caused by extraneous bodies, irritating vapours, gastro-oesophageal reflux and other harmful materials that may be accidently inhaled.

Chapter 14

Building the Instrument

The Cartilages

In a passage that could have been written by Meano in 1964, Fussi and Gilardone contend that the cartilaginous structure of the larynx is comprised of five principal cartilages: three single cartilages, the cricoid, the thyroid and the epiglottis, and the paired thyroarytenoid cartilages. The epiglottic cartilage takes the form of a curved leaf with its stem fixed firmly to the thyroid cartilage below by the thyroepiglottic ligament. It projects superiorly above the thyroid cartilage that determines the opening to the laryngeal cavity. In the second phase of deglutition the epiglottis functions as a protective valve. In fact, it folds over the orifice to the larynx ensuring that food passes over the trachea and finds its way to the oesophagus.

The Thyroid Cartilage

Fussi and Magnani believe that the thyroid cartilage is the major cartilage in the vocal organ. The thyroid is constituted by two medially conjoined laminas culminating in an angle formed posteriorly at two levels opening at the back. The margins of the lateral posterior of the laminas culminate into two elongated formations: the superior and inferior tubercles. The lateral surface of the thyroid lamina provides the site of insertion for the sternothyroid, thyrohyoid and the inferior constrictor muscles of the pharynx.

On the superior border of the concave cartilage, we find the insertion for the thyrohyoid membrane, which resides on the external margins of the superior horn, and is arranged into a system of jagged fascicles that comprise the thyrohyoid ligament. Inferiorly, on the margins that possess a concave shape at its margin or rather the lateral portion and convex at the centre, the cricothyroid ligament that connects to the cricoid cartilage is detached. On the inferior margins, which are concave in shape on the lateral portions and convex in the central part which separates the cricothyroid ligament and which is connected to the cricoid cartilage.

The inferior horn is connected through a small synovial formation that acts as a pivot for the rotation and movement of the respective cartilages [Fussi & Magnani, 1994: 17].

Many years later, Fussi and Gilardone declared that the thyroid cartilage is formed by two quadrilateral cartilaginous laminas that connect upon the median line to form an obtuse angle. The anterior connection of these two wings form the anterior portion of the thyroid, also colloquially known as 'Adam's apple'. The structure of these thyroid plates allows for the insertion of the thyrohyoid muscle descending from above, and the sternothyroid muscle ascending from below. These muscles are inserted on to the oblique crest on each external aspects of the thyroid cartilage. Posteriorly, the quadrilateral lamina is projected upward through the connection between the great horn and the thyroid membrane, and inferiorly via the connection between the small horn of the thyroid cartilage and the cricothyroid membrane which connection facilitates its articulation with the cricoid cartilage [Fussi & Gilardone, 2009: 12–13].

The Cricoid Cartilage

With respect to the cricoid cartilage, Fussi and Magnani declare that in its morphology, the cricoid resembles a signet ring with its apex reversed posteriorly, located upon its vertical axis which is between to 2 to 3 cm. in size. The quadrangular lamina that constitutes the thicker chestnut end is characterised by two depressions which serve as attachment for the two posterior cricoarytenoid muscles. These depressions are on either side of at the angles of central protuberance upon which superior border we find two oval-shaped, concave articulatory facets that are connected to the inferior facet of the arytenoid cartilage. This is the site where the cricoid lamina is connected to the thyroid arch, and upon which we find the cricoarytenoids [Fussi & Magnani, 1994: 17].

Many years later, Fussi and Gilardone (2009) would describe the cricoid cartilage as follows: The cricoid cartilage is connected inferiorly to the trachea via the tracheal membrane. The cricoid represents the base of the laryngeal skeletal. It takes the form of signet ring with the posterior part considerably thicker than the anterior, and which is colloquially referred to as the chestnut, but anatomically better known as the body of the cricoid cartilage. The external wall remains the site of the two small articulatory facets upon which the small horns of the thyroid cartilages are connected. Anteriorly, we observe the cricoid arch upon which superior border we find the points of insertion for the cricoarytenoid muscles. On the cricoid arch proper, we also find the cricoid tubercles, a protrusion upon which, we find inserted the bilateral cricothyroid muscles [Fussi & Gilardone, 2009: 14].

The Arytenoid Cartilages

The arytenoid cartilages are situated upon the median line in the posterior part of the cricoid and have their base on the body of the cricoid cartilage upon which they articulate by means of the cricoarytenoid articulatory muscles. These cartilages take the form of a triangular pyramid and present a medial side, and posterior facet upon which we insert the posterior interarytenoids and the anterolateral facet upon which we insert the inferior thyroarytenoid muscle. From the angle of the pyramidal base we find two projections: one directed anteriorly and the other directed laterally, upon which we find the insertion for the vocalis muscle and the muscularis respectively. The vocal apophysis (processes) represents the site of insertion for the vocalis (the true vocal folds), whilst the lateral apophysis (processes) becomes the site of insertion for the muscularis, the lateral cricoarytenoid and posterior cricoarytenoid muscles.

The Epiglottic Cartilages

The epiglottic cartilage (epiglottis) takes the form of a curved leaf presenting the apex downward. It is fixed to the thyroarytenoid cartilages by the thyroepiglottic ligament. Above, we find it projecting from the superior border of the thyroid cartilage that determines the form that marks the beginning of the laryngeal cavity. The epiglottis functions as a protective valve to the airways in the second phase of deglutition. During deglutition, in fact, the epiglottis floats over the orifice to the larynx, permitting the correct passage of food to the oesophagus [Galignano, 2013: 65]. Like the rest of the laryngeal mechanism, the epiglottis possesses a variable mobility, generally determined by the subject's general state of health. The epiglottis has a major function and that is to act as a sphincter protecting the airways during the second phase of deglutition [Galignano, 2013: 67].

Marco Galignano and Cartilages

Following in Fussi and Gilardone's footsteps, Marco Galignano contends that the larynx is a complex structure formed by a combination of eleven cartilages, which are manoeuvred by the intrinsic and extrinsic laryngeal muscles as well as a number of ligaments and membranes.

Galignano's description is almost identical to that provided by Fussi and Gilardone. However, it finally remains a more complete description, simply because Galignano adds the smaller paired cartilages such as corniculate cartilages or the cartilages of Santorini which sit above the arytenoids, and the cuneiform cartilages or the cartilages of Wrisberg, which are situated inside the aryepiglottic folds and are of minimum dimension. He acknowledges the fact that neither the cartilages of Santorini, nor those of Wrisberg play any part in sound production. [Galignano, 2012: 71].

The Arytenoids

Marco Galignano contends that there are three major single cartilages, namely the cricoid, the thyroid and epiglottis and the three paired and symmetrical cartilages. All of the single cartilages play an important role in voice production, but the arytenoids are the only paired cartilages to make a great contribution to voice production are.

According to Galignano, the two arytenoid cartilages are situated several ml. apart from each other on the superior posterior margins of the body of the cricoid. These arytenoid cartilages take the form of a pyramid and present a medial aspect upon which we insert the inter-arytenoid muscles. This also represents the inter-lateral facet, which becomes the site of insertion for the inferior thyroarytenoid muscles, also known as the muscularis. From the angles at the base of the arytenoid pyramid we find two processes, one directed anteriorly and the other laterally, also called the vocalis and muscularis processes (apophysis) respectively [Galignano, 2013: 72-3].

This is simply because the vocal apophysis is the site of insertion for the vocalis muscles, also known as the medial thyroarytenoid, whilst the lateral apophysis, remains the site of insertion for the muscularis, the lateral cricoarytenoid and the posterior cricoarytenoid. Thanks to the structure of the arytenoid cartilages and their ability to move along their base in several directions, including rotating, inclining, and moving closer together or further apart, actions that help to either adduct or abduct the vocal folds with a concomitant effect on sound quality [Fussi & Gilardone, 2009: 11 to 25].

Anatomy and Physiology of the Vibratory System: Larynx

Anatomically, the larynx extends from the pharynx to the trachea; it is situated in the neck just below the hyoid bone, in front of the lower cervical vertebrae. It is formed by a large number of cartilages that articulate upon each other with ligaments and muscles, the larynx is the anatomical organ dedicated to sound production.

The Cartilages

The cartilaginous structure is comprised of five principal cartilages: two are even and three are uneven.

For reasons of individuation and control during the teaching voice, the larynx can be subdivided into three different levels, so as to better understand the interdependent state of play between anatomy and the function during sound production.

The supraglottic plane constitutes the vestibule of the larynx. It represents a conduit that takes the forms a funnel that narrows below at the level of the real vocal folds, in which the anterior aspect corresponds to the posterior aspect of the epiglottis when this is closed

The space of the laryngeal vestibule opens above by means of the superior laryngeal orifice, and when the epiglottis is open, the inferior part of the vestibule is framed below by the closing and opening of the vocal folds.

As we observe the internal aspects of the vestibule from above, we notice the vocal folds, the arytenoid cartilage, and adjacent wrapped by a mucosa and connected to a portion of the musculature involved with the laryngeal mechanism, the so called false vocal folds, a board of membranous tissue above the vocal folds. The false vocal folds are utilised in artistic research for particular vocal production (suffocated voice) whilst they are a cause of illness when they are too closed above the true folds, or when they are made to vibrate as a substitute for the true vocal folds, provoking the typical rough voice (voce rauca) [Galignano, 2012: 67].

At the glottis plane, so called the glottis, is formed by the combined space between the vocal folds, when these remain apart or when they are adducted. Surrounding the vocal folds, we find the vestibular folds or the false vocal folds.

At the subglottic level, that is, at the level below the vocal folds, we find the proportion of the larynx that widens the space below. It is the attachment of the cricoid cartilage to the trachea that creates the air passage to the lungs. It represents the space adjacent to the vocal folds seeing from below. The larynx is innervated in every angle by the superior laryngeal nerve, both of which are branches of the vagus nerve [Galignano, 2013: 69].

The Cricoid Cartilage

The structure of the larynx is situated upon the trachea, with which it is continuous through its attachment with the cricoid cartilage. The cricoid cartilage has the shape of a signet ring with its greatest dimension, which is even thicker, and which is often referred to as the cricoid chestnut, turning posteriorly behind the cervical vertebrae of the dorsal spine. The cricoid represents the foundation of the laryngeal skeleton and is connected inferiorly to the trachea via a membrane. Anteriorly, (Posteriorly) we observe the cricoid arch, upon which superior board we find the point of insertion of the cricoarytenoid cartilages and the cricoid processes, upon which projection we insert the bilaterally cricothyroid muscles [Galignano, 2013:69].

The Thyroid Cartilage

The thyroid cartilage is the largest in the larynx, externally visible at its anterior apex, particularly in the male in whom it is recognised as the Adam's apple. The thyroid cartilage takes the form of a shield, often looking like a visor or a helmet that protects the glottis at the larynx. It is structured by two lateral vertical laminas, inclined obliquely.

On the posterior plane, the quadrilateral lamina of the thyroid cartilage projects superiorly via the two great horns that insert into the thyroid membrane. Inferiorly, they connect to the minor horns of the thyroid through which the thyroid cartilage articulates with the cricoid below. This articulation is possible as a result of the support offered by the cricothyroid membrane. During phonation, it shifts depending on the register. For instance, in the production of the lower register, it covers the anterior part of the vocal folds, whilst during the execution of the high register it juts forward, revealing the vocal folds in their entirety [Galignano, 2013: 71].

The Arytenoid Cartilages

Perched on the superior posterior margins of the cricoid, we find the two pyramid cartilages placed several millimetres from each other. The arytenoids are capable of moving along the base, rotating, inclining and moving close together.

Above the arytenoids we find the corniculate cartilages, often referred to as the cartilages of Santorini, they are minimum dimension and together with the cuneiform cartilages or the cartilages of Wrisberg situated inside the aryepiglottic folds, between the arytenoids and the epiglottis. Neither the corniculate nor the cuneiform cartilages are involved in voice production. The arytenoids are situated posteriorly upon the median line of the cricoid, upon which they articulate via the cricoarytenoid. These cartilages take the form of a pyramid and present a medial aspect and a posterior aspect upon which we insert the interarytenoid muscles, the anterolateral muscles, the site of insertion of the inferior thyroarytenoid muscles, also known as the muscularis.

From the angles of the base of the arytenoid pyramid we find two processes, one directly anteriorly and the other directed externally, also respectively referred to the vocal apophysis and the muscularis apophysis [Galignano, 2013: 71-3].

The vocal apophysis is the site of insertion of the vocal folds, whilst the apophysis muscularis is the site of insertion of the lateral cricoarytenoid muscles.Thanks to this structure, and their rotating ability, the arytenoids act as handles to adduct and abduct the vocal folds.

The laryngeal muscles are divided into the intrinsic and extrinsic muscles of the larynx. During phonation, the intrinsic muscles determine all the small and delicate movement of the vocal folds, whilst the global movement of the cartilages, is regulated by the extrinsic muscles of the larynx [Galignano, 2013: 73].

The Extrinsic Laryngeal Muscles

The extrinsic muscles of the larynx, including the hyoid muscle, upon which we will elaborate shortly in our discussion of the hyoid bone, have the responsibility for both supporting and articulating the larynx through their connection to the muscles emanating from the sternum, the hyoid bone and the pharyngeal wall [Galignano, 2013: 75].

The extrinsic laryngeal muscles move the entire larynx altering the relationship between adjacent structures, whilst the intrinsic laryngeal muscles move each cartilage in relation to the others. As the names suggest, the extrinsic muscles are situated externally to the cartilaginous scaffolding, allowing the elevation of the larynx. These movements modify not only the inclination and distance between cartilages, but they also alter the length of the intrinsic muscles. These significant variations in position alter in a substantial way the level of tension of both the vocal folds and the vocal cavity, with a concomitant impact on vocal quality.

Amongst the most important extrinsic muscles we find the thyrohyoid, and the sternothyroid, and the inferior constrictor muscles of the pharynx [Sanchez Carbone, 2005: 162]. In addition, the digastric, the stylohyoid, and the hyoglossus muscles fix the larynx, allowing the intrinsic muscles to better react.

Schindler reminds us that the paired thyrohyoid muscles connect the hyoid bone to the thyroid: with fixed connection to the hyoid bone, they lift the larynx (for the emission of the high register) or, alternatively lower they lower the hyoid bone into the larynx.

The sternothyroid muscles represent the ring of connection between the thyroid and the sternum, from the posterior facet of the manubrium of the sternum to the sides of the respective laminas of the thyroid cartilage. They lower the larynx (for the emission of the lower notes). The laryngeal cartilages then are interconnected thanks to a complex system that included muscles, membranes, ligaments and articulation. The membranes that involved are the thyrohyoid, cricothyroid, cricotracheal and the elastic membrane of the larynx, whilst the ligaments are thyrohyoid, the cricohyoid and the aryepiglottic and thyroarytenoid superior and inferior [Schindler, 2010: 42].

The larynx is connected to the pharynx via the inferior constrictor muscles internal of the pharynx that, when necessary in the phase of relaxing the pharyngeal muscles, for example) their position it posteriorly. These muscles are innervated by the glossopharyngeal nerve.

The collective responsibility of the digastric, stylohyoid, and hyoglossus muscles fix and support the larynx until the intrinsic muscles are in a position to better respond [Galignano, 2013: 75].

The Intrinsic Muscles of the Larynx

The intrinsic muscles of the larynx are with one exception all situated within the laryngeal scaffolding, they fibres running from one cartilage to the next. The exception refers to the cricothyroid muscle, which in the anatomical literature is regarded as an intrinsic muscle, but it does have an attachment to the external part of the thyroid cartilage. However, its function must be considered as that of an intrinsic muscle, and we will therefore treat it as such.

Beyond the actualisation of the true vocal folds, the intrinsic muscles articulate most the movement pertaining to the various laryngeal cartilages.The intrinsic laryngeal muscles accomplish three subtle functions on the vocal folds:

1. They adduct the vocal folds, with a concomitant narrowing of the glottis.
2. They abduct the vocal folds with a concomitant dilation of the glottis.
3. They extend the vocal folds, an action that facilitates vocal fold vibration [Galignano, 2013: 77].

These muscles are controlled by the inferior laryngeal nerve, which is also known as the recurrent nerve, which is an internal branch of the vagus nerve.

In the following, Galignano describes an anatomical, schematic, of the intrinsic muscles of the larynx. This description is designed to facilitate the visualisation of this process.

The Posterior Cricoarytenoid Muscle

The point of insertion and arrival: from the posterior facet of the cricoid nut to the posterior/internal facet of the muscular apophysis of the arytenoids. Its function is that of dilating the glottis through the condition of the external vocal apophysis [Castellani, 2012: 21].

The Interarytenoid Transverse Muscles

The point of insertion/arrival for the transverse muscles begins at the posterior facet of one arytenoid to the posterior facet of the other arytenoid. Its function is as a glottal constrictor, it adducts the vocal folds, through the narrowing of the arytenoid cartilages.

The Oblique Interarytenoid Muscle

The point of insertion/arrival: from the posterior internal facet of one arytenoid to the superior extremity of the other arytenoid. Its function: a glottal constrictor, it functions as a stabiliser of the related to the movement of closure of the vocal folds.

The Aryepiglottic Muscle

Point of insertion/arrival: it originates as the continuation of certain fibres of the inter-arytenoid muscles that follow the folding of the glottis arytenoids, from which it gains the name the muscle in question. Its function: it is to lower the epiglottis.

The Thyroarytenoid Muscle Superior

The point of origin and insertion of the thyroarytenoid muscle runs from the superior angle of the thyrohyoid cartilage to insert at the anterior external part of the muscular apophysis of each arytenoid. Its function is that of a glottal constrictor.

The Inferior Arytenoid Muscle

It inserts in the angle of insertion of the thyroid cartilage and then divides into two branches directing: The external strand; arytenoid cartilages, folding into the aryepiglottic, and the lateral border of the epiglottis, then the internal strata; inserts posteriorly on the external side of the vocal apophysis and on the antero/external facet of the arytenoid. It functions as a glottal constrictor.

The Suspensory Mechanism: The Connection to the Hyoid Bone

The larynx is situated in the neck at the same level as the vertebral column and is fixed, in suspension to the hyoid bone. The hyoid bone becomes the site of insertion for many muscles that together form the supporting apparatus of the larynx, generally referred to as the suspensory mechanism. The hyoid bone, uneven, floating has a shape of a horseshoe with the aperture facing the posterior wall, in the neck, where it is situated in the median plane below the mandible. It occupies a super facial position, so as to be able to be seeing or palpated with the external fingers. The role of sustaining the larynx is accomplished by the hyoid bone through the ligaments thyrohyoid later, and the median thyrohyoid [Galignano, 2013: 78].

The body of the hyoid bone consists of an osseous lamina flattened anteriorly/posteriorly and it projects towards the both sides with those that are called the great horns. The union of the superior borders of the hyoid bone body on each of the great horns forms small osseous projections that are called small horns. Thanks to its particular anatomical form, the hyoid bone is the connection or the passage to a number of muscles oriented in various directions, of which determine the position of the larynx within the neck. The hyoid muscles (extrinsic muscles) the part of the muscular suspension system is represented by the extrinsic laryngeal muscles, that a subdivided into suprahyoid and infrahyoid muscles. All of these muscles have in some way something to do with the hyoid bone, either because their take their origin from it, or because their lean on it, finding the right resistance to alter direction in that long bent passage that goes to the external mandible (petto/collo/mandibola).They allow the movement of the larynx in a vertical direction such as occurs during phonation [Galignano, 2013: 79].

The Infrahyoid Muscles

The infrahyoid muscles represent the vertical musculature anterior to the neck and they connect the larynx to the superior part of the thorax, it is joined to the hyoid bone and the thyroid cartilage, and forming below a lower and superficial plane: The lower plane is constituted by the external thyrohyoid muscles, and the thyrohyoid cartilages, whilst the superficial plane is external to cleidohyoid and omohyoid.

The function of the infrahyoid muscles is that of lowering the larynx, taking the lower the hyoid bone and the connected thyroid cartilage [Fussi & Gilardone, 2009: 21].

The Suprahyoid Muscles

There are four muscles that either connect to the mandible or the hyoid bone, and which combine with those muscles that extend to the base of the cranium, and these are the diagastric muscle, the stylohyoid muscle, and the mylohyoid and geniohyoid muscles that constitute the foundation of the buccal cavity. Their function is to elevate the larynx, or, in the case of a forced aperture of the mouth, to lower the jaw (lower mandible). These are superficial muscles in the body, some are in direct contact with the skin as such it is possible to intervene directly upon their function through manipulation (knowingly) to relax them, warm them, and to minimise fatigue [Fussi & Gilardone, 2009: 21].

Having dealt with the Anatomy and functional physiology of the larynx, it is now time to put it into action by once again reminding ourselves of the unity of the instrument, the various physiological configurations involved in the different registers of the vocal instrument.These are combined with the technique of 'copertura' which is the technique used to pass seamlessly from one register. This particular function involves not only the formation of registers, and the particular vocal qualities involved with each register, but also explore a number of techniques including 'copertura' in the pursuit of the seamless blending of these registers.

Interaction Between the Thyroarytenoid and Cricothyroid Muscles

The laryngeal cartilages are connected by a complex system of membranes, ligaments, and articulatory muscles.

The major membranes involved in forming these connections are: the thyrohyoid, the cricothyroid, the cricotracheal, and the elastic laryngeal membrane (cover).

The major ligaments are: thyrohyoid, cricothyroid, the aryepiglottic ligament, and the thyroarytenoid superior and inferior, that is, the vocalis and muscularis respectively.

There are two principle membranes or ligamental articulators. They are even, symmetrical and work together. These muscles of articulation are known as the cricothyroid and the thyroarytenoid muscles: the articulation of the cricothyroid with those of the cricoarytenoids [Fussi &Gilardone, 2009: 16].

The Cricothyroid Muscle

External to the laryngeal scaffolding, we find the cricothyroid muscle. This muscle tilts the thyroid cartilage both forward and down, distancing the anterior commissure from the arytenoids and thereby increasing the length and tension of the vocal folds.

These muscles contribute to the support of the laryngeal structure and are positioned, for the major part, external to the larynx, but in as much as they help to stretch the vocal folds in a direct way by widening the glottis, they are considered intrinsic muscles. In particular, the cricothyroids articulate and facilitate the movement between the thyroid and cricoid cartilages. The cricothyroids insert into the anterior external facet of the cricoid arch and their posterior attachment is on the anterior border of the small horn of the thyroid cartilage. The external laryngeal nerve innervates the cricothyroids [Galignano, 2013: 77]. Fussi and Magnani agree that the cricothyroids connect the two external aspects of the cricoid arch to the inferior aspects of the small horns of the thyroid cartilages posteriorly, but they also elaborate on their physiological function. Contraction of the cricothyroids increases the tension of the vocal folds, expanding the distance between the two points of insertion, and allowing for the tilting of the thyroid cartilage. Contraction of the cricothyroids brings the cricoid and thyroid cartilages closer together [Fussi & Gilardone, 2009: 16].

Sanchez Carbone confirms that the cricothyroids are comprised of two parts, the pars recta and the pars oblique. When contracted they move the thyroid cartilage and cricoid cartilages in a tilting manner that facilitates the articulation of these cartilages upon each other. That is, they bring the anterior part of the cricoid and the inferior part of the thyroid closer together, closing the gap between these cartilages and stretching the vocal folds. This results in longitudinal tension (lengthening) of the vocal folds, and contributing to the control of the frequency being emitted. They are especially involved in the higher register, that is, frequency above 650 Hz [Sanchez Carbone, 2005: 165].

The Thyroarytenoid Muscles

Fussi and Magnani (1994) state that the physical and psychoacoustic aspects of voice production are directly influenced by what happens at the glottal level. With that in mind, there is no more important regulatory muscle than the thyroarytenoid muscle. It extends from the posterior wall of the thyroid cartilage and the cricoid ligament to the anterior base of the arytenoids, where their insert into the vocal processes and the muscularis, coursing in a posterior, lateral and superior direction. The contracting muscular fibres lower and adduct mainly membranous part of the vocal folds, thereby shortening, and thickening them whilst also rounding their free borders, thinning the lamina propria and the epithelium, rendering the body of the vocal more tonic. Their contraction produces a lowering of the fundamental frequency [Fussi & Magnani, 1994: 19].

By 2009, Fussi and Gilardone were able to declare that the body of the vocal fold is constituted by a striated muscle called the thyroarytenoid, (vocalis muscle). Contraction of the thyroarytenoid causes a shortening of the vocal folds with a consequent increase in the width of the vocal fold body, and a rounding of its free border. When the subglottal airflow meets the adducted vocal folds, it is forced to confront a considerable glottal resistance caused by the adduction of the vocal folds. This is the result of the action of the vocalis muscle, which adducts the surface of the free borders of the vocal folds. Its action shortens the vocal folds but lengthens and stretches them vertically. As a rule, the various vocal postures and every laryngeal muscular action that reduces the glottis also determine an increase in glottal resistance. As a consequence, the number of times in which the expiratory air is capable of opening the glottis will be reduced resulting in the production of low tones which correspond with a low vibratory frequency [Fussi & Gilardone, 2009: 23].

Its action provides an ample contact of the vocal folds at the midline. Contraction of the thyroarytenoid muscle primarily shortens, thickens and increases its mass, but it also and importantly collaborates with the LCA in the adduction of the vocal folds.

Fussi and Gilardone continue by stating that the base of the arytenoids are connected upon the superior border of the posterior part of the cricoid cartilage, a structure that allows for the movement of the processes either medially or laterally, facilitating the abduction and adduction of the vocal folds [Fussi & Gilardone, 2009: 16].

Angela Castellani gives us a concise but effective description. She argues that the thyroarytenoid muscle is the principal muscle of phonation, and extends horizontally from the angle of the thyroid shield to the vocal processes of the arytenoids. This muscle divides into the internal thyroarytenoid or vocal muscle and the external thyroarytenoid. Its contraction shortens the vocal folds, given origin to the ensuing lower frequency tones [Castellani, 2012: 21].

The anatomical site of the entire intrinsic muscular system of the larynx is situated in the region above the trachea at the point where it narrows, and at which it coincides with the raising of the internal mucosal cover so as to form the two vocal folds just above the cricoid cartilage. The two vocal folds are defined as two elongated muscular formations on the internal surface of the larynx. They are rather thick behind in the part that is constituted by the vocalis muscle, and thin anteriorly at the point where the two rims meet each other. They take the form of mucosal foldings residing within the internal cover of the larynx, and are therefore fixed on one side of the laryngeal mucosa whilst remaining free at their internal border. They are comprised of various levels of muscular fibres (internal and external) superimposed and interdigitating with fibres diverse orientation and different direction, and which are symmetrically inclined towards the angle of the thyroid cartilage. This is the site where one attaches to the right side of the median line whilst the other attaches to the left side [Castellani, 2012: 21].

They shut down the orifice found on the higher part of the trachea, which is very similar to two membranes stretched between the two internal walls of the laryngeal tube and the central line that divides them into two, upon which these two membranes meet at their borders. They present as two ribbons or sashes that are pearly white in colour. They extend form the internal surface of the thyroid cartilage near the median line to the vocal processes, part of the arytenoid cartilages continuing under the conus elasticus. They are constituted by the vocal muscle, the vocal processes of the arytenoid cartilages, and the vocal ligament, which is represented by the superior border of the thick membrane previously referred to as the *conus elasticus* that has its origin on the superior surface of the cricoid cartilage. The *conus elasticus* is a powerful structure that supports the vocalis muscle and the vocal folds.

Angela Castellani agrees and declares that:

> The internal surface of the larynx is delineated in its inferior portion by a membrane called the *conus elasticus* that extends from the superior border of the cricoid cartilage up to the vocal folds, which resemble two small elastic bands stretching horizontally in the form of a V, from the angle of the thyroid shield to the arytenoid cartilages. On the other hand, the superior portion is delineated by the so called quadrangular membrane that extends vertically from the level of the vocal folds connecting with the sides of the margins of the arypeglottic folds, and the thyroid and arytenoid cartilages. The ligaments that constitute the external aspects of the quadrangular membrane are known as the ventricular ligaments. They are passive structures that are situated laterally in relation to the true vocal folds, and are referred to as the false vocal folds. Between the false and true vocal folds, we find a small space that constitutes the ventricles of Morgagni [Castellani, 2012: 17-18].

Fussi and Magnani (1994) give a similar description but they approach it from the opposite end. They state that under the laryngeal mucosa we find a fibroelastic tissue that is the true element that bonds the laryngeal cartilages together. This fibroelastic membrane is generally categorised into a superior and inferior membrane, which in turn is known as the quadrangular and triangular membrane respectively. The superior part of the membrane is distinguished by its quadrilateral shape and hence its name. The quadrangular membrane extends from the space between the vocal processes, to the posterior corniculate and the lateral border of the epiglottis, up to the anterior insertion on the thyroid cartilage. The superior border of the quadrangular membrane corresponds with the aryepiglottic folds. On the other hand, the inferior border extends to the vestibular ligament that is situated inside the false vocal folds.

The inferior part of the fibroelastic structure, which is called the triangular membrane, or conus *elasticus*, is connected inferiorly to the superior border of the cricoid cartilage, and superiorly to the internal aspect of the thyroid cartilage. Anteriorly, the membrane forms the median ligament. The free superior border of the triangular membrane becomes progressively thin and sharp, forming the vocal ligament which extends from the thyroid cartilage to the arytenoids. The anterior connection of the two ligaments at the thyroid angle and the mucosal cover constitute the anterior commissure [Fussi & Magnani, 1994: 19].

The vocalis muscle remains the main layer in the body of the vocal fold and also the only muscle in the human body capable of producing sonorous vibrations. The strands of muscle fibres are capable of contracting either alone or in concert with each other and are responsible for the various tensions of the vocal folds, the equilibrium with the other muscles of the larynx, and the muscular dimensions that produce sound.

Chapter 14 — Building the Instrument

The vocalis muscle is undoubtedly the most important vocal muscle, in as much as its complicated structure allows it to accomplish all the necessary configurations and contractions that modify tension, thickness, width and length of the vocal folds as they relate to their phonatory function, and the intonation of various sounds [Sanchez Carbone, 2005: 172–174].

Angela Castellani confirms the above and adds that the vocal folds are two small elastic bands of variable dimension and length, depending on age and sex (17 to 22 mm in men and 12 to 17 mm in women), they extend horizontally in the form of a V at the angle of the thyroid-shield and the arytenoid.

The vocal folds are comprised of the vocal ligaments, and the intrinsic muscles known as the thyroarytenoids. These muscles control the state of tension, the variations in length and the movement of adduction and abduction of the vocal folds. The vocal ligament finds its anterior surface of the triangular shape of the arytenoid cartilage referred to as the vocal processes, where it extends horizontally to its point of attachment on the angle of the thyroid shield. She confirms that the thyro-arytenoid muscle, also known as the vocal muscles, has its insertion on the lateral surface at the base of the arytenoid, also known as the muscular process, extending horizontally to the angle of the thyroid known as the 'Adam's apple' [Castellani, 2012: 20].

The Vocal Folds

The more superficial aspects of the vocal folds present two stratified elements that possess important properties that influence the quality of the sound: these are the epithelium and the lamina propria. Epithelium may be compared to normal skin and is embodied in the superficial layer of the vocal ligament, conferring upon it its typical grey-white colour, and not the pink colour normally associated with other parts of the body, provided that the surface is not bounded by an abundance of capillaries.

The lamina propria on the other hand is comprised of three separate components: the superficial layer, the intermediate layer and the deep layer. The superficial layer of the vocal folds resembles a clear gel which connects it to the epithelium immediately above; whilst the intermediate and deep layers embrace and protect the vocal ligament, conferring upon it its elastic properties which facilitate the lengthening and shortening of the vocal folds providing it with its characteristic white colour. These elements can be reclassified into the body/cover model, in which the cover is constituted by the epithelium and the superficial layer of the lamina propria, whilst the intermediate and deep layer of the lamina propria combine with the vocal ligament and the thyro-arytenoid muscle to form the body of the vocal folds [Castellani, 2012: 20].

Sanchez Carbone elaborates on the size, shape, physiology and activity of the vocal folds, which in the female are not only shorter but also thinner, whilst in the male they are rounder and of greater mass, ensuring that a larger area comes into contact when the vocal folds meet at the midline during the closing phase of the vibratory cycle. The anatomical differences of the vocal folds are responsible for the differences in vocal quality between the male and female voice. It is not only the length of the vocal folds but also the mass of the fold set into vibration that determines vocal quality.

The insertion of the vocal folds on the thyroid cartilage is of a rather fixed nature, but not so those of the posterior arytenoids which remain mobile and responsible for the adduction and abduction of the vocal folds and therefore for the posterior approximation of the vocal folds. Stroboscopic examination reveals that in a loser type of vocal fold approximation the vibratory movement is of an ondulatory type or mucosal wave. In contrast, however, a firmer posterior-occlusion results in a cessation of the ondulatory vibrations, or mucosal waves, and a shortening of the vocal folds, reducing the vocal fold mass set into vibration and increasing fundamental frequency. Abductory laryngeal muscles, the posterior cricoarytenoids, abduct the vocal folds. Contraction of the posterior cricoarytenoid (PCA) opens the arytenoid cartilages and therefore the vocal folds, producing a space between them that is triangular in form. Its summit corresponds with the anterior point of insertion of the vocal folds on the thyroid shield and its base at the space comprised of the two arytenoids: this is the rima glottides. During adduction of the vocal folds, which is due to the contraction of the very robust vocal muscles, including the lateral cricoarytenoid and the interarytenoids, which take place during expiration and is accompanied by the formation of the vocal sound. The two arytenoids approximate each other in a manner that brings their internal surface of the vocal processes together into mutual contact with each other and their processes. The vocal folds follow this movement by approximating each other and thereby forming a slim horizontal fissure which runs directly through the anterior posterior median line created by the free borders of the vocal ligaments [Sanchez Carbone, 2005: 178].

This is limited anteriorly at the summit of the thyroid cartilage, posteriorly at the arytenoid processes, and laterally by the vocal ligaments. Firmly related, this fissure is known as the *rima glottides*, or glottis. The anterior three/fifths of the glottis are known as the intramembranous part, whilst the posterior two fifths of the glottis are known as the intercartilagenous part of the glottis. In the adduction phase, the longer intermembranous part is reduced to a fissure whilst the two fifths of the cartilaginous part take the form of a triangle.

During phonation, the intermembranous part vibrates whilst the posterior intercartilaginous part remains in apposition. The act of adduction induces the vocal muscles fibres to contract, shorten and thicken, forcing the vocal folds together to meet at the midline. The force of adduction is variable and it is possible that the internal face of the arytenoid may come together without achieving a complete and perfect contact but it remains a little ajar. When applying a strong adductory force, the vocal folds meet much more energetically and close hermetically. We can state that there is a direct relationship between the adductory force and the intensity of emission, that is, the stronger the adductory force the greater the intensity [Sanchez Carbone, 2005: 179].

The Lateral Cricoarytenoid Muscle

Galignano confirms that the lateral cricoarytenoid functions to approximate the vocal folds and close the rima glottides. He also adds that lateral cricoarytenoid is innervated by the recurrent nerve [Galignano, 2013: 77].

Posterior Cricoarytenoid Muscle

The posterior cricoarytenoid muscle is regarded as a very important muscle, some authors believe the most important muscle, because it is the only major muscle of abduction, it is vocal fold dilator. It has its origins on the posterior wall of the cricoid cartilage and inserts on the muscular process of the arytenoid cartilages.

Galignano declares that contraction of the posterior cricoarytenoid (PCA) muscle opens the vocal folds during respiration, causing the cessation of sound. Galignano reminds us that it is the anterior branch of the recurrent nerve serves to innervates the posterior cricoarytenoid [Galignano, 2013: 77].

The Interarytenoid Muscles

The interarytenoids are two uneven muscles interposed between the two arytenoids. These are constituted by two muscle strands, one transverse and extends from one arytenoid cartilage to the other, covering the posterior and lateral surfaces of each, and the other an oblique strand that crosses the transversal strand from the base of one cartilage to the summit of the other, in the shape of a crossover x. Contraction of these muscles contributes to the closure of the cartilaginous portion of the glottis through the approximation of the arytenoid cartilage [Sanchez Carbone, 2005: 164]. Sanchez Carbone confirms that the interarytenoid muscles are constituted by a combination of the transverse and oblique arytenoid muscles that approximate the arytenoids in such a manner that sees the medial surfaces not only touch each other but in doing so close the triangular opening that remains even when the vocal processes and therefore the vocal folds oppose each other.

Frequency

Fussi and Magnani (1994) contend that the fundamental frequency of the vocal folds is equal to the frequency of vibration of the vocal folds. This is generally measured by the number of cycles (opening and closing cycles) per second. This process is controlled by the laryngeal musculature responsible for modifying the mass, tension and length of the vocal folds: the more stretched the folds the greater the increase on the surface of the glottal area, and the more developed the effect of subglottal pressure the faster the beginning of the vibratory cycle. This configuration corresponds with an increase in fundamental frequency and a shorter vibratory cycle. On the other hand, the shorter and thicker the vocal folds the more difficult their separation, and the greater the resistance to the glottal airflow, meaning that the vibratory cycle is prolonged and the fundamental frequency is reduced [Fussi & Magnani, 1994: 23].

As already mentioned, the frequency at which the vocal folds vibrate per cycle is determined by the length, and tension of the vocal folds, through the respective modulation of the elasticity, length, thickness and mass of the fold set into vibration. By stretching, lengthening and thinning the vocal folds and increasing their tension, we alter the forces of glottal resistance that reflect an increase in frequency of vibration. This has repercussions on laryngeal morphology. For instance, in singing a high note the vocal folds are long and thin, on the other hand, when singing a low note, they are relaxed, short and round. The force applied at the muscular level is commensurate with the increase in fundamental frequency, but is not in direct relationship. That is, muscular energy increases with fundamental frequency in a way which is not directly proportional: it is at a minimum on the lower part of the voice, when the vocal folds are short, but it increases enormously even for small differences on the acute (high) part of the range. For this reason, the falsetto register, characterised by long, and thin vocal folds, is the one that utilises the greatest expenditure of muscular energy. The lengthening of the vocal folds is mainly due to the muscular activity of the cricothyroids muscle, which moves the anterior part of the cricoid cartilage up and in, thereby diminishing the angle between the thyroid and the cricoid. This causes an increase in distance between the anterior and posterior insertions of the vocal folds, which take place at the thyroid cartilage and the arytenoid cartilages respectively. The arytenoids are connected to the superior/posterior aspects of the cricoid body. Contraction of these muscles is responsible for the tension, compactness and stiffness of the vocal folds, all of which impacts on frequency.

The medial fascicles of the thyroarytenoid muscles act antagonistically with the cricothyroid muscles, and the lateral cricoarytenoids to stabilise the laryngeal muscles and increasing adduction during an increase in fundamental frequency [Fussi & Magnani, 1994: 24].

Falsetto

With the passage into falsetto register, there is a discontinuity of coordinated contraction of the laryngeal muscles, making it less predictable and indicating a more complex regulation of fundamental frequency. It would appear that in falsetto register the main responsibility shifts from the laryngeal muscles to the muscles responsible for subglottal pressure. This pressure is more a function of the antagonistic action of the respiratory muscles. Experimental research reveals very different and sometimes contradictory results with respect to the production and emission of falsetto. These varying results may well be a testament to the various modalities or techniques of producing falsetto. These different techniques are generally noted perceptively by musicians who are well trained to perceive the differences between a professional male soprano or contralto, from a well-prepared singer who occasionally and only for an effect, sings falsetto in almost any register [Fussi & Magnani, 1994: 25].

Lowering the Frequency

Lowering fundamental frequency in singing in a descending scale between the high and medium register is essentially due to reduction in contraction of the cricothyroid muscles. On the other hand, a reduction of fundamental frequency in the medium register is determined by an active contraction of the lateral thyroarytenoid muscle (muscularis) and the external laryngeal sternothyroid muscles that lightly induce a forward inclining movement of the thyroid cartilage, with an ensuing shortening and thickening of the vocal folds.

The thyroarytenoid muscle that extends between the thyroid cartilage anteriorly and the arytenoid cartilages posteriorly performs two important functions: the first is that of contacting the medial bundle of the muscle that constitutes the vocalis muscle which increases the compactness and tension of the vocal folds, the second is that of contraction the lateral bundle of the thyroarytenoid muscle (muscularis) responsible for shortening the vocal folds. The latter activity is also fundamental to everyday life. Physiologically the vocal vibratory cycle follows a regular course, can be observed through the images displayed through the stroboscopic light [Fussi & Magnani, 1994: 25].

The collision of the superior surface of the vocal folds generates an undulating movement known as the mucosal wave that proceeds anteriorly on the direction of the thyroid cartilage. At such a frequency, the vocal folds open uniformly low, relaxed and lose. On the high register on the hand, the vocal folds appear to be long, tense and thin, the mucosal wave are not clearly visible and closure tends to be simultaneous but still minimally from the inferior edge of the vocal folds to the superior. In the falsetto register, they do not achieve a complete closure. The glottal area increases and diminishes without ever reaching zero [Fussi & Magnani, 1994: 25].

The result of the vibrations of the vocal folds is the production of sound comprised of a fundamental equal to the frequency of vibration and a number of harmonic partials. These are integers of the fundamental and together theses frequencies form a harmonic series. This laryngeal product (voice source) determines in part the final acoustic result influencing in a complex way the resulting emission [Fussi & Magnani, 1994: 26].

Intensity

Intensity is essentially and primarily determined by subglottal pressure: the greater the subglottal pressure, the greater the amplitude, that is, the swing of the vocal folds on the opening phase of the cycle at the glottal levels. This amplitude corresponds with intensity.

Galignano declares that vocal intensity is determined by amplitude due to the variations of periodic pressure of the sound wave. This depends above all on subglottal pressure, which as we know, is regulated by respiratory forces, muscular/elastic or intentional. He suggests that as we look around, we may assess that there are same voices that emphasise the ultra-high harmonics and others that a flabby, both are hard to listen to for any length of time. The one thing they have in common is a miscalculation of the importance of the intensity of the voice. To reorganise the balance of vocal intensity, is essentially the coordination of the flow with the relative phonation through the assiduous audio-vocal control [Galignano, 2012: 118].

I like Silvia Magnani's treatment of vocal intensity (2017). She contends that intensity of sound (amplitude) and audibility (loudness) are related to the amplitude of the signal obtained at the glottal level. This amplitude is in turn proportional (but only for soft onset) to subglottal pressure created by the air-current under the vocal folds. Consequently, we can say that modifying subglottal pressure is the equivalent of varying vocal intensity.

Magnani submits three different modalities for examination. She states that it is possible,

1. To increase airflow by developing voluntary inspiration;
   She suggests that we probably have all experienced this modality at one time or another, especially at a time when we are preparing to yell. The preparation for yelling involves a deep and spontaneous inspiration, very similar to preparation required to blow the candles out on a birthday cake. Unfortunately, this method

of inspiration does not allow for the type of subglottal pressure control required for competent classical singing.

2. The second respiratory modality is represented by that paradigm which artists call respiratory *sostegno*. She refers to this modality as vocal athleticism.

3. The third modality is another spontaneously actuated paradigm in which intensity is reached during speech level conversational. In fact, the continuous alteration in vocal intensity constitutes, at least in part, the integration of the musicality which is obtained only accessing one's own unconscious and natural talent for adjusting the glottal resistance in accordance with the expressive requirements. This requires the singer to modulate the level of contraction applied to the adductory muscles, and also to lightly alter the vertical laryngeal position. We should recall that the lowering of the larynx produces an increase in vocal fold mass and a concomitant increase in the glottal resistance that opposes the air current. It is also appropriate to recall that the falsetto register has a great deal of inherent resistance [Magnani, 2017: 31].

With respect to falsetto, Magnani contends that, in the production of falsetto, a process known as damping-closure is affected. In this process, the vocal folds are decisively approximated on their anterior half and only the posterior half that remains mobile, generating the compressions and rarefactions of the air. Given that the anterior part is functionally disabled, we can say that the glottis is anatomically shortened [Magnani, 2017: 29].

Magnani rightly concludes therefore that in this modality the course of intensity is one of limited amplitude.

Breathy and Pressed Phonation

The other parameters that are essentially determined by the interaction between glottal resistance and subglottal pressure are the various quality of tone ranging from breathy or loose phonation, through to a desirable firm phonation, through to a tight production which is in extreme versions sometimes distorted or pressed phonation.

A breathy sound refers to a type of loose production which is the result of an incomplete glottal adduction, allowing the escape of air and generating a noise in the medium frequency. Notwithstanding the relative simplicity with which one overcomes the given perception associated with escaping transglottal air, the global effect obscuring the noise created by the glottal signal makes it difficult to evaluate the adequacy of the fundamental. This increases the risk of attributing inferior values to those that are effectively produced. The instrumental valuation provided in Hz is the only safeguard we have against an erroneous valuation. This adductory model, with its characteristic dispersion of airflow, has very little intensity. In fact, the singer who fails to achieve complete glottal closure cannot obtain adequate levels of subglottal pressure to satisfy the phonatory demands for a firm tone. This singer is consequently obliged to compensate with additional muscular action in order to achieve adequate glottal adduction.And in this way, give the impression of 'yelling without voice'. In addition, the impossibility of attaining a level of glottal resistance, such as that achieved when the thyroarytenoid muscle is in a state of tonicity, impedes an even moderately intense emission. Consequently, the singer is forced to use the voice in a manner that produces a very slight level of intensity. Breathy sound is characteristically representative of a number of pathologies [Fussi & Magnani, 2010: 238-9].

Pressed Voice

Pressed phonation is a type of glottal adduction obtained through the maximum activity of the intrinsic muscular system responsible for glottal adduction. This quality of vocalising is characterised by a high level of glottal resistance. Pressed voice is accompanied by a reduction in fundamental frequency and an increase in subglottal pressure and intensity of emission. The proportionality directed at these last two vectors is effective only at levels of contraction that do not apply extreme pressure on the system of adduction including the thyroarytenoid muscles. The exaggerated involvement of the musculature which generates increasing levels of resistance, the yield in intensity with a decreasing return of intensity, due to the incremental rigidity in the system, which rises fundamental frequency in sympathy with the elevation of the larynx [Fussi & Magnani, 2010: 239].

Alongside these two polarities of breathy or pressed phonation, the Italians have a third or median modality that they refer to as efficient vocalising. Fussi and Magnani describe efficient voice production as the result of a concentrated effort towards the realisation of a type of voice production which is not only efficient, but also eloquent, and propitious. The above should be achieved whilst minimising both effort and the risk of vocal damage. This highly efficient physiological behaviour is designed not only to increase vocal audibility, but also obtaining the most efficient access to vocal tract formants so as to reinforce the higher harmonics and attain maximum acoustic penetration without having to resort to either increasing intra-glottal pressure (amplitude), or the time duration at which the vocal folds are in contact during the vibratory cycle.The criteria of vocal efficiency can also be applied to muscular work being accomplished, independent of its efficacy or its functional economy [Fussi & Magnani, 2010: 200].

Conclusions to Quality: Vocal Timbre

With respect to vocal timbre, I must say that the treatment presented by both Damiani (2003) and Sanchez Carbone (2005) resonates greatly. They suggest and I agree that vocal timbre is dependent on the number of and relative strength and intensity of the harmonics contained within that particular tone. The vocal folds produce what Sundberg has referred to as a bouquet of harmonics, which is comprised of a fundamental and a series of harmonics, which are integers of the fundamental frequency. Together they form a harmonic series which relative strength is reflected on the sound spectrum. Vocal timbre depends primarily on the approximation or adduction of the vocal folds. They both suggest that much of the individual characteristic of the voice comes from the anatomical cavities of the resonator, and the arrangements of the articulators.

The adduction of the vocal folds can be more or less perfect, so that by increasing glottal adduction we produce a richer, more brilliant and biting vocal timbre; the opposite is true with a loser glottal setting and an imperfect adduction, which issues into a breathy, dull, veiled sound.

The vocal folds close quicker, firmer and for a longer duration during the production of the richer, more brilliant tone relative to the production of dull, veiled tone. The latter, veiled tone is accompanied by an incomplete, less firm adduction and a closing rate that is much shorter, issuing into a breathy, noisy, veiled timbre.

The thickness of the vocal folds at the time of adduction also plays an important part in vocal timbres, in particular because it determines register.

Chapter 15

Vocal Quality and Registers

Carlo Meano suggests that before discussing registers, intensity, frequency, vocal quality, and laryngeal position, we should examine the vocal instrument at length with a view to gaining a thorough knowledge of the anatomy of sound production.

Having discussed the breathing process in the previous chapter, Meano simply reinforces its importance to the act of singing before moving on to a lengthy discussion of sound production. He begins by inviting his reader to analyse certain aspects of vocal anatomy so as to better facilitate a deeper understanding of voice production, especially in the region of the vocal membrane (squamous epithelium), which possess certain characteristics that are particularly conducive to sound production [Meano, 1967: 52].

Meano emphasises the importance of the adduction of the true vocal folds as well as the indispensable stretching of the vocal membrane, forming a canopy over the laryngeal tube, which is its natural position during the production of sound. That is, to the process of converting breath-energy into acoustic energy requires the interaction of subglottal pressure and glottal resistance. He informs us that the central division of these two membranes form the *rima glottides* that opens in inspiration and must close for the production of sound: the degree of closure is responsible for the quality of sound ranging from breathy quality through to pressed. Meano reminds us that anatomically the ventricles of Morgagni and the false vocal folds lie above the true vocal folds and may be observed from above when the *rima glottides* remains open during inspiration. The importance of the vestibular chamber as the first resonator cannot be overestimated.

According to Meano, there is only one mode of vocal fold production, and this mode is based on a column of air passing through what he refers to as 'the limited marginal rims of the true vocal folds in contraction and approximation' [Meano, 1967: 57]. These muscular contractions are caused by nervous impulses which prepare the vocal folds for the production of sound as the pulmonary pressure overcomes the resistance offered by the vocal folds: this causes the contracted vocal folds to vibrate. He refers to this process as the physical origin of sound [Meano, 1967: 57].

Rachele Maragliano Mori reminds us that as far back as the 13th century, Gerolamo da Moravia recommended that the note should be set high in order to be heard far away, it should be gentle to delight the listener and clear so as to satisfy the ear.

Meano then examines the manner in which man, who reasons and performs every action guided by the brain, also speaks and sings under the influence of cerebral impulses, thereby producing sound at the vocal folds. He contends that the brain is the seat of every voluntary impulse transmitted into action. He states that our brain thinks of a predetermined sound or pitch and then commands the vocal folds the vocal organs to produce it. This command is transmitted from our brains and radiates through the nervous system until it reaches the vocal folds, causing them to contract and approach each other in a manner that will allow the pulmonary pressure to set them into vibration.

Meano's influential contemporary, Rachele Maragliano Mori, wrote her *Coscienza della Voce* in 1970 and in many respects, she echoes a number of ideas already depicted in Meano's book.

In the following dissertation, Mori asserts that although a number of theories have been developed and debated, but in the end 'it is the generally accepted opinion that in the final analysis it is the product of two antagonistic forces'. One is the result of the expiratory column of air directed from the base of the lungs towards the vocal folds, the other is the antagonistic force offered by the resistance of the vocal folds. The vocal folds, through their movement, adduction and tension oppose the force of the expiratory column of air.

In reality, the vocal folds are two small muscles inserted in the mucus membrane that covers the larynx. These muscles are more appropriately called the thyroarytenoids which are anteriorly connected to the thyroid cartilage, and posteriorly to the arytenoid cartilages. Mori contends that the expiratory airflow is the indispensable element in whichever vibratory modality we accept, whether it has its genesis in either the myoelastic or the neurochronaxic theory. Either can be the phonic vehicle for the sound originating at the larynx and rising through to the adjoining resonating tube in which the original signal is transformed into voice, enriching all of its characteristic timbres [Mori, 1970: 13].

The myoelastic theory singles out the origins of the vibrations in the periodic interruptions of the equilibrium between the muscular adductory tension that determines the closure of the glottis and the subglottic pressure that opens it.

The neurochronaxic theory allows for the regulation of the vocal fold vibrations (pulse by pulse) by means of the efferent information originating in the central nervous system. The vocal folds are the physiological element that, animated by the muscular dynamism, combined with other physical element (expiratory air current and the position of the resonating cavities), gives way to the phenomenon of the voice [Mori, 1970: 13].

According to Fussi and Gilardone, the larynx has three fundamental roles, and these are:

1. its involvement in respiration
2. it guarantees the protection of the airways
3. it remains the organ of phonation par excellence.

The sphincteric activity is undoubtedly its principal function because it is through it that we derive not only the protective function, but also such inherent functions as sneezing, hiccoughing, crying, laughing and other physiological dimensions such as parturition, defecation, and weight lifting, all of which demand an increase in intra-thoracic pressure.

The protection of the airways may be realised through laryngoscopic reflex caused by foreign or extraneous reflexes, or irritating vapours or gastro-oesophegeal reflux.

In an effort to explain not only vocal fold vibrations but also the mechanism through which it may control or modify it, vocal scientists have developed a number of theories. The various theories seem to converge into an overwhelming support for the myoelastic/aerodynamic theory. The myoelastic component of this theory combines the muscular and elastic forces which are connected to the intrinsic muscular function and the characteristic structure of the vocal folds. This tends not only to adduct the vocal folds but also coordinates them with the subglottal pressure which is the base of the rhythmic movement of the vocal fold cover often called the free border of the mucous membrane.

On the other hand, the aerodynamic aspects of the theory are determined by the pulmonary bellows, which in the expiratory phase provide the subglottal pressure required to overcome the resistance of the vocal folds in their closed phase. This interaction results in varying degrees of glottal opening. As a result of the escaping transglottal-airflow, we can confirm a rapid reduction of subglottal pressure, and increase in kinetic energy, with a consequent increase in the myoelastic adductory forces of the vocal folds. The airflow across the subtle fissure of the glottis determines the expiration that gives origin to the glottal mucosal wave that is propagated from the inferior phase of the vocal folds right up to the ventricles which simultaneously contribute to the closure of the vocal folds. This represents the basis of the vibratory cycle (the opening and closing of the vocal folds), the number of which correspond to the fundamental frequency of the sound emitted. This also corresponds to other acoustic characteristics such as intensity, timbre and duration.

Intensity, for instance, is determined by amplitude and variation of periodic pressure of the sound waves, which is primarily dependent on subglottal pressure, which in turn is regulated by the expiratory force summoned by the elastic muscular force of the expiratory muscles.

Fundamental frequency by the speed of the sound waves, which depends on the tension, shape and mass of the vibrating portion of the vocal folds, through the modulation of length, thickness, and elastic tension of the vocal folds.

Every increase in the elastic tension of the vocal folds results in an acceleration of the vibratory cycle. In fact, the greater the tension of the vocal folds the greater the subglottal pressure required and the more rapid the vibratory cycle. This process increases the difficulty of abduction, lengthens the vibratory cycle which in turn reduces fundamental frequency, (F_o).

The thyroarytenoid muscles constitute the body of the vocal fold, which is also known as the vocal muscle. The vocal muscle is comprised of a striated muscle which contraction results in the shortening, thickening and rounding of the vocal fold body, especially at the free border of the vocal folds. These actions result in a substantial vertical contact at the point where surface of the vocal folds meet at the median line. In addition, contraction of the thyroarytenoid muscles not only shortens, thickens and increases the mass of the vocal folds, but it also contributes to the adduction of the vocal folds.

As a rule, vocal fold postures as well as the action of the laryngeal muscles that reduce the area of the glottis contribute greatly to glottal resistance (generally, the smaller the glottal area (the area between the closed vocal folds, the greater the resistance). As a consequence, we can say that the number of times the expiratory air-current manages to open and close the glottis corresponds to fundamental frequency. For instance, the shorter, thicker and the greater the mass, the lower the frequency and by contrast the longer, thinner and tenser the vocal fold mass the higher the fundamental frequency.External to the laryngeal scaffolding we find the cricothyroid muscles. This muscle tilts the thyroid cartilage forward and down, lengthening the space between the arytenoids and the thyroid cartilages, increasing the length and tension of the vocal folds.

Registers

There is no better example in the Italian literature of the deference and affection for the historical Italian School, combined with a thorough forward looking scientific orientation than that which we find in Mori's work. Nor is there a better analysis of the interrelationship between registers, timbre, resonance, laryngeal posture and vocal fold configuration than that which we find in Mori's treatment of registers.

Mori begins by stating that the term register must have had its origins in the terminology of the organ. The register of the organ serves to alter the timbre the nature of the notes of the instrument. So, we can state that a change in vocal timbre is commensurate with a change in vocal register. Mori contends that,

> In the didactic of the singing voice the term register refers to a series of sounds equal in timbre, produced by the same mechanism of the larynx, in equilibrated relationship with the gestures of the resonance cavity [Mori, 1970: 75].

Mori believes that there is a close organic and harmonic relationship between the various organs of phonation during speech. For example, she states that

> There is a limit to the action of the soft palate in the formation of speech, in vocal articulation and in the determination of timbre depending on the larynx. The posture created by the closure of the vocal folds at the point where air pressure and velocity flow meet the adducted glottis is continuously regulated. These impulses are so well located that they contribute to the regulation of respiration [Mori, 1970: 75].

Mori continues:

> It is from these biological facts that we derive the concept of functional harmony that constitutes the philosophical concept relating to vocal registers, which consist of a heavy register and a light register; these are separated by an intermediate or mixed register in which it is more difficult to realise the necessary correct posture.

Mori continues thus:

> Every era, in one way or another, has signalled the presence of registers. Medieval singers cite voices of the head and those of the throat, and singers of the classical period such as Caccini, Tosi and Mancini also mention two registers: chest and falsetto. For them, however, falsetto was synonymous with head register. And falsetto and chest registers referred to a preponderance of one of the two resonance cavities, and not to the exclusive dominion of one over the other [Mori, 1970: 76].

Register Terminology

The term register had its origins in the terminology of the organ. Organ registers serve to alter the timbre and nature of the notes of that instrument. Beginning with this concept, it is easy to conclude that when the voice changes register the vocal sound necessarily changes its timbre and nature. In the didactic of the singing voice, by the term register we intend a series of sounds of equal timbre, which are produced by the same laryngeal mechanism, in a balanced relationship with the adjustment of the resonance cavities. In such a manner, we ensure a close functional harmony with the verbal organs (articulators) and those of phonation [Mori, 1970: 76].

According to Mori, it would appear that the theoreticians of the 16th century had an altogether limited view of registers; this however, only serves to reflect the fact that at the beginning of the 16th century the extension of the vocal range explored by composers was little more than the spoken range. This limitation was designed to achieve the effect of *recitar cantando*, the ideal vocal style of the period. Caccini and his contemporaries all recommended the transposition of their songs in the key that most naturally suited the singer's voice, but without resorting to *voce finta*.

In the 18th century, with the development of *'stile fiorito'*, vocal emission was set on a level of such lightness and fluidity, that the mechanism of the registers was comprised almost entirely of its own mechanism, combining the various timbres of the vocal range, in which substance we find the results of the various registers. It is worth mentioning that it was during this period that Mancini, although fleetingly, mentioned the existence of the medium register.

It is important to acknowledge that there is little agreement with respect to registers. There are some who question the existence of registers at all, let alone the controversy attached to the number and nature of vocal registers. Mori suggests that there are many who would prefer to forget the problem, simply because some singers are so naturally talented and intuitive that they manage to blend their registers anyway. On the other hand, the educated voice is able to develop strategies that hide the breaks often experienced at the *passaggio* from one register to the other. These singers are capable of blending to such an extent that they seem to deny the existence of registers altogether. Mori believes that the truth about registers is revealed by the raw, uneducated voice; it is in the uneducated voice that the majority of difficulties are exposed and particularly highlighted in the process of seamlessly blending registers [Mori, 1970: 76-7].

The term *passaggio* refers to the moment in which the singer prepares the posture and then flexible modification of the vocal folds. It is these different and variable vocal fold gestures that are responsible for the production and blending of registers. According to Mori, a thick and round vocal fold shape corresponds to the thick or heavy register, often referred to as chest register; whilst for the thin or head register, the vocal folds are more stretched and more closely adducted. As the sound proceeds towards the high register, the vocal folds undergo various alterations in posture and a constantly changing interrelationship between the thyroarytenoid and the cricothyroid muscles; until finally, at the extreme high range of the voice only the anterior portion of the folds is still vibrating whilst the posterior part is occluded and therefore inoperative [Mori, 1970: 77].

To avoid any sense of antagonism at the *passaggio* between one vocal posture or register and another, the singer must never reach the limits of that register, but rather prepare the *passaggio* by slightly lightening the emission and mildly modifying the form of the vowel.

The *arrotondimento*, that is, the rounding of the mouth cavity, especially the anterior portion of the resonator, also referred to as covering the vowel, protects the pharynx from the progressive but natural reduction of the pharyngeal space, which naturally occurs in an ascending passage. For instance, Mori cites a personal communication with one of her students, a mezzosoprano, who writes the following:

> When I cover correctly on the E and the F natural, I feel that the head register comes out quite naturally and I have the sensation that the sound begins outside of me, in the surrounding air [Mori, 1970: 77].

She continues by suggesting that whenever we sense an antagonistic conflict between the chest register and head register, then we can be sure that the *passaggio* is defective. Mori declares that head voice demands a major resistance from the vocal folds to the air-pressure issuing from the lungs, and this should be combined with a major and cohesive adjustment of the resonating cavities.

Mori suggests that theoreticians of the 16th and 17th century had a limited interest in registers. The reasons were twofold:

1. The first is that the range employed by Caccini and his colleagues was limited to the spoken range.

2. The second reason was that they also recommended the transposition of their songs and arias into a tonality that allowed the singer to maintain his natural *voce piena* (modal register) as opposed to indiscriminately flipping into *voce finta*. This meant that the singer essentially remained in the speaking range, representing the idealised style of the period *recitar parlando*.

By the 18th century, with the development of the *stile fiorito* (floral style: decorated) of singing, vocal emission evolved to a level of lightness and fluidity that all register problems seem to have vanished quite naturally.

Mori is aware of the ongoing controversy with respect to vocal registers. Consequently, she concludes that registers are a phenomenon that good singers are conscious off, even though they do not possess precise knowledge [Mori, 1970: 77].

During the romantic period and the later verismo style, registers cause singers to become increasingly conscious of the onerous demands this style made on the vocal folds. This highlighted the existence of vocal *passaggi* and the necessity to modify the vowels (arrotondimeneto) in order to facilitate the process of register blending. It is important to realise that belcanto singers hardly considered the phenomenon of registers. In fact, they had almost ignored them, believing implicitly that with few exceptions, register breaks were inevitable. They believed that registers occurred naturally in certain zones of the voice, and that this was the price you paid for the full exploration of the vocal range [Mori, 1970: 78].

Mori makes an important point here, and that is that many vocal problems can be camouflaged as long as we don't make great demands on out instrument. Problems are only revealed and put under the spotlight when we attempt to use our instrument in an elite manner, and there are so few singers who attempt to maximise they gifts today. If you don't put your voice under pressure you will never learn how to eliminate the problems that a spawned by elite demands.

Mori contends that there were other reasons for much of their success:

1. The teacher's intuition and the calm environment they provided for their students over a long period of time;

2. The continual contact that created the conditions for the fine-tuning of the instrument;

3. The memory training required to recreate the sensations elicited by correct singing (proprioceptive sensations) that were concentrated at points of maximum sympathetic vibration (acoustic energy). These sensations sustain the singer in their effort to overcome all obstacles to register blending [Mori, 1970: 78].

Mori recalls García's precepts on register blending.

The three-register mechanism (long, medium and short cord), enables the vocal folds to produce an extended series of sounds). Consequently, we conclude that through this three-register mechanism, singers have learned how to simultaneously increase the range of the voice, whilst also producing an infinite variety of colours.It was not until García invented the laryngoscope that the nature of the diverse mechanisms was revealed to us. Before García, we knew the effect of these registers but not the cause [Mori, 1970: 78].

García's observations taught us that we must not alter our vocal technique of singing to accommodate the subtle alteration we sense in the mechanism as we ascend the scale. The solution to the problem is connected to the principal of equalisation. The singer must seek uniformity of respiration, a steady and moderate laryngeal position and constant resonance (Mori believes that the latter is perhaps the most important), so that the voice might be reflected in its definitive anterior position and there maintained by the airflow leaning against the diaphragm. It is only then that the vocal folds begin to enjoy that elasticity and tranquillity that is essential to the free modification of their movement without sudden changes or register breaks that we so often hear in inferior singers. Otherwise, register changes do not occur imperceptibly as is necessary and the rough change between one register and the other becomes very perceptible [Mori, 1970: 78].

In passing from one register to another, the vocal folds are activated by a subtle and antagonistic interrelationship of tensions that are regulated by the thyroarytenoids (internal tensors) and the cricothyroids (external tensors).

Mori reminds us that whichever mechanism dominates at a certain point in time, we obtain either the so-called chest register, or the head register. As we progressively ascend the scale, the medium register is characterised by the gradual diminution of the internal tensor (vocalis) and a concomitant increase in tension on the external tensor (cricothyroid). The increase in tension is regulated by the contractible fibres of the vocal folds which alter their shape but not their volume. For instance, the contraction of the vocalis muscle alters the shape by shortening, rounding and thickening the folds but does not in essence alter the volume [Mori, 1970: 79].

Laryngeal position is another important element in the technique for blending registers. There are authors such as Wicart that believe that the larynx should be maintained in an elevated position, whilst others recommend a lowered and stable laryngeal position. Both of these positions are related to a particular and idealised sound world. These two laryngeal positions are representative of the chiaro/scuro paradigm so beloved of the Italian School [Mori, 1970: 79].

Generally, the high larynx position is best represented by the forward, brighter vowels such as the [i] and [e], whilst the lower larynx is represented by the darker and rounder [o] and [u] vowels. Mori regards the [a] vowel as being perfectly equilibrated and a more balanced and mediated position. The larynx is not only more balanced but it's also more flexible and dynamic depending on frequency and register [Mori, 1970: 79].

In comparing the above discussion with the precepts developed by the belcanto singers of the past which was responsible for the concept 'ascending whilst descending' and 'descending whilst ascending', Mori concludes that in order to achieve a balance between the antagonistic muscular interplay from which we derive an even and graceful emission, the larynx cannot assume a stable and definitive position, except perhaps at the extreme parts of the range and vocal timbres [Mori, 1970:79].

Consequently, Mori concludes that laryngeal position is lower for the darker, lower and intense sounds and higher in the clearer, brighter sweet sounds. The difference, however, is to understand how to do it at relevant points. The velocity, fluidity and delicacy of movement of the vocal organ during vocal and musical production make it difficult and dangerous for the instrument to find a definitive absolute position, save but in rare moments. In this sense, the aphorism of the belcanto singers seems to express great wisdom, in as much as 'descending whilst rising' signals the utilisation of the antagonistic opposition to the natural, progressive resistance of the vocal organ in ascending the scale. It would be logical, but dangerous to also allow the spontaneous ascension of the diaphragm and the larynx. Equally, in 'rising whist descending', we must remain alert to the necessity of increasing muscular energy at the pharynx, the palate, the thorax and the abdomen. This surge of muscular energy is designed to counter the tendency to lower the larynx too severely and too rapidly, an action that could cause a loss of resistance on the part of the breath. Unbalancing this configuration may lead to a loss of edge to the sound, which is particularly important to the carrying power in the lower part of the register [Mori, 1970: 80].

We should recall that Mori, in line with her great predecessors, ranging from García and Lamperti, through to Marchesi and Stockhausen, adheres to the three-register model. This model is characterised by a thicker and rounded chest register, a bright and brilliant head register, and a mixed register that separates these two and which is much more difficult to balance. She contends that there are teachers who still don't acknowledge the middle register in the male voice. In fact, she reminds us that the ancient teachers didn't even mention it. Naturally, she acknowledges that the mixed register doesn't have the colour of the chest register nor the penetration of the head register, it is rather a mixed colour and easy on the voice [Mori, 1970: 83].

In the gradual transition between the tension sustained by the glottis in the chest register (internal tensor) and the more relaxed position of the throat in the chest head register, we find the balance between these extremes embodied in the mixed register, which mechanism also offer the vocal organs a point of equilibrium. It is for this reason that many of the great schools of the past advise paying particular attention to it. In fact, they went as far as referring to this mixed register 'as the homeland of the voice' [Mori, 1970: 83].

In a more technical description, Mori describes the medium register as one in which the tensions of the vocal folds (internal tensions) gradually diminish and is substituted by the steady increased activity of the external tensors. This is generally called the mixed register or half chest register (mezzo petto) [Mori, 1970: 83].

Antonio Juvarra

Following Mori's excellent dissertation, the only other author that could rightly be described as building a bridge or a connection between modern vocal science as embodied in the work of Oskar Schindler (2015), Fussi and Magnani, and Fussi and Gilardone and the Italian empirical studio in the post Rachele Mori era is Antonio Juvarra. His 1987 book *Singing and its*

Techniques, whilst not as elaborate as some of the later books that we will also be discussing in this chapter was nonetheless a substantial breakthrough in the connection between vocal science and the empirical singing studio. Juvarra's objective was very similar to Mori's, which was to incorporate the science of his time into his teaching and writing, and he does this very well.

Nonetheless, whilst the science is definitely more advanced than that which Mori had available to her, I don't believe his work is as elaborate, balanced and complete, nor as nuanced as Mori's was nearly twenty years earlier, nor as Sanchez Carbone's twenty years later. Nonetheless, by virtue of the overall quality of the work and the fact that he was the only Italian singing teacher of substance to share his knowledge and thoughts with us in the period between Rachelle Maragliano Mori, and Nanda Mari who both published in (1970), and the big trio of the early 21st century as represented by Bruno and Paperi (2001), Battaglia Damiani (2003) and Sanchez Carbone (2005), places him in a unique historical position amongst Italian singing teachers of the late 20th century. Interestingly, Juvarra makes considerable amendments for his omissions with the publication of his second book *I Segreti del Belcanto* published in 2006, and a later revision of his book *Singing and its Techniques*.

Juvarra begins his dissertation by suggesting that the indispensable point of departure in order to obtain control of the vocal mechanism is a brief but accurate description of the vocal organs involved in phonation. This needs to be presented in a manner that emphasises clarity and precision. As has been suggested in the introduction, singing is a holistic phenomenon involving both 'psyche' and 'soma' in a perennial dance of reciprocal conditioning that involves many organs forming a phonatory sensibility in the memory. This holistic approach must take account of every serious and equilibrated didactic method and even if as sometimes is suggested it is possible to educate the vocal instrument with indirect methods born of the imaginative psycho/somatic suggestion, it is also true that in these cases development is rather slow and precarious. 'According to Juvarra, 'this lack of progress is also in evidence when we fail to substitute the generic invitation to '*appoggiare*', or to 'open' or 'darken' with more precise instructions' [Juvarra, 1987: 23]. In fact, from the moment in which for the first time we penetrate the 'passaggio, we have the impression that we reach a new dimension of sound where the normal laws that govern voice production do not seem to apply. Whereas, previously the intonation of the ascending notes was associated with the physical sensation of a vertical rising, and a firmer closure of the glottis, in ascending further beyond the passaggio, the sensation suddenly becomes horizontal or it may seem altogether a descending sensation, 'in ascending descend' [Juvarra, 1987: 43].

It is important that the teacher is able to choose strategies, and combine, and graduate the type of intervention necessary for a student's development, depending on the temperament, talent and particular or inherent problems.

According to Juvarra, the phonatory vocal organs consist of the larynx, pharynx, nasal cavities, the mouth and lungs. He believes that the function of the diaphragm, the abdominals and even the facial muscles are extremely important to the development of the voice.

The larynx is the source of sound production, whilst the pharynx, mouth, nasal, and paranasal cavities form the resonating vocal tract.

The Larynx

The larynx, which is very complex, takes the form of a cartilaginous scaffolding (the Adam's apple). The thyroid or shield cartilage dominates the anterior part, which is clearly observable with the naked eye. We can also distinguish the cricoid cartilage, which takes the form of a ring, and is the foundation and sustaining skeletal element of the larynx. The two arytenoid cartilages form a triangular pyramid which is predisposed towards a lateral movement, whilst the epiglottic cartilages which is attached to the anterior/interior surface of the thyroid cartilage, and whose function it is to close access to the lungs from above, remains both mobile and flexible [Juvarra, 1987: 24].

The Vibrator

Within the laryngeal cavity, we find the two vocal folds that together constitute the glottis. The vocal folds adduct in order to realise their phonatory function, which is to set them into vibration. Above all, the vocal folds can assume a number of different positions and conformations, depending on the various extrinsic laryngeal muscles that activate them (Juvarra is suggesting that laryngeal position is not only a function of the extrinsic muscles, but also of the diaphragm, which Sundberg confirms plays an important part in vertical laryngeal position). The configuration of the vocal folds themselves although influenced by laryngeal position, is primarily a function of the intrinsic laryngeal muscles. These muscles are mainly (the TA) tensor, the (CT) stretcher, and the adductors (IA) and (LCA), whilst the posterior cricoarytenoid (PCA) sometimes referred to as the posticus, remains the most important muscle of abduction [Juvarra, 1987: 24-5].

The muscles responsible for this process are the (TA) muscles that vary both the length and thickness of the vibrating part of the vocal folds, effecting both pitch, and glottal adduction but only in the lower range. In an ascending scale, only the contraction of the cricothyroid muscles that lengthen the vocal folds is responsible for an increase in frequency.

Finally, in its entirety, the larynx is conjoined to the hyoid bone via the thyrohyoid membrane, which is turn joined to the internal surface of the mandible, at the base of the cranium and the root of the tongue. It is a mobile organ that can be lowered and raised and participates passively with all the movements of the cervical column. The correct position of the larynx in the singing voice is the base position which will be defined shortly.

The sounds formed in this manner are amplified by the resonatory apparatus, which consists of the mouth, the pharynx, the nasal cavity and the paranasal. The tongue, the lips, the soft palate, and the larynx proper, provided that it takes a low position, assume considerable importance in the amplification of the source signal [Juvarra, 1987: 25-6].

Juvarra on the Vocal Registers and Passaggio

Covering

The importance of covering the voice at the passaggio, according to Juvarra, is to be found in the ensuing benefits, which are: protecting the vocal folds, facilitating access to the high notes, and modulating the vocal musculature in a way that allows the singer to develop the full extension of the range. This can only be achieved when at a certain frequency the singer learns how to execute the mechanism called passaggio.

Other names for this technique are 'copertura della voce', covering the voice; 'girari i suoni', turning the voice; 'passare in testa', passing into head voice', each of these suggestions is based on particular subjective perception.

Whilst this technique originated in Italy, it was exported at the beginning of the 18th century. Husson studied the passaggio in considerable depth at the Sorbonne in Paris in the 1960s. In so doing, he was able to clarify both its function and action. Juvarra also credits Husson for bringing the mechanism to light, branding it as 'a fundamental element of laryngeal protection in a more general theoretical system. This technique is designed to stabilise the larynx, offering a level of technical and vocal security' [Juvarra, 1987: 43].

Covering the voice at the passaggio is not a mechanism that functions automatically, but is rather the result of difficult, prolonged, and patient work. This passaggio is characterised by an artificial feel about it, allowing the singer to experience sensations that are generally not part of the normal consciousness of vocal emission, which is typically a more instinctive production. Juvarra believes that the importance of *copertura* or covering the voice, rests on the fact that it protects the vocal folds, it facilitates the entry into the high register (head voice), and it modulates the musculature in such a way as to allow the singer to develop the full extension of the voice. The first time the singer penetrates the passaggio, he gains the impression that he is entering a different vocal dimension, a dimension in which the normal laws of voice production do not apply.

Like Mori before him, Juvarra declares that in ascending a scale from the lower to medium register, rising frequency seems to be accompanied by a concomitant mental and physical vertical ascension, as well as a firmer closure of the glottis. Singing beyond the passaggio, the sensations become more horizontal and in extreme cases, they give the impression of descending, and hence the old school adage suggesting that 'in rising we descend'. This sensation is the result of a lowered larynx, and a widening the pharynx, which ensure a steady breath flow through the glottis, approaching the passaggio with extreme facility and lightness of emission (open throat and closed vowel). Failure to comply with the laws of the passaggio inevitably leads to an unhealthy open sound that will in time prove ruinous. This kind of technical failure can also lead to incorrect voice classification [Juvarra, 1987: 43].

Some of the benefits of a covered voice are, its extreme facility, fluidity of emission, and the power of the voice, which is also the result of correct *appoggio*. The question is how does the passaggio manifest, and how do we recognise it? [Juvarra, 2015: 60].

Raul Husson explains the passaggio by working through the example of a tenor singing an ascending scale in chest register on an open vowel.

He contends that if we begin on C3, and proceed beyond C4 and D4 without problems, we then find that around the E4 and F4 natural the voice becomes lighter and white, and the sound is characterised by a regrettable constriction, such as was previously alluded to. This type of sound appears to be too open, resulting in a sound that borders on being strident.

To proceed by excluding these persistent and pernicious sensations something has to change, and that something is the passagio. The singer becomes aware of these alterations which take the form of a switch and which for a moment seem to interrupt the vocal line, only for it to quickly reappear with a very different timbre. This is characterised by a certain muscular softness, a lightness of touch, and a darker tonal colour which has the effect of closing the vowel [Husson in Javarra, 2015: 60]. At this point, it is even more important to know the internal modifications upon which this mechanism is built, and these are:

1. The contraction of the cricothyroid muscle that inclines the thyroid cartilage forward and down.

2. The lengthening of the vocal fold, the larynx as a whole is more relaxed, allowing for an increase in the amplitude of vibrations of the vocal folds.

3. The larynx is lower and the pharyngeal space is expanded enormously.

4. The dorsum of the tongue moves forward.

5. The soft palate is slightly lowered.

These modifications increase the intensity of certain harmonics and expanding the pharynx that reinforces the fundamental. The different modes of emission (open and closed tone) should therefore be a point of departure from the normal [Juvarra, 2015: 61].

At this juncture, we are ready to begin the work of equalising the two registers by managing the break at the passaggio. The teacher should have a definite vision of what she is trying to achieve. This vision is formed and clarified by studying the great singers who seem to have a natural and instinctive ability to realise the passaggio [Juvarra, 1987: 44-5].

Having studied this mechanism, we are now able to understand the various elements that constitute it. At this point we should add that the contraction of the cricothyroid muscle does not pertain to a voluntary action, even though it intervenes automatically during the execution of the [i] vowel, which is the vowel that most exercises these muscles on the high notes. We do, however, experience some acoustic and visible signs, alerting us not just to the passaggio notes, but rather as Miller suggest a broader setting called the zona di passaggio.

The signs by which we recognise the passaggio, according to Juvarra, are:

1. Above all, the mechanism that covers the voice is characterised by its ability to close all the vowels (collect the vowel is better). This covered sound makes it impossible to simultaneously sing on an open vowel.

2. The execution of the passaggio corresponds with a moderate lowering of the larynx, which is easily confirmed by just placing a finger at the zone designated as the Adam's apple.

3. During the execution of the passaggio notes, it is possible to see the dorsum of the tongue rising with a consequent increase in pharyngeal space [Juvarra, 1987: 45].

The realisation that it is impossible to sing beyond the passaggio on an open vowel can be most disorienting to singers who are not fully aware of the problems confronting them. This is simply because their limited experience has taught them that in an ascending scale the vowel must be gradually opened in order to lighten and brighten the sound (allowing the larynx rise). Consequently, we can say that ascending exercises are counter indicated in terms of developing the passaggio technique of *copertura*.

That is, unless the teacher, in an effort to prevent these traps has made the student particularly aware of the difficulties confronting him, whilst at the same time ensuring that the student does not eschew those difficulties involved in smoothing the passaggio by enforcing at any cost the need to collect the vowel. In fact, in this type of exercise, the most important requirement is that of uniformity of emission and melodic legato. In order to realise this, the student is instinctively drawn to conclude that he must avoid the staccato on the passaggio. If only because before becoming a reflexive act, the mechanism of copertura involves for each of its executions a conscious control of the resonators. In the case of an ascending scale, it is possible that a preoccupation with maintaining evenness and agility of tone leads to an open emission which mentally conditions the student, thereby retarding his progress to a covered tone. It is therefore desirable that before ascending a scale, the student is taught to ascend the notes of the passaggio in isolation, training herself to alternate a closing last note with an open first one [Juvarra, 1987: 45-6].

According to Juvarra, lightening the voice in the critical range known as the *zona di passaggio* in an ascending scale is a necessary condition for the smooth execution of the passaggio, but it is not the only one. The other condition for lightening the voice is that it must not be obtained by brightening the sound, or allowing the larynx to rise, but rather by slightly darkening the tone (lowering the larynx) in the zone immediately before the passaggio. This preparation for the zona di passaggio is also the best way to disguise any interruption of the vocal line. The result *cantando piano* or 'singing softly' represents the unmistakable softness of timbre that characterises the medium zone of the scale. Rising beyond the passaggio, the voice becomes darker still, this is the 'dark colour' described by García (voix Sombrè). Although at this point, this lightening effect is automatic and associated with the vowel modification connected to the mechanism of *copertura* [Juvarra, 1987: 45-6].

If the copertura is not activated, the singer seeks to obtain the characteristic colour of the *copertura* by applying alternative strategies to the open sound in this pre-passaggio zone. Typically, the technique applied is vowel modification, which tends to compensate by darkening the vowels which endow the sound with some qualities associated with *copertura*. This sound is induced by a technique which often results in a sound which is either *intubato* (giving the impression that it is emerging from a tube), or is alternatively associated with a sound that resembles a scream. Neither of these are techniques should be confused with covering.

Juvarra suggest that confusion is inevitable when the teacher is not aware of any other technique for developing the voice other than that of chest voice, or when the teacher, or sometimes the overly ambitious student, pretend that a voice is what it is not by masquerading it as a darker and more dramatic voice than it is in reality in order to sing bigger more dramatic roles. This technique tends to confine the resonance to the posterior palato/pharyngo zone through an incorrect tongue position (retroflex tongue) and mouth position. In such cases, according to Juvarra, a best and most expedient way of negotiate the passaggio is to channel the voice towards the superior resonating cavities through a regime of nasalised exercises.

Nasalisation refers to the act of lowering the soft palate and thereby placing the cavity of the pharynx in communication with the nasal and paranasal cavities, and consequently altering the vocal tract.

Juvarra informs us that the lowering of the soft palate can be either complete or partial. According to him,

1. It is complete when we sing with a closed mouth: the intensity of the vibratory energy as perceived in the nasal zone (the index of the level of nasalisation) will at this point be at its maximum. It is possible to maintain the same level of nasalisation. When opening the mouth, the tongue dorsum rises touching the soft palate and forming a bridge that excludes the mouth. If in the emission of an [a] vowel with the mouth open progresses from a position of a raised soft palate (nonnasalised sound) to one in which the soft palate is lowered (complete nasalisation), it is possible when we look in the mirror that in addition to lowering the palate we will also see the raising of the tongue dorsum. This movement of the tongue is the same action, although less accentuated, as the one involved in the execution of the passaggio.

2. The partial lowering of the soft palate during vocal emission results in a sound that is nasalised. A good example of this results when we attach the nasal consonant or the [n] continuant to a vowel, the sound will be nasalised. The majority of exercises produced in the best vocal studios are based on consonants that open the nasal cavity. In the majority of these cases they lead to the discovery of a truly new resonance cavity, whereupon the voice (quite apart from any resulting aesthetic judgement) can find some respite thanks to the physiological beneficial effect of nasalisation on the vocal folds [Juvarra, 1987: 46; 2015: 64].

Juvarra believes that a light level of nasalisation such as we experience in a vocalise that is preceded by a nasal consonant, can be beneficial to the voice by direction the emission towards the mask [Juvarra, 1987: 46-7].

He concludes that a low level of nasalisation combined with a lightness of emission facilitates the exploration of the complete vocal range, whilst also guaranteeing a level of protection of the vocal folds, and whilst this configuration does not automatically determine the passaggio, it most certainly facilitate it. Having arrived at this point, it is more a question of becoming aware of the different types of emission that give origin to particular sonorities, and associating it with certain concepts and mental images that vary with each individual.

Finally, Juvarra warns us that having succeeded in actuating the passaggio does not mean that we have automatically ensured correct vocal emission. To achieve correct vocal emission, we need to also ensure an adequate *appoggio*, an absence of tension in the throat and the maintenance of the resonance focal point in the mask [Juvarra, 1987: 47].

Juvarra addresses the myoelastic/aerodynamic model of vocal fold vibration. He acknowledges the three-register model, but does not treat each of them in in detail as would be expected in major book of vocal pedagogy. What he does manage, however, is the elaborate treatment of the two competing strategies for changing registers: the first is a strategy of blending registers in which there is a minor lightening of the vocal mechanism in preparation for the change of register, followed by a minor darkening of the voice at the passaggio proper, register blending. The second strategy refers to copertura (covering) the passaggio notes in order to penetrate the head register. This strategy requires the lowering of the larynx and widening of the pharynx at the level where the sound changes register, and this Juvarra does very well.

A 21st Century Scientific View of Registers

With respect to vocal registers, Fussi and Magnani contend that whilst the definition and number of registers is still hotly debated, there is a great deal of agreement as to the existence of registers. There is also a great deal of agreement that registers are an acoustic and perceptive reality for singers. Fussi and Magnani acknowledge that dichotomous nature of registers, they are often defined primarily on the basis of their mechanical laryngeal properties, which together form a series of sounds that are perceptively similar and which are produced by a precise configuration of the vocal folds set into vibration, whilst other researchers define them on the basis of vocal quality that is perceived as been maintained at a certain level of frequency and intensity. In other words, just as some define registers from the point of view of the laryngeal mechanism, others prefer to base their understanding of registers on the quality of tone emitted, with respect to the singing voice we tend to categorise register terminology into two grand categories in relation to vocal source behaviour. Beginning with the female voice, we find that it is distinguished by its modal register which is sometimes referred to as heavy register, incorporating chest and medium voice, and mixed voice which integrates both medium and high voice (head register), and above this we find the female falsetto, or whistle register. On the other hand, the male voice is termed as chest voice, head voice or mezza voce, and the register beyond this which is called falsetto. A register classification based purely on laryngeal phenomenon fails to consider the great timbrel variations realised by the singing voice.

It is necessary for us to define at least two registers with respect to human phonation simply because the human voice is characterised by discontinuity or involuntary transitions during the production of voice. The transitional phenomenon that occurs between registers maybe the result of perceptual variations of timbre, and may or may not be related solely to laryngeal alterations [Fussi & Magnani, 2015: 68-70].

Fussi and Magnani on Vocal Registers

The definition and number of registers in the singing voice is still much debated. Although, it must be said that there is also much agreement on the fact that registers are an acoustic reality that is related to the singer's perception. Registers are often defined on the basis of their laryngeal and mechanical properties, combined with a series of notes perceived as being produced in the same way by a vibratory glottal model, whilst at times there are perceived as being maintained by a certain frequency and intensity range.

In other words, whilst some define registers only on the basis of their laryngeal and mechanical principals, others give greater weight to the quality of the sound emitted in particular register.

Fussi and Magnani categorise the female voice as heavy and medium voice, medium and high sounds, and falsetto and flute; the male voice on the other hand, they categorise as voce di petto; voce piena in testa, and mezza voce for modal register, and falsetto or falsettone for the highest male register.

They also contend that register classification with laryngeal phenomenon does not sufficiently take into account the many variations of timbre that may be attained through a good technique. The reason we recognise at least two registers in the human voice is derived from the phenomenon of a discontinuity or rather the transitions that occur involuntarily during voice productions [Fussi &Magnani, 2015: 70].

Fussi and Magnani inform us that the transitional phenomenon between registers may also be the result of various perceived timbrel differences, which may not be correlated to laryngeal alterations. The truth is that most timbre transitions are associated with changes in spectral energy in the superior part of the spectrum, but there are some timbrel transitions that are the result of crude alterations of vowels. It is important to realise, however, that not all phenomena associated with timbrel shifts is due to either glottal or acoustic alterations, often there is a third cause involved, and this is dependent on the psychoacoustic properties of perception. This is definitely the case with a transition of periodicity, simply because in part we perceive the phenomenon of glottal impulses as individual events, something that happens only when the frequency is below 70 Hz rather than hearing it on a continuum, such as is the distinction between vocal fry and modal register [Fussi & Magnani, 2015: 70].

The authors remind us that in order to fully comprehend what we define as modal or full register, as distinguished from falsetto, it is important that we recall how the muscles involved in the vibratory cycle interact to the extent that they render physiological equilibrium between the vocal folds and their respective tensing mechanism [Fussi & Magnani, 2015: 71].

In an ascending scale from the low notes to the high register we transition from modal register, commonly called lower register, into falsetto register, perceiving a sudden change in quality as we ascend to falsetto. This signifies that the tonal field has realised certain auto-functional laryngeal modifications. This sudden change is accompanied by rapid variations of the vocal fold mass set into vibration. This is due to the alteration of vocal fold tension that causes the decoupling of the vibrating layers, and the variations of the open quotient of the vocal fold cycle as measured by electroglottography. This perceptible *passaggio* should be gradually and consciously-managed by the experienced singer during this tonal transition, through the dominant modality of the tensor muscles and glottal contact time. If we desire that the process of register transition is to appear seamless, then, these gradual glottal alterations must be accompanied by a gradual and sympathetic adaptation of the vocal tract.

If every primary register covers a determined range of phonatory frequency that the singer can produce, in order to change imperceptibly from one mechanism to another, some sounds within that range possess the type of emission that undergoes a gradual modification in order to transit towards the high register, depending on the vibratory modality that establishes the relationship between the tension of the intrinsic and extrinsic laryngeal muscles to different levels of subglottal pressure and different postures of the pharyngeal cavity (vocal tract).

The perceptive effect of this modality is the illusory coherence of means and a uniformity of phonatory timbres along the entire glottal range. But registers do exist, both in singing and in speech, and they should be recognised as the result of the mechanical function of the vocal folds. Their perceptible acoustic effect may be compensated through the technical understanding of blending, which is considered necessary the for the equalisation between one register and another, such as happens in classical singing or as is otherwise exploited and exhausted in certain aesthetic models, such as modern singing [Fussi & Magnani, 2015: 71].

Fussi and Magnani contend that at the origin of vocal registers, which could be defined as a laryngeal reality, there exists a mechanical correlation between the vibratory characteristics of the vocal folds which have been designated and described as four (4) mechanisms.

1. In the mechanism defined as M the vocal folds are short, thick and the layers that constitute the cover (mucus, epithelium, and superficial layer of the lamina propria) are all relaxed and mobile, easily separating themselves from the muscular body underlying the vocal folds (vocalis). The muscular activity of the thyroarytenoid (TA), the cricothyroid (CT), and the interarytenoid (IA) is at its minimal whilst the glottal closing rate is very long. This mechanism is usually associated with the production of the lowest notes of the vocal extension.

2. In the laryngeal mechanism designated as M1, the vocal folds are thick and vibrate in their entire length, with a substantial vertical phase difference and a substantial involvement of the amplitude of the vocal fold mass. The vocal fold body is stiff relative to the vocal fold cover. The action of the thyroarytenoids (TA) dominate that of the cricothyroids (CT), whilst their combined activity increases with increasing frequency. The closing phase of the vibratory cycle is often longer than the opening phase. This is the mechanism employed by both men and women in the lower and middle part of their extension.

3. In mechanism M2 vibrations are reduced with respect to the preceding mechanism and there is no substantial vertical phase in the vibratory movement. All the stratified vocal fold layers are stretched, but the collagen fibres of the vocal folds are maximally stretched and tense. The muscular activity of the cricothyroid (CT) dominates that of the thyroarytenoid (TA), and the opening phase of the vibratory cycle is longer than the closing phase. This mechanism is used by both men and women, and in the medium and higher extension of the voice.

4. The mechanism designated as M3 is comprised of the flute and whistle register, in which the vocal folds are characterised by a thin, tense and highly reduced vibratory mechanism, with respect to the previous mechanism, which includes a lack of contact at the edges of the vocal folds. It has been hypothesised that the vibration of the vocal folds may be induced by a vortex of periodic turbulence interacting with the resonators [Fussi & Magnani, 2015: 72].

An important characteristic of these categories is that in the range of dominance of both principal mechanisms (M1 and M2) we superimpose a predetermined range of frequency that allows the singer to choose between one or other mechanism. The range we speak of is between 165 to 370 Hz in men and 196 to 392 in women. As a consequence, in this range we have a choice of which mechanism we choose. Such choices are tied to the stylistic requirements of the piece, which will be satisfied in relation to the characteristics of the glottal flow. The most capable classical singers know how to attain certain modifications of this type of vocal quality by adjusting the vocal tract in a favourable manner, as is the case in the perceived mixed voice or register. This means that at least from the laryngeal point of view the singer uses a precise mechanism, that is, M1 is the dominant modal in men and M2 the dominant model in women. The success of both modes requires some modification of the vocal tract adept at masking the perceptible transition of register [Fussi & Magnani, 2015: 72].

In returning to the role of laryngeal tensor muscles which determines the two laryngeal mechanisms, we recall that the thyroarytenoid muscle (TA) seems to be essential to the regulation of registers, demonstrating greater activity in the modal register, whilst decreasing its activity during the *passaggio* from modal to falsetto register.This muscle group inserts into both the thyroid cartilage and the arytenoids, and depending on the frequency being sung, or the volume or intensity aimed at, the throarytenoid muscle will proportionally oppose the cricothyroid (CT) muscles. The thyroarytenoids (TA) are also very active during increasing intensity and or diminishing frequency [Fussi & Magnani, 2015: 73].

To compensate for the (CT) cricothyroids inability to regulate dynamic intensity and render a fuller sound, even in the tonal range pertaining to mechanism 2, it is evident that the tension of the arytenoid muscles must increase, resulting in an increase in the contact time of the vibratory cycle. The demands made on the mechanism, require a major level of subglottal pressure whilst maintaining intonation. In fact, if we increase intensity of tone, that is, if we increase subglottal pressure, the activity of the cricothyroids alone would not be able to control the incremental pressure without simultaneously raising fundamental frequency (Fo), at least not without the regulatory tension on the part of the opposing muscles of the vocal folds that allows the singer to maintain intonation, as occurs when we suddenly increase volume in speech [Fussi & Magnani, 2015: 73].

Consequently, we may conclude that it is the arytenoid system that compensates for the inability of the cricothyroids to maintain the vocal folds in the adductory position whilst resisting the increased level of subglottal pressure that accompanies every increase in intensity. The function of the intrinsic laryngeal muscles that inserts into the arytenoids induce the following effect:

1. They maintain the adduction of the vocal folds at the glottal level. Contraction of these laryngeal muscles determines the diverse contact time, which result in different vocal qualities often perceived and defined as laryngeal registers.

2. These muscles also oppose the antagonistic action of the cricothyroid muscles which tend to abduct the vocal folds especially during the elevation of fundamental frequency (Fo), and even more so during a time of maintaining the M1 mechanism.

3. They also regulate the intensity of the central or middle register by regulating the thickness and vibrating surface of the vocal folds, and by allowing an increase in the contact time which gives the perception of fullness of tone so characteristic of M1.

4. They function to differentiate the tension on the highest notes, when the cricothyroids (CT) reach their limit of contraction (a mixture of mechanism 1 and 2).

5. They also regulate variations in intensity in response to the difference in subglottal-pressure. Determining a vocal quality that in the absence of the activity of the cricothyroids is perceived as chest voice (mechanism 1).

When the closed glottal phase is longer than the opening phase of the cycle, it assists with the creation of a number of harmonics which determine the richness of vocal timbre, intensity and fullness of sound (voce piena), We use the term chest voice to describe the ensuing sensations directed towards the thoracic cage. It is through the contractile function of the vocalis muscles and the arytenoid muscle system in general that the vocal folds are shortened, thereby increasing their mass.

The authors remind us that chest voice (voce di petto) refers 'to that perceptive phenomenon that we perceive as fullness of tone that provokes in the singer sensations of substantive vibrating consonance that are muscularly directed towards the thorax' [Fussi & Magnani, 2015: 74].

In the course of ascending a scale, the cricothyroid muscles gradually increase their activity, thereby lengthening the vocal folds (longitudinal tension), whilst the continued antagonistic activity of the thyroarytenoid muscles (tensors) allows the singer to avoid the elevation of the larynx with its concomitant reduction in resonating space. In this manner, the vocal folds are allowed to vibrate in their full amplitude, and the tone maintains its acoustic quality of fullness. Given that the longitudinal tension has thinned vocal folds, the subjective vibratory sensations are directed towards the head cavity, and are termed *voce piena in testa*.

If on the other hand we sing an ascending scale without covering the sound at the passaggio, we obtain a spontaneous elevation of the larynx, resulting in a state of muscular contraction experienced as a sense of constriction and phonatory fatigue (we refer to this as voce spinta), that brings us to a point in which it is impossible to achieve an equilibrium of the muscular forces involved without incurring a vocal break [Fussi & Magnani, 2015: 74].

Since the change of frequency is also reflected in a change in the relationship between the cricoid and the thyroid cartilages, we can confirm that the neck muscles that also effect the position of the larynx can collaborate with the cricothyroid to create longitudinal tension. In fact, it is instinctive for the muscles to raise the larynx in sympathy with frequency. On the other hand, the cricoid is partially anchored to the oesophagus and trachea [Fussi & Magnani, 2015: 75].

Fussi and Magnani explain this as an instinctive rising of the larynx is associated with incorrect vocal function, although, it is sometimes a stylistic choice amongst pop singers. They proceed by explaining that the corrective action for this defect, especially with respect to classical singing, relates to the mixing of M1 and M2 or vice versa. In these circumstances, contact time remains inferior to 40% of the vibratory cycle and the mucosal wave expands but a little upon the vocal folds. The resulting vocal timbre is rather poor in harmonics, weak in intensity and is often perceived as a fixed vocal sound. The falsetto register is used by tenors in polyphonic music, other light tenors, yodelling and folk singing and falsetto [Fussi & Magnani, 2015: 75].

Medium Register

In between modal register, or *voce piena* and falsetto, there exist a number of intermediary possibilities distinguished by more moderate levels of tension than offered by the two tensor muscles that characterise the medium and high notes in the female voice and the high register of the light lyric tenor voice, and which can be managed either by beginning from mechanism 1 or mechanism 2. This modality, which is defined as medium register, should be considered as common ground in both the singer of light melodic music and the classical singer, and remains indispensable for the correct execution of *mezze voci* and pianissimo in classical singing [Fussi & Magnani, 2015: 75].

Intensity of tone is mainly determined by the management of airflow, and it is as well to recall that airflow is itself a function of subglottal pressure.

Consequently, we may conclude that when values of subglottal pressure are increased, airflow is much more elevated. These variations in pressure are necessary even for modifying the fundamental frequency of the note being emitted: in fact, in ascending towards the higher register, it is necessary to lengthen the vocal folds, a physical requirement which is achieved through an increase in subglottal pressure.

The singer must regulate and control the level of subglottal pressure in accordance with the intensity and frequency we wish to obtain. We have established that an increase in intensity requires an increase in subglottal pressure, altering the interrelationship between the laryngeal muscular systems resulting in different acoustic outcomes.

The relationship between register and intensity becomes even more evident when we focus our attention on the *passaggio* notes, for example at the end of the middle register in an ascending passaggio towards the upper *passaggio*, or in a descending scale, the lowest notes that we are able to execute in falsetto. One major element of evidence of an unbalanced voice placement is when the lowest notes of mechanism 2 become increasingly weaker as we travel towards the domain of M1. Since the high notes of the chest register, that is, the middle notes heading towards the upper *passaggio* become more intense as we ascend the scale, it becomes obvious that we must find some sort of accommodation if both parts are to work together in a homogenous and harmonious manner. The procedure necessary to reconcile such discrepancies depends largely on the regulation of intensity between these 2 modalities in this tonal zone. In such a case, the level of intensity produced with chest register must be reduced, a procedure that unites perceptively the two mechanisms grounded in functional unity. The level of lighting the chest register depends most probably on the repertoire and the vocal topology of the singer, oscillating in the middle register in mechanism 1 mixing with 2 or mechanism 2 mixing with 1; that is, between a voice that may be perceived as fuller (minor lightening) and a voice that is perceived as medium register (major lightening) [Fussi & Magnani, 2015: 76].

Within the realm of the medium register, intensity may be seen as a catalyst to the alteration of frequency. Only because change in the level of vocal intensity results in an abrupt alteration to the mechanism that defines laryngeal registers [Fussi & Magnani, 2015: 76].

The voice, therefore, cannot be homogenous until these registers are integrated and finely balanced. The influence of intensity tends to be mediated by the artist's ability to adjust the mechanism. These are the reasons we encounter difficulties when we attempt to execute the *messa di voce*, which alone maybe attributed to the changes within the laryngeal musculature in response to intensity. If diminishing or augmenting the volume of a single tone were to be the product of a single register mechanism, the *messa di voce* would not be such a problem [Fussi & Magnani, 2015: 77].

The authors contend that it is particularly difficult to comprehend this process if we first don't understand the need to achieve a dynamic but perfect transition in the relationship between the cricothyroid and thyroarytenoid muscles as a means of changing the physical dimensions of the vocal folds. The break that is usually exhibited at the *passaggio* between a piano and a forte (filato) occurs when the physical dimensions of the vocal folds change from long and thin for low intensity singing to short and thick for high intensity singing. This creates a dynamic muscle contraction at the level of the tensor muscles: in particular the activity of the arytenoid system during an increase of intensity [Fussi & Magnani, 2015: 77]

As with intensity, frequency and resonance, are amongst the elements that provoke a perceptible tonal quality due to the change in dynamics between piano and forte, which are also associated physiologically with the mechanism associated with register change. This must be considered an important element in the development of these coordinated relations, and also with the perceptive terminology of registers, which may have summarised as follows:

There is broad agreement that the scientific paradigm known as modal register, is generally comprised of a combination of chest, medium or mixed voice, and head register, and represents a significant characteristic of classical singing. We have established two paradigms, a covered and an open register, depending on the posture of the vocal tract. That is, a long and ample pharynx refers to the covered register, and a short, less ample pharynx for the open register.

The inherent deficiency in the activity of the cricothyroid (CT) must be compensated for by an increase in tension on the part of the arytenoid group because the capacity to lengthen the vocal folds through their contraction reaches a physiological limit: as a consequence, in the very highest notes the arytenoids become the regulatory mechanism that manages the level of intensity and frequency. It achieves this by increasing glottal resistance, and therefore the impedance to the glottal airflow, managing subglottal pressure, and reducing the vibratory portion of the vocal folds (posterior occlusion).

It is important to discriminate between the different modalities of emission for both the male and female voice. In the male voice, a number of different modalities have been demonstrated. For instance, in the light register we encounter a number of descriptive and perceptual differences. These modalities depend heavily on the activity of the arytenoids and this is the factor that most distinguishes the falsetto with certain characteristics pertaining to the M2 mechanism, from the falsettone (a mix of M1 and M2) perceptively and spectrographically analogous to the light lyric soprano, and is produced by the male voice with extreme involvement from the arytenoid group (posterior occlusion) in producing the highest notes with a healthy intensity [Fussi & Magnani, 2015: 78].

Fussi and Magnani, warn us about carrying the full voice (M1) too high in the chest voice or *voce piena gridata,* which is associated with belt or rock singing, and can create hyperactivity in the muscles involved in the vocal *passaggio.* This type of production is characterised by an increase in contact time, elevation of the larynx, and an increase in subglottal pressure [Fussi & Magnani, 2015: 78].

Transition from the Empirical System Towards the Scientific Method

We saw above that vocal science in Italy was well represented by Meano and Bellincione in the fifties and sixties, whilst singing teachers were at least twenty years behind the times. For instance, it was not until 1970 that Rachele Maragliano Mori and Nanda Mari, both respected singing teachers, directed Italian vocal pedagogy on a very different course by adopting a more scientific, objective approach. More recently we saw a flurry of scientific activity with respect to vocal science, which involved Mari and Schindler, Fussi and Magnani, Ruopoli and Schindler, Fussi and Gilardone and more recently Fussi and Turli. Collectively, these works represent a wondrous body of knowledge, and as expert a body of vocal science as we are likely to see anywhere in the world.

The big difference this time around is how quickly and extensively singing teachers have responded to this body of scientific knowledge. It is also interesting that with few exceptions whilst their English and American counterparts are quite happy to sit back and just work from the material that has been translated into English, the Italians are not only working from the considerable Italian literature but are also translating and incorporating English, Spanish, French and German literature as well as Scandinavian, making them more proactive in their search for new knowledge than many of their English-speaking counterparts. Authors such as Juvarra (1987), Bruno and Paperi (2001), Damiani (2003), and Sanchez Carbone (2005), all revere the literature from the far past but also unconditionally embrace new scientific knowledge. With this in mind, we can say that the beginning of the 21st century has been a most productive period for adoption of vocal science by Italian singing teachers. In short succession, we saw the publishing of three major works. The first was Bruno and Paperi's *The Singing Voice* (2001), the second was Battaglia Damiani's *Anatomy of the Voice* (2003) and the last of the three and probably the most impressive is Sanchez Carbone's *Vox Arcana: Theory and*

Practice of the Voice (2005). These works are all impressive volumes, but probably the one that is destined to be the most influential and enduring is last of the three: Sanchez Carbone's *Vox Arcana* runs to nearly 950 pages and is detailed and well curated in every sense of the word.

Fussi and Magnani give us as good an explanation of the myoelastic/aerodynamic model of vocal fold vibration as you are likely to read, and the detailed explanation of registers how their work and how there are blended or joined together is very much its equal. I like Fussi and Magnani's work very well indeed.

Chapter 16

Modern Masters on Registers

Bruno and Paperi (2001) declare that registers represent a series of notes with the same timbrel characteristics. The timbres differences that we discern between the various registers are the result of proportional modifications created by the zones of resonance, and laryngeal muscular tension. These authors suggest that it is not their intention to discuss how registers have been understood in various eras, a subject that has been well treated by many contemporary authors, instead they prefer to concentrate on how today's singer may confidently approach the subject of managing timbres and registers. This should be the starting point in the quest to obtain the colour between the various registers, so as to homogenise the complete vocal range through the combined action of the intrinsic laryngeal muscles, whilst retaining certain characteristics of each individual register [Bruno & Paperi, 2001: 114].

Bruno and Paperi next address the *passaggio*. They state that even though the *passaggio* which is the most intensely scrutinised element of registers, should be thought of as a way of facilitating the seamless coordination of the larynx and its corresponding resonators at the time when the product of the voice source is traversing between the 'medium or mixed register' and the 'head or high register'. Any technical deficiency at this level will manifest as an obstacle in the quest to seamlessly blend these registers.

The authors argue cogently that the *passaggio* is a very individual process, and even two tenors of the same type and vocal weight will find minor individual differences with respect to the frequency upon which register change should occur for each particular vowel. This process generally requires *copertura*, a slight vowel modification, or *arrotondimento* which translates to a rounding off of the resonators.

More about these methods of blending registers further on in this chapter under the heading of *copertura*. According to the authors there are many reasons for these differences, but issues of nationality, internal physiology, the relationship between the larynx and resonators, but also the level of efficiency achieved through quality teaching.

For now, let us pursue an explanation of the accepted modern view of registers. This paradigm is generally comprised of three registers, i.e., low, medium or mixed, and high. Although, the authors argue that these divisions are more valid for women and other high voices than men. According to them, the full lyric tenor and bass/baritones are more likely to unite the low and medium register. The authors dismiss falsetto by ignoring it all together.

I can understand this because falsetto register fails to engage the vocalis muscle (the body of the vocal folds), combined with the failure of its ligaments to meet at the midline, can be regarded is an illegitimate register. Even when it does meet at the midline, it is generally with a minute portion of the ligament and it does not manifest any phase difference. Consequently, we can say that it lacks upper harmonics.

I am less sanguine about the notion that males essentially combine only the low and medium mechanism. I know that in principle this statement is correct, but as it stands it does not explain the art of releasing the lower mechanism thyroarytenoid (TA) muscles whilst gradually increasing the stretching and tensing cricothyroid (CT) mechanism. This is the traditional head register mechanism that Vennard believed was much more a mixture of medium and falsetto rather than low and medium. Whilst Bruno and Paperi are not wrong, because strictly speaking, even a full blooded top C needs to combine the action of the cricothyroid (CT) with the antagonistic action of the vocalis muscle, i.e. the medial portion of the thyroarytenoid (TA), the level of cricothyroid contraction, however, needs to be closer to falsetto register rather than middle register. I am personally more inclined to align myself with Vennard in this issue.

The Low Registers

Bruno and Paperi refer to the lower register as one that emphasises the lower resonances whilst not excluding the regulated participation of the medium and higher resonators: these last observations are very important for the development of a homogenised tone throughout the vocal range.

The authors ask us to remain conscious of level of laryngeal descent in the lower register, with a view to training our muscle memory as to exactly how far we lower it as we approach this register. They also make us aware as to whether the larynx inclines anteriorly or posteriorly, or whether it remains in a horizontal position. In a close analysis of these strategies, Bruno and Paperi conclude that lowering the larynx whilst maintaining a horizontal level should be the privileged position. This, they believe, facilitates the muscular balance, which allows the larynx to respond to the situational requirement.In this strategy, the jaw must remain completely free and disengaged from the larynx, and the sound pressure level within the oropharynx must be proportional to the subglottal pressure applied by the expiratory muscles [Bruno & Paperi, 2003: 114].

Medium or Mixed Voice

It would be easier and more convenient to locate and activate the mixed range zone of the voce. This is particularly true of dramatic sopranos, mezzos, contraltos, and white, clear male voices male. In order to maximise the intermediate voice, which is the register between low and high register, the voice must be well trained. Further, the authors contend that this medium register is best joined to the lower register. They also suggest that we should not over emphasise the primo passaggio between the low and medium register, such concentration could lead to a compromised outcome. The smooth connection between the low and medium register should be given due consideration but in its execution, it needs to be smooth and natural.

The authors believe that the singer needs to prearrange the shape of the instrument by ensuring an appropriate position of the palate, and throat, combined with an adaptable subglottal pressure. This facilitates the production of mixed tones in continuous evolution, combined with a certain stability of emission that does not to betray the characteristic timbre of the voice (this process will be helped by the retroactive influence of the auditory system). The authors suggest that the progressive variation of tension is due to the antagonistic action of the laryngeal muscles, which must also be balanced with the lower and higher resonators. In so doing, we facilitate the ascension of the voice towards the higher register.

Bruno and Paperi believe that in the mixed register it is easier to quantify the energy issuing from the subglottal pressure, which is commensurate with the comfortable glottal resistance that it is responsible for creating. The acoustic energy, which is the product of the encounter between subglottal pressures and glottal resistance, is then directed into the vocal tract in the form of sound and words. The authors recommend not over inflating (overblowing) nor covering the medium register, but rather to educate it and execute it with care, controlling the sfogato (outpouring of sound) so that it does not come at the expense of a well-focused sound in the mask. In fact, according to Bruno and Paperi, we should never consciously push the sound out. With respect to warming up the voice, the authors recommend always beginning in the middle register, because in this register it is easier to locate the diaphragm and elicit from it its principle activity, which is as a regulator of airflow [Bruno & Paperi, 2001:15]. This allows us to coordinate the various parts of the instrument. The uniform production of all the notes that constitute the mixed register must be the first priority of every student before rushing to fully develop both the low and high registers. These registers may well exist in their potentiality, but their full development must be approached from a well-established and focused medium register. Since the medium register is the one that is most involved in arias and roles that a particularly well chosen for a given voice, then it becomes particularly important that this register be well defined and established. In fact, there are a number of authors who regard the medium register as the home of the voice. Having established the medium voice, the interpreter may subject the voice to a great variety of sounds required to express diverse emotional situations [Bruno & Paperi, 2001: 115].

The Higher Register

This register represents that part of the voice that needs to be well educated by paying particular attention to the quality of the sound, beginning with those notes that precede the passaggio notes. If the singer becomes accustomed to loading the laryngeal muscles, with a concomitant participation of the neck muscles, it will then become difficult to establish the muscular balance necessary to produce the malleability required for phrasing in this vocal zone. This requires a stable but sensitive laryngeal position capable of responding to individual stimulation. The authors exhort the student to develop this register gradually, a little at the time, beginning with a smooth mezzo forte, first on the vowels and then on the syllables, whilst also maintaining instrumental agility, dramatic intent and vocal legato, which is the indispensable element of quality phrasing. For certain voices, it is advisable to lighten the emission so as to eliminate tension (all the while being careful not to sing piano), whilst maintaining the efficient laryngeal action balanced with *sostegno* or *appoggio*.

It is important to pay attention to the participation of the body whilst training this vocal register. There may be certain postural tensions that may emerge in the process, as often occurred with incorrect reflexive movements. This could engender a great deal of rigidity on the lower jaw and the chin [Bruno & Paperi, 2001:16]. This configuration produces a tense sound, which is often accompanied by raised shoulders, a consequent hardening of the muscles and excessive activity in the external laryngeal muscles. This may involve an uncontrolled pressure on the thorax, which is sometimes contrasted by an excessively relaxed state that involves the dropping of the choice, preventing it from participating in the formation of the high register. There are many pedagogues that that continue the old terminology, i.e., 'head voce instead of 'high register' These authors believe that this is an expression that derails the perception of the sound in its entire complex, because for a balanced sound we are really required to use all of the resonators and that can only come from the most propitious position of the articulators [Bruno & Paperi, 2015: 116].

The 'head voice' was much more identifiable in the vocal technique that dominated the period beginning just prior to the early years of romanticism. With respect to falsetto, which is easily differentiated from 'falsettone', especially, when the falsetto is appoggiato on the breath. Supported falsetto is still used today by some famous international tenors. Bruno and Paperi refer to falsetto as a vague term, connected with a style that is generally used for a special effect. Although, they do believe that it can be useful in the development of the highest notes of the female range. This is a very different function to the female falsetto than that which was originally attributed to it by García and his immediate predecessors of the *bel canto* period. García referred to the notes located between the end of chest voice, on F natural, and the beginning of the first passaggio on D flat, as the female falsetto.

When the singer is required to sing *passagi* of high and brilliant agility, or very rapid intervals and jumps, it is useful to utilise a particularly high focus or projection whilst ensuring diaphragmatic and laryngeal coordination in order to mediate the effects of the passaggio, and as a consequence modifying the manner of collecting the sounds, so that they may be directed towards the facial resonators. Even so, it is appropriate to perceive a preordained type of singing, a sound that is determined by breath flow. In ascending the scale, it is important not to exaggerate the concept of thinking small on the highest sounds, simply because exaggeration will impact vocal quality [Bruno & Paperi, 2001: 116].

Damiani on Registers

Damiani, along with Meano, Mori and more recently Sanchez Carbone informs us that the term register is derived from those of the church organ: in the organ, every note corresponds to a certain length of pipe, and each pipe determines a characteristic timbre or register. The organist must choose the next appropriate pipe for the pitch he is playing: bringing in certain registers and excluding others.

Damiani, like most Italian authors, going back to Caccini, Tosi, and Mancini, subscribes to the theory that the human voice is comprised of two fundamental registers, which corresponds to the action of the diverse configuration of the various laryngeal muscles. Most of these muscular configurations were discussed at length by Fussi and Magnani above and will not be elaborated at this point.

Damiani believes that registers are important because they are a congenial means by which the larynx may fully exploit the vocal folds. The more we cultivate and support the vocal instrument in general and the vocal folds in particular, the more they are inclined to respond to the demands of the high register. Common sense, however, informs us that even the most favourable glottal configuration must reach its limits, if only because the contractile action of the vocal muscle (vocalis), which both thickens and shortens the body of the vocal folds, acts antagonistically to the lengthening and thinning function of the cricothyroids, preventing the full stretch associated with the longitudinal tension of the vocal folds as long as the voice remains in modal register. This limitation, however, is easily resolved as the singer learns to gradually relax the vocalis muscle (the body of the vocal folds), whilst simultaneously contracting the cricothyroid stretcher, which allows it to passively stretch, thin and tense the vocal folds without too much force, a glottal setting that is ultimately responsible for the production of the upper modal or high (head) register [Damiani, 2003: 234].

According to Damiani this changing of the guard between the laryngeal muscles represents a delicate moment in the development of the singing student.

Damiani is absolutely right about the above statement. My own ideas are reflected in the above statement. I believe that the art of seamless register equalisation is the art of gradually releasing the contraction of the (TA) thyroarytenoid muscles, allowing the (CT) cricothyroids to stretch and tense the vocal folds, whilst creating a commensurate level of midline compression, involving both the (IA) interarytenoid muscles and the (LCA) lateral cricoarytenoid muscles.

In my view, this can only be accomplished when the laryngeal mechanism as a whole aided by the extrinsic laryngeal muscles finds its ideal vertical position within the larynx, and the whole laryngeal mechanism is well supported by the respiratory musculature, in a manner that eschews rigidity whilst ensuring a balance between subglottal pressure and steady breath flow. Note that this is a different concept to that often-encountered exhortation to support the voice, which is a physical impossibility, simply because sound travels at 1130 feet per second and cannot be supported, whereas the present exhortation embraces the imperative of physically supporting the vocal instrument.

Daniela Battaglia Damiani embraces vocal science and has an excellent knowledge of it, but she does so with some reservations, believing that it is often overstated and exhibiting a reluctance to part with the traditional Italian school.

Registers and Voice Classification

Damiani contends that at some point the stabilisation of the passaggio becomes clear and with it also the classification of that particular voice.

To the point of voice classification, the location of registers in the extension of the voice and the location of the *passaggio* at a certain degree of the scale, especially when combined with vocal timber and vocal extension, can be considered amongst the most trusted indication of voice classification.

Heavy Register

According to Damiani, in heavy or low register, the laryngeal function is represented by a configuration of the vocal folds that vibrates to the full extent of the vocal lips. In this register the vocal muscle (vocalis) contracts and the vocal folds vibrate in all their amplitude. In this configuration, the vocalis muscle vibrates in its entirety, slowing down the vibratory cycle, the closing phase predominates over the opening phase, and the cricothyroids remain relaxed. On the other hand, the high or acute register corresponds to a vocal fold function represented by relatively thin (lamelle) strands. The two registers coexist largely on a particular frequency.

As we gradually proceed from the heavy register to the medium and high register, we note a gradual reduction of contraction in the thyroarytenoid muscle and a concomitant increase in contraction of the cricothyroid muscle. For many years now, we have known which muscles are involved in the change of register (passaggio) [Damiani, 2003: 239].

Chest Register

When the vocal muscle (vocalis) is tense and contracted, it participates in the vibration of the vocal folds, and the ensuing production is known as chest voice. On the other hand, when the vocal muscle is relaxed, it is not apt to participate in vibration, a vocal fold configuration that confines the vibrations to the edge of the vocal folds (the vocal ligament), which produces a falsetto sound. The transition from heavy to light register requires a different vocal fold configuration; this is a function of the relaxation of the vocalis muscle which allows the cricothyroid to contract and passively lengthen and thin the vocal folds. [Battaglia Damiani, 2003: 239].

A great number of vocal exercises have been directed towards equalising the sonority of vocal timbre in the various registers and gaining control over the '*note filate*'. As well, these exercises modulate the mezza voce, and regulate the crescendo and decrescendo, and intensity of the sound, releasing contraction of the vocalis in a manner, which does not alter tonality (frequency).

Mixed Register

Having acknowledged both the high and low registers, also known as chest and head register, Battaglia Damiani concedes that many authorities add a third, the medium or mixed register, which mechanical configuration corresponds to the seamless transition or *passaggio* between low and acute register.

The medium or mixed register requires a most perfect level of coordinated, and equilibrated interaction between the thyroarytenoid (vocalis muscle) and cricothyroid.This interaction requires that the contraction of the (TA), the vocalis muscle is gradually released, whilst that of the cricothyroid muscle is progressively increased [Battaglia Damiani, 2003: 239].

Through an intelligent approach and an awareness of available techniques, the singer employs these exercises to ensure an unusually high level of equilibrium. It is the quest for equilibrium and balanced registers that often represents the greatest level of technical difficulty for the artist.

Battaglia Damiani cites Bilancioni as her authority in terms of vocal fold occlusion and medial compression.Bilancioni suggest that during the emission of chest voice, the vocal folds are closed for a period that exceeds 50% of the vibratory cycle; whilst in falsetto register they close for only about 40% of the vibratory cycle. The consequences of the length of vocal fold closure may be heard in the sound, in which the chest register, which has the greater length of closure, produces a much richer bouquet of harmonic partials. Sound quality is also impacted by the general emission of the sound; it can be either *'aperto'* or *'coperto'* (opened or closed). To fully comprehend the significance of these vocal styles, it is important to determine the meaning of the term *'aperto'* or *'coperto'*. These terms refer to the acoustic sensation produced by the sound [Battaglia Damiani, 2003: 240].

Voce aperta (open voice) is characterised by an elevated larynx, a constricted, a base of the tongue that approximates the posterior wall of the pharynx, and an elevated soft palate. Voce coperta, on the other hand, is characterised by a comfortably lower larynx, a more open pharynx, the base of the tongue is further away from the posterior wall of the pharynx, and the soft palate remains in a highly elevated position.In covering the sound, the singer is attempting to find equilibrium in his passaggio notes, *note di passaggio.* These sounds are referred to as being covered because they assume a darker colour. Covered sounds allow us to graduate the muscular action of the extrinsic and intrinsic laryngeal muscles, by calling into action the cricothyroid muscles. Covered sounds are extremely rich in harmonics. If we fail to activate the correct vocal mechanism at the *passaggio* between registers in a timely manner, it will certainly spawn problems at the laryngeal level. When the beginner singer does not yet possess the technique required to impact the *passaggio,* that is, the notes between registers, in particular between the medium and high register, the voice may well develop register breaks [Battaglia Damiani, 2003: 240].

Damiani's big achievement, in terms of registers, is the comprehensive literature review which allows her to extrapolate from previous historical knowledge and register structures.

Damiani begins her literature review with a substantial appraisal of Manuel Patricio García's work on registers.

Damiani addresses a number of theories, including those generated by Juvarra, Fussi, Dupers and Garneau. According to her, an analysis of the selected texts reveals considerable differences, many of which may generate confusion for the student. In such cases a discussion with the teacher who should best know the individual voice of the student with respect to registers would be appropriate. Finally, the student should be conscious of the fact that even though assiduous work and the generation of valid theories is important, there is no escaping individual differences from one singer to another.

Sanchez Carbone on Registers

Sanchez Carbone agrees with Bruno and Paperi that many singers define registers on the basis of the subjective vibrations created by the phenomenon of proprioceptive sensations induced by resonance. Consequently, Sanchez Carbone believes that the low register of the human voice is generally defined by singers as the chest register simply because this type of vocal emission produces proprioceptive sensations around the thoracic cage: that is, 'the superior part of the chest and the inferior part of the neck, provided that it is situated lower than the larynx. These sensations are transmitted towards the thoracic cage through the infra-laryngeal muscles' [Sanchez Carbone, 2005: 289].

The author maintains that generally the vocal timbre in this register, (which is dominated by contraction of the thyroarytenoid muscle), is rich in harmonics yielding an increasing intensity of sound as we ascend the scale and traverse the register. On the other hand, the high register (head register) involves an increased contraction of the cricothyroid and a gradual decrease of the vocalis muscle. The lateral cricoarytenoids (LCA), the posterior cricoarytenoids (PCA), and thyroarytenoids (TA) are all collectively responsible for adduction, abduction, and medial compression. As we proceed in an ascending scale, at some point the voice switches into falsetto the body of the vocal folds (vocalis) is eliminated, which effectively means that the vibrating vocal ligaments do not meet at the midline, there is virtually no phase difference, a closed phase, and on the rare occasion when the vocal ligaments do meet at the midline, they do so with considerable posterior occlusion [Sanchez Carbone, 2005: 288–290].

Sanchez Carbone argues that vocal registers have for long been hotly debated. In every era, theories relating to registers have created disagreement amongst singing teachers with respect to the nature, number, and origin of registers.

Sanchez Carbone believes that laryngeal position is dynamic, exhibiting not only a particular and different position for every register, but also making minute but significant adjustments of its position for every note that comprises that particular register. She considers that this laryngeal position must be maintained irrespective of the varying tension of the vocal folds caused by the increasing and decreasing length of the vocal folds. We have already confirmed that every sound corresponds with a particular laryngeal position (the larynx in entirety, or with the intrinsic muscles of the larynx in particular), but it is also important to stress that the position of the resonators is also critical. It is after all the resonatory system that modifies the vibrating column of air in accordance with the vowel and source frequency (the feedback system (inertial reactance) into the vibrating glottis can be either beneficial or detrimental).

For instance, in the high register the resonator decreases in amplitude in all its direction. This is due to a gradual raising of the larynx, shortening the vocal tract and diminishing the length of the air column. This shortened air column is designed to accommodate the already shortened sound waves. These are not only shorter but also simultaneously increase in number in response to rising frequency. Sanchez Carbone encapsulates the dilemma pertaining to registers, when she asks, 'are vocal registers simply a function of vocal folds configuration or are there supraglottal elements involved (inertial reactance), generated by the adjustment of the vocal tract? According to Sanchez Carbone, up to this point we do not have a satisfactory answer to this question Sanchez Carbone, 2005: 306].

In 1953, however, Van den Berg and Vennard made a film called The Vibrating Larynx, which created a great deal of interest and which went a long way towards clarifying the confusion surrounding many of these issues. The film showed clearly the action of the vocal folds both in the lower thick register and in the higher light or thin register. It demonstrated clearly the changes in vibrating modality between the thick and the thin or light and heavy registers.

With respect to registers, Van den Berg's was able to use the film to conclude the following about chest register:

> In the phonatory position, contraction of the vocalis muscle abducts the glottis and this requires a compensatory medial compression. Furthermore, contraction of the vocalis muscle tends to shorten the glottis and to tilt the thyroid cartilage. With shortening beyond a critical value, this requires a compensatory contraction of the cricothy-

roid muscles, which increases the length of the vocal folds. This increase is limited, however, and length is only slightly increased beyond the resting length or not at all. Therefore, the longitudinal tension in the vocal ligaments remains negligible compared with the longitudinal tension in the vocalis muscle (the body of the vocal folds). The large patterns, large amplitudes and long closure of the glottis during the cycle are thus primarily determined by the body of the vocal folds and not by their margins [Van den Berg in Sanchez Carbone, 2005: 304].

Sanchez Carbone considers that singing is a process of coordination and, if the mechanical response is somewhat deficient, one of the methods of confronting the problem consists of correcting the lack of equilibrium present in the registers.

She is aware also that in the singing voice, the variation of tone is far more important than it is in speaking, and the larynx must be capable of emitting sounds of an extension of 2 or 3 octaves. In fact, a singer that begins an ascending scale in the middle register at a certain point is sure to encounter difficulties with the various characteristics displayed by their sound. These difficulties are due primarily to the various positions adopted by the constituent parts of the vocal mechanism. Above all, in an untrained singer, the quality of theses sounds appears so different from the others that it becomes evident that somehow they must be reunited in a group of their own, because they are similar in nature and quality and are produced by the same laryngeal mechanism.

The theoretical technicians distinguish with the term register that series of consecutive sounds produced by a particular predetermined functionality of the vocal organ in its various parts and their combination.

Registers are therefore represented by a particular laryngeal attitude and vocal fold configuration assumed by the vocal organs in response to the frequency and intensity of the sound. In fact, there is a direct correlation between vibratory frequency and vocal fold length, mass and elasticity [Sanchez Carbone. The variable difference in the length, mass and elasticity of the vocal folds creates a number of sonorous, but differentiated qualities, each quality corresponds to a different but well-defined register [Sanchez Carbone, 2005: 285–286].

Well that may well be, but notwithstanding a lack of definitive evidence with respect to register mechanism, Sanchez Carbone concludes and I concur that registers are essentially determined by the action of the intrinsic laryngeal muscles assisted by a number of neck muscles that are responsible for sustaining the function and structure of the laryngeal musculature. These elements are combined with subglottal pressure, control of breath flow, the coupling of the larynx with supraglottal resonator, and finally the amount of damping of the vocal folds. Damping or posterior occlusion is responsible for diminishing the length and amplitude of the vibratory portion of the vocal folds with increasing frequency [Sanchez Carbone, 2005: 286].

Contemporary theory suggests that more often than not if the singer has a problem with the *passaggio* notes into head voice it can be traced back to the fact that the mixed voice or middle register is too heavy, that is, that there is too much vocalis muscle (too much vocal fold mass) at the expense of cricothyroid contraction, which stretches and thins, and tenses the vocal folds and the more specifically the vocal ligament. The remedy for this problem is to release the tension on the vocalis muscles (medial part of the thyroarytenoid), allowing the cricothyroid to stretch the vocal folds, a process that creates longitudinal tension. By starting with a comfortable head voice and the right antagonistic balance between vocalis and cricothyroid contraction, the vocal folds are sufficiently stretched whilst simultaneously reducing their mass and forming a greater connection between the vocal fold body and cover. In this manner, the singer can educate the intrinsic muscles of the larynx to produce the appropriate vocal fold configuration in order to negotiate the difficult *passaggio* notes. This can be particularly difficult in some male voices. The singer should start vocalising around a B♭ for high voices and around a G or an F for lower voices, and gradually descend with the same quality. It will not be possible to retain the initial configuration, nor is it desirable because vocal fold adjustment needs to remain flexible and dynamic, but the sheer effort of trying to retain a similar quality will not only educate the laryngeal and breathing muscles, but will also be artistically rewarding [Talia, 2017: 132–133].

Fussi and Magnani enlighten us as to the laryngeal position and the 'passaggio'. These authors separate the 'passaggio' phenomenon into primo and secondo 'passaggio', suggesting that we should note that as we move from chest, to mixed register and then head register, there is a considerable difference in quality between registers. This is due mainly to increasing glottal tension, a gradually ascending larynx, and the characteristics imparted by the resonator. With respect to laryngeal position, Fussi and Magnani found that in an ascending passage from the lowest to the highest notes of the scale, the position of the larynx rises progressively until the change of registers (Passaggio). At which this point it descends a little, only to rise again as it ascends into 'head register' [Fussi & Magnani, 1994: 102–103].

Chest Register

Sanchez Carbone maintains that chest register is more important in the male than it is in the female voice, only because it occupies two thirds of the extension or the male range, whereas in the female the situation is reversed, that is, the female executes only one third of her extension in chest voice, whilst the remaining two thirds is executed in mixed head voice (register) [Sanchez Carbone, 2005: 306].

In using the chest mechanism to emit the high notes, the laryngeal and cervical muscles are tensed, and subglottal pressure becomes very important producing an elevated intensity of tone.

High Register

In proceeding to the high register with the same mechanism, the singer becomes aware of certain difficulties, including a sudden and unplanned change into falsetto. Sanchez Carbone contends that the high register is characterised by thin, long and tense vocal folds, produced by the stretching action of the cricothyroids combined with medial compression produced by the lateral cricoarytenoid (LCA), and the thyroarytenoid (TA) muscles, and the antagonistic abductor muscle, the posterior cricoarytenoid (PCA). It is worth recalling that Miller (1996) informs us that when the vocal folds achieve a full and sharp abduction (PCA), the adduction that follows is naturally firmer and more complete. This mechanical process of singing an ascending passage is designed to decrease the contraction of the thyroarytenoid whilst gradually increasing the contraction of the cricothyroid muscles, allowing the (LCA) to loosen its adduction creating greater swing or amplitude. Although such increases are not necessarily synchronised with increased levels of frequency [Miller, 1996: 25].

Such discrepancies derive from the capacity of the vocal organ to produce a variety of very different and contrasting sound qualities determined by a number of factors. Amongst the most important are the temperament of the singer, the dimension, the form, the condition and mechanical response of the vocal organ, depending on the change of vowel sounds or intensity.

Medium Register

Within the polarity represented by the two principal registers which corresponds to the two principal vibratory modalities, that is, either heavy or chest register which is dominated by activity of the thyroarytenoids, or the high and falsetto register, which is dominated by the activity of the cricothyroids, there is a third vibratory modal: one that is born from the admixture of these two extremes. We are referring to the so-called medium or mixed register, which is generally considered a separate register: a register in which the thyroarytenoid and cricothyroid muscles perform a delicate antagonistic dance aimed at balance.

Vennard confirms that the mixed register is the result of the combined action of the cricothyroids which produce the falsetto register, and the vocalis muscle which produces the chest register. The interaction of these two muscle groups is not only responsible for blending registers but also for the execution of the *passaggio*. Consequently, Vennard believes that the *passaggio* between these two registers is controlled by the contraction of the cricothyroid (CT) on the one hand and the antagonistic actions (TA), which is the register controlling muscle par excellence, on the other. These combine with the antagonistic action of the (LCA) lateral cricoarytenoid (adductor), the (PCA) posterior cricoarytenoid (abductor) and the cricothyroid (CT) muscles (stretcher).

On the question of vocal registers, Sanchez Carbone states that Hirano, throws considerable light by studying the physiologically and histological characteristics of the vocal folds. Each vocal fold is constituted by three distinct layers, each comprised of a particular texture and with very different mechanical properties. These layers have come to be known as the cover, the transition, and the body of the folds (vocalis). That is, the mucus membrane, and vocal ligament immediately below, the lamina propria, and connective tissue, and the body of the vocal folds which is comprised of the vocalis muscle [Sanchez Carbone, 2005:307].

The above is correct as far as it goes, but I feel that an elaboration is required. It is true that Hirano maintains that the vocal folds are not uniform but rather a layered structure, which is quite different to other instruments. This is how he describes each of the five layers:

1. The vocal fold is comprised of a thin epithelium capsule. Below the epithelium we find the three layers of the lamina propria.

2. The first layer is referred to as the superficial layer, or Reinke's space, which is a gelatinous matrix, permitting the epithelium to glide over the vocal ligament. Hirano believes that this loose fibrous component is not only the most pliable but also the most important for the singing voice, simply because if any of this layer becomes stiff, the singer is in danger of losing the professional sound.

3. The intermediate layer is comprised chiefly of elastic fibres that resemble something like soft rubber bands.

4. The deep layer of the lamina propria consists primarily of collagenous fibres that resemble cotton thread. The intermediate and deep layers of the lamina propria combine to form the vocal ligament.

5. Underneath the lamina propria, according to Hirano, we find the vocalis muscles, the main body of the vocal fold. When this muscle contracts, it may be regarded as a bundle of stiff rubber bands [Hirano, 1988, 52].

Hirano then proceeds to break this then to the cover body model, which can also be very useful in terms of the impact the body has on the tension or lack thereof on the cover.

Following this interesting deviation, which undoubtedly enriches our understanding of registers and makes greater sense of the elaboration of the body/cover paradigm, let us return to Sanchez Carbone. She contends that normally when we contract the cricothyroid muscles, the entire vocal muscle is extended, including the mucus membrane and the vocal ligament. This is the result of the longitudinal stretching (tension) of the striated muscle strands that constitute the vocalis. On the other hand, when the (TA) muscle is contracted we note a shortening off and an increase in the thickness of the thyroarytenoid (TA), which is in direct relationship with the intensity of the sound being produced. Moderate contraction of the vocalis muscle, combined with a small pressure, releases the tension in the intermediate muscle fibres, which will also release and relax the cover.

Hirano found that when the vocalis muscle was observed to dominate the cricothyroid, the vocal fold cover was seen to be flexible in its movement, when the cricothyroid muscles dominated the vocalis, the vocal folds were stretched and tensed, thereby producing the higher register. (Let us clarify that these higher notes are still in modal register, engaging the vocalis muscle, and not falsetto. Falsetto is generally characterised by a complete disengagement of the vocalis muscle, leaving only the vocal ligaments to vibrate. It was also observed that the vocal ligaments do not meet at the midline, there was an absence of vertical phase, and therefore mucosal wave. In many cases, there was also considerable posterior occlusion.

On the other hand, contraction of vocalis muscle shortens, thickens and rounds the vocal folds, producing the lower register. In this register the vocal folds adduct completely and for a long percentage of every vibratory cycle, thereby creating a mucosal wave.

Mixed Register

In the mixed register, contraction of the thyroarytenoid (TA) dominates the cricothyroids, which offer very little resistance to either the thyroarytenoid (TA) or the air current. Consequently, there is very little tension on the vocal ligament. In the execution of an ascending scale, the tension on the vocal muscle gradually increases. The amplitude of the vocal folds ensures that they execute a full excursion away from the midline, whilst vibrating in all their length and thickness.

The contraction of the thyrovocalis is limited to the position fibres of the vocalis. The opening and closing of the vocal folds begins at the inferior edges.

As we ascend the scale in this register we experience the increased contraction of the thyroarytenoids, which are aided by the antagonistic actin of the cricothyroid (CT), and the adductory action of the (LCA), and (IA), all of which offer greater glottal resistance to the airflow. Critical in maximising the effect is the correct laryngeal position, which leads to an appropriate adjustment of the resonators.

On the other hand, in the high register the action of the thyroarytenoids is no longer the dominant partner but rather increasingly more equal with the antagonist contraction of the (CT), whilst the (IA), and (LCA) work to adduct the vocal folds. As we ascend the scale, the (TA) begins to relax, giving way to an increased contraction of the (CT) muscle. The free margins of the vocal folds are very thin and in contact with each other at the midline. Van den Berg suggests that:

> In this register, the longitudinal forces in the vocal ligaments are no longer negligible compared to those of the vocalis muscle, but are rather of the same order of magnitude. To achieve this, the contraction of the vocalis must be submaximal, because these muscles are antagonistic to the cricothyroid muscles which passively stretch the vocal folds and thus the vocal ligaments. This adjustment requires a somewhat stronger contraction of the interarytenoid muscles and a medial compression beyond a minimal level, otherwise the glottis becomes too wide, and the vocal folds cannot be thrown into vibration by the air. In this register, the vibratory patterns are determined by the body of the vocal folds and their margins [Van den Berg in Sanchez Carbone, 2005: 305].

In fact, in the emission of the high notes only the vocal ligaments are set into vibration, thereby producing the falsetto voice. It could be said that the muscular fascicles of the vocal folds are almost excluded from the phonatory act, allowing only the margins to be set into vibration.

The contraction of the thyroarytenoid vocalis is confined to the anterior portion of the vocal folds.

The closure of the glottis is brief, small and incomplete as a result of the considerable tension on the vocal folds; suffice to say that the opening of the glottis is shortened and eventually reduced to the anterior part of the vocal folds (interligamental), whilst the posterior part (intercartilaginous) remains closed, as a result of the contraction of the LCA and the thyrovocalis [Sanchez Carbone, 2005: 305].

During an ascending scale, only the elliptical fissure of the glottis moves forward, causing an increased contraction of the CT muscle.

In the production of the high register the only portion set into vibration refers to the muscular fibres inserted into the anterior part of the vocal folds.

The sound emitted in this register possesses few harmonics partials. Consequently, every increase in frequency brings about a major increase in tension of the LCA, PCA and CT, and vocalis muscles.

The combined action of these elements influences the physical adduction, whilst also rendering the vocal folds longer, thinner and capable of supporting a major tension:

Registers are determined by the intrinsic laryngeal muscles, which are in turn influenced by some neck muscles involved in supporting the laryngeal muscles, as well as subglottal pressure, airflow, and the coupling of the vocal source with the supraglottal resonators. Registers are also a function of the level of damping that determines the length and amplitude of the part of the vocal fold set into vibration as a result of the pressure applied to the vocal folds by an elevated frequency [Sanchez Carbone, 2005: 306].

For the singer, it is important to know how and when this regulatory mechanism of the vocal folds takes place – that is, exactly where in the extension of this scale this change occurs. If this change occurs in a rough or brusque manner, the singer will manifest a variety of different voices. A good singing teacher is charged with the responsibility of correcting these disorders by demonstrating to the singer how to overcome these breaks at the *passaggio* between registers, leading to the impression of having one register with sounds of equal quality but of different frequency. The activity of the vocalis muscle, (the medial part of the thyroarytenoid), is of primary importance, since if it does as not release its tension whilst the cricothyroids contract, we will find an excessive muscular antagonism and therefore the regulation of these muscles becomes rough, sudden and uncontrolled, leading to a break in the voice.

When a singer pushes the chest voice too high towards the upper register, it will bring about an excessive tension in the vocal muscles and the singer brings a heavy register into the high register where the light register should obtain. This produces vocal strain, muscular fatigue, and in the end, may cause nodules in the vocal folds [Sanchez Carbone, 2005: 308].

Sanchez Carbone is very thorough in every aspect of the myoelastic/ aerodynamic theory of vocal fold vibrations, as well as each of the registers and strategies for their equalising.

Conclusions to Register

The ancient Italians believed in a two-register paradigm, that is, chest and falsetto or head register. This paradigm is not unlike the one supported by vocal scientists today, which centres around modal register and falsetto. The big difference is that for the ancient Italians falsetto began at the passaggio on G natural or A flat, the modern version teaches us that modal register is constituted by a series of notes ranging from chest to head voice, or voce *plena in testa*, a range that engages the vocalis muscle, which is the mechanism associated with the modal register. In this scenario, the falsetto register which utilises a very different mechanism begins on D flat above top C5. Falsetto is the result of a very different mechanism, involving only the edges of the vocal folds and not the body. Generally, the vocalis muscle drops off at the top C5, leaving the mechanism to experience an incomplete closure of the vocal folds and a gradual posterior occlusion. This is a process in which the vocal folds are gradually and firmly occluded posteriorly, preventing that particular section from vibrating. There some cases of falsetto in which the vocal folds refuse to adduct altogether, creating a breathy, veiled falsetto.

These basic models spawned a number of others paradigms, many of which included up to six or seven registers such as lower thick, higher thick, lower medium and higher medium registers followed by lower thin and higher thin, and falsetto or whistle register. García created further confusion by renaming the female medium register as the female falsetto. Fortunately, and notwithstanding the confusion, modern masters have found an accommodation which comprises the chest register, followed by mixed register (which is comprised of chest and head register) and the head register above. The falsetto register in the male and the whistle register in the female are located above. Even with the extensive knowledge of registers available in the 21st century, the blending of registers can still be problematic.

Modern teachers have essentially settled on two major strategies: the first strategy is the one utilised by the ancient singing masters, involving the preparation of the instrument for the blending of registers. In this strategy, the passaggio was prepared by a minor adjustment of the intrinsic laryngeal muscles, accompanied by slight rise of the laryngeal mechanism and a rounding of the vowel. The other technique for managing the passaggio is the one that is most prevalent today especially in the more dramatic repertoire. The technique referred to here is the *copertura* technique which involves the lowering of the larynx and the expansion of the pharynx.

Chapter 17

Vocal Onset in the Modern Italian School

Sanchez Carbone is scientifically speaking the most up-to-date of our contemporary Italian authors, but in her monumental (2005) book *La Voce Arcana*, she also displays a good knowledge and good sense of history. Sanchez Carbone contends that every vocal (school) technique has paid attention either directly or indirectly to the position assumed by the vocal folds before the emission of sound. The existence of such a prephonatory position has been confirmed by electromyography, that is, by monitoring the electric activity of the relevant muscles.

In addition, she agrees with Mori (1970) and Juvarra (1987) on two points with respect to vocal onset: (1) the importance of onset to the long-term health of the voice; and (2) the decisive effect that different types of onset have on the ensuing vocal emission. She believes that the attack of the sound 'is decisive in maintaining freedom and relaxation for the whole duration of phonation.' Consequently, it must be said that the way in which the sound is initiated and launched 'is extremely important because it conditions all of the successive emission' [Sanchez Carbone, 2005: 236].

A substantial review of prominent Italian writers on singing over the last 50 years reveals two important findings: (1) that there is agreement amongst them with respect to important issues pertaining to vocal onset; (2) that with few exceptions, Italian pedagogues have an entirely different and more holistic approach to the issue of vocal onset than their English-speaking counterparts.

The first issue where we find broad agreement is that the attack or onset is generally regarded as probably the most difficult and troubling issue to address, let alone teach.

Two general difficulties have been identified. The first is learning how to teach onset in a holistic manner, which involves not only the attack at the vocal folds, but also breathing, resonance, the singer's temperament and psychological and emotional state, and the repertoire to be performed;

The second problem relates to language. Too often the language to describe the 'onset' or 'attack', as the Italians call it, is at best inadequate and at worst confusing. In fact, in terms of confusion 'the onset' is only marginally less controversial than that other rather vexing issue of singing, 'vocal registers'. This applies to both nomenclature and execution.

Mori regards the attack as obtaining its start from the cerebral impulse that regulates the elements responsible for producing the sound. This, she contends, requires a supreme act of concentration on behalf of the singer if he or she is to coordinate the mental and muscular forces required to balance the rhythmic elasticities of the subglottal and supraglottal pressures [Mori, 1970: 63].

Nanda Mari agrees and contends that the problem of the attack has its roots in various issues, including an excessive breath pressure, and a high level of mental distraction, leading to an attack which is characterised by scooping instead of a decisive and precise attack. This type of attack is characterised by 'a lack of mental concentration, a failure to open the throat, and paucity of good breath management' [Mari, 1975: 69].

Sanchez Carbone adds her considerable knowledge by stating that the difficulty with teaching the vocal attack lies in the fact that 'the sensations we attach to it are altogether subjective. It is a matter of eliciting a muscular function over which we have no conscious control from the very beginning. Consequently, we risk either using too much muscular contraction (adduction), thereby producing a throaty attack, or too little adduction and thereby produce a breathy or false voice. Beyond this the vocal attack demands (a) particular care because it is the prelude to a more intense and prolonged muscular action' [Sanchez Carbone, 2005: 236].

Therefore, it can be seen that Sanchez Carbone (2005), Mori (1970), and Mari (1975), all conclude that every attack consists of two elements: the mental and the physical. In addition, Bruno and Paperi (2001) also add their considerable voices with respect to the mental and physical elements of onset. Let us examine their thoughts below:

Bruno and Paperi suggest that prior to vocal onset, the singer should form a habit to reclaim a mental concentration such as would grant him the opportunity to simultaneously consider both technical and emotional issues. At the moment of inspiration, the larynx, the tongue, the palate and the pharynx all adopt a certain posture that is determined by the mental preparation with respect to the frequency to be sung, the mental concept of the sound, the vowel to be sung, and the expressive content of the phrase to be sung [Bruno & Paperi, 2001: 104].

Bruno and Paperi exhort the student to use her imagination and creativity in order to develop a vivid mental concept of their own personal sound world. This imagined sound world is a function the physical state of the instrument and the mental/physiological approach to vocal onset.

Bruno and Paperi (2001) also recommend the mental and physical preparation of the instrument before attacking the tone. They contend that in substance the vocal folds are subjected to a double stimulus: the first refers to the cortical command and the second to the pressure exerted by the entire column of air [Bruno & Paperi, 2001: 103].

Sanchez Carbone argues cogently that the mental and physical elements required for good singing are generally combined. She contends that:

> At the beginning of each emission these two elements are virtually synthesized, because at a certain point in time one becomes the expression of the other. Before the vocal attack the vocal organs are in a state of general relaxation. Their only function up to this moment was that of respiration [Sanchez Carbone, 2005: 236].

Even all of the above mental and physical preparation, however, is insufficient for the Italians, who traditionally included posture, breathing and preparation of the articulators as part of the attack. The new breed of Italian masters, such as Mori (1970), Mar1 (1975), Juvarra (1987), Bruno and Paperi (2001), and Sanchez Carbone (2005), all seem to go further in their preparation for vocal attack. They now include such elements as 'priming the instrument', 'timing and coordination', 'apnea or suspension', and finding the natural 'resonance focal points'.

Prephonatory Preparation, Breathing and Focal Points

Bruno and Paperi contend that the best technique for priming the instrument is to assume a position 'similar to a yawn'. This, they inform us, is the position in which the antagonistic breathing muscles, aided by a firm adduction of the vocal folds produce an optimal subglottal pressure, which the singer perceives as a container of compressed air at his/her disposal. This they contend is a suitable preparation for the firm attack of the sound, which should not be allowed to deteriorate into either a 'dry attack' or García's controversial *coup de glotte* [Bruno & Paperi, 2001: 103]. Commenting on Bruno and Paperi's reservations about the dry attack, I can say that it is perfectly understandable. This refers to the type of attack in which the breath is so compressed that insufficient breath is allowed to flow through the vocal folds. Consequently, there is no breath cushion between the vocal folds, resulting in a pressed and dry attack.

Their reference to the *coup de glotte* is less understandable because they are all for the *coup de glotte* with respect to staccato and other ornamentation, but seem to be against this type of onset when followed by a sustained sound.

I can only conclude that this position is conditioned by ignorance and fear. How can it be safe to use the coup de glotte on 20 consecutive staccatos and picchettati tones in a few seconds and then imagine that it is dangerous to execute one 'medium hard attack' followed by a twenty-second beautiful legato line before you have to execute another *coup de glotte?*

On the other hand, Juvarra (1987) believes that too often the element of disturbance that invades the moment of onset is caused by incorrect mental preparation, in which the dominant thought is conditioned by the idea that we must employ a different and distinct vocal attack for singing than we normally do for speaking. Juvarra contends that this is not the case, declaring that at the laryngeal level the attack for singing must be natural and relaxed and similar to that employed for speaking. Obviously, at the beginning this is only possible in the middle voice and consequently that should be our starting point [Juvarra, 1987: 65].

In this instance, I respectfully disagree with Juvarra. I don't believe that the type of onset he advocates is an appropriate attack throughout the scale, with different levels of intensity and in all styles of singing, nor with all personality types. This, for me, represents too narrow a view of vocal attack, one which is not only prescriptive, but also unnecessarily cautious. The type of attack recommended by Juvarra is related to speech and therefore only appropriate to 'cantar parlando' or *'speech level recitative'*. It is not appropriate for either the high register or at great intensity.

I personally believe that if the timing and coordination of the execution are well synchronised much of the muscular contraction will adjust itself to the naturally appropriate level and there is no need for such an inflexible and overly prescriptive attitude. The truth is that vocal attack will alter to accommodate not only pitch, intensity and register, but also musical style and characterisation. The singer's temperament and psychology also play a part in vocal attack. Finally, it must be remembered that greater vocal adduction is accompanied by greater breath pressure. It is therefore not appropriate to suggest that the spoken attack is relevant to singing outside of a very small range of pitch and intensity.

Finally, I remind the reader that the vocal folds adduct more firmly, creating more glottal resistance as we ascend the scale; consequently, they are naturally much firmer for the high register relative to the middle. Consequently, we must conclude that no matter how relaxed one might be, or how mentally and emotionally tranquil one may feel, you will still require more breath energy to overcome the natural increase in glottal resistance.

With that in mind, I believe it is desirable to explore those most important elements of singing: physical and mental coordination, timing and coordination, 'apnea' or suspension, and resonance focal points. We will now elaborate on each of these in turn before addressing the Italians' view on the different types of attack.

To begin, Bruno and Paperi contend that before the attack, the singer should cultivate 'the habit of mental concentration that allows the coordination of both technical and emotional affects.' This prephonatory phase is followed by an emission of the sound that benefits enormously from being guided towards 'a good focal point for the arrival of the sound (face, zygomatic arch, or forehead). If this focal point is properly understood and assisted by an appropriate breath, it will serve to attenuate the excessive attention that is often placed on the larynx at the time of the attack' [Bruno & Paperi, 2001: 104].

According to Bruno and Paperi, it is the coordination of the cortical command with the pressure on the air column that forges a balanced relationship between 'the breath, the correct glottal resistance and the appropriate adjustment of the resonators. It is thus that the sound and the word are literally formed not only by the vocal folds, the larynx, the tongue and the soft palate, but also by a free and suitable jaw articulation; it should permit us to guide the sound with its expressive content right up to our favourite focal point' [Bruno & Paperi, 2001: 103].

This last idea, that is, the brilliant notion of creating a synthesis between separate elements of vocal technique and combining them with the psychological and emotional elements, all the while encouraging the resulting proprioceptive and sympathetic vibrations towards a singular focal point, does not originate with Bruno and Paperi. Nor did it originate with Rachele Mori (1970) whose great contribution to singing was the dissemination of this vocal synthesis into a facial focal point throughout Italy and Europe, some 40 years ago. The idea of focal points was first popularised by Lilli Lehmann and Giovanni Battista Lamperti, at the turn of the 19th century. Originally it was designed as a useful guide, providing the student with a general idea as to where the sympathetic vibrations may be felt to impinge at different pitches and with different vowels. Lamperti generalised correctly that the student should guide the middle voice against the zygomatic arch and face, whilst the head voice was more appropriately aimed towards the front part of the head, but not as far forward as the forehead. It was Lilli Lehmann who took this idea to ridiculous lengths and in an altogether too inflexible and prescriptive a manner. Mori's greatest influence, however, was not Giovanni Lamperti, nor Lilli Lehmann, but rather a García scholar, Herman Klein whom she cites at length. The following is what Klein wrote in 1923:

> The solution of the problem lies in uniformity — uniformity of breathing, of 'singing position', of resonance — the last is perhaps the most important. So long as the voice is securely reflected in its ultimate forward position and is sustained there by the breath, supported from the diaphragm, the vocal cords will enjoy the elasticity and freedom essential for modifying their action, without that sudden change or 'break' which is commonly heard [Klein, 1923: 29].

Mori was too intelligent and intuitive not to immediately understand the importance of the synthesis of so many vocal principles embodied in Klein's brilliant synthesis of vocal ideals. Having understood the value of this synthesis, she then assimilated it into her own teaching before disseminating it in the Italian literature.

Mori reminds us that the singer has at her disposal a variable and infinitely flexible resonator towards which she can direct the expiratory column of air. These flexible but subjective resonating points are very different to the fixed resonator applicable to most man-made instruments. They are also very different to the objective *appoggio* which is constituted by diaphragmatic breathing.

Mori argues that the expiratory column of air finds its base primarily in the *appoggio* provided by the elastic resistance of the expiratory muscles, that is, the diaphragm, the abdominal girdle, and thorax. However, in order to become vocally significant, Mori tells us that the column of air must find an equally valid and opposite pole of resistance at a variable place within the resonance cavity. It is only when the sound is reflected in the most appropriate but subjective angle that it becomes resonance efficient. Consequently, it may be concluded that if the singer is to attack the sound in an efficient and healthy manner, he must incorporate a stable focal point known in the Italian school as the *appoggio* of the sound, and this focal point will vary with pitch, vowel and register. This ultimate focal point towards which the voice is directed is also influenced by education, taste, and style, all of which create a fluid and complex problem, for both vocal pedagogues and phonetic scientists.

These varied and subjective focal points include aiming the soundwaves towards the head, the sinuses, the mask and the back of the neck, which Mori refers to as the 'nuca' [Mori, 1970: 69–70]. Coincidentally, this last focal point was one of Caruso's favourite focal points.

In this context, Mori cites the phonetic scientist Wicart, who asserts that the *appoggio* of the 'resonance focal point' is subjective, whilst the *appoggio* of the diaphragm is objective.

Wicart explains that diaphragmatic *appoggio* is obtained through deep breathing, resulting in a dilation of the abdomen and tracheal pull. In this type of breathing, we inflate the abdominal area before cleanly stopping inspiration and then emitting the sound whilst maintaining the inflated and expanded abdominal position as long as possible. This is in line with Lamperti's exhortation to remain in the inspiratory position as long as possible. The only difference is that Lamperti also incorporates the thorax and lower ribs in his breathing strategy. Diaphragmatic breathing alone is not sufficient, nor is it muscularly balanced.

Mori then proceeds to explore a different and earlier system of breath management, which according to her involved a retraction of the abdomen, whilst dilating the base of the thorax. This system of breath management which was discussed earlier in the Mengozzi chapter corresponds to what García, Lehmann, or Bonnier referred to as the '*sostegno* system' of breath management, which they defined as *sostegno* based on lower costal breathing. This system of breath management is characterised by a high chest and expanded lower costals but without either hardening the chest or exerting undue breath pressure. This type of breathing has the added advantages of accessing the lower pharyngeal resonator and inducing a natural and stable diaphragmatic position [Mori, 1970: 70].

This system was discussed at length, and the following is meant only to serve as a reminder of this time-honoured traditional system. The *sostegno* system we recall was characterised by 'the retraction of the abdomen, the dilation of the thorax, the stable and natural position adopted by the diaphragm, and the lowering of the trachea' (tracheal pull), all of which according to Mori favour 'the opening of the lower resonance cavity' [Mori, 1970: 70]. The old Italians knew about the resonance advantages ensuing from 'tracheal pull' the way sound is initiated but they generally didn't speak too much about resonance.

Having discussed the three important objective elements of *appoggio*, that is, diaphragmatic *appoggio* and *sostegno*, which are generally agreed to be objective, and the subjective *appoggio* associated with resonance 'focal points', we are now in a position to examine another important element of the vocal attack: timing and coordination.

Prephonatory Preparation: Timing and Coordination

With respect to the timing of the vocal attack, Bruno and Paperi perfectly understand its critical importance to a good and healthy vocal onset. They exhort the singer to cultivate the habit of allowing the briefest possible time between the breath pressure impinging at the vocal folds and the release of the breath through the glottis, the pulses of which create the primary sound.

Following a brief suspension of the breath, which Mori (1970), Bruno and Paperi (2001) and Sanchez Carbone (2005) refer to as an '*apnea*', and which Mori defines as '*a brief moment of the suspension of the breath flow*' accumulating under the vocal folds, the breath must be allowed to burst through the resistance of the vocal folds without further interference, ensuring what *Titze* refers to as its convergent, divergent journey through the vocal folds, which is in fact the means by which the vocal folds attain *self-sustained* oscillation. Any attempt to prolong the closed phase of the vocal cycle, according to Mori, will not only create tension at the glottis but also unnecessary breath pressure, which will then burst forth, creating a violent plosive attack as opposed to *'the incisive, neat and clean attack'* described by García with respect to the *'coup de glotte'.*

Bruno and Paperi concur with Mori when they advocate the following:

> We are of the opinion that unless there is a specific dynamic indication, the anticipation of the vocal onset must be very brief, even after a long breath, and the sound produced must not be either too hard, nor too lacking in energy so as to appear relaxed (morbido).
>
> It is for this reason that there must be no negative muscular interference either upon the vocal folds or the muscles of adduction, but rather a coordinated and balanced action beginning with the sostegno: in this manner, the image of the sound visualized before the attack will be more easily transferred to the larynx [Bruno & Paperi, 2001: 104–105].

Ideal Onset Begins With Apnea

According to Sanchez Carbone and Mori the ideal attack must be preceded by a slow and ample nasal inspiration followed by 'a very brief physiological apnea', which aids with adequate muscular preparation of the sound to be emitted in combination with a brief prephonatory and momentary closure of the vocal folds, acting in opposition to the airflow. If this attack is well executed it will result in a neat, clear, incisive adduction free of tension.

This brings us to another important issue to be addressed and this pertains to the central idea often referred to in the literature as *'Apnea'*, which has already been touched on. Apnea is also the beginning of the physiological, psychological and mental synthesis which converges into one single act, manifesting itself as 'the vocal attack'. This takes place at the moment the air accumulates under the vocal folds building subglottal pressure and then bursting through the glottis setting the vocal folds into vibration.

In my view, this is an idea that demands elaboration and further clarification. I personally like Mori's definition of apnea.

Mori refers to *'apnea'* as that instant of suspension of 'expectant attention' that precedes every attack conceived with intense concentration and is 'noted by very good orchestral conductors and practiced by excellent interpreters as a means of controlling the attack. This is often achieved almost without conscious realization'. According to Mori, 'To avail oneself of the "apnea" before the principal attack serves not only the mental and emotive concentration, but also as a means of gauging the space to be confronted and the gap to be bridged, that is, the quantity of energy required for the dynamic launch necessary for the development of the phrase…' [Mori, 1970: 29].

Lest we believe that 'apnea' on its own is sufficient, Mori also reminds us that there are, in all, four elements that are indispensable to producing a good attack:

- The first element is that the attack must be preceded by a slow, ample respiration through the nose.

- This full breath must be followed by the 'apnea' that is, as already stated, 'a brief moment of suspension of the breath' (this refers to a brief moment of suspension when the singer is neither inhaling nor exhaling).

- The act of bringing into conscious memory the image of a well-established sound sensation.

- The establishment of the indispensable stabilisation of the larynx (this point follows directly from the second: suspension of the lowered breath) [Mori, 1970: 64].

Psychological Aspects of Vocal Attack

As we saw above, Bruno and understand perfectly well the importance of the physical aspects of vocal attack. They do not, however, believe that addressing the physical aspects of vocal attack is in itself sufficient. Consequently, these authors suggest that to attain a good vocal attack, the student should dedicate him/herself to acquiring a technique that depends not just on the general state of health but also takes account of the mental and psychological state of mind. Bruno and Paperi go further, placing emphasis 'more on the psychological than the physiological state, removing all negative mental and emotional resistance' [Bruno & Paperi, 2001:105].

Sanchez Carbone concurs, believing that 'the personality and the psychological state of the singer or speaker may have an effect upon the muscular activity of the larynx' [Sanchez Carbone, 2005: 236].

Conclusions to the Italian Approach

In conclusion, it is clear that the Italians have a more holistic approach with respect to vocal onset.

They accept three types of onset, but they consider the two extreme versions, that is, the 'breathy' and the 'hard' onset as being unsuitable for sustained elite vocalism.

On the other hand, and in solidarity with their English counterparts, Italian authors have also arrived at a great level of consensus with respect to the soft or coordinated onset. In general, there is also a great level of support for the *'coup de glotte'* with respect to virtuosic, bel canto floral and coloratura vocalism, and also for the execution of the verismo repertoire.

From a technique point of view, these authors are apt to address more broadly the impact of breathing strategy and subglottal pressure on vocal attack; they also give greater consideration to supraglottal events, including more general use of resonating focal points.

They seem to have a greater reluctance to separate the vocal trinity of the instrument: breath, source and resonance. However, whereas in the English literature much of the emphasis is on the firmness of glottal closure, the Italians place more value on the timing of the onset. They believe that the longer the glottis remains closed before release the greater the expulsion. Consequently, for a soft and smooth onset, the subglottal pressure should be directed through the folds almost simultaneously with their closure.

Artistically, they seem to understand that whilst the soft attack is the safest, the 'coup de glotte' is very important to the execution of virtuosic singing. This includes trills, staccatos, picchettati and other virtuosic ornaments. They also consider that the *'coup de glotte'*, which they often and mistakenly use synonymously with the 'hard attack', is more desirable for the Verismo repertoire and the depiction of certain characters.

They also place much greater value on the importance of mental preparation, which they believe induces a more precise and natural physical response.

Finally, the Italians believe that the singer's psychological state of mind and personality traits play a large part in the muscular response during vocal attack.

Conclusions

Vocal onset is one of the most important and controversial issues in singing, not only historically but even still today. I hope that this study has revealed and enlightened my reader with the facts about the *coup de glotte*, because it is only by demystifying the so-called secrets of the great masters that we can confront our problems with energy and confidence. In so doing, we can fulfil our true potential without using fear and personal prejudice as an excuse for failing to fulfil our artistic destiny.

Finally, I believe that at a time when pop singers and Broadway crossover singers, and classical singers such as Pavarotti, Freni, Caballe, Sutherland and more recently Placido Domingo are or were all singing into their late sixties and seventies, and sports medicine is making unprecedented demands on our athletes, it is no longer acceptable for classical singers and singing teachers to be jumping at shadows. As we saw in our brief examination of the vocal fold structure, the vocal folds are well equipped to manage the everyday demands made on them with respect to healthy vocalism. The evidence is that the vocal instrument if properly used is tremendously resilient, so singers need to get on with what they are paid to do, sing. If they are not sure as to whether they are on the right track, they should find a mentor who knows his/her business and be guided by them. Thanks to the works of the Old Masters, and that of our contemporary vocal scientists, we now have sufficient real knowledge to bring our gifts to fruition without too much guesswork. Remember that nobody succeeds on their own so surround yourself with the best people you can find in the different aspects of our art. As for the rest, the world is littered with great voices that never come to fruition because their owners either settle for second best or are too arrogant to ask for help. Either way, there is no particular virtue in being the owner of an excellent gift that has never been brought to fruition.

Voice Quality Ensuing From Vocal Onset

Having provided an analysis, and I hope also a defence, of García's *'coup de glotte'*, all that is left for us to remember is that the vocal onset has an influence far beyond just the onset of sound; it is actually a great and accurate determinant of the ensuing sostenuto sound. According to Ingo Titze (1994), each of the three vocal onsets discussed is associated with a particular muscular glottal setting, and each of these glottal settings is responsible for a certain quality of sound, ranging from breathy to pressed vocalisation.

To summarise then, there is great support amongst singing teachers and scientists for a model of attack consisting of three different types of onsets, each being the prelude to a particular kind of sound. The first amongst these acceptable qualities, according to Gauffin and Sundberg (1989), is the breathy tone:

- Breathy singing results from an incomplete adduction of the vocal folds; that is, an adduction in which the vocal folds never close completely. Consequently, part of the breath escapes with the sound, making it breathy and hooty, resulting in a 'rounded glottal pulse' that emphasises the lower harmonics on the spectrum at the expense of the 'higher spiked ones';

- The second quality or mode of phonation is flow phonation in which the vocal folds combine a complete glottal closure with the highest amplitude possible, even when compared to speech mode. This mode of vocalisation is very efficient as it still converts all of the breath to tone without the wastefulness of the breathy mode, but it does so with a fairly loose glottal setting, preventing rigidity and allowing maximum amplitude to take place, resulting in the most economical and efficient aerodynamic to acoustic energy conversion, and a gain of energy (volume) in the vicinity of 12 dBs. This sounds like an excellent glottal setting, except that quite often the sound reveals a high level of breath admixture with deleterious consequences for the purity of sound.

- The third quality or mode of vocal fold vibration is pejoratively known as pressed vocalisation, mainly because, according to Callaghan, it produces the type of tone that misguided singers use when they require increased loudness, brightness, or excitement (this quality is associated with a tight, metallic sound, often bordering on the shrill). This type of vocalisation, according to Gauffin and Sundberg (1989), combines high subglottal pressure with a high level of vocal fold adduction, resulting in a low amplitude glottal pulse, and a tight production. I agree with Callaghan, she is absolutely right in her assessment. This is the type of sound which is only used by misguided singers who believe that they are producing a more voluminous and brilliant sound. However, the opposite is true, because this type of tight sound does not have the amplitude or the swing at the vocal folds required to produce a voluminous sound, and its focus is far too tight and narrow to allow the harmonics to vibrate naturally, thereby giving the sound a tight, shrill and dry quality. There is no warmth, no roundness and no beauty in this type of sounds.

What Gauffin is describing in this third quality is an extreme version of pressed phonation, which sounds very much like the result of the second type of 'hard onset', which is eschewed by singing teachers and scientists. The problem is that what Gauffin is describing has nothing in common with 'medium hard onset', or its equivalent 'firm phonation', which are the result of 'medium hard onset' followed by a sustained vocal fold maneuverer designed to maintain the sound first created on vocal onset. Consequently, a word of caution is here issued about the cavalier dismissal of 'firm phonation' in favour of so-called flow phonation, which in reality often borders on breathy or soft phonation. Firm phonation, which I have argued lies somewhere between flow and pressed vocalisation, produces a firm, ringing, and round vocal quality whilst remaining the most economical, efficient and brilliant sound.

Richard Miller represents my argument perfectly with respect to pressed (vocalisation) phonation when he contends that:

> There are advocates of flow phonation who risk reducing vocal-fold resistance to such a point that breathiness intrudes; hooty, breathy vocalism is the outcome. Scientific information without a profound understanding of the nature of the professional voice is as dangerous as ignorance regarding function. Some persons who advocate free flow phonation themselves demonstrate a nonprofessional timbre far removed from the voce completa of the trained performer. They admire the "relaxed sound" of the amateur, the folksinger, and nonprofessional chorister, who show high incidences of breath admixtures. The sturdy, operatic voice often displeases advocates of "flow phonation [Miller, 2004: 59].

I agree with Miller with respect to glottal settings and the energy and body work required for what he terms as voce completa, or elite operatic singing. The artist's task is to judiciously maximise his/her talent for the benefit of the audience and fans and ultimately for his/her own career, whilst remaining within the boundaries of aesthetic good taste, and healthy and safe vocalisation.

The Elite Singer's Zone

It is important to remember that whilst it is necessary to respect boundaries and conserve good taste and healthy vocalisation, an obsession with these parameters can interfere with the drive to excellence. This alone should be the primary objective of any artist, other things being important but not defining. My thesis is that anybody can play it safe by operating efficiently at about eighty per cent capacity, but it takes a creative, intuitive, determined and intelligent artist to operate at ninety per cent and beyond.

My point here is that being a great artist is not for people who lack talent, ambition, or drive and a great capacity for sustained work.

As I was writing this, I came across a wonderful interview with Marilyn Horne in Jerome Hines' excellent book, *Great Singers on Great Singing*, which confirmed the point I was trying to make. In it, Hines was so impressed with the depth of Horne's knowledge and the richness and clarity of her ideas that he was moved to say, 'You have just reconfirmed my opinion that successful singers who endure are endowed … upstairs'. Hines was struck by Horne's comment that *'Singing is ninety-five percent brains'.* Hines contemplates the question and concludes that 'singing is ninety-five percent brains, ninety-five percent talent, ninety-five percent perseverance, (and) ninety-five percent guts' [Hines, 1994: 143].

I agree and would also add that the singer needs to bring a sense of excitement, a willingness to take chances, a daring to overcome obstacles, and an impeccable technique that can facilitate the singer's artistic intentions.

These ideas are not new. From the beginning of solo singing, all the great masters have used them to inspire their students towards great success.

For instance, William Vennard, Horne's teacher, addressed the issue most eloquently in his 1970 monograph 'Developing Voices'. According to Vennard, the first challenge comes when an advanced student takes the necessary leap into becoming a professional artist. Vennard states that there is a dangerous moment in every young singer's life, occurring when he/she begins to transition from an advanced student into a professional singer, demonstrating a professional quality. He claims that generally it is best to wait until the student demonstrates a fundamental freedom in technique before introducing 'the aggressive quality' which is a necessary ingredient of the professional voice [Vennard, 1970].

I take Vennard's statement to mean that in the early years the teacher is mainly concerned with developing the student's physical instrument, through judicious vocalising, as well as dispensing knowledge pertaining to the prevailing performance practices, repertoire and style. At this stage, the student is generally happy to produce a fresh, attractive sound that displays a certain flexibility and ease of production. The head register seems to be developing nicely but the sound is still white, light and underdeveloped, lacking core, power, and brilliance. The student is still avoiding the chest voice for fear that they will either hurt themselves or worse they are not sufficiently skilled to execute the passaggio back to the middle register without gurgles and cracks. This sound is not complete, and it is not sufficient to fill a large theatre over a substantial orchestra.

What I understand by Vennard's aggressive sound, is that sound described by Lodovico Zacconi as *'Voce Mordente'* that is, *'a voice with a pungent, biting quality'* that can be heard over a large chorus and orchestra. This sound must have a core throughout the range and at every level of intensity (the singer's formant). This dangerous sound possesses firmness, roundness, a variety of colours, and high level of brilliance.

The professional sound should have a well-developed chest voice and a powerful and ringing head voice, all combined with a balanced chiaroscuro, as recommended by the old masters.

I think the above would be Vennard's basic requirements for a professional operatic voice, with the vocal and artistic refinements still to come as part of the ninety-five percent quest for excellence.

At some point, the intelligent and responsible teacher knows that if the student wants to become a professional singer, it is no longer just about the student; the vision must also incorporate external considerations, such as the composer's intentions, audience reaction and the discipline imposed by the market place.

So, a good teacher must work to bridge the gap between the student's natural gifts and the demands of the composer and the market place, because if the student can't meet these demands, he is doomed to fail in professional circles, let alone stepping up to the ninety-five percent elite singer's zone.

Richard Bonynge is one of the few authors in the literature to address audience demands and their subsequent reaction. He is referring specifically to bel canto opera, but I believe the same argument can be made for other genres as well.

The following are Bonynge's thoughts:

> The audience that goes to bel canto opera is going to a vocal circus. The critics say that against it, but I say that for it. The singers need to tread the high wires; they are doing vocal gymnastics. If they are big singers and bring it off well, it can be exciting. And there is always that element of doubt whether they will make it. A singer just may crack on that high E-flat and fall flat on her face [Bonynge in Adams, 1980: 75].

I agree with Bonynge because I believe that at the very highest levels the art of singing is really a blood sport. People are divided between applauding you and booing you off the stage. Bonynge was referring to the bel canto operas and there are certainly many opportunities to fail in those. However, the principal relationship between talent maximisation and stardom remains the same whether we refer to a bel canto opera or the later dramatic repertoire. It is all about putting everything on the line to the degree that the audience wonders whether you are going to overcome the obstacles of a particular role.

Chapter 18

The Physiological Elements of Supraglottic Events

The Vocal Tract

The vocal tract is comprised of all the cavities situated on the supraglottal plane. These are also known as the resonating cavities designed to amplify the sound issuing from the laryngeal source, which in its unamplified state is comparable to a raspberry. The amplification of this primary sound is generated when the subglottal pressure is sufficient to overcome the resistance of the vocal folds setting them into vibration, thereby creating a continuous current of sound waves. From the point of view of both music and acoustics, Sanchez Carbone affirms that the laryngeal sound constitutes the fundamental tone and a series of upper harmonics that are multiples of the fundamental and responsible for the final timbre of the voice. She further reminds us that the harmonic series is the same structure, that is, the fundamental is always followed by the first harmonics and then come the second and third and so on, all are multiples of the fundamental. These higher harmonic partials become increasingly weaker relative to the strength of the fundamental. The exception being those higher harmonic partials that contain major acoustic energy and intensity that corresponds to the frequency of the resonator: these are enhanced, whilst those that are not attenuated. The effect of exciting the resonances of the vocal tract result in peaks in the spectrum (Fourier analysis), known as formants [Sanchez Carbone, 2005: 353].

It is important to recall that just as the fundamental and its harmonic series are a product of the collision of the vocal folds as they are set into vibration by the subglottal pressure produced by the respiratory muscles, the formants are a product of the excitation of the air in the vocal tract as shaped by the articulators. Sanchez Carbone contends that this process of matching harmonics with the formants of the vocal tract represents the cooperation of the two fundamental mechanisms responsible for the production of sound, that of the vocal folds which produce the primary sound originating with the vibrations of the vocal folds, which in turn excite the air within the vocal tract as part of the filtering process. All of these elements are indivisible and act together in a synergistic manner. Consequently, we can say that the success of this filtering process is dependent on the complex of muscles that constitute the resonating tube (vocal tract), and must assume a position that is synonymous and synergistic with the laryngeal system, thanks to the activity of the intrinsic and extrinsic laryngeal muscles [Sanchez Carbone, 2005: 353].

Castellani confirms Sanchez Carbone with respect to many basic vocal elements, including the fact that fundamental frequency is controlled by the intrinsic laryngeal muscles which are responsible for the tension, and elongation(and therefore thickness) of the vocal folds: the longer and thinner they are, the greater the number of vibrations in the cycle, (the shorter and more rapid the vibratory cycle); on the other hand, the shorter and thicker the vocal folds, the greater the reduction in the number vibratory cycles per second (opening and closing cycle) and therefore the greater the reduction in fundamental frequency (the longer and slower the vibratory cycle) [Castellani, 2012: 25].

When these soundwaves traverse the highly modifiable cavity, the vocal tract naturally selects the frequencies of the harmonic partials closest to its formant frequencies. The formant frequencies themselves are a function of various configurations of the mobile articulators, including the tongue, the jaw, the lips and the soft palate. The placement of these articulators modifies the shape and volume of the vocal tract, and in so doing, they alter the formant frequencies to match the frequency of the harmonic partials generated by the vocal folds. When the partial frequencies are matched to the frequencies of vocal tract formants, the result is a sonorous sound, rich in harmonics and definition, representing the unique vocal identity of each person.

It is important to underline that all objective resonators reside in the supraglottal area, making their way to the external environment. All other sensations accruing in other cavities such as the thorax, the chest, the trachea and other parts of the body are only sympathetic vibrations reflecting the vibrations produced at the vocal folds. They are not, however, involved in either the production of sound at the source level, nor as a primary resonator. In fact, these are just subjective reflected sensations (proprioceptive vibrations) [Castellani, 2012: 25].

Strictly speaking, the vocal tract is constituted by the three principal cavities called the laryngopharynx, the oropharynx and the nasal pharynx that together form the unique structure we call the pharynx. These three components that constitute the resonating and articulating cavities can be modified in infinite ways by the articulators, including the tongue, the jaw, the lips the soft palate (velum), uvula and the lowering and raising of the larynx which either shorten or lengthen the vocal tract with significant modification of the vocal tract formants.

The Pharynx

In a 1967 statement that predates James McKinney almost identical passage by nearly thirty years, Carlo Meano declares that:

> The pharynx is important in the production of sound because, anatomically, it is the first area to contain the sound waves produced in the larynx during their projection and amplification, and contributes towards the formation of timbre or quality. The pharynx extends from the top of the larynx and oesophagus to the posterior nasal openings. The section in the region of the larynx is called the laryngopharynx; opposite the back of the mouth, the oropharynx; and opposite the posterior nasal openings, the nasopharynx [Meano, 1967: 35].

According to Meano, the oropharyngeal cavity consists of a narrow passageway to the mouth, which is known as the fauces, colloquially referred to as the throat. The fauces represent the passageway between laryngopharynx and the oropharyngeal cavity. The posterior part of the throat is composed of the velum (soft palate), the uvula, with its pendula tip hanging into the mouth, and the pillars of the throat which are comprised of the palatopharyngeus and palatoglossus arches, which together form the faucial arches. In between these arches, we find the palatine tonsils.

Meano continues, the tongue, which is constituted by the geniohyoid, the mylohyoid and the genioglossus muscles, forms the floor of the mouth; whilst the roof of the mouth is comprised of the immobile hard palate anteriorly and the mobile soft palate (velum) posteriorly.

Meano contends that:

> The mouth cavity, with its extremely elastic and mobile walls, notably influences the quality of the sound and forms a natural 'hi-fi', or amplifier, which gathers the sonorous vibrations and amplifies them during their outward projection. The nasal cavities behind the nose and above the faeces participate directly in the function of this natural sound amplification [Meano, 1967: 36].

As we saw above, Meano subdivides the pharyngeal cavity into the laryngopharynx, the oropharynx and the nasopharynx with palatopharyngeus and palatoglossus arches as its passageway.

Castellani confirms Meano, stating that the vocal tract is constituted by a series of three principal cavities (the laryngopharynx, the oropharynx and the nasopharynx) that together constitute the pharynx. This unique structure is comprised of a muscular tube that extends from the base of the cranium to the superior margins of the oesophagus and to the inferior margins of the larynx [Castellani, 2012: 26].

She further contends that the primary sound issuing from the vocal folds may be compared to a raspberry, a phenomenon generated by the vibrations of the vocal folds when the air pressure from the lungs overcomes the resistance offered by the vocal folds and projects the soundwaves into the supraglottic cavities or resonating cavities, the site of amplification of the original laryngeal sound [Castellani, 2012: 25].

Battaglia Damiani (2003) agrees with Meano and Castellani's pharyngeal subdivisions and even more importantly with Meano's interpretation of the musculature that constitutes the pharyngeal cavity. In addition, however, Damiani emphasises the importance of the inferior, medius and superior constrictor muscles. These constrictor muscles are stacked into each other from the top down, forming the posterior and lateral pharyngeal wall. It is widely accepted that contraction of the constrictor muscles generally reduces the pharyngeal space.

Battaglia Damiani clarifies and amplifies on the relationship between the various muscles and their effect on pharyngeal resonating space. She contends that whilst contraction of the constrictor muscles reduces the volume of the pharynx, contraction of the stylopharyngeus muscles expands it. Further, she contends that the responsibility for shortening the pharynx is due to the contraction of the palatopharyngeus, and the thyrohyoid muscles, which together raise the larynx thereby shortening the pharynx, whereas responsibility for the elongation of the pharyngeal cavity remains with the sternothyroid, which contraction lowers the larynx and lengthens the pharyngeal cavity. The shortening of the pharynx creates the condition for privileging the higher formants whilst lengthening the pharyngeal space privileges the lower formants [Battaglia Damiani, 2003: 228].

Silvia Magnani (2017) addresses the impact of lowering and raising the larynx on the sound source. She contends that certain vocal tract gestures are responsible for generating change to the shape of the vocal folds. For instance, an elongation of the vocal folds obtained by lowering the larynx (mainly through contraction of the sternothyroid) generates an increase in vocal fold mass and a decrease in length, with a concomitant reduction in Fo; whilst a shortening of the vocal tract obtained by raising the larynx at the vocal fold level generates a stretching of the vocal folds through a separation of the anterior commissure of the arytenoids with a concomitant increase in Fo, and stability of adduction [Magnani, 2017: 49].

Sanchez Carbone agrees with the above but also maintains that the vocal resonator is very different to other instrumental resonators. For instance, the vocal tract does not have a fixed structure, but is rather a flexible system of resonance, capable of assuming diverse forms. It is a resonating chamber that is both 'alive and active'. Sanchez Carbone, continues:

The cavities that comprise the resonator are neither precisely determined nor defined. They are variable, flexible and determined by the articulatory movement of the larynx, which with its ascending and descending movement alters the length and volume of the pharynx. It also influences the action of the mandible, the lips and the tongue. As a result of its variable flexibility, the resonating cavity is capable of assuming an infinite number of dimensions and configuration. The direct muscular control that the singer may exercise over the resonator is somewhat imprecise, given that the necessary adjustments are realised above all via phonetics. That is to say, through the formation of vowels and consonants and diction [Sanchez Carbone, 2005: 350].

From the muscular interrelationship presented above, we have gained a lightly sketched picture of the anatomical and physiological function of the vocal tract. We will of course obtain a more vivid picture as we explore in more depth all of the principal articulators such as the tongue, the jaw, the soft palate and the lips, each of which plays an important part in the formation of the various configurations of the vocal tract that are responsible for the formation of all the vowels and consonants. But we are getting a little ahead of ourselves, for now let us concentrate on discovering more about how the pharyngeal cavity operates as a whole, and its potential influence on voice quality.

With this objective in mind, let us return to Fussi and Gilardone in an effort to better understand the resonator, and the effect a particular morphological configuration has on the quality of the sound.

Fussi and Gilardone maintain that in the field of verbal or vocal communication the vocal tract has two distinctive functions: the first is articulation and the other is resonance. The vocal tract is a specific type of resonator or filter upon which the volumetric parameters are extremely flexible and variable thanks to the notable mobility of the anatomical components, comprised of the articulators. These include the lips, the mandible, the tongue, and the soft palate, all of which are capable of modifying the characteristics of the vocal tract.

Fussi and Gilardone contend that even though the supraglottic vocal tract has only two distinctive functions, that is, resonation and articulation, the manipulation of the different articulators provides us with an infinite number of vocal tract configurations, each resulting in an ever so slightly different vocal quality [Fussi & Gilardone, 2009: 34].

Sanchez Carbone, on the other hand, whilst accepting the theoretical distinction between resonance and articulation, emphasises the fact that in practice there is no real separation of activity between articulation and resonation: 'the activity of the articulators has a direct influence on the shape and size of the resonator' [Sanchez Carbone, 2005: 351].

Fussi and Gilardone also assert that the direct control we are able to exercise over the resonator is limited and imprecise. The best and only way the singer can control the resonator is through phonetic measures – that is, through the formation of vowels and consonants. It is important to remember that even a minor alteration in muscular behaviour, or to the walls of the vocal tract cavity, creates a corresponding alteration in vocal quality and timbre [Fussi and Gilardone, 2009: 35].

The oropharyngeal cavity is not only the principal resonator, but it is also the cavity that contains the major articulators. The air current which is transformed into sound when the air is chopped by the vibrating vocal folds, then flows through the vocal tract either as an articulated sound or as a vocalised sound. The first, which creates consonants, is caused by a constriction within the vocal tract; whilst the latter, which is characterised by the uninterrupted production of sound, is responsible for the production of vowels and voiced consonants. The main articulators, the mandible, lips, tongue and soft palate are responsible for the essential modification of the vocal tract that influences in a major way the final acoustic product.

The consonants are produced by the interruption of the airflow, creating voiced or unvoiced consonants by means of the pharyngeal and oral constrictions that generate a sound.

When the free air traversing the vocal tract behaves in a certain manner, it can enhance the complex harmonic partials that constitute the sound wave, thereby creating characteristic vocalic sounds.

Righini on Sound Waves and Formants

For elaboration of these soundwaves their length, duration, and cycles per second, let us turn to Pietro Righini, one of Italy's foremost acousticians.

Righini informs us that when two waves moving in a medium either meet or collide at a certain point of that medium, their respective energies are actually combined into one major wave. The movement of these waves is influenced by new impulses that produce vibrations that consist of frequencies that are multiples of the fundamental. These are considered the originators of this phenomenon and are therefore called harmonics.

These overtones that arise from this vibratory motion are better known as the first, second, third, fourth and so on harmonics. The frequencies of these harmonics are respectively double, triple and quadruple frequencies; whilst the duration of the sound travels in the opposite direction. That is, with each harmonic the frequency increases and consequently the duration or the time it takes to complete each cycle manifests as a half, a third, or a quarter.In short, the lower the fundamental frequency the longer the duration of the cycle; in contrast, the higher the fundamental the shorter the duration [Righini, 1994: 26]. For instance, Sundberg has calculated that the frequencies of the first four formants lies in the vicinity of 500, 1500, 2500, and 3500 cycles per second. With respect to the length of the sound waves, following Sundberg's seminal work in the area of formants, there is now wide acceptance that the human vocal tract is about 17.5 centimetres long in the average male. In terms of the relationship between the sound waves and the length of the vocal tract, Righini suggests that we can fit a quarter wave length within the vocal tract, which represents the first formant, and a three-quarter wave for the second formant, a one and quarter wave for the third formant, and a one and three-quarter wave for the fourth formant and so on. Fussi and Gilardone concur [Righini, 1994: 26; Fussi & Gilardoni, 2009: 132].

Definition and Importance of Resonators

There is now broad agreement that every instrument requires a resonating chamber to amplify its original sound. Certainly, where the voice instrument is concerned there is incontrovertible evidence that the originating sound lacks of substantial volume. In fact, Righini maintains that:

> The vibrations of the vocal folds, however, do not develop sufficient energy to generate sounds of the required volume. Consequently, it is the task of the resonating cavities that by varying their volume in accordance with the frequency, promote the amplification, and the intensity of the sound, transforming it from the weakest sound into the most powerful singing voice [Righini, 1994: 39].

There is also broad agreement in the Italian literature that intensity and timbre are amongst the most important elements of singing and both are a function of the relative strength between the fundamental and harmonic partials. These elements are ultimately controlled by the interrelationship between subglottal pressure and glottal resistance. It is important to remember that this whole discussion about resonance, intensity, vocal timbre and its relationship with the relative strength of the harmonic partials can only take place within the paradigm of excellent breath management and the influence that the interrelationship between subglottal pressure and glottal resistance has on vocal quality. It is this relationship, in fact, that is responsible for most of the parameters associated with vocal strength and acoustic power.

I believe that the relative strength of these harmonic partials is a function of the interaction between subglottal pressure, amplitude, closing rate, duration and the abrupt termination of airflow, all of which impact on the skewing of the waveform and enrichment of the upper harmonics. Consequently, we can say that the structure of the sound wave is established well before it enters the vocal tract.

According to Fussi and Magnani, if we are to achieve this objective, it is necessary to consider some fundamental principles pertaining to the physics of vocal acoustic. In consideration of these principals we can say that:

1. The more-ample or long the vocal cavity, the deeper the vocal frequency, whilst a reduction of the size or a shortening of the vocal tract has the opposite effect, that is, it results in a high frequency and a brighter sound.

2. The firmer and tenser the walls of the vocal tract, the higher the resonance frequency and the lighter the resulting sound. On the other hand, a reduction in muscular vocal tract tonus has the effect of darkening the ensuing vocal sound.

3. The smaller the diameter of the cavity, the greater the degree of vocal dampening on the other hand, an increase in diameter allows for optimal increase in intensity.

4. We may generate some complex diameters of the cavity for which any small alteration of muscular behaviour upon the walls of the vocal tract creates a corresponding alteration in vocal quality and timbre [Fussi & Gilardone, 2009: 34].

In this chapter, we will discuss in considerable detail both the anatomy and functional physiology of the vocal tract articulators. But let us defer that for a moment until we address the pharyngeal cavity as a whole.

Fussi and Gilardone (2009) elaborate that the vocal tract is a specific type of resonator or filter upon which the volumetric parameters are extremely flexible and variable thanks to the notable mobility of the anatomical components, such as the lips, the mandible, the tongue, and the soft palate, all of which are capable of modifying the characteristics of the vocal tract [Fussi & Gilardone, 2009: 35].

Let us elaborate on each of these major articulators.

The Tongue

The tongue constitutes the floor of the mouth. It is an organ capable moving in an almost global direction due to the fact that it is attached to the hyoid bone which is situated deep within the neck. It has inserted to the hyoglossus and the mylohyoid, whilst at the base of the cranium, it is joined to the styloglossus and palatoglossus muscles. The tongue is particularly rich in intrinsic muscles such as the traverse, vertical and longitudinal muscles [Galigliano, 2013: 95]. Castellani reports that the tongue is constituted by thirty-two different muscles which occupy a major part of the space that comprises the oral cavity, as well as accomplishing other fundamental roles, such as deglutition and mastication. Its movements determine perceptible alterations in articulation and quality of sound. If anteriorly oriented, it will produce a rise in the frequency of the second formant, and potentially also the first. On the other hand, a retroflex tongue, that is, a tongue retracting towards the soft palate generates a lowering of the second formant, which results in a darkening of timbre [Castellani, 2012: 28].

According to Fussi and Gilardone, the tongue remains the principal articulatory organ and is mainly responsible for balanced resonance changes. The authors make the connection between lingual and mandibular relaxation and the corresponding commensurate relaxation at the pharynx. The movement of the tongue is responsible for a modest degree in either raising or lowering the larynx. The lowering of the larynx facilitates the production of the back vowels such as [o] and [u] and the raising of the larynx facilitate the [e] and [i]. We should also remember that the larynx, being a mobile organ, is also responsible for the modification of the vocal tract. The elongation of the vocal tract obtained through a lowering of the larynx produces an overall lowering of all the formant frequencies, especially if it involves a protrusion of the lips, a configuration that strengthens the intensity of the fundamental and lower harmonics [Fussi & Gilardone, 2009: 36].

I contend that, even though the above is correct, it lacks the sophistication associated with elite singing. We should recall Righini's earlier statement previously cited in these pages suggests that we cannot in the case of singing always apply indiscriminately the results of scientific research to vocal technique. He continues by suggesting that the teacher's ear becomes indispensable for the adoption of scientific knowledge, and I concur.

In this instance, even a perfunctory glance at the situation would tell you that good singers have developed a high level of muscular independence which they combine in a seamless and holistic manner. So, they learn how to focus on and educate the individual organs of the instrument before combining them in a holistic way. Mori gives the example of instrumentalists such as pianists and the violinist and the hours they spend practising their fingering and familiarising themselves with their instrument, and then asks why singers should do less with respect to practising and honing familiarity with the individual parts of their instrument, such as their breathing, their articulation and studying the exact nature of their resonator [Mori, 1970: 29–32].

The first thing to say is that the vocal tract articulators such as the tongue, lips, mandible and soft palate are far more flexible and active in the formation of vocal tract resonances, otherwise known as formants, than the raising and lowering of the larynx would suggest.

In large part, the larynx is responsible for the gross adjustments of the vocal tract, as well as the production of the singer's formant. However, in terms of forming the vowel formants, it remains a minor player. It is generally reduced to lowering the larynx for the darker vowels, and rising it for the brighter ones. Lowering the larynx generally lowers all the formant frequencies, especially if it is accompanied by a protrusion of the lips, whilst raising the larynx raises all the formant frequency, and more so if it is accompanied by a hint of a smile. With respect to the vowel formants, they are literally formed by the mouth articulators, mainly the tongue, the lips and the jaw.

It is true that in the strict sense the larynx tends to rise with the lateral vowels [i] and [e] and lower for the round and darker vowels [o] and [u], but elite singers know that the rise and fall associated with vertical laryngeal position must be controlled. Elite singers do not allow the larynx to bop up and down indiscriminately with every phonemic alteration. These singers learn to find a stable and moderately low laryngeal position maintained by sub-laryngeal forces such as a lowered diaphragm and greater breath volume. It is also further stabilised by the action of the external depressor muscles (strap muscles). So, in time, elite singers learn through training to gain a high level of independence between the movement of the larynx and that of the vocal tract articulators, allowing for a subtle laryngeal mobility underpinned by an overall laryngeal stability.

It is only through this independent control that the singer can learn to maintain a relatively lowered larynx position combined with a tongue that is flexible and in a high enough vertical position to form the [e] and [i] vowels, but without ever becoming excessively high. Let me emphasise that there is no rigidity or a fixing of any vocal organs involved in this manoeuvre, it is just a small aid to nature to resist the raising of the larynx by maintaining a low diaphragm at the same time as the tongue is apt to raise the larynx. This antagonistic action between a lowered diaphragm and rising larynx has the effect of controlling the rise and fall of the larynx, because it is driven by the antagonistic action of the breathing muscles, thereby ensuring a stable but moderately low larynx, and a smooth transition between vowels which maintains a seamless legato line.

The opposite treatment is necessary of the darker round vowels, which quite often exhibit a laryngeal position that is too low, lowering all the formant frequencies indiscriminately and resulting in sound that is too dark. In these conditions, the opposite strategy is indicated. That is, both the tongue and the larynx are elevated and a brighter colour is infused into the sound. For instance, the [o] is infused with a small percentage of the vowel [a] quality and the position of the mouth is a little more horizontal rather than the usual oval or vertical position generally associated with the [o] vowel. I believe that our predecessors called it the 'Art of Singing' for a reason, because it requires imagination and creativity within the constraints of naturalness. If all we are going to do is open our mouth and go with nature, we will never be great artists. We certainly must consult nature's intentions, but that is not the same as surrendering to its fickleness and incompleteness. Sometimes we just need to forge our own destiny by helping nature along. We should understand that most vocal instruments, good as they are, have inherent limitations. A great deal of our training is directed towards overcoming these limitations. In the end my friends, there is no substitute for hard work, imagination, creativity, and forging your own pathway to success. And finally, and this is for the really smart ones, surround yourselves with the very best and listen. There is no need to invent the wheel someone else has already done that for you. All you have to do is use it intelligently.

Let us return to the position of the tongue appreciably alters the capacity of the vocal tract, and because of its sheer size, flexibility and capacity for voluntary control, the tongue remains the most important articulatory organ of the vocal tract.

According to Sanchez Carbone, the most important lessons from observing the tongue during singing are:

- Learning to reduce tongue tension during singing.

- Seeking to maintain the tip of the tongue against the surface of the lower teeth during the formation of the various vowels;

- In educating the voice we must observe and influence two elements: the first is the position of the tongue and the second is the shape of the tongue caused by its own contraction.

The muscular component of the tongue is comprised of a base, the dorsum and the tip of the tongue. The singer should realise that the position of both the tongue dorsum and the tongue tip are a function of muscular activity, which can be verified through the mirror. During the process of vocalisation, the tip of the tongue moves in an active manner from superior to inferior position during the execution of consonants, but remains in the anterior part of the mouth, that is, against the surface of the lower teeth, during the production of vowels [Sanchez Carbone, 2005: 360].

In the process of executing the high register, the tongue tip undergoes a slight retraction, but this retraction should never become excessive.

Every exaggerated contraction of the tongue acts as an obstacle to the proper function of the larynx and the movement of the articulators.

Battaglia Damiani largely concurs with the above and reports on an extensive study by Di Girolamo to make a compelling argument with respect to the connection between the tongue, pharyngeal space, and the resulting formants and therefore vowels. Here are her thoughts:

It has been observed that in singing the [a] vowel, the base of the tongue caused constriction at the pharyngeal cavity; on the other hand, during the emission of the [i] vowel it was observed that the space in the pharynx was much more substantial and the muscular contraction was most concentrated between the tongue and the hard palate. With respect to the 'u' vowel it was found that the dorsum of the tongue was raised and the constriction was found at the level of the soft palate. In the same study, it was found that upon increasing the intensity of the sound, the singer was required not only to increase subglottal pressure, but also to drop the jaw, thereby increasing the space between tongue and the palate [Di Girolamo in Battaglia Damiani, 2003: 220].

Schindler's contribution came in the form of emphasising that whilst vowels are distinguished by both first and second formants, it is really the second and dramatically higher formant that finally differentiates the vowels [Schindler in Battaglia Damiani, 2003: 220].

Sanchez Carbone suggests that the source sound generated at the level of the larynx may be distorted by an incorrect tongue position. She believes that:

> This effectively means that somewhere along the line we need to find an accommodation designed to compensate for an erratic position of the tongue on the acoustic load of the vocal tract. This erratic tongue position can alter the singer's formant, and influence the perception of exact intonation. This type of vocal tract posture generally disturbs the natural and efficient function of the instrument and demands a maximum effort from the larynx at the vocal fold level [Sanchez Carbone, 2005: 360].

It would appear that an erratic tongue position influences not only the adjustments of the articulators with an immediate impact on the formants, but also impacts acoustic reactance, which in turn influences the posture and function of the vocal folds.

Sanchez Carbone has identified a number of incorrect tongue positions that occur during singing, and which impact on both the formants of the vocal tract and the vibratory function of the vocal folds. The most important amongst these are:

- Placing the tip of the tongue too far down the lower teeth instead of the recommended superficial part of the lower teeth. This excessive lowering of the tip of the tongue has the effect of curving the tongue body into a higher position of the mouth. When this occurs, the space between the hard palate and the tongue is reduced in a similar way as the space between the soft palate and the posterior part of the tongue. This space reduction results in the loss of the higher harmonic partials, which is perceived as a weakening of the sound and often as a lowering of pitch.

- The tongue towards the upper palate and pulling it back towards the hard palate, a position that distorts the vowel and reduces the clarity of the timbre.

- The retroflex tongue, that is, a posture in which the tongue acting through the hyoid bone forces the larynx down until it assumes an excessively low position. This vocal tract configuration causes a heavy and dark vocal production.

- The next incorrect tongue configuration is one in which the singer lifts the tongue until it comes into contact with the upper molars.

In such a position, one tends to maintain the acoustic position which is characteristic of the 'I' vowel. This muscular behaviour results in an exaggerated brilliance of the sound and a harsh timbre because this configuration augments the upper harmonics associated with the vowel. This configuration also induces a particularly high laryngeal position, serving to shorten the vocal tract and eliminate the darkness of the sound (lower acoustic energy).

In general, we might say that during the execution of the front vowels, the tongue body rises towards the hard palate whilst in the execution of the back vowels the anterior part of the tongue is lowered and the posterior part rises. We conclude from the above that all types of tongue tensions are then transmitted to the larynx through the muscles connected to the hyoid bone from which the larynx is suspended.

Bruno and Paperi on the Tongue

Bruno and Paperi also believe that the most important and often undervalued organ of articulation is the participation of the tongue. The tension, which is frequently associated with the tongue, is often caused by the wrong emission of the voice. This will require the singer to both stimulate the tongue's mobility on the one hand and take corrective action on the other (Bruno & Paperi, 2003: 111).

In order to ensure that the negative effect on these organs will disappear, the singer should avoid any contraction of the various organs associated with phonation, such as an excessive amount of pressure on the larynx and excessive tension of the tongue. Ultimately, the singer should aim to attain a high level of relaxation and elasticity of the tongue starting with the base, which should resolve the problems of tension.

We must seek to keep the tongue very loose and flexible in order to start the sound from a position that is from the beginning well suited to the position of a 'MA', that is clean but warm which although born out of the larynx completes its formation comfortably high between the soft and hard palate. Bruno and Paperi warn the singer not to involve the jaw muscles to guide the vocal sounds in a convergent shape towards the facial resonators.

The preparatory movement will be divided between a larynx that is lower and a soft palate that rises in order to allow the tongue to extend forward towards the lower teeth.

Bruno and Paperi contend that if a singer pursues an extremely loose articulation which is allowed to migrate towards a number of vowels or consonants produced at varying frequencies, then such loose sounds will naturally migrate towards the formation and projection of the [A] vowel. In order to achieve the aesthetic richness and reach a comfortable and ample oropharyngeal space, some students will have to begin with the 'MI' or 'IMMI'. The authors ask us to remember that:

> A flattened tongue, a retroflex tongue, a tongue with its tip raised is not appropriate to good resonance or clean pronunciation, simply because it is difficult for a tongue in this position to move freely, making the necessary adjustments as required [Bruno & Paperi, 2003: 111].

Many students, according to Bruno and Paperi:

> Believe that they can simultaneously solve the problem of the tongue and oropharyngeal space by arching the tongue down; others sing with the tongue in a curved position believing that they can create adequate space by forcefully dropping the jaw. All of which tends to obstruct the amplitude of the pharynx, modify the quality of the sound, and interfere with the clarity of the word [Bruno & Paperi, 2003: 112].

Bruno and Paperi believe that the singer should avoid channelling the tongue in such a way as to produce a dark or heavy sonority that can have a negative influence on the epiglottis. On the contrary, the tongue should be extremely adaptable to change even at the base and should not at all linked to the lower jaw, in order to modify imperceptibly the articulation as required by any given passage. The tongue needs to collaborate in the efficient projection of the sound, at first vertically and later gently towards the facial resonators.

The Lips

The lips act as a sphincter, in the sense of a functional valve, closing the vocal tract horizontally. As such, it participates in important communicative functions, such as forming the vowels and the phonoarticulatory functions. The protrusion and rounding of the lips indicates a darkening of timbre, and lowers all the formants [Fussi & Magnani, 2015: 62].

Castellani agrees with Fussi and Magnani and adds that the use of the lips can produce a variety of sounds. For instance, the protrusion and rounding of the lips that determines a darkening of the timbre and a lowering of the frequency of the third formant, whilst the lengthening associated with lip protrusion has the effect of increasing the intensity of the first formant [Castellani, 2012: 28].

As stated above, the lips play a considerable part in the closure of the horizontal portion of the oro-vocal-tract. Consequently, we may recall from the previous pages that protruding the lips we extend and elongate the vocal tract with a consequent darkening of the timbre and eventual potential dampening of the resonance.

In contrast to this vocal tract elongation, the stretching of the lips laterally (just a hint of a smile) produces a shortening of the vocal tract, resulting in a lightening of vocal timbre, and a consequent increase in carrying power.

Bruno and Paperi contend that in a gently relaxed state, the lips tend to reveal the upper teeth, which is still considered the most individual automatic characteristic of this position. In combination with an overall relaxed face, especially in the middle register, the lips should adopt an almost smiling position. In this position, both the lips and the face should always be ready to render both word and sound into a reflexive zone where the sensations are reflected back to the singer. On the other hand, any distortion of the face muscles or even a forced smile would not allow for an easy recruitment of the muscles necessary for the proper amplification of the facial resonance. We may add that a mouth combined with a softer facial attitude verging on a smile, can, in some expressive moments, answer the requirements of the bel canto style.

In conclusion, and in keeping with the principles of acoustic physics, an ample aperture of the mouth favours the high frequency resonances (the higher formants), whilst a small opening of the mouth and a narrowing of the angle of the lips is generally associated with a degree of lowering of the larynx, and consequently favours a lowering of the resonating frequencies of all the formants.

Sanchez Carbone contends that the lips form two such articulatory positions: the first is one in which the lips are pulled back into a smile, resulting in the shape of a letterbox and from which sound issues forth with a clear, whitish quality, lacking in vibrato; the second position is one in which the lips are protruded forward, resulting in a constantly dark emission, deep and intubated sound. In this instance the voice becomes thick, 'smorzata', that is, the upper harmonics are dampened, and the voice becomes excessively doughy and badly articulated. It follows that the facial features (muscles) must adopt a posture that promotes maximum naturalness and relaxation so as to favour the variation of timbre, the ease of articulation and the emission of the voice. Sanchez Carbone states that 'a common error amongst singers is to believe they can alter the oral cavity by manipulating the lips, but this manoeuvre only serves to distort the sound' This type of distortion dampens both high and low frequencies. Depending on the position adapted by the lips, the sound may lose its fullness. Any excessive tension on the facial muscles around the lips will have a detrimental effect on the quality of the tone [Sanchez Carbone, 2005: 359].

Two other elements that contribute to harmonic formation and resonance balancing, according to Castellani, are the level of mouth opening and the vertical laryngeal positioning. The controlled lowering of the jaw benefits mouth opening, rising the first formant, whilst closing the mouth lowers the first formant. In lowering the vertical laryngeal position, we lengthen the vocal tract and lower the fourth and fifth formant, whilst rising the larynx will shorten the vocal tract and rise these formants [Castellani, 2012: 28].

Angela Castellani, contends that formants, which are function of the position and postural attitude of the articulators discussed above, generally represent the timbrel characteristics of the voice. Formants can also be understood as combination of frequency peaks within a range that determine vowel intelligibility (first and second formant), brilliance (third formant) and penetrating, and carrying power (fourth and fifth formant — otherwise known as the singing formant) [Castellani, 2012: 28].

Fussi and Magnani, declare that the characteristic timbre of the emission is tied to the formants which in turn are connected to the position of the articulators and organs of resonance. Modifications to the spectral composition of the voice are dependent on the following rules:

1. The value of F1, which is generally in the range of 250 to 800, may be elevated proportionally to the opening of the mouth and mandible,
2. The value of F2, which is in the range of 600 to 2000, maybe elevated by projecting forward of the tongue tip against the lower teeth, but is lowered with the retroflex tongue,
3. The value of F3, which is in the frequency range of 2500 to 3600, is mainly concentrated in the oropharynx and may be elevated through the protrusion of the lips and by maintaining the apex of the tongue against the lower teeth,
4. The value of F4 and F5, which is in the frequency range of 2800 to 3600, is concentrated in the larynx and oropharynx and both are generally lowered by the lengthening of the vocal tract by lowering the vertical laryngeal position [Fussi & Magnani, 2015: 55; Castellani, 2012: 28].

Castellani reminds us that the first and second formant provide us with the recognition of balanced vowels, whilst three, four and five form a cluster of formants which provide the sound with brilliance and penetration and which are known as the singer's formant.

In conclusion Fussi and Magnani (2015) maintain that the vocal tract plays an extremely important role in the final vocal product. The glottis signal is characterised by the presence of the fundamental (Fo) which contains a high level of intensity, followed by harmonic overtones which are integers of the fundamental frequency, and which in the lower and central part of the spectrum display a decreasing level of intensity. There are some harmonics that are placed at the extremely high level of the frequency spectrum that also display a high level of acoustic energy.In their journey from the originating voice source to the labial lips, these harmonics are subjected to a filtering process by the vocal tract, in which some harmonics are amplified whilst others are attenuated.

The characteristics of the original signal are therefore mainly influenced by the fundamental which happens to be the dominant acoustic element.

These authors contend that even though the supraglottic vocal tract has only two distinctive functions, that is, resonation and articulation, the manipulation of the different articulators provides us with an infinite number of vocal tract configurations, each resulting in an ever so slightly different vocal quality [Fussi & Magnani, 2015: 55].

Soft Palate

According to Sanchez Carbone, the buccopharyngeal cavity reinforces all the constituent partials of a sound, provided that they are within the natural range of its resonances. In particular it reinforces the fundamental and the lower harmonics, which are normally more intense than the upper harmonics, even allowing for the fact that a particular configuration of the vocal tract will automatically favour certain harmonic partials.

Sanchez Carbone, the majority of singers produce their vowels in such a manner that even though the soft palate is raised, a certain amount of sonorised air passes through the nasal cavities and the posterior part of the nose: this has the effect of beautifying the sound. If the amount of air is excessive, due to a defective soft palate, or through an erroneous technique, the emission will become nasal [Sanchez Carbone, 2005: 358].

The soft palate is a mobile structure that may best be understood as a functional valve which is capable of separating the oral cavity from the nasopharyngeal cavity. It is to its elevation that we owe the possibilities of producing phonemes that have an exclusive oral quality (all the Italian vowels and most of the consonants). An inadequate separation, either due to an incapacity or morphological inadequacy would induce the presence of a nasal quality in those sounds that would normally have an absence of nasality [Fussi & Magnani, 2017: 60]. Consequently, we can confirm that raising the soft palate separates the oral cavity from the nasopharynx, beneficial to some French vowels and the nasal consonants. However, for the execution of the nasal consonants the sound waves need to be deviated towards the nasal cavity. This can only be achieved through a lowering of the velum and an opening of the velopharyngeal port, not a vocal tract configuration that enhances most other vocal sounds.

According to Fussi and Gilardone, for the production of all other vowel sounds and consonantal sounds, the soft palate remains elevated, otherwise we would speak of maintaining an open velopharyngeal port. This configuration suggests a preference for nasality in the vocal sound. In the event that the source signal is simultaneously radiated across the oropharynx and nasal cavities, there is a reduction of intensity [Fussi & Gilardoni, 2009: 35].

Carlo Meano (1967) confirms that 'the nasal voice is due to the prevalence of resonance in the nasal cavity. In this case the velum in the oral cavity does not rise sufficiently towards the nasal posterior opening during phonation. Therefore, the sonorous waves go directly to the superior resonating cavity and are impeded in the effort through the mouth'

There are two reasons for this reduction in intensity. The first is that by enlarging the overall size of the resonating vocal tract we diffuse the acoustic energy; the second follows from the well-known fact that there is a very high level of acoustic energy absorption by the walls of the vocal tract.

It follows from the above that the greater the vocal tract volume, the greater the damping levels. If the resonances emphasise some harmonic elements (formants), the anti-resonances abate them. Therefore, resonances and antiresonances interfere variably, arriving at a mutual cancellation. The nasalisation therefore reduces or cancels the increase in intensity of important harmonic groups (the singer's formant) and determines the decline in quality of emission. The paranasal sinuses are functionally excluded from the resonating cavity in as much as the minute orifices of communication with the nasal cavity are under normal conditions collapsed or blocked [Meano, 1968: 36].

The elevation and backward position of the soft palate involves a lengthening of the posterior section of the horizontal vocal tract, resulting in a darkening of the vocal timbre, a reduction of carrying power and penetration, and a quality of voice that is best characterised as a backward production. The backward elevation of the palate, combined with the high and lateral position of the faucial arch (palatopharyngeus and palatoglossus arches) increased notably the long distance carrying power of the voice, and contributed substantially to the formation of the singing formant [Meano, 1968: 37].

Definition and Importance of Resonators

Meano informs us that the pharynx, which extends from the larynx to the posterior nasal opening, and referred to as the laryngopharynx, is closely connected to the oropharynx opposite the back of the mouth, the nasopharynx which resides opposite the posterior nasal opening. Meano believes that the pharynx is one of the most important cavities in the production of sound, simply because anatomically it is the first area to contain the soundwaves produced in the larynx during their projection and amplification, thereby contributing to the formation of timbre or vocal quality [Meano, 1968:35]. Fussi and Gilardone agree, they believe that vocal timbre represents a most important element in vocal sound. At a psychoacoustic level, the quality of a particular voice is based above all on the quality of its timbre. From the point of view of physics, timbre depends on the number and relative intensity of the harmonic series. The frequency of the harmonics corresponds to multiples of the fundamental. Another component of timbre depends on the adduction of the vocal folds and in part on the anatomical characteristics of the resonating cavity. We These authors conclude that when there is an increase in adduction of the vocal folds, vocal timbre is enriched and the sound gains in ring and brilliance. On the other hand when vocal fold adduction is incomplete, the sound is said to be breathy, and veiled and is perceived to be altogether of poor quality or timbre [Fussi & Gilardone, 2009: 25].

Fussi and Gilardone suggest that the articulatory and resonatory apparatus (vocal tract) is constituted by a number of structures and a cavity that is situated just above the vocal folds, and which diverse and variable conformations determine and modify the signal from the glottal spectrum. The element that vibrates within the resonating cavity is none other than the air which is apt to resonate in the presence of the fundamental frequency (Fo) which is generated by the vibrations of the vocal folds. In reality, the resonator is nothing more than the air contained within the cavity and not the cavity per se. The resonance cavity is constituted by the spaces containing the air that, when charged with a soundwave, produces a sound comprised of a frequency band (harmonics) containing peaks which are centred around the natural frequency of the resonating cavity through which it is being filtered. Depending on the conformation and posture assumed by the cavity receiving the soundwave, the filtering process enhances certain harmonics and attenuates others. Those harmonics that fall within the bandwidth that has been selected for reinforcement are known as formants [Fussi & Gilardone, 2009: 25].

Sanchez Carbone concurs with the above, but concentrates on the physical aspects of the resonating cavity rather than the air contained within. She suggests that a resonator consists of a cavity which dimensions and shape, give it the ability to collaborate with another vibrating body capable of transmitting its vibratory frequency to the air contained in the resonator. 'In order to achieve this acoustic phenomenon, it is important that the length of the wave transmitted by the vibrating body coincide with the dimensions of the resonating cavity' [Sanchez Carbone, 2005: 249].

When we accomplish this process of matching frequencies, the intensity of the original sound is multiplied in accordance with the capacity of the resonator. She reminds us that in the human resonator, it is the nasopharynx, the buccopharyngeal cavity and the paranasal sinuses that are mainly responsible for determining the intensity and timbre of the sound. For these reasons, Sanchez Carbone is moved to declare that 'the resonating system is no less important than that which produces the original sound' [Sanchez Carbone, 2005: 349].

Sanchez Carbone rightly believes that the amplitude and mobility of the resonators are related in a major way to the extension of the voice.

She cites the importance of raising the soft palate not only for various pitches, but also in order to separate the nasopharynx from the (mouth) oropharynx, through to the more complex and subtle movement of the pharynx and larynx. Further, she reminds us that the vocal apparatus extends from the vocal folds to the lips, mandible, tongue and soft palate through to the zygomatic arch and larynx. Sanchez Carbone believes that we have limited direct control over the resonator. The best and only way the singer can control the resonator is through phonetic measures – that is, through the formation of vowels and consonants [Sanchez Carbone, 2005: 351].

We have addressed the two main elements of voice production: the first is the primary source which originates in the vibration of the vocal folds, and the second is due to the vibrations of the air in the vocal tract. All of these elements are indivisible and act together in a synergistic manner.

We recall that Castellani compared the primary sound generated by the vocal folds as no more than a raspberry.

Certainly, Righini maintains that where the vocal instrument is concerned there is incontrovertible evidence that the originating sound is lacking of substantial volume. In fact, he suggests that it is the task of the resonating cavities to promote the amplification, and the intensity of the sound. In so doing, transforming a weak sound into a powerful singing voice [Righini, 1994 39].

Consequently, we may conclude that the resonating vocal tract is critical in the modification, enhancement and amplification of the original laryngeal sound stream.

Juvarra declares that the control of the resonators is a function of the manipulation of the soft mobile articulatory organs, such as the tongue, the mandible, the lips and the soft palate. To the above, we may also add the larynx. As a result of its capacity to rise and fall, the larynx can modify the size and shape of the vocal tract, either elongating or shortening it with very important acoustic and phonetic effects. From the above, we may conclude that the acoustic cavity is theoretically capable of assuming an infinite number of positions, but the direct muscular control that the singer may exercise upon it is rather of a gross nature, the more refined adjustments depend on the phonetic adjustments or on vocalic formation [Juvarra, 1987: 48].

Antonio Juvarra suggest that:

> Resonance maybe defined as the transmission and amplification of the originating sound as produced by the larynx, which is subsequently filtered through vocal tract, that is, the oral cavity, the pharynx and nasals, of the initial sound as produced by the larynx [Juvarra, 1987: 48].

According to Juvarra, this is an acoustical phenomenon of major importance, simply because it:

1. Contributes to, and determines in large part the quality of the voice.
2. It can either facilitate or obstruct the proper function of the vocal folds.
3. Finally, he contends that resonance can be controlled by the singer, but only by using the auditory and vibratory to continuously verify the correctness of his emission.

Juvarra contends that the resonators can only be controlled through the adjustment made on the mobile parts of the vocal tract. That is, the tongue, the mandible, the lips and the soft palate. To these, we should also add the larynx, which as a mobile organ capable of rising and falling within the pharyngeal tube, can modify in a sensible manner the dimensions of the vocal tract. It achieves this by lengthening and shortening it, which has considerable influence not only on the phonetics, but also on the acoustics of the vocal tract [Juvarra, 1987: 48].

Battaglia Damiani (2003) essentially agrees with Juvarra with respect to resonators, but defines the resonating cavity in slightly different terms. She deals more with sympathetic vibrations, suggesting that:

> Resonators are comprised of elastic bodies that co-vibrate spontaneously when excited by a soundwave that possesses a similar frequency to its own. Some resonators have a limited range of sensibility, vibrating only within a strict frequency band; others are capable of responding to a much wider range.

> An acoustic phenomenon consistent with the ability, on the part of an elastic body, to spontaneously co-vibrate when it is excited by the external vibrations

of another vibrating body that happens to coincide with the frequency of the said resonators. As with all elastic bodies, resonators co-vibrate spontaneously when they are excited by a sound wave of the same or similar frequency. All musical instruments take advantage of the principle of resonance [Battaglia Damiani, 2003: 207].

Damiani suggests that some resonators have a limited range of sensibility, vibrating only within a narrow band of frequency, whilst others are capable of responding to a much wider frequency range.

Further, and in line with Carlo Meano (1967), Damiani (2003) reminds us that when we listen to musical sounds issuing from a hi-fi, one can modify the brilliance, that is, the high frequencies of the spectrum and the lower frequencies are responsible for the *oscuro* aspects of the tone, but either way the pitch cannot be altered, according to her, the brilliance depends on the relative strength of the relevant (higher) partials frequencies.

The control of the resonators is a function of the manipulation of the soft mobile articulatory organs, such as the tongue, the mandible, the lips and the soft palate.

The resonator can also be controlled through the natural rise and fall of the larynx, which modifies the size and shape of the vocal tract by elongating, lowering and shortening it. This laryngeal rise and fall tends to shape the vocal tract into a very important acoustic and phonetic device. Thus, the lowering of the larynx results in García's voix sombré whilst raising the larynx is corresponds to Garía's voix claire [Battaglia Damiani, 2003: 207–208].

The acoustic cavity is theoretically capable of assuming an infinite number of positions, but as we discussed above, the direct muscular control exercised by the singer is rather of a gross nature, the more refined adjustments depending on the phonetic and vocalic formation.

According to Sanchez Carbone, the resonating system is no less important than that which produces the original sound. It is now well established that the nasopharynx, the buccopharyngeal cavity and the paranasal sinuses are mainly responsible for determining the intensity and timbre of the sound. Just a note of caution with respect to the nasopharynx: absent a raised soft palate, which closes the nasopharynx, it is now scientifically proven that an open nasopharynx can dampen the soundwaves.

Sanchez Carbone contends that:

> Given that the level of activity at the vocal folds remains constant, then quality and timbre of the sound we produce will be dependent on the emphasis we give to one or other of the resonators, that is, the nasopharynx, or the buccopharyngeal cavity, will determine the final timbre. Beyond this however, and notwithstanding the influence of the tongue with respect to expression, the type of vocal placement we end up with will be dictated by the particular physical and morphological makeup of the singer.

If for the sake of simplicity, we allow that it is possible to treat the nasal resonators (nasopharynx) as a separate and distinct resonator from the buccopharyngeal resonators, we may then be able to concentrate on the pharynx and the buccal resonating cavities, both of which possess a particular and separate resonance frequency. The walls of these two resonators are elastic, allowing for flexible changes in shape and volume.

The configuration of the pharynx depends on the position of the larynx, the tongue and the soft palate, whilst that of the buccal cavity depends on the opening of the mouth (lowering the jaw and raising the zygomatic arch), as well as the position of the tongue and the lips. The coupling of these resonators modifies the frequency of both resonators [Sanchez Carbone, 2005: 370]. In the chiaroscuro model, so beloved of the old Italian school, we generally associate the pharyngeal cavity with the formulation of the *scuro* aspects of the sound, that is, the first formant frequency which lends the sound its depth, roundness and colour; whilst the buccal cavity is associated with the second formant and lends the sound its characteristic brightness and brilliance, or the *chiaro* aspect of the balanced operatic sound.

The various vowels differentiate themselves from each other by choosing to emphasise the different resonance cavities that vary the timbre of the sound originating in the laryngeal source through the voluntary modification of the mobile parts of the articulatory apparatus.

Sanchez Carbone cites studies conducted by Raul Husson at the Sorbonne in Paris in 1956 which recognise that the buccopharyngeal cavity is capable of several fundamental functions. The most important of these are the absorbent function, the inertial impedance function, and the proprioceptive function. Let us examine each of these in detail.

Absorbent Function

According to Raul Husson, the acoustic energy absorbed by the vocal tract is enormous.

With respect to intense singing the absorption rate is mainly due to the softness of the walls of the cavity, as well as the turbulence and the viscosity. Titze (1994) and Fussi and Gilardone (2009) have confirmed Husson with respect to pharyngeal energy absorption, viscosity and turbulence aspects of interference. With respect to intense singing the absorption rate is mainly due to the softness of the walls of the cavity, as well as the turbulence and the viscosity.

Inertial Impedance Function

Husson maintains that during phonation these resonating cavities confer upon the larynx a relevant impedance (in the form of inertial reactance), which is constantly changing in accordance with the instantaneously varying vocal tract configurations.

This impedance, which as a result of inertial acoustic reactance is now a much closer match to glottal impedance, exercises a protective function that is efficacious on the fine neuromuscular mechanism of the glottis. In this manner, we can obtain maximum intensity at every moment by increasing the value of this rebounding impedance.

This idea of acoustical impedance, which has proven to be is so beneficial to the smooth vibrations of the vocal folds represents quite a complex concept and not altogether easy to explain. Loy's description of the various elements that create impedance are worthy of elaboration.

Loy concludes that:

> The first thing to say is that 'inertial reactance', which is defined as 'the inertia of the air mass, and is therefore called 'inertance', opposes change in volume velocity. This opposition to applied force because of inertia is called inertial reactance. It impedes the applied force because of the inertia of the air. Because an air mass stores energy by accelerating, it is called an acoustical inductor' [Loy, 2011: 360].

Inertial reactance, therefore, is the energy contained in an air mass and acts in opposition to the acoustic charge. This acoustic current, or acoustic charge, consists of the volume velocity of a particular airflow. Consequently, we can say that the acoustical charge is characterised by the total amount of air moved in a particular time. The power of the charge is determined by the strength of the current and the length of time the charge is applied for.

Air pressure may best be defined as the energy contained in a volume of air – which is also known as energy density. This energy density is really the energy contained in a particular air pressure.

Inertial reactance, then, may best be defined as 'the inertia (movement of air) inherent in an air mass which opposes change in volume velocity'. The main characteristic of inertial reactance is that it acts in opposition to the applied force of the breath flow and is therefore an impedance to the applied force. Therefore, inertial reactance maybe defined as a function of the air mass that acts as an impedance to the applied force.

In summary, it is the inertial reactance inherent in the air mass that impedes the force applied by the acoustical charge in the air current, which according to Husson, and more recently elaborated on by Martin Rothenberg and Ingo Titze, is so beneficial to the vibratory function of the vocal folds and massively contributes to an acoustically strong voice.

Proprioceptive Function

The internal sensibilities originated by the walls of the resonating cavity during phonation exercise important effects: they increase the tonus of the laryngeal musculature via reflex actions, which flow into the consciousness of the singer allowing her to examine and control the phonatory flow.

I agree with all three points, and believe that the advantages issuing from vocal tract reactance are an enormous boon to the singer with respect to quality of sound and economy of coordinated effort. These benefits ensue from the abrupt termination of the airflow as a result of the almost instantaneous closure of the vocal folds and have the effect of skewing the glottal airflow and exciting the upper harmonics which, when filtered by the vocal tract, endow the voice with its brilliance and ring. This can best be achieved through a combination of firm glottal closure (vocal fold collision), a high level of subglottal pressure, and a large value of acoustic reactance being fed back towards the glottis.

I certainly agree with Righini with respect to the importance of the resonator, and the benefits of vocal tract reactance. The truth is that absent the vocal tract the human voice would be no more than a buzz. We here recall Righini's comments with respect to the diminutive size of the vocal sound absent the resonator.

Consequently, we can confirm that through the intelligent deployment of the variable inertial reactance, the vocal tract is capable of forging a stronger source/tract connection, leading to an unusual ease of vocal fold vibration and a stronger acoustic output. It achieves this by lowering the larynx, elongating the epilaryngeal tube, and widening the pharynx.

This strong source/tract connection lowers the threshold level, skews the glottal waveform and leads to maximum flow declination rate (abrupt glottal closure), which as discussed above, has the effect of exciting and strengthening the higher source harmonics which have a great impact on the vocal intensity and timbre.

All of the above is now common knowledge but I am happy to report that the better Italian schools, led by Oskar Schindler, Franco Fussi and Silvia Magnani, through to Mara, Juvarra, Damiani, and Sanchez Carbone have all adopted this relatively new knowledge.

I agree with Juvarra (1987) Battaglia Damiani (2003), Sanchez Carbone (2005), and other Italian authors.

Having said that, I believe it is important not to overstate the extent and influence ascribed to the resonator. The human resonator (vocal tract) undoubtedly plays a major part in enhancing vocal quality and timbre. It also plays an important part in the feedback element which facilitates vocal fold vibration. Nonetheless, it remains a fact that the human resonator can only enhance the harmonic partials contained in the sound waves produced by the voice source (vibrator). Whilst it is true that the vocal tract imparts its own characteristic and personal voice quality to the sound through the process of matching and enhancing the harmonic partials issuing from the voice source to the formants of the vocal tract, it is not of itself capable of producing the originating harmonic partials.

It is worth remembering that the relative strength of the harmonic partials is produced at the source. Once these leave the voice source, they cannot be altered. The resonator can only enhance whatever partials are swept through it; it cannot, as Rothenberg reminds us, make a weak partial strong. It cannot convert a breathy, veiled sound into a brilliant one.

Titze (2009) contends that there are only two primary means of producing source harmonics:

1. The first is to adduct the vocal folds sufficiently so as to facilitate their collision, and the greater their collision the greater the number of harmonics and the greater the relative strength of these harmonics.

2. The second is to cause the acoustic energy of the vocal tract (acoustic reactance) to go back towards the glottis, thereby altering the glottal flow. Both strategies cause a distortion of an otherwise simple glottal airflow that would normally only produce one harmonic, the fundamental [Titze, *Nats Journal,* May 2009].

The first strategy, vocal fold adduction, is the result of greater subglottal pressure and greater glottal resistance.

The second strategy involves the lowering of the larynx, the elongation and narrowing of the epilaryngeal tube and the widening of the pharynx. I agree with Titze (2009) when he says that typically both strategies are deployed simultaneously [*Nats Journal,* May 2009].

There is also broad agreement in the Italian literature that intensity and timbre are amongst the most important elements of singing and both are a function of the relative strength between the fundamental and harmonic partials. These elements are ultimately controlled by the interrelationship between subglottal pressure and glottal resistance. It is important to remember that this whole discussion about resonance, intensity, vocal timbre and its relationship with the relative strength of the harmonic partials can only take place within the paradigm of excellent breath management and the influence it has on glottal resistance. It is this relationship, in fact, that is responsible for most of the parameters associated with vocal strength and acoustic power.

I believe that the relative strength of these harmonic partials is a function of the interaction between subglottal pressure, amplitude, closing rate and the abrupt termination of airflow, all of which impact on the skewing of the waveform and enrichment of the upper harmonics. Consequently, we can say that the structure of the sound wave is established well before it enters the vocal tract.

Having said that, it is also true that the standing waves travelling back and forth along the vocal tract creating a variable inertial reactance have considerable influence on threshold pressure and can either facilitate or dampen the vibrations of the vocal folds, but this influence is secondary and not as direct as the interaction between subglottal pressure and glottal resistance and the resulting mode of the vocal fold vibration. The resulting harmonic partials are enhanced by the vocal tract, but it is this combined source/tract fusion that imparts the personal and unique characteristics to the voice.

Vocal Timbre

Damiani (2003) agrees with the concept that glottal adduction has a great deal of bearing on the types of sound we produce. For instance, she rightly insists that the timbre and character of the human singing voice depends not only on the number but also the relative intensity of the harmonics. These harmonics correspond to multiple frequencies of the fundamental that superimpose themselves in particular relationships as represented on the sound spectrum.

Battaglia Damiani postulates that, with respect to timbre, this is not only a function of the vocal resonators but also a function of the shape of the vocal folds, as well as the mode of vocal fold vibrations, and how these elements are adjusted relative to one another. She confirms that when the vocal folds are more firmly occluded, vocal timbre is enriched and is often described as having more bite. From a physiological point of view, the closure of the vocal folds occurs more briskly and for a shorter duration. In this mode of vibration, the sound wave is more linear, manifesting itself on the acoustic spectrum as an enrichment of the higher partials. On the other hand, whenever vocal fold occlusion is more relaxed and incomplete, the resulting sound is both breathy and veiled.

At this point, Battaglia Damiani emphasises the fact that the occlusion of the vocal folds is indeed very important not only because of its impact on the relative intensity of the harmonic partials and thus on vocal timbre but also because when combined with the size and shape of the vocal fold thrown into vibration, it is a determinant of vocal registers [Battaglia Damiani, 2003: 206–209].

Carlo Meano (1968), an Italian ENT specialist and vocal physiologist of international stature, lends his considerable voice on the subject. He contends that when we listen to a musical instrument, such as a piano, sounding a particular pitch, we also perceive the sound of other notes, always higher and gradually decreasing in intensity. Each harmonic tone sounds like an echo of the fundamental tone, but increasing the number of vibrations by a factor of two, three, four and five. This is the internationally accepted wisdom of the day, but since we are dealing with Italian authors, I choose to cite Meano.

According to Meano, these tones are supplementary harmonic overtones of the initial fundamental sound.

According to Meano, 'Our ear hears the supplementary harmonics blended into a unified sonorous sensation through an involuntary and natural process of synthesis, establishing a characteristic timbre for each sound' [Meano, 1968: 20].

Without harmonic overtones, the fundamental sound may be characterised by a weak or highly diminished intensity.

Meano elaborates with even more precision:

> It is the harmonics which create that indispensable resonance in the so-called 'resonating chamber' of all musical instruments and also in the human body during vocal production [Meano, 1968, 20].

Fussi and Gilardone make a substantial contribution when they state that:

> The timbre of the voice depends in part on the mode of occlusion of the vocal folds and partly on the anatomical characteristics of the vocal tract and the morphological organization of these. When we increase vocal fold occlusion, vocal timbre is enriched and we say that that the voice has gained 'bite' or squillo [Fussi & Gilardone, 2009: 25].

On the other hand, these authors contend that,

> When glottal occlusion is reduced and incomplete, the vocal folds generate a breathy sound which produces a timbre that is perceived as being poor and 'veiled' [Fussi and Gilardone, 2009: 25].

With respect to resonators, Fussi and Gilardone make an important distinction between the resonator itself and the air contained in the resonator, which is set into vibration by the excitation force exercised by the source vibrations originating at the vocal folds. These vibrations are contained within the issuing sound waves and are constituted by the fundamental tone and a complete harmonic series. According to Fussi and Gilardone:

> If the air in the resonator is excited by a particular sound wave, it produces a sound composed of a frequency band which is comprised of the natural peaks pertaining to the vocal tract being traversed [Fussi and Gilardone, 2009: 25].

These spectral peaks are called formants and the singer's task is to match as closely as possible the frequency of the harmonic series with the corresponding frequency of particular vocal tract formants [Fussi & Gilardone, 2009: 25]. All of the above is in line with the accepted wisdom, and indeed this book is not seeking to prove that the Italian singing master possesses any particularly superior knowledge, but rather it seeks to examine how they adapt the available scientific knowledge.

Battaglia Damiani contends that the human resonator can do it all: it increases the volume of the voice, enhances the quality, and above all it emphasises the timbre that distinguishes not only one voice from another, but also one person from another. She believes that no two voices are the same, not even amongst identical twins.

The timbre of the human voice, when properly placed, is determined by the formants of the singing voice. Damiani is adamant that when a student arrives at this understanding, she will never again feel the necessity to scream in order to amplify the sound. She rightly insists that the timbre and character of the human singing voice depends not only on the number but also on the relative intensity of the harmonics. These harmonics correspond to multiple frequencies of the fundamental that superimpose themselves in particular relationships as represented on the sound spectrum.

Battaglia Damiani defines resonance as 'an acoustic phenomenon consistent with the ability, on the part of an elastic body, to spontaneously co-vibrate when it is excited by the external vibrations of another vibrating body that happens to coincide with the frequency of the said resonators' [Battaglia Damiani, 2003: 207].

There is broad agreement that the human instrument is very different from other instruments, simply because the vocal tract resonator does not have a fixed structure, but remains a rather flexible system of resonance, capable of assuming diverse forms. It is a resonating chamber that is both 'alive and active', and in which by altering the combination and frequency of the formants we produce different vowels, and often at the passaggio a slightly modified version of those vowels.

In summary, we may state that the cavities that comprise the resonator are neither precisely determined nor defined. They are rather variable and flexible and are determined by the articulatory movement of the larynx, which with its ascending and descending movement alters the length and volume of the pharynx. The vocal tract is also influenced by the movement of other articulators such as the action of the mandible, the soft palate, the lips and the tongue. As a result of its variable flexibility, the resonating cavity is capable of assuming an infinite number of dimensions and configuration.

Formants and Vocal Tract Resonances

Van den Berg contends that the interaction between the breath and the voice source results in 'puffs or rushes of air escaping through the glottis', creating sound waves and proving conclusively that 'the glottis is the primary source of sound' [Van den Berg, 1957: 230]. It is the nature of this interaction that determines the timbre (quality) of the voice source spectrum: a flat, round spectrum signifies a breathy voice lacking in upper harmonics; whilst a sharp, tall, spikey signal signifies a brilliant, penetrating sound that is rich in upper harmonics. Sundberg found that when the frequency of these source harmonics is matched to the frequency of the formants of the vocal tract, the singer gains a synergistic boost of acoustic energy. He believes that these vocal tract formants 'are of paramount importance to the voice sound. They totally determine vowel quality, and they give major contributions to the personal voice timbre' [Sundberg, 1998: 47].

The skill and imagination with which the artist combines the mechanical elements with the aesthetic elements of singing (musicality and poetic sensitivity), tell us a great deal about the artist's intelligence, creativity and ability to fuse the physiological, emotional and aesthetic elements.

The value of the vocal tract is due to the fact that it not only reinforces the sound but also regulates and serves to excite other regions of resonance. The proof of the statement is demonstrated by the fact that during the act of singing the sound waves travel beyond the vocal tract, reaching out to the face, the forehead, in the head and all the way back to the neck, such diffusion contributing greatly to the resonances of the voice.

Sanchez Carbone makes a compelling argument about formants, stating that the regular harmonic structure for a sound issuing from the voice source can best be described as triangular, but by the time it has been filtered through the vocal tract, it is no longer linear but rather displays an uneven surface. This does not mean that the fundamental will be the strongest note, on the contrary, often it is the second harmonic which is stronger than the fundamental simply because the resonating vocal tract comes into play, enhancing certain partials and attenuating others. These resonances, which are known as formants, determine the vowel.

Sundberg states that the vowel we pronounce or sing whether it be an [a] or an [i] has a great deal to say about the constituent harmonics. Johan Sundberg confirms that there are 4 or 5 formants produced by the laryngeal vestibule and vocal tract in combination with the articulators such as the lips, the tongue, the pharynx and the soft palate. In particular, he postulates that lowering the larynx and protruding the lips lengthens the vocal tract, thereby lowering all formants; whilst raising the larynx pulling the lips into a smile has the opposite effect, that is, it shortens the vocal tract and raises all the formants [Sanchez Carbone, 2005: 385].

Schindler believes that the process of either singing or speaking, is characterised by constant minor alterations in the length of the vocal tract. These various and continuous changes in laryngeal position and the also the shape of the mouth, are a function of the sound and vowel being sung [Schindler 2010: 75].

Sanchez Carbone goes directly to the source, citing Johan Sundberg. She suggests that we tune these formants by intelligently manipulating the vocal tract to attain different configurations and therefore, different vowels. We achieve this by manipulating the component parts of the vocal tract; that is, the pharynx, the tongue tip and tongue blade, the jaw and the lips. We will deal with vowel formation in a later section.

Each of these configurations affects a particular formant:

1. The jaw for instance, affects the first formant and dropping it generally raises the first formant. This is typically achieved by the articulation at the tempora-mandibular joint which provides the only free movement within the skull: specifically, it is responsible for the diverse movement of the Jaw so critical to both articulation and resonation.

2. Manipulation of the tongue body generally alters the second formant, which is particularly dependent on the tongue shape.

3. For most vowels, it is the tip of tongue that influences and alters the third formant; for most vowels, it is the tongue tip that influences the third formant.

4. And lowering the larynx and widening the pharynx, expanding the ventricles and widening the laryngeal collar affects the fourth and fifth formants. Sundberg, has found that a cluster of the third, fifth and fourth formants represents the configurations which manifests itself as the 'singer's formant'.

Before going further, we should explore an understanding of such concepts as formants, formant tuning, and the singer's formant.

We should explain that 'formants' may best be described as areas of heightened concentrations of acoustic energy, which are found within the vocal tract and are determined by a particular configuration of the articulators. Each specific vocal tract configuration corresponds to a particular resonance frequency known as a 'formant', and the different combinations of first and second formants therefore form a corresponding vowel with its own individual colour. With reference to spectrograms, formants manifest themselves as peaks of energy displayed on the spectrum.

These peaks of energy vary widely, depending on which vowel is being sung. Vowels are the function of the first and second formants of the vocal tract.

We know that the soundwave issuing from the vocal source is a complex sound consisting of fundamental and harmonic partials or overtones. When these harmonic partials are fed through the glottis and into the vocal tract, the partials are impelled towards a matching frequency amongst the formants residing in the vocal tract. When these frequencies finally find their match, the result is that the first formant is mainly responsible for vocal colour and the second formant is largely responsible for vowel definition, while the cluster of formants 3, 4, and 5 provides the sound with focus, brilliance, and a characteristic timbre, which was so prized by the traditional Italian school with its concept of chiaroscuro.

Formants and Formant Tuning

Opening the mouth for top notes has the effect of raising the first formant to the level of the fundamental, which in high register of the female voice is considerably high than the first formant. If we fail to match the frequencies of the source harmonics with those of the formats, we will never achieve optimum vocal resonance.

The fourth formant is ever dependent on the laryngeal vestibule and is found in the frequency range between 1700 Hz 3500 Hz — the other two formants display considerable variations.

It is clear from the above that the actual configuration of the articulators within the vocal tract is not only the ultimate determinant of vocal resonance, but is also responsible for the fine-tuning of all the formants. Given the importance of these articulators and their specific association with particular formants, I believe it is now imperative that we should examine each in detail, but with particular attention to the Italian school.

Antonio Juvarra on Formants

According to Antonio Juvarra, the acoustic cavity is theoretically capable of assuming an infinite number of positions, but the direct muscular control that the singer may exercise over it is of a gross nature, the more refined adjustments depend on vocalic formation.

Juvarra subdivides the formation of the vowels in accordance with the position of the tongue and lips, and the creation of the space within the vocal tract. He categorises them into forward and backward vowels, laterals and rounded vowels, and open, closed and mixed vowels.

For each vowel, the distribution of energy between the fundamental and the formants that constitute that particular vowel is different.Consequently, we speak of higher and lower resonances or strong or weak resonances. For instance, the [u], [y] and [i] all share the same lower resonance (first formant) but are distinguished by different high resonances or (second formant).

Battaglia Damiani (2003) agrees with Juvarra (1987) and states that whilst phonemes or vowels are distinguished by both first and second formant, it is really the second formant that is most significant to the differentiating the various vowels. The reason is simple, whilst there are several vowels that possess a first formant frequency of a similar value the real difference is in the frequency value of the second formant that swings dramatically with the different vowels [Battaglia Damiani, 2003: 220].

Juvarra declares that the mastery of the singer over his instrument depends in large part on his ability to harmonise the harmonics produced at the source (the fundamental and its integer partials) with the formants of the vocal tract that provide vowel definition roundness and colour. This essentially means matching the fundamental frequency with the first formant, or one of the higher partial with the second and third formant (brilliance). Juvarra informs us that every pitch has a number of multiples of its fundamental frequency, which may or may not coincide with the frequencies that constitute the vowel formants.

Matching Formants in the Female Voice

We will see later that an important part of our work as singers is to match these frequencies, and given that we can't change the frequency of the note (pitch) we must then resort to altering the formant frequencies. This is particularly so in the female voice which, in the high register, sings well above the frequency of the first formant. Consequently, in order to match these two frequencies, we have no alternative but to drop the jaw which has the effect of rising the first formant.

When fundamental frequency or one of its harmonics falls within the bandwidth of a vocal tract formant, then there is consonance between the source harmonics and the and formant frequency of the vocal tract. This does not happen often because whilst the fundamental and the relevant harmonics are changing constantly, the frequency band of the formants remains fairly fixed within each vowel. Given that the fundamental cannot be changed because the notation represents the composer's intention, then there is only one way to match the fundamental to the formant frequency and that is to alter the formant frequency by lowering the jaw or through moderate vowel modification.

Fussi and Magnani explain the process of matching the first formant to the fundamental being sung. The following is their description of the process:

> The difference between the female singing voice and the female speaking voice is more distant than it is in the male, but than again so is the intensity produced by the female voice. When the female voice sings at high frequencies, it is difficult to understand which vowel is being sung, simply because the degree of mouth opening required to

accommodate the high register is more dependent on the frequency being sung than it is on articulation. Consequently, we can say that the soprano opens her mouth in an effort to elevate the frequency of the first formant to match the frequency of the fundamental being sung.

So that in cases where the first formant is lower than the frequency being sung, which is generally true of all the soprano high register, that formant is altered and repositioned in a way that its frequency approximates the value of the fundamental. This is achieved through the modification of the vocal tract by opening the mouth, a manoeuvre that produces an increase in vocal intensity. This is the result of the acoustic law stating that the closer the approximation between a formant and its matching fundamental, the greater the intensity of sound [F M, 1994:40].

In short, we can say that some vowels function well (that is, they create a favourable acoustic reactance), facilitating the oscillation of the vocal folds whilst other vowels act as an obstacle. It is clear from the above that the singers' task is to continually adapt the space of the vocal tract in such a manner as to facilitate the best results through a balanced outcome between the lower formant which provides the colour and roundness, and the upper formants which are responsible for the brilliance.

Damiani on Vowel Formants

Damiani is most eloquent with respect to the formants that constitute the vowels. She contends that acoustically speaking the elements that most specifically characterise the human voice are represented by the first harmonic or the fundamental which frequently is to be found in the frequency bandwidth between 100–125 Hz for male voices and between 200–250 Hz for female voices. The fundamental frequencies then are to be found in the zone of the lower notes, whilst the frequencies that distinguishes the phonemes or words are to be found in the zone of the high or acute zone of the voice. These frequency areas are in the zone of 250 or more; that is:

- 250 to 500 low frequency band
- 500 to 2000 medium frequency band
- 2000 and anything above are regarded as higher-frequency-bands.

Battaglia Damiani cites a number of authorities with respect to formants and the part that the individual articulators play in their formation. She is influenced by Di Girolamo and associates and even more so by Schindler whom she cites at length.

Di Girolamo's contribution came in the form of MRI photographs in which the subject was asked to sing the corner vowels (a, i, u).

Formants and Timbres

The pharyngeal resonating cavity increases the sound level of the harmonics which frequency is harmonised with the pharyngeal frequency. This is generally somewhere between 100 and 2500 Hz, depending on the shape and volume of the bucco-labial opening.

It follows, as we have already argued, that every sung vowel when issuing from the mouth is produced by two principal formants that typically give it its particular characteristic. The bucco-pharyngeal vocalic formants are different in the singing voice than they are in the speaking voice. This is due to the rapid alterations occurring in the shape of the acoustic cavity during articulation of the spoken word.Acoustic studies have revealed that the timbre of the singing voice is different to that of the spoken. The expert singer is always seeking the best match between the frequencies issuing from the voice source and those formed by the vocal tract.

Formants are characterised by bandwidths of frequencies generated by the vocal tract and generally excited by the sound waves issuing from the vocal source. Battaglia Damiani defines 'formants' as a narrow band of frequencies that an instrument or indeed the human voice has the natural aptitude to excite for the purpose of enhancing resonance. These natural narrow bands of frequencies may be considered as the fingerprints of that particular voice or instrument [Battaglia Damiani, 2003: 220].

In addition, the formants differentiate the sound source by enriching certain harmonic partials that confer timbre to the voice. Damiani reminds us that in the case of the [u] vowel the first formant is around 250 and the second is around 500 Hz, whilst the first formant of an [i] vowel is also around [250]: the second formant, however, is above the 2000 Hz zone, well above the frequency of the soprano C6 [Schindler in Battaglia Damiani, 2003: 220].On the other hand, with respect to the [i] vowel, the elevated anterior position of the tongue diminishes the volume of the mouth space and augments that of the pharynx. It follows that the superior part of the spectrum will be raised. That is, the high harmonics are strengthened and emphasised on the spectrum. On the contrary, with the [u] vowel the posterior part of the tongue is raised towards the soft palate, reducing the pharyngeal space and augmenting the buccal cavity, thereby reinforcing the lower formants [Battaglia Damiani, 2003: 220].

The Singer's Formant

A particular frequency of great interest to the singer is the so called 'singer's formant' to which we attribute the 'squillo' of the voice, that is, the brilliance and carrying power of the elite singing voice. The 'singer's formant' cannot be considered as a formant in the strict sense of the term, simply because it is common to all vowels and independent of the articulators, and can therefore be regarded as a normal vocalic characteristic as may be observed in the spectrum. The singer's formant, however, provides the singing voice with the capacity to be clearly heard over an orchestra.

Scientists have demonstrated that in the professional voice vowel recognition depends on the lower formants, whilst the characteristic aesthetic quality of the voice is determined by a formant that is only present when the voice is emitted at great intensity. This peak has been defined as the singer's formant and is regarded as an appropriate parameter to define the aesthetic character of the voice, often referred to as 'squillo'.

This singer's formant is therefore a frequency zone which reinforces the resonances and which can be found between 2300–2500 and 3200 Hz for vocalic sounds. In addition to providing clarity and relevance to the voice, the singer's formant also contributes to the differences in timbre.

Fussi and Magnani describe elegantly the physiological process that induces this very powerful mechanism. Here is their description of the Singer's formant:

> Since the fourth formant, which is the principal formant constituting the singer's formant, varies in relation to the diameter of the larynx, its decline or development may be obtained by lowering the organ (this causes an increase in the volume of the vestibular ventricles and pyriform sinuses and an elongation of the vocal tract) it is possible to understand the often-repeated exhortation by teachers to their male students to maintain a low laryngeal position during singing. These teachers exhort their students to preserve that lowered laryngeal position even as the fundamental frequency ascends. This technique counteracts the physiological raising of the organ in the highest level of the tessitura [Fussi & Magnani, 1994:40].

Conclusions

I have discussed the anatomy and physiology of the resonating vocal tract, and we have concluded that it is the various configurations of the articulators within the vocal tract, that is, the tongue, the lips, the jaw and the soft palate produce the different vowels. The soft palate is particularly important in separating the oral cavity from the nasopharynx. Failure to close the nasopharynx by raising the soft palate produces nasality in the sound. The tongue is particularly important to the formation of the second and third formant, whilst the mandible remains the best option for raising the frequency of the first formant.

I have argued throughout this chapter on the vowels, as constituted by different formants, remain very important to the process of resonation.

There is good agreement amongst vocal scientists and the better singing schools that vowels are constituted by the first two formants, and that these formants are the result of the size and shape of the vocal tract, which in turn is a function of the different configuration of the articulatory organs. With respect to formants, it is worth remembering that the first formant provides the vowel colour, depth and roundness, whilst the second gives the tone brightness and brilliance (chiaroscuro). The cluster of formants 3, 4, and 5 constitutes the singer's formant, which gives the singing tone that constant ring or carrying power (squillo) irrespective of the vowel or frequency being sung. Unlike the vowel formants which are created by the articulators within the vocal tract, the singer's formant is a function of the activity and shape of the epilaryngeal tube. It involves lowering the larynx, widening the pharynx and the vestibular sinuses.

Chapter 19

Consonants and Articulation

Mori contends that so many good as well as inferior singers have repeated the axiom that articulation helps the voice that it has become a commonplace. Mori laments that so many say it but very few do it, and many of the better singers who do it, do so instinctively, without really knowing what they are doing. Only a few select singers know what they are doing and are also aware that the mouth fulfils the function of harmonising with the harmonics from the voice source.

The fact that it is not just the movement of the tongue, but also the soft palate, the lips, the cheeks and so on, can modify the oral cavity, which in turn influences in the most diverse manner the articulated sound. This should not only interest the singer, but also induce her to explore the means that offer the best possibilities of modifying the sound.

Since the sung word is the effect of a synthesis of multiple activities competing to produce, it is right that we should meditate upon the reasons that produce or destroy the effect. This intelligent analysis should attract the singer in a similar manner to an artist on a quest to conquer his colours and form [Mori, 1970: 41–42].

Mori proceeds by classifying consonants into voiced and unvoiced consonants. She informs us that, voiced consonants are accompanied by the vibrating vocal folds, whilst the unvoiced are characterised by an articulatory constriction within the vocal tract that produces a pure rumour. For example [p] and [t] are unvoiced and therefore caused by a momentary constriction somewhere within the vocal tract, whilst [b] and [d] are produced in conjunction with vibrating vocal folds. She further classifies consonants into:

- labials (p-b-m)
- labio-dentals such as (f-v) which are semi-occlusive-fricatives
- lingua-dentals are represented by (d-t-l-n-r-s-z)
- palatals are represented by (c-g-gn-gl-se)
- velar consonants are represented by (c-g).

Mori believes that each of these classifications will have its own flavour that needs to be studied, at first with the help of a good teacher and later on one's own with the aid of a mirror. These exercises are to be performed for short periods daily, until the singer becomes more aware of the deviations within each classification. It is clear that consonants cannot be produced without some sort of occlusion or restriction somewhere with the vocal tract. This constriction can take place at the lips (fricatives) or by leaning the tongue in a predetermined position in the mouth, on the palate or in the pharynx [Mori, 1970: 42].

Sanchez Carbone advances those and other important themes with respect to consonants with rare incisiveness and clarity. She states that it is important to understand that any form of vocal sound must be defined as a response to laryngeal action, whereas any other form of noise created at the level of the supraglottic cavities is the result of an articulatory function. From the point of view of general acoustic communication, there is a clear distinction between the laryngeal function and that of the articulators, even though in practice they are intimately linked.

The laryngeal function, that is, the production of sound at the level of the vocal folds has a major significance in terms of emotional communication. On the other hand, the articulatory function, that is, the production of noise at a supraglottal level of resonance and articulation also possesses an autonomous communication, but it is rather at the intellectual level.

From the point of view of phonemics, the laryngeal function is destined to aid the production of vowels, for which we experience laryngeal vibrations without involving the constrictive organs of articulation, and which vibrations are then reinforced by the resonating cavity.

The Oropharynx

The oropharyngeal cavity is the principal vocal resonator; it is also the receptacle of the major articulators. The current of air which is transformed into sound when the air is chopped by the vibrating vocal folds and then flows through the vocal tract either as an articulated or as a vocalised sound. The first is caused by a constriction within the vocal tract, which creates consonants, whilst the latter, which is characterised by the uninterrupted production of sound, is characteristic of the production of vowels. The main articulators, the mandible, lips, tongue and soft palate are responsible for the essential modification of the vocal tract that influences in a major way the final acoustic product.

The consonants are produced by the interruption of the airflow, which are caused by a pharyngeal and oral constriction that ultimately generates a sound. These consonants or sounds can be either voiced or unvoiced.

When the free air traversing the vocal tract behaves in a certain manner, it can enhance the complex harmonic partials that constitute the soundwave, thereby creating characteristic vocalic sounds.

Nasopharynx

Raising the soft palate separates the oral cavity from the nasopharynx, an action which is beneficial to vowels and some consonants; however, for the execution of the nasal consonants the soundwave needs to be deviated towards the nasal cavity, this requires a lowering of the velum and an opening of the velopharyngeal port.

Oskar Schindler concurs with the above and elaborates further.

He informs us that the levator palatini muscle is mainly responsible for the elevation of the soft palate, whilst the tensor palatine muscle is responsible for the tensing of the palate. The palatoglossus muscle lowers the soft palate and raises the tongue, whilst contraction of the palatopharyngeus moves the palate in a dorsal caudal direction, which also influences the lateral wall of the pharynx. When the above combination is added to the contraction of the levator palatine muscle and the superior constrictor of the pharynx, they combine to close the velopharyngeal sphincter during phonation.

Finally, Schindler informs us that the velopharyngeal port regulates the closure of the nasopharynx, particularly during the execution of the m and n consonants, or nasal continuants. Its relaxation allows the nasalisation of these consonants, whilst its contraction excludes nasalisation from the phenomenon of resonance. This is a particularly important in determining vocal colour [Schindler, 2010: 76].

Fussi and Magnani also address the issue of nasality by suggesting that we need to remember that the soft palate is a mobile structure that functions as a valve which is capable of separating the oral cavity from the nasopharyngeal cavity. Its elevation produces phonemes that have an exclusive oral quality (all the Italian vowels and most of the consonants). If the separation between the oral cavity and nasopharynx is inadequate, then it will induce a nasal quality [Fussi & Magnani, 2017: 60].

Consequently, we can state that during the execution of the nasal consonants the sound waves need to be deviated towards the nasal cavity. This can only be achieved through a lowering of the velum and an opening of the velopharyngeal port, not a vocal tract configuration that enhances most other vocal sounds.

According to Fussi and Gilardone, for the production of all other vowel sounds and consonantal sounds, the soft palate remains elevated. In the event that the source signal is simultaneously radiated across the oropharynx and nasal cavities, there is a reduction of intensity [Fussi & Gilardoni, 2009: 35].

As we saw above, Sanchez Carbone laments the unruly tongue and how difficult it can be to aducate it to find its rightful place without creating tension. She recommends a remedial strategy in which we use the consonants that brings the tip of the tongue against the lower teeth. For example, the [v] fricative consonant, in which the upper incisors meet the lower lips (labio-dental), whilst the tongue remains in contact with lower teeth. Another family is represented by the [z] and [s] buzzes which induce the neutral position of the tongue. Even when the vowel changes, the tip of the tongue remains in contact with the lower teeth, as long as it is preceded by such consonants.

On the other hand, if the vowel is combined with such consonants as [v], [f], [b], [p], [z] and [s], the lingua-dental position of the tongue must be maintained during all vocal emission. Once the tip of the tongue has been conditioned to remain in contact with lower teeth, the vowels may retain that position without the aid of the consonants.

Sanchez Carbone also reminds us that during the emission of the vowels that follow these phonemes with consonants such as [v], [f], [b], [p], [g], [m], [s], and [z] the tip of the tongue must also remain in contact with the upper surface of the lower teeth. Any part of the vocal instrument that remains in a fixed or static state disturbs the triple mechanism constituted by the tongue-hyoid-bone-larynx, all of which form an anatomical unity. Normal phonatory behaviour allows total freedom for these three elements. [Sanchez Carbone, 2005: 362].

Sanchez Carbone continues:

> A clear articulation of consonants allows both precision of diction and continuity and uniformity of sound. This is obtained when the singers realises that a major part of the consonants are produced in a rapid and precise manner, with the apex of the tongue on the inferior surface of the lower dental arch. It is also true that insufficient energy of consonantal articulation causes an absence of precision and clarity in linguistic sound and rhythm. This defect maybe generated by various causes: such as concentration of all energy on the attack of the sound, leaving too little for the rest of the phrase. In part this is the result of how one manages the airflow [Sanchez Carbone, 2005: 468].

Finally Sanchez Carbone acknowledges that there are times when the constituent parts of the instrument are not sufficiently or correctly developed and here she provides us with a remedy. She contends that if the lips, tongue and mandible are insufficiently flexible, the remedy can be found in a programme of exercises connecting certain consonants with the appropriate articulatory organs. In acquiring the necessary elasticity and flexibility, we can be of great help to the emission of both vowels and consonants, and in the process we will almost certainly improve the overall quality of vocal emission [Sanchez Carbone, 2005: 469].

Finally, Sanchez Carbone maintains that a language that is rich in vowels is more conducive to a placement that is more oriented towards emotive elements and laryngeal virtuosity; whilst languages that are more consonant driven, are generally oriented towards articulation of consonants, precision of diction and comprehension of text.

Bruno and Paperi concur with Sanchez Carbone above, particularly with respect to the tongue. They further declare that if the tongue does not occupy the correct position and configuration within the mouth, it will only cause vocalic distortion. This configuration must be compatible with the vowel being sung. Any lingual tension, or a deficient functional filter will interfere with harmonics being swept through the resonator, will distort the vowel. Bruno and Paperi suggest that the importance of the tongue in singing is often underestimated. Tension in this organ can be detrimental to the overall sound produced. Such tensions are almost always the result of incorrect voice production. Bruno and Paperi declare that we should aim for a great deal of freedom and flexibility in the tongue, if we are going to begin our study with an ideal postural position. This is best achieved by using a clear but warm [MA] that is born in the larynx, but completes its formation between the soft palate and the hard palate. We will become aware that we should not use the mandibular muscles to converge the vocalic sound towards the facial resonators. The preparatory movement is divided between a larynx that is descending and a soft palate that is rising, allowing the tongue to extend its tip towards the lower teeth [Bruno & Paperi, 2001: 111].

Control of the tongue is the principal technique for releasing the excessive tension that often accumulates in the buccal cavity.

In a description that recalls Rachelle Maragliano Mori, Battaglia Damiani on the other hand reminds us that consonants are the product of air traversing a restriction of the vocal tract either at the pharynx or the oropharynx. She mentions the fact that these constrictions can produce a second source of periodic sound that generates turbulence or a noise.

The essential element that characterises correct diction is due to the very distinct articulation of the consonants. The intelligibility of a conversation depends in part on intensity but above all on the mode of producing these consonants, and this is valid for all languages. The listener should not have any difficulty perceiving and identifying the phonemes [Damiani, 2003: 255].

The above is also in line with Meano. He contends that during the emission of most consonants, the tongue rises against the palate, thereby closing the passage of the expiratory current of air, causing a characteristic fricative noise. Consequently, we can say that consonants are produced by a fricative noise caused by constrictions of the air current as it flows through the phonatory tube.

Meano suggests that consonants should be classified in two ways:

- their mode of production, or how the obstacles occur during the passage of sonorous air current through the phonatory tube, and
- their zone of articulation or point of formation.

There are five modes of production:

- Fluid consonants or glides, the point of the tongue presses against the inferior alveolar ridge.
- Vibrant Consonants (R) the dorsal part of the tongue is elevated towards the palate whilst the point presses against the inferior dental incisors, creating a repetitive closure and opening for the expired passage.
- Occlusive consonants (plosives) — the point of the tongue presses against the upper alveolar ridge forming an obstacle which the column of air overcomes abruptly.
- Sibilant consonants or Fricatives (f, v, s, z, th, h) — the sonorous air column is restricted to a thin passage through the tightening of the phonatory tube.
- Nasal consonants (m, n) — the sonorous air column passes into the nasal cavity due to the lowering of the velum, constraining the entrance to the oral cavity [Meano, 1967: 126–127].

Battaglia Damiani is in line with Meano when she reiterates that consonants are no more than an acoustic noise that can be classified on the bases of articulation, that is, the restrictive area which is marked by the location where the expiratory current is disrupted on its way to the exit. As we have said, consonants can be classified on the basis of articulation or on the basis of mode of vibration. Those classified on the basis of articulation are:

- The labials — (p- b- m);
- The labio-dentals — (f -v);
- The dentals — (d- t- s- z);
- The alveolar — (r- n- l);
- The palatala are such as (Gi- Ge- Ci -Ce, Gn- Sc- Gl- Ch- Gh).

They can also be classified on the basis of mode of vibration which include the occlusive, explosive p, t, b, d, ca, ga, m, n, gn, le; and the nasals such as m, n, and g.

Appoggio may be best described as the focal point against which the soundwave vibrations impinge upon (proprioceptive sensations), these include the following focal points, facial *appoggio*, and the dentals, labials, and nasals.

Bruno and Paperi believe that with respect of *appoggio* and placement, we need to develop the capacity of our resonator by accessing all the parts at its disposal before the voice can be set free to reverberate in the external environment.

Consequently, we need to consider not only the more fixed walls of the vocal tract, but also the mobile parts, such as the mandible, the tongue, the epiglottis, the soft palate, the zygomatic arch and the lips.

In order to enhance the sound, we need to understand how to intervene in the oral cavity, the pharynx, and consequently the facial zone (the mask) upon which we must concentrate the arrival of the final product — variations of the final product.

We only mention this fact because there is a danger that we rather too quickly send both sound and word directly to the mask without allowing either time or space for all the harmonics to gain in amplitude and richness in a semi arch that can only be attained when the sound waves vibrate in the pharyngeal arch (faucial Isthmus). We should remember that in singing we also utilise the area above the soft palate.

In some instances, for example as when we execute the 'picchettato', the sound must find a vertical direction, which focal point is to be found in the large arch produced by raising the soft palate, before radiating towards the zygomatic arch and forehead. This is especially the case with coloratura sopranos.

However, we must keep in mind that the trajectory of the voice is not only vertical. In fact, most vocal styles, once having found the ideal position of the larynx, pharynx and soft palate, must learn to shape the vocal tract in order to enrich both sound and words, and any melody that does not possess the intensity of the 'picchettato' and which can withstand the modification of its projection during the passaggio. Consequently, it is better to become accustomed to controlling the voice as perceived not only in the air (atmosphere) but also internally (proprioceptive sensation) [Bruno & Paperi, 2001: 110].

Conclusions to Consonants

Consonants are produce by means of the air current traversing a restriction at some predestined point within the vocal tract. Consonants are generally classified as either voiced or unvoiced. Voiced consonants are characterised by the continued vibrations of the vocal folds irrespective of the constriction being created in the vocal tract, whereas unvoiced consonants are a function of the constrictions or occlusion at some point in the vocal tract, and therefore result in a pure rumour or even a turbulence. So we can say that consonants can be classified in two ways:

1. The first is the mode of production, or how the restrictions, or obstacles occur during the passage of the airflow through the vocal tract.
2. The second is the area of articulation or mode of vibration. These include glides, occlusive or plosives, fricatives and nasal.

The configuration of the tongue dorsum and tongue tip is different for each of these classifications and varies a little within each configuration.

Finally, we dealt with the notion of nasalisation, and we discovered that it is a function of a lowered soft palate, which allows the soundwaves to deviate into the nasal cavities or nasopharynx. Learning how to elevate and tense the soft palate, which is a function of the contraction of the levator and tensor palatine, will close the velapharyngeal port denying the sound waves access to the nasopharynx.

Final Conclusions

This book was inspired by a desire to critically evaluate the Modern Italian School of bel canto, its sources of knowledge, a blending of the old bel canto school and modern vocal science, and its techniques.

Having written extensively on both, the Old Italian bel canto school and contemporary vocal science, the fascination for me was to discover how a school, which is the fountainhead of such deep knowledge and enduring affection could move forward into the 21st century. I believed it would be a challenge to manage the transition and this study has proven that the challenge is real. However, the Italian School is making very good progress in terms of incorporating objective and scientific knowledge into its school. There are many excellent authors who have written a great number of erudite books, demonstrating an excellent knowledge of both the old school and contemporary science. In fact, it would not be an exaggeration to claim that their knowledge is the equal of any of their contemporaries anywhere in the world. The problems that we all have, which is not national but rather an international one, is how do we propagate this knowledge amongst teachers who are less enthusiastic about the physiological and scientific progress being made through vocal science than they should be. This is not an Italian phenomenon, but rather an international one, simply because there is no remedy for ignorance, and self-satisfied complacency, nor is there a cure for arrogance, and for people who have been infected with the malady known as 'I know it all'.

The book is structured in two sections the first part deals with the two periods of bel canto: the first refers to the Baroque period, which was dominated by the castrati and their teachers and composers, and the second was dominated by that formidable genius who reformed bel canto singing as much as he reformed opera, Gioachino Rossini.

Italians share a great awareness of the old bel canto school and its glorious achievements. Internationally, we have analysed all the available techniques of the old school extensively, but very few people seem to know what is happening in the Italian bel canto school of today. Consequently, I felt that it would be advantageous to investigate the modern Italian School, and in so doing, fill a considerable gap in our knowledge of the Italian School.

The idea for this book came to me whilst translating certain selections from the Italian literature into English for my previous books. It occurred to me that there were a number of excellent Italian authors who were exploring and writing about contemporary vocal research in Italy. However, their books were not available in English, and yet these writers are in direct line to Porpora, Manual Garcia, Francesco Lamperti and Mathilde Marchesi.

Consequently, I began translating substantial selections of their work into English in order to obtain an overview of the legendary school in transition, and thereby assessing its progress and current position. I discovered a thriving scene in which more and more vocal science research is being undertaken by first-rate scientists and assimilated into the Italian singing studio by such excellent teachers and authors as Rachele Maragliano Mori, Nanda Mari, Antonio Juvarra, Bruno and Paperi, Battaglia Damiani, and Maria Luisa Sanchez Carbone, and more recently, Delfo Menicucci. Vocal scientists are also prominent in Italy. Vocal scientists and acousticians such as Oskar Schnidler, and Fussi and Magnani, Gilardone, Ruoppolo, Righini and many others are very prominent indeed. It is true that most of these authors still speak of the old school with great affection, but how could you not? We have seen in these pages what was achieved by artists such as Farinelli, Caffarelli, Pistocchi, Bernacchi, Carestini, Senesisino, David, Nozzari, Garcia, Cuzzoni, Colbran, Malibran, Pasta and countless others. We all have much to learn from such artists and their techniques but current teachers and researchers understand vocal science and they know that it is not necessary to choose one or the other, but rather one and the other. These teachers are just as enthusiastic about contemporary vocal science as they are about the old school.

The objective of this book is to explore the trajectory of the old empirical bel canto school, with its proven techniques, vocalizzi and ornamental *fiorit-*

ura, as it progresses towards a new, modern Italian School dominated by scientific knowledge and methodology and physiological objectivity.

The element that unites these two paradigms is a common sound world.

Both the earlier masters and those of the modern Italian School profess a continuity, as both understand the importance of a good forward ringing tone that begins with a firm simultaneous onset and ends with a clear and spontaneous release. The result is a voice of good size and substantial range, capable of executing the two pillars of the bel canto style, *canto spianato* and *canto fiorito*.

These teachers seek to bring forward many of the proven techniques of that august school. However, they teach those techniques in very different ways to their predecessors. Not only do they incorporate an increasing amount of science into their teachings, but they also use a very different and more precise language. However, the essential ideas have not changed as witnessed by the substantial chapters in this book on respiration, voice source, registration, onset, resonation and articulation.

There is undoubtedly a lingering influence from the bel canto school in the modern Italian School, not just in terms of the continuity of a familiar sound world, and many proven techniques, but also in the enriching and humanising of the modern school. This, however, does not prevent modern teachers from moving towards a Modern Italian School. This new knowledge, this more precise and incisive language provides not only the foundations for the new Italian School but also a sense of continuity, a sense of that history which naturally evolved into the Modern Italian School, the aim of which is to incorporate and assimilate, not divide. There is an understanding that it takes more than a good voice and a good technique to make a wonderful career. It takes temperament, intelligence, subtlety, musicality, and a strong winning psychology. This is a school that understands that ultimately it is the richness of our humanity that makes each performance a unique experience.

APPENDIX A

Muscles of Respiration

Accessory Muscles of Inspiration

Seikel et al. contend that in order to develop an understanding of the respiratory function, we need to attain a good knowledge of the skeletal system. This is a proposition that I agree with.

It is important to remember that the lungs, which are the motive force of all sound production, are contained within the thoracic cage. The thorax is suspended from the vertebral column which doubles as the conduit for the spinal cord, and its nervous system supply for the body and extremities. It is bordered superiorly by the first rib and clavicle, and inferiorly by the lower floating ribs as shown here.

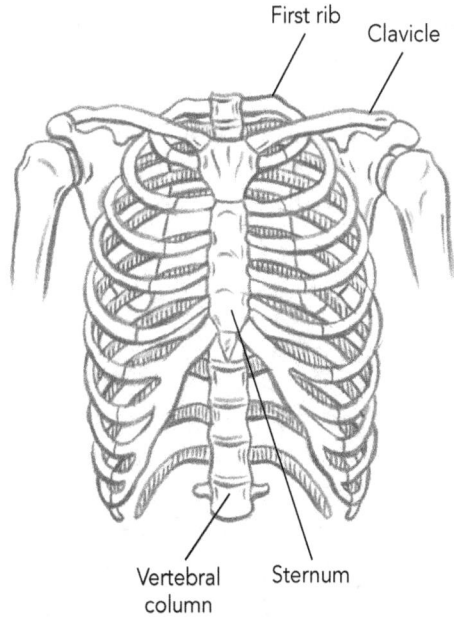

Figure 1 – Anterior view of the thorax.

The lateral and anterior aspects of the thorax are comprised of the ribs and sternum. All but the two lowest floating ribs are attached to the sternum through cartilages.

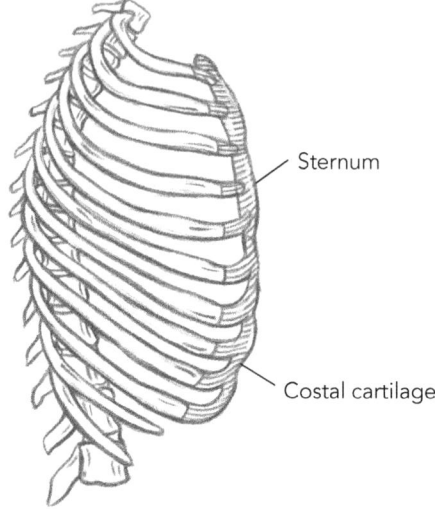

Figure 2 – Lateral view of rib cage showing relationship among ribs and sternum. Note that the rib cage slants down in the front.

We can see from the above lateral view of the thorax that the rib cage generally moves back and down but during full inspiration the rib cage are elevated and thrust forward. This, according to Meribeth Bunch Dayme, is representative of the pump handle strategy. Bunch offers an alternative strategy, which she calls the bucket handle strategy, in which the the lateral movement of the thoracic cage becomes prominent.

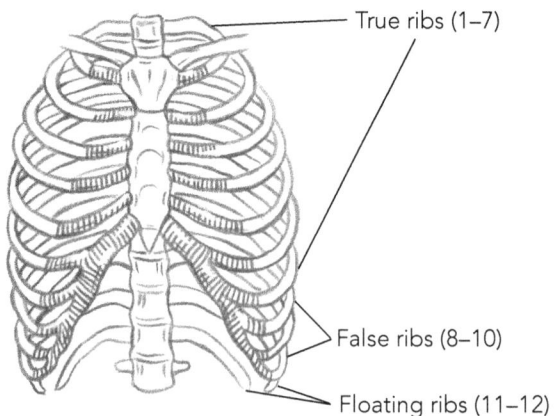

Figure 3 – Schematic of the relationship between the true, false and floating ribs.

While the diaphragm remains the central inspiratory muscle, it needs and receives assistance from its accessory muscles such as the external intercostals, contraction of which raises the ribcage forward. The external intercostals are a critical aid to the diaphragm and although the diaphragm remains the main muscle for inspiration, the external intercostals provide a significant increase in the capacity of air being processed.

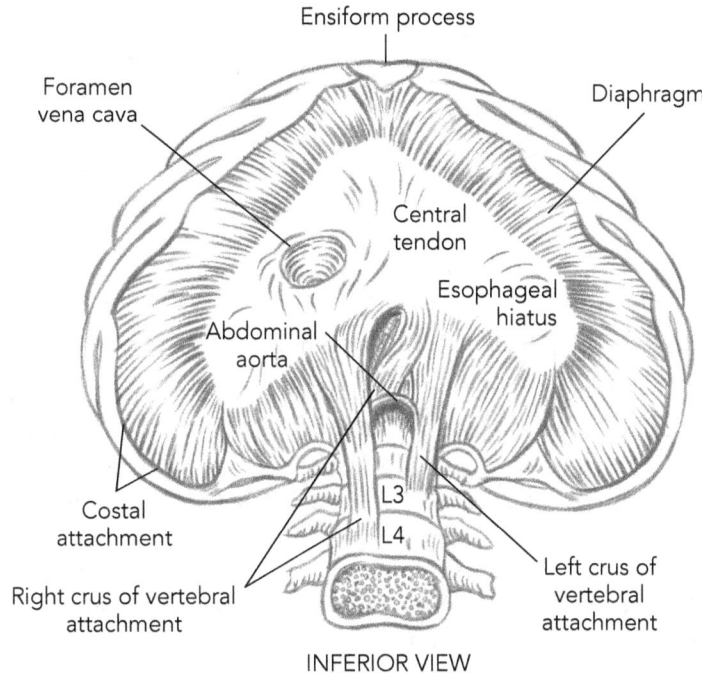

Figure 4 – Inferior view schematic of diaphragm, as seen from the abdominal cavity.

Posterior Thoracic Muscles of Inspiration

We will now examine the function of the different sets of muscles including the posterior thorax muscles, the accessory muscles of the neck, the muscles of the arm and shoulder, the muscles of forced expiration, the anterior and lateral thoracic muscles including the anterolateral abdominal muscles, and the posterior thoracic muscles.

The chief posterior thoracic muscles are the levator costarum and the serratus posterior superior. These muscles may appear to be muscles of the back but in fact are generally considered to be part of the thoracic framework.

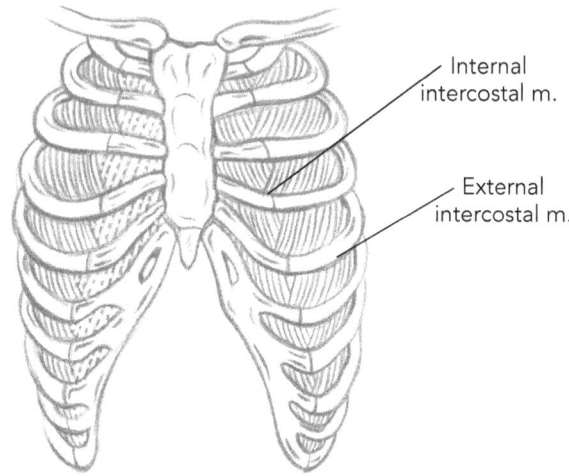

Figure 6 – External and internal intercostals.

Muscles of the Thorax, Back and Upper Limbs

Due to their attachment on the sternum and ribs these muscles are believed to assist the external intercostals in elevating the ribs and therefore aid with inspiration. At this point, we need to stress that the function of some of these muscles has not been confirmed through physiological studies.

The pectoralis major is a large fan shaped muscle that originates from two heads: the sternal head attaches to the costal cartilages, while the clavicular head is attached to the front clavicle. In respiration, the pectoralis major elevates the sternum and thus increases the transverse dimension of the ribcage. Seikel et al. (1997) contend that the pectoralis minor performs a similar function, although this has not yet been verified.

Serratus anterior muscles arise from the ribs 1 through 9 along the side of the thorax, converging on the inner vertebral border of the scapula. It is believed that the contraction of these muscles may also elevate the ribcage.

The subclavius muscle originates at the inferior margin of the clavicle and courses its way obliquely and medially to insert into the superior surface of the first rib at the chondral margin. It is believed that the subclavius elevates the first rib during inspiration, but the evidence to support this claim is rather inconclusive.

The rhomboideus major and minor, together with the trapezius and levator scapula muscles all provide support for the upper body, as well as assisting with elevation and control of the head and neck. These are vertebroscapular muscles, which according to Miller rotate the scapula, but do not play an important role in breathing (Miller, 1986: 275). In general

Appendix A — Muscles of Respiration

then, it is believed that these muscles assist with elevation of the ribs, and consequentially assist with inspiration.

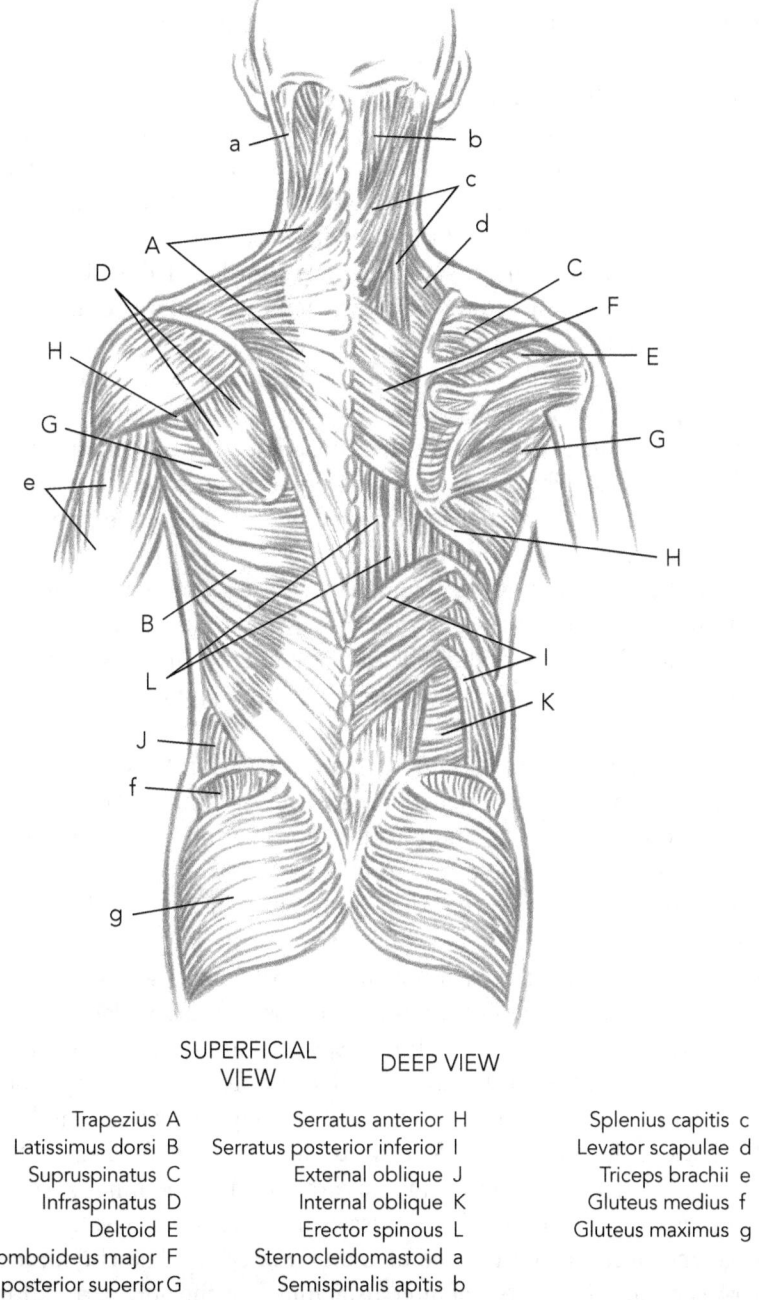

SUPERFICIAL VIEW

Trapezius A
Latissimus dorsi B
Supruspinatus C
Infraspinatus D
Deltoid E
Rhomboideus major F
Serratus posterior superior G

DEEP VIEW

Serratus anterior H
Serratus posterior inferior I
External oblique J
Internal oblique K
Erector spinous L
Sternocleidomastoid a
Semispinalis apitis b

Splenius capitis c
Levator scapulae d
Triceps brachii e
Gluteus medius f
Gluteus maximus g

Figure 7 – Posterior thoracic view.

Muscles of Forced Expiration

Muscles of the Thorax: Anterior and Lateral

It is believed that the internal intercostal, the innermost intercostal, and the transversus thoracic muscles almost certainly act in concert to pull down the ribcage and aid with forced expiration.

The internal intercostal muscles, sometimes called Intercostalis Interni, are pervasive throughout the thorax. They begin at the sternum, in between the cartilages of the true ribs and extremities of the cartilages of the false ribs. These muscles descend from the floor of a costal groove and adjacent costal cartilage and insert into the upper border of the rib below. These muscles are thickest around the cartilaginous or parasternal area. Their fibres run obliquely and almost at right angles to those of the external intercostal muscles. The muscles continue to the posterior costal angles, at which point they are replaced by the internal intercostal membrane. This aponeurotic membrane (a big sheet of tendon) is continuous posteriorly with the anterior fibres of a costotransverse ligament and anteriorly with the fascia between the internal and external intercostal muscles. These muscles are conspicuously absent in the posterior aspect near the vertebral column. While there is still considerable debate about the role of the internal and external intercostals, it would appear that the authoritative opinion is now heavily weighed towards the belief that the internal intercostals play a major role in depressing the ribs and therefore aiding expiration (*Gray's Anatomy*, 1995; Last, 1988).

When combined, the internal and external intercostal muscles, the latter running nearly at right angles to the internals, provide significant protection for the ribs, support the ribcage and maintain rib spacing, functions of considerable importance in forced expiration. The external intercostals consist of eleven pairs of muscles which extend from the tubercles of the ribs, where they blend with the posterior fibres of the superior costotransverse ligaments, almost to the costal cartilages, where each continues forward to the sternum as a large sheet of tendon called the external intercostal membrane. These muscles, which are thicker than the internal intercostals, pass from the lower border of one rib to the upper border of the rib below. Their muscle fibres run obliquely downwards and laterally at the back of the thorax, and downwards, forwards and medially at the front.

The transversus thoracic muscles are found in the inner surface of the rib cage. Contraction of these muscles tends to resist elevation of the rib cage and decrease the volume of the thorax cavity. The chondral portion (parasternal) of the internal intercostal muscle is the only part of this essentially expiratory muscle that is active during forced inspiration. The muscle is capable of partial contraction while the rest remains relatively relaxed.

In general, it would appear that the above muscles are involved in the lowering and the diminishing the thorax cavity and are therefore muscles of expiration.

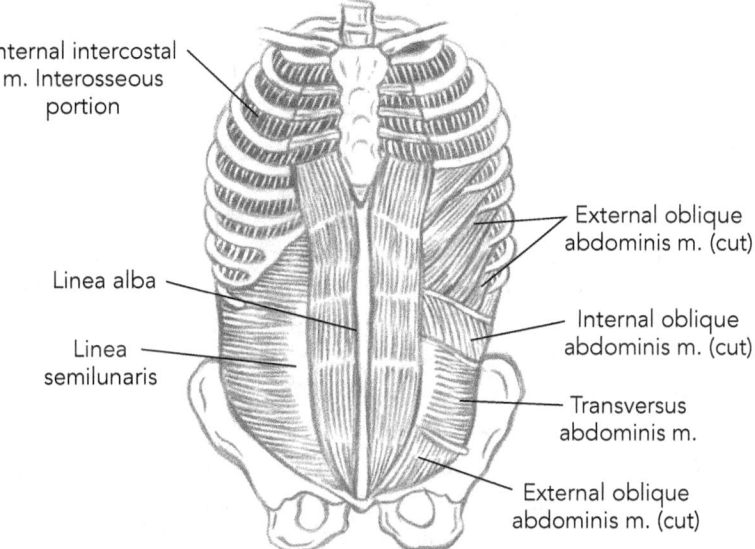

Figure 8 – Anterior view of the abdminals and accessory muscles.

Posterior Thoracic Muscles

All the available evidence suggests that the following muscles combine to depress the ribs and assist the anterolateral abdominal muscles with the act of forced expiration. Let us examine these muscles and ascertain how on the basis of their anatomical structure they help with forced expiration.

The subcostal muscles, which are found in the inner posterior wall of the thorax and take the same course as the internal intercostals, are unlike the intercostal muscles; the subcostals may span from the internal surface of one rib to the internal surface of the second or third rib below. The most probable function of the subcostals is to depress the ribs, hence aiding expiration (*Gray's Anatomy*, 1995: 815).

The serratus posterior superior: contraction of these muscles almost certainly contributes to the elevation of the ribcage and therefore assists with inspiration.

The serratus posterior inferior muscles originate on the spinous processes of the T11, T12, L1 through L3 and make their way laterally to the lower five ribs where they insert into the lower margin. The function of the serratus posterior inferior muscle is to pull down the ribcage, and assist with expiration (Last, 1988: 215).

The serratus posterior superior: contraction of these muscles almost certainly contributes to the elevation of the rib cage and therefore assists with inspiration.

The course of the innermost intercostals runs parallel to those of the internal intercostals. The internal intercostals are attached to the internal aspects of two adjoining ribs. They extend mainly through the middle three quarters of the lower intercostal spaces and are considered to be in the same plane as the transversus abdominis: that is a third layer. It is presumed that these muscles act with the internal intercostals.

The latissimus dorsi muscle originates from the lumbar, sacral and lower thoracic vertebrae with fanlike fibres inserting into the humerus. Its primary role is the movement of the upper extremity, but it also plays a role in chest stability and perhaps in aiding expiration.

The quadratus lumborum performs a function similar to the latissimus dorsi muscle, and is located in the dorsal aspect of the abdominal wall. These muscles originate along the iliac crest and fan up to insert into the transverse process of the lumbar vertebral and inferior border of the 12th rib. Unilateral contraction assists lateral movement of the trunk, whereas bilateral contraction frees the abdominal wall in support of the abdominal compression. This function is generally identified with forced expiration.

Other muscles suspected of providing abdominal support for forced expiration, according to Seikel et al., are the psoas major and minor muscles and the iliacus muscle: evidence for these suspicions is scant because of the difficulty in attaining physiological recordings of these muscles (Seikel et al., 1997: 109).

In general it may be said that the function of the posterior thoracic muscles is to pull down the ribs and decrease the thorax cavity, thereby aiding in expiration. The most active muscles in this group are: the internal intercostals, the subcostals, the innermost intercostals, the transverse thoracis, the serratus posterior inferior, the latissimus dorsi and quadratus lumborum.

The Anterolateral Abdominal Muscles

The function of the abdominal muscles of expiration is determined by compressing the abdominal viscera, a function that also promotes defecation, vomiting and childbirth (vocal folds are tightly adducted).

The transversus abdominis are the deepest of the anterior abdominal muscles. They run laterally from the posterior aspect of the vertebral column to the transversus abdominis aponeurosis. This also runs on the inner surface of ribs 6 through 12 at which point it interdigitates with the fibres of the diaphragm. Contraction of the transversus significantly reduces the volume of the abdomen.

The transversus abdominis also constricts the abdomen and compresses its contents. Zemlin (1988) believes that on the basis of its architecture, the transversus is probably the most efficient and effective abdominal muscle in forced expiration (Zemlin 1988: 72).

The internal oblique abdominis muscles are located between the external abdominous and the transversus abdominous. The muscles have their origin on the inguinal ligament and iliac crest and they course through the cartilaginous portion of the lower ribs and part of the abdominal aponeurosis lateral to the rectus abdominous. Contraction of the internal oblique abdominals assists in rotation of the trunk if unilaterally contracted or flexion of the trunk when bilaterally contracted. This muscle compresses the abdominal contents and assists with forced expiration.

The external oblique abdominis muscles are the most superficial of the abdominal muscles, as well as the largest of the group. These muscles originate along the osseous portion of the lower 7 ribs, and fan downwards to insert into the iliac crest, inguinal ligament, and abdominal aponeurosis. Bilateral contraction will flex the vertebral column, while unilateral contraction results in trunk rotation. The external oblique compresses the abdominal content and raises the intra abdominal and intrathoracic pressures (Zemlin, 1988: 72).

This muscle characteristically shows contraction immediately before the production of sound and in phasic quality towards the end of articulation, especially in staccato vocalises. When sustained voice was produced there was also sustained contraction (Astraquillo et al., 1977: 504).

The rectus abdominus muscle is the prominent muscle in the middle of the abdominal region. The rectus abdomens originates at the pubis and inserts into the xiphoid process of the sternum and the cartilages of the lower true and false ribs. Contraction of this muscle also compresses the abdominal contents. The rectus abdominis muscle assists the act of expiration by pulling down on the ribs, thereby depressing the thoracic cage (*Gray's Anatomy*, 1995: 828).

The Muscles of Expiration

In general we may conclude that the action of the posterior thoracic muscles, and the anterior and lateral thoracic muscles combined with the anterolateral muscle group provides a firm but elastic wall which assists the abdominal viscera in opposing the action of gravity and assisting with forced expiration. This is mainly the function of the internal intercostals and the oblique muscles, especially the internal oblique whose contraction exercises a compressive force on the viscera which provided that the thorax and the pelvis remain fixed, plays an important part in expiration. If the pelvis and the vertebral column are fixed, then the external oblique is also activated, depressing and compressing the lower thorax, an action which also aids expiration. In general it appears that the obliques and the transversus are mainly concerned with compression; the recti are mainly concerned with tension, as are the pyramidalis whose action is responsible for tensing the linea alba. The latter muscle remains absent in one in five people, it cannot therefore be considered as critical to respiration (*Gray's Anatomy*, 1995: 827). The evidence seems to suggest that the external oblique is the most active of the anterolateral group of muscles.

These then are the muscles which collectively are responsible for the expansion and contraction of the space available to the lungs. They are also responsible for the erection and support of the vocal instrument. It is obvious from this analysis that respiration requires considerable muscular effort. It is the control exercised over these muscles that largely determines the efficiency of respiration.

APPENDIX B

Laryngeal Musculature

The most important cartilage in the larynx is the cricoid, the only complete cartilaginous ring in the whole air passage, and the base upon which the arytenoid cartilages and the thyroid cartilage are articulated by the synovial joints. The cricoid is therefore the foundation of the larynx. The anterior of the cricoid is known as the arch; the posterior, a quadrangular flat part, is known as the lamina. The inferior horn of the thyroid cartilage attaches to the cricoid near the junction of arch and lamina. The latter has sloping shoulders, which carry articular facets for the arytenoids.

A shallow concavity on each side of the lamina accommodates the posterior cricoarytenoid muscle, whilst the vertical ridge forming the concavity becomes the attachment for the longitudinal muscle of the oesophagus.

Attached to the cricoid cartilage are the twin arytenoid cartilages, which are shaped like pyramids and whose rotating action is of enormous importance to securing the abduction (opening) and adduction (closing) of the vocal folds so critical in singing.

Each pyramid shaped cartilage has three surfaces, two processes, a base and an apex. The transverse arytenoid muscle covers the posterior surface; the anterolateral surface contains a crest near the apex; this apex curves back, down and then forward to the vocal process. This is the process upon which the true vocal folds are attached. The lateral angle constitutes the muscle process, and is the attachment for the attachment to the posterior cricoarytenoid muscle behind and the lateral cricoarytenoid muscle in front. The medial surface is covered by a mucosa and the lower edge forms the lateral boundary of the intercartilaginous part of the rima glottidis. The vocal ligament is attached to the forward projecting vocal process (*Gray's Anatomy*, 1995: 1641–2). Abduction and adduction of the vocal folds is, however, secured only by the movement of the cricoarytenoid joints, which rotate as a function of the contraction of the cricoarytenoid muscles (abduction), and the lateral cricoarytenoid muscle, and the interarytenoids (adduction).

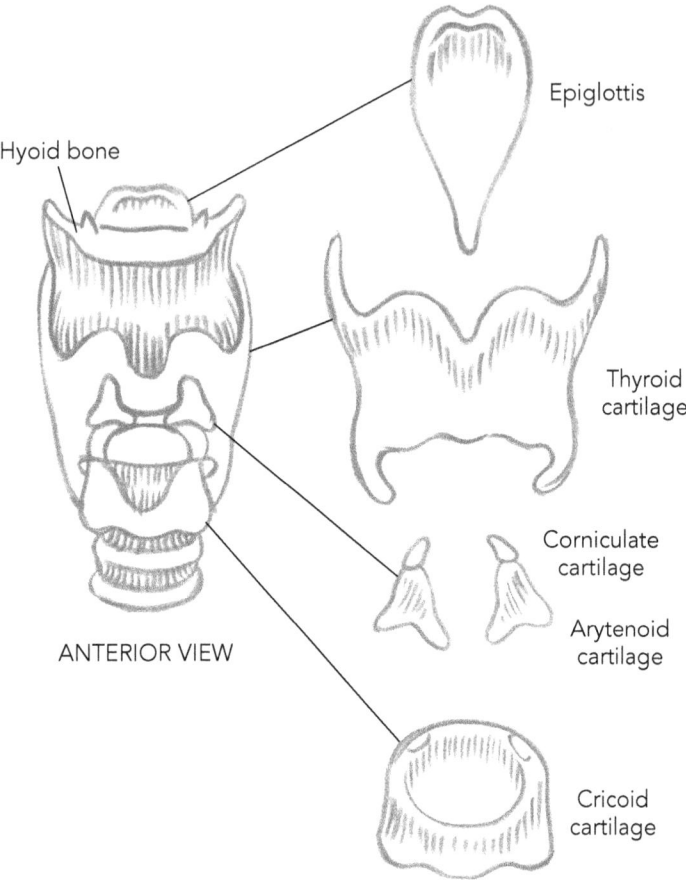

Figure 9 – Anterior view of the larynx, and its constituent cartilages.

The larynx is suspended from the hyoid bone, which in turn is suspended from the stylohyoid ligaments, which are attached to the styloid processes of the temporal bone.

The larynx tube is partially housed within the pharynx, a wider, longer tube. Towards the bottom of the pharynx, on the left and right respectively, we find two pear shaped cavities, known as the pyriform sinuses. These are situated between the pharynx and the larynx. At the bottom of the pharynx, at the posterior part of the sinus pyriform, just behind the arytenoids, is the opening to the stomach system, the oesophagus. The cervical vertebrae constitutes the back wall of the pharynx, the constrictor muscles constitute the sidewalls, and the anterior wall comprises a scaffolding which includes the larynx tube at the bottom, the epiglottis in the middle, and the tongue at the top. The tongue originates in the hyoid bone, and is composed of a number of muscles. Its root sits well below the upper tip of the epiglottis, creating a cavity (the valleculae) between the root of the tongue and the upper part of the epiglottis. The ceiling of the pharynx cavity is constituted by the velum (soft palate) which serves as the gate to the nasal cavities and forms the most posterior part of the mouth.

Suspended within the pharyngeal structure, we find the larynx, a small tube shaped cavity. The bottom of the larynx is limited by the glottis, which is defined as the variable opening between the vocal folds (Zemlin, 1988: 117).

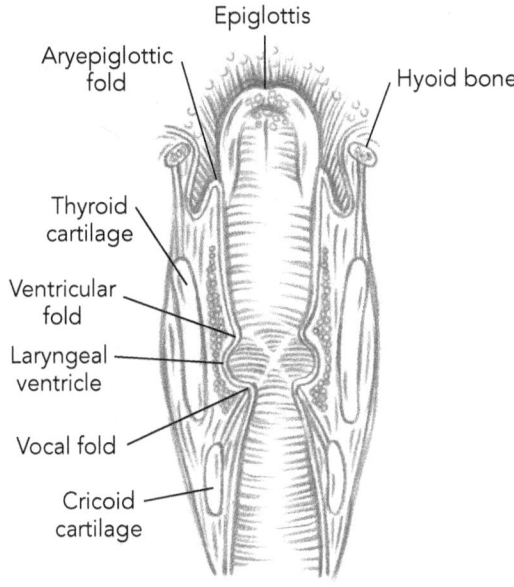

Thyroartytenoid m.

Figure 10 – Cavity of the larynx.

The posterior part is limited by the arytenoid cartilages; the anterior by the thyroid cartilage and the inferior part of the epiglottis, while the tissues, which join these structures, constitute the internal lateral wall, with the thyroid and cricoid cartilages constituting the external casing of these walls. The thyrohyoid membrane, for instance, forms the lateral wall of the pyriform fossa, whilst the laryngeal vestibule, from the aryepiglottic folds down to the ventricles, is also covered by mucous membrane. The two quadrate membranes and the lower half of the epiglottis constitute the walls of the laryngeal vestibule.

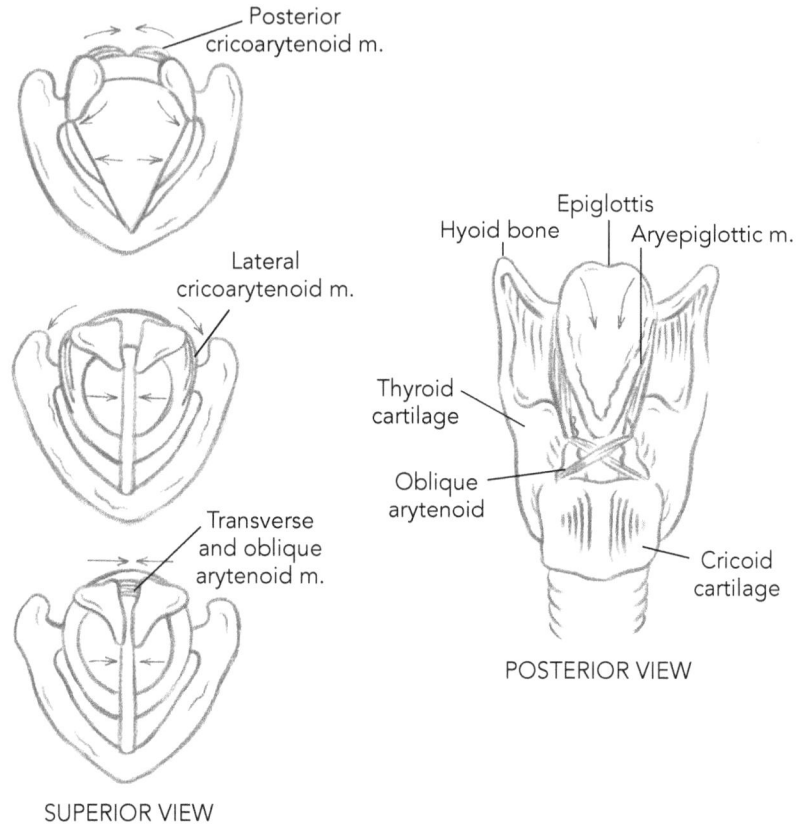

Figure 11 – Intrinsic muscles of the larynx.

Halfway down the cartilaginous laryngeal tube, below the epiglottis, we find the vocal folds: a membrane of fibro-elastic tissue whose strands run in different directions. The vocal folds are capable of withstanding a lot of pressure both from above and below. They are also capable of abducting (opening) and adducting (closing), as well as lengthening and shortening, a function designed to increase and decrease tension with a corollary effect on pitch.

The Abductor: Posterior Cricoarytenoid

Because of its function as the only dilator muscle of the rima glottidis, Last (1988: 428) regards the posterior cricoarytenoid muscle as the most important single muscle in the larynx and possibly the whole body. The posterior cricoarytenoids, sometime referred to as the posticus, are the only laryngeal muscles which open the glottis, rotating the arytenoid cartilages laterally around an axis passing through the cricoarytenoid joints (*Gray's*

Anatomy, 1995: 1644), thus separating the vocal processes and the attached cricothyroids to tense the vocal folds.

The posterior cricoarytenoids arise from the concavity on each side of the lamina of the cricoid cartilage. The muscle fibres converge on the muscular processes of the arytenoid cartilages: the upper fibres are almost horizontal, the lateral fibres almost vertical. The horizontal component draws the arytenoids towards each other and rotates them, generating a diamond shaped aperture of the glottis. The vertical component draws the arytenoids downward on the sloping shoulders of the cricoid, thus separating them without rotation, generating a V shaped opening of the glottis (Last, 1988: 428).

Adductors: The Lateral Cricoarytenoid and Interarytenoid Muscles

The lateral cricoarytenoid muscle is smaller than the posterior cricoarytenoids. It arises from the upper border of the cricoid arch and its fibres ascend obliquely backwards to the front of the muscular process of the arytenoid cartilage at the same side. The action of the muscle in drawing the muscular process forwards is to cause the vocal processes to approximate each other by rotation of the arytenoids, thus opposing the horizontal component of the posterior cricoarytenoid muscle. Its secondary function is to assist the vertical component of the posterior cricoarytenoid to draw the arytenoid downwards on the shoulder of the cricoid lamina: an action which dilates the muscle of the larynx, a function it can never fulfil on its own. The lateral cricoarytenoids close the glottis by rotating the arytenoids medially, to approximate their vocal processes. The transverse arytenoid pulls the arytenoid cartilages toward each other, closing the posterior (intercartilaginous) part of the rima glottidis (Last, 1988: 428).

The interarytenoid muscle combines the transverse and oblique arytenoids and consists of a strong mass of transverse fibres, which connect the posterior, and part of the medial surfaces of the arytenoid cartilages to each other. Contraction of this muscle draws the arytenoid cartilages upward along the sloping shoulders of the cricoid lamina, approximating them without rotation. The muscle is simply an opponent of the vertical action of the posterior cricoarytenoid muscle (Last, 1988: 428).

The Intrinsic Muscles of the Larynx

The epiglottis is a slightly curled, leaf-shaped cartilage, which is prolonged below into a slender process, and which is also attached to the midline below the notch of the upper border of the thyroid cartilage. The epiglottic cartilage leans back from its attached stalk to overhang the vestibule of the larynx. The prominence on the posterior surface below the apex, the cushion of the epiglottis, is produced by the shape of the cartilage, enhanced by an overhanging collection of mucous glands (Last, 1984: 426).

The aryepligottic folds represents the inlet of the larynx and are constituted by the upper border of the quadrate membrane. The aryepiglottic folds, which contain the cuneiform cartilage, constitute the vertical, oval shaped aperture of the larynx. (Last, 1984: 427).

The aryepiglottic folds contain muscle fibres which connect the side of the epiglottis to the muscular process and posterior surface of the opposite arytenoid cartilage. The two muscles cross each other behind the transversally running fibres of the intraarytenoid muscles. The contraction of the transverse and oblique arytenoid muscles draws the epiglottis down to bring its lower half into contact with the arytenoid cartilage, creating a constriction. Vocal scientists from García through to Bunch have recognised that aryepiglottic constriction is a major contributor to the vocal quality known as *squillo*, which is directly responsible for the ring in the voice (Bunch, 1997: 86).

The muscle fibres that attach the thyroepiglottic muscle to the upper border of the thyroid cartilage lie outside the quadrate membrane, on which they run to be inserted into the side of the epiglottis. The posterior third of the tongue also slopes down to the epiglottis, where a midline flange of mucous membrane, the glossoepiglottic fold, is raised between them.

Tensors

The cricothyroid muscle consists of two parts: the pars recta and the pars oblique. These form a triangular shape which fans backwards from the arch of the cricoid towards its insertion on the lower border and inferior horn of the thyroid lamina respectively. Contraction of the pars recta tilts the cricoid cartilage upward and the lamina backwards, approximating the thyroid and cricoid cartilages, which increases the distance between the thyroid and arytenoid cartilages. Contraction of the pars oblique also increases the distance between the thyroid and the cricoid cartilages by sliding the cricoid cartilage forward (Sundberg, 1987: 9). In conclusion then, contraction of these muscles causes the arch of the cricoid and the thyroid to either approach or separate from each other. It is necessary to stress that while theoretically it is just as possible for the cricoid to rise towards the thyroid, in practice it is more common for the thyroid cartilage to be tilted downwards towards the relatively fixed cricoid arch. The reason being that during phonation the cricoid is usually held immovably against the vertebral column by the cricopharyngeus. In practice then, it is more likely that the cricothyroids stretch the vocal ligaments, which are located within the body of the corresponding vocal fold, forming the medial portion of that fold, by tilting the thyroid cartilage forwards and downwards on the cricoid. The vocal ligaments are characterised by free thick margins and share a common point of attachment with the vocal folds: the anterior angle of the thyroid cartilage and the vocal processes of the cricoarytenoids (Zemlin, 1988: 113). Because the arytenoid cartilages are anchored to the cricoid lamina by the contraction of the cricopharyngeus the forward tilting of the thyroid cartilage increases the distance between the vocal processes and the anterior angle of the thyroid, so lengthening the vocal ligaments and therefore the vocal fold, a process that has significant consequences on tension and fundamental frequency (*Gray's Anatomy*, 1995: 1645).

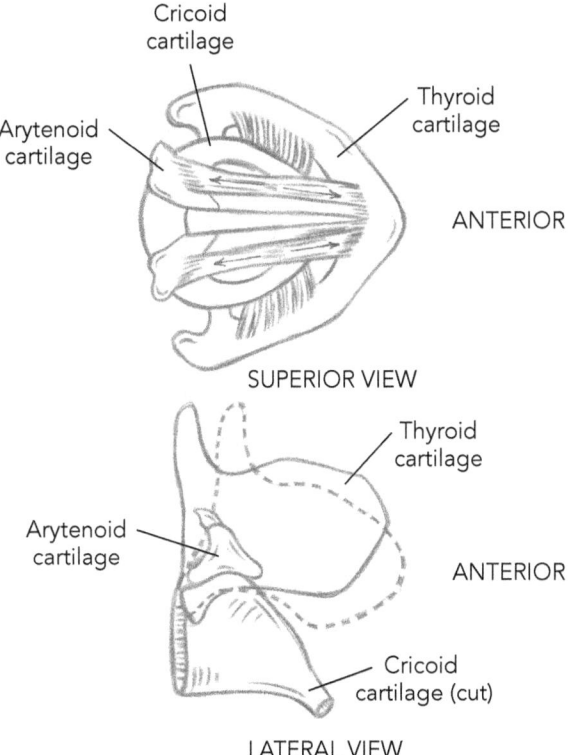

Figure 12 – Action of the cricothyroid in alteration of fundamental frequency of vibrations.

The muscles responsible for the important task of elevating and depressing the larynx in its entirety are called the sternothyroid and the thyrohyoid.

APPENDIX C

Head and Neck Muscles

The Suprahyoid Muscle Group

The larynx is suspended from the hyoid bone by a complex of membrane and muscles, both of which elevate the floor of the mouth and therefore the larynx. In addition it possesses its own elevators. The anterior and posterior belly of the digastric muscles, combine with the geniohyoid and mylohyoid muscles to form the anterior part of the suprahyoid sling. The contraction of this muscle group pulls the hyoid bone anteriorly and slightly upward, depending on position of jaw.

The digastric is a two-part muscle consisting of a posterior and anterior belly. Contraction of the anterior belly pulls the hyoid bone anteriorly and slightly upward; whilst the posterior belly pulls the hyoid bone upward and posteriorly [Zemlin, 1988: 122].

Contraction of the mylohyoid also has a dichotomous function: it elevates the hyoid body and retracts it posteriorly, depending on position of jaw.

The geniohyoid is a also a paired cylindrical muscle located over the surface of the mylohyoid muscle. Contraction of the geniohyoid pulls the hyoid bone anteriorly and slightly upward.

The hyoglossus enjoys a close relationship with the geniohyoid, and both are acknowledged tongue depressors. Contraction of the hyoglossus muscle depresses the tongue.

The thyropharyngeus muscle is part of the inferior constrictor. Its fibres arise from the the thyroid cartilage and the sternothyroid combine to form the thyropharyngeus. Contraction of this muscle helps to elevate the larynx whilst constricting the pharynx, and narrowing the laryngeal space.

The cricopharyngeus muscle is also part of the inferior constrictor. Contraction of this muscle also elevates the larynx [Zemlin, 1988: 157].

The stylohyoid is an elevator muscle. Contraction of this muscle elevates and retracts the hyoid bone, and can also aid tongue movement [Zemlin, 1988: 122].

The Infrahyoid Muscle Group

Laryngeal Depressors

Contraction of the infra-hyoid muscle group has the effect of lowering the larynx, which in turn lengthens the vocal tract, and lowers all the formants of the vocal tract. This configuration is also amenable to the production of the singing formant. Contractions of this muscle group restrain the movement of the thyroid cartilage, altering its relationship with the cricoid cartilage. This impacts on the mass, length and tension of the vocal folds, and according to their shape and configuration, they will impact pitch, loudness and register.

The thyrohyoid is a thin muscle that lies deep to the omohyoid. It originates at the oblique line of the thyroid lamina, coursing its way to the lower border of the greater horn of the hyoid bone. If the hyoid is fixed, contraction of this muscle elevates the thyroid, but its function normally decreases the distance between the thyroid and hyoid, especially anteriorly [Zemlin, 1988: 120].

The sternothyroid is a long, thin muscle lying on the anterior part of the neck (See figure 14). It originates at the posterior surface of the manubrium of the sternum and the first costal cartilage, inserting on the oblique line of the thyroid cartilages. Contraction of the sternothyroid pulls down the thyroid cartilage and opens the pharynx, and impacts on the opening of the laryngeal collar or the epylarynx [Miller, 1996: 251]. The sternohyoid is a thin muscle lying on the anterior side of the neck. It originates on the posterior side of the manubrium of the sternum and the end of the clavicle, inserting into the lower border of the body of the hyoid bone. Its contraction pulls down the hyoid bone and larynx [Zemlin, 1988: 124].

The omohyoid is a long, narrow, two-part muscle situated on the anterior and lateral surface of the neck. The omohyoid has two bellies both of which are joined at an intermediate tendon.

The inferior belly originates along the upper surface of the scapula, inserting on the intermediate tendon, whilst the superior belly inserts into the border of the great horn of the hyoid bone. Contraction of both bellies pulls down on the hyoid bone, although the superior belly has a more pronounced effect in this direction than the inferior belly [Zemlin, 1988: 124]. According to Miller, the omohyoid not only depresses the hyoid bone, but also steadies it and and may also be involved in retracting and epressing the larynx [Miller, 1996: 252].

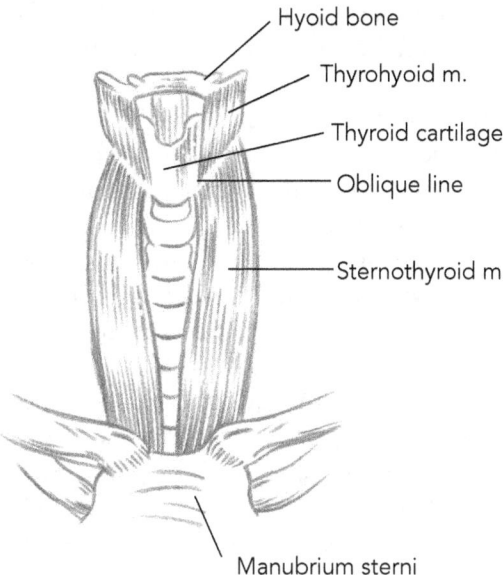

Figure 13 – The sternothyroid and thyrohyoid muscles.

The Constrictors

Contraction of the superior constrictor muscles pulls the pharyngeal wall forward constricting the pharyngeal diameter and closing the velopharyngeal port.

The middle constrictor originates from the angle between the lesser cornu and the greater cornu of the hyoid bone. Its fibres diverge widely as they course around the pharynx to end in the median raphe. The middle constrictor narrows the diameter of the pharynx.

The uppermost fibres, according to Last (1984), reach the pharyngeal ligament and enclose the superior constrictor, whilst the lower fibres arch down to the level of the vocal folds. The gap between the middle and inferior constrictors is filled and closed by the pharyngeal membrane. Accoding to McKinney, what is often forgotten is that contraction of these relatively slender longitudinal strands of the constrictors tends to shorten anfd lengthen the pharynx with considerable consequences on all the format frequencies of the vocal tract [McKinney, 2005: 131]

The inferior constrictor arises from the oblique line of the lamina of the thyroid cartilage, and from the side of the arch of the cricoid cartilage. These two separate parts are known as the thyropharyngeus and cricopharyngeus. These muscles form part of the inferior constrictor, which is rounder and thicker than the other flat constrictors.

The thyropharyngeus arises from the oblique line of the thyroid cartilage and courses around the midline raphe, enclosing the mid and superior constrictor.

The cricopharyngeus part of the inferior constrictor is rounder and thicker than the other flat constrictors. It extends from one side of the cricoid arch to the other around the pharynx. This muscle acts as a sphincter at the lower end of the pharynx [Last, 1984: 412]. The main function of the cricopharyngeus in singing, however, is to anchor the cricoid cartilage against the vertebral column, thus preventing it from slipping forward under pressure from a contracting cricothyroid: an action which creates the resistance necessary for the stretching of the vocal folds [Gray, 1995: 1645].

The tensor palati arises from the sphenoid bone between the lateral and medial Pterygoid plates, just lateral to the wall of the eustachian tube. Its fibres course down forming a tendon that passes around the Pterygoid hamulus, expanding to become the palatal aponeurosis. Contraction of this muscle tenses and flattens the soft palate and opens the eustachian tube [Zemlin, 1988: 263–4].

The levator palati is a paired muscle that arises from the apex of the *petrous* portion of the temporal bone and from the medial wall of the eustachian tube cartilage, comprising the bulk of the soft palate and body of the velum. The levator palati courses down and forward, inserting into the palatal aponeurosis of the soft palate lateral to the musculus uvulae. Contraction of the levator palati raises the soft palate and velum, also retracting the latter.

The musculus uvula originates at the posterior nasal spine of the palatine bones and from the palatal aponeurosis. Its fibres run the length of the soft palate on either side of the midline, inserting into the mucous membrane cover of the velum. Contraction of this muscle raises and bunches up both the uvula and soft palate. Gray's suggests that the primary action of this muscle is to elevate the almost vertical posterior part of the soft palate and pull it slightly backwards [Gray's, 1995: 1689].

The thyropharyngeus muscle originates at the front from the anterior portion of the hard palate, and its posterior fibres arise from the midline of the soft palate and velum posterior to levator palatine, which is attached to the palatal aponeurosis. These fibres course their way laterally and down to insert into the posterior thyroid cartilage. In so doing they form the posterior faucial pillars, better known as palatal pharyngeal arch. Contraction of these paired muscles assists in narrowing the pharyngeal cavity and lowering the soft palate.

Appendix C — Head and Neck Muscles

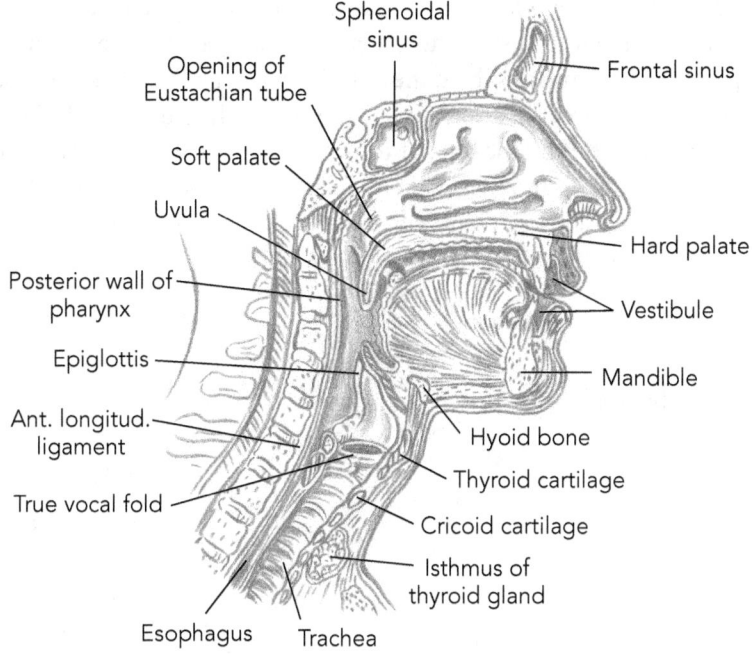

Figure 14A – Vocal tract sagittal section.

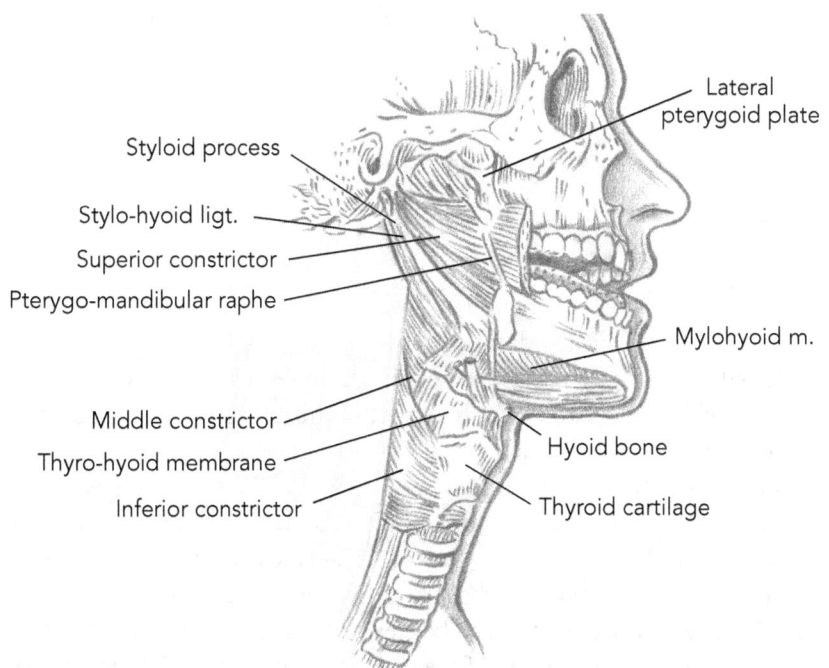

Figure 14B – Constrictors of the pharynx – Lateral view.

The palatoglossus muscle originates at the anterolateral palatal aponeurosis, and runs down to insert into the sides of the posterior of the tongue. The palatoglossus muscles form the anterior faucial pillars, better known as the palatoglossal arch, just forward of the palatopharyngeal arch. The two arches are separated by the palatal tonsils that lie between the two arches. Contraction of these muscles will either depress the soft palate and velum or raise the back and sides of the tongue, depending on which end the muscle is the most stable [Seikel et al., 1997: 318–326].

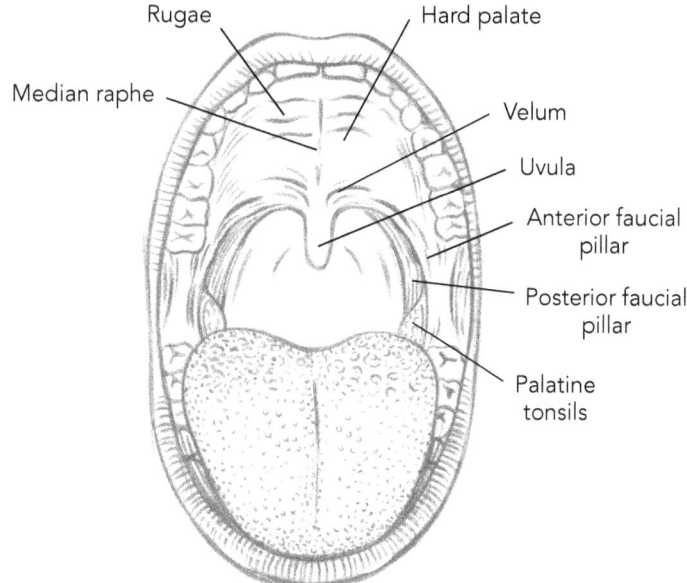

Figure 15 – Anterior view of the oral cavity including the soft palate, tongue, and vocal tract.

The Soft Palate

In order to complete any discussion of the pharynx, the soft palate must be included (even though it is involved in articulation as well). Although continuous with the hard palate, the structure of the soft palate is comprised of an aponeurosis that is acted upon by several muscles in order to alter its shape and position. According to Last (1984), as the soft palate is raised or lowered, it modifies the general configuration of the resonant characteristics of the vocal tract. Normally the soft palate is elevated for the production of vowels and lowered for what we refer to as nasal sounds [Last, 1984: 421–2]. The soft palate may also be elevated, tensed or relaxed. Elevation is accomplished by contraction of the levator palati muscles. The tensor palati muscle tenses the palate by pulling it horizontally. Both actions are most important to singing because this creates more resonating space in the oral pharynx and blocks off the nasal pharynx, preventing an undesirable nasal tone. When relaxed the soft palate hangs downward, leaving the nasal port open. This leads to an ugly hypo-functional vocal production.

Modifying the laryngeal inlet is the task of the medial muscle of the styloid apparatus (stylo-pharyngeus) assisted by salpingo-pharyngeus and palato-pharyngeus raises the larynx and the pharynx.

Tongue Muscles

The mylohyoid muscle constitutes the floor of the mouth. The posterior fibres and midline raphe of the mylohyoid are attached to the body of the hyoid bone. Its construction flattens the angle between its two halves and elevates the hyoid bone.

The main function of the mylohyoid, however, is to form a stable and mobile floor for the mouth and support the thrust and weight of the tongue and hyoid bone. With the movement of the mandible, already examined, the tongue remains the principal articulator and its movement is indispensable to articulation and resonance.

The tongue is a bundle of striated muscle, the bulk of which is constituted by the genioglossus muscles, which lies directly above the mylohyoid. It contains some vertical, longitudinal, and transverse intrinsic muscle fibres. Contraction of its fibres draws the tongue forward altering its shape and consequently that of the resonator:

- Contraction of its longitudinal fibres shortens the tongue.
- Contraction of the transverse muscles narrows and elongates the tongue.
- Contraction of the vertical fibres produces a midline groove.

The other main articulators are the lips, the jaw and the soft palate. Having dealt with their essential musculature we will now deal with their function. Contraction of this muscle tends to constrict the oropharynx [Last, 1984: 413; Gray's, 1995: 1724].

The Cavities of the Vocal Tract

The vocal tract consists of five distinct cavities named the buccal, oral, and pharyngeal as well as the two nasal cavities.

The Buccal Cavity is a small space limited by the lips and the cheeks externally and the gums and teeth internally. The buccal cavity communicates with the mouth or oral cavity.

The oropharyngeal isthmus represents the port that communicates with the pharyngeal and nasal cavities.

The pharyngeal cavity: the pharynx consists of a muscular-membranous complex running from the back of the skull to the sixth cervical vertebrae behind the cricoid cartilage. It is about twelve centimetres long and is larger and oval-shaped in its transverse plain.

The pharynx may be divided into three interrelated sections: the nasopharynx, oropharynx and laryngopharynx. We will now investigate each of the three sections of the pharyngeal resonator beginning with the upper part: the nasal pharynx.

The nasopharynx is bound by the rostrum of the sphenoid and the pharyngeal protuberance of the occipital bone, and is limited inferiorly by the soft palate.

The nasal pharynx has a number of functions and characteristics. The most important according to Bunch are:

- Amplification of nasal consonants and vowels.

- When closed off by the mobile soft palate, it prevents food from entering the nose; it is also critical to the production of certain kinds of sounds.

- The eustachian or tympanic tube opens into the nasal pharynx, a fact that contributes considerably to the difference in sound as perceived by the performer and the actual sound heard by the listener, although the conduction of vibrations by bone to the middle and inner ears also contributes to the difference between perception and actual sound.

The sinuses and tear ducts draining into the nasal cavity often cause congestion of the nasal mucosa.

The oropharynx is limited superiorly by the soft palate and inferiorly by the hyoid. The oropharynx communicates with the oral cavity through the palatoglossal and palatopharyngeal arch.

The middle or oral section of the pharynx extends from the soft palate to the inlet of the larynx and is the largest of the resonating spaces. Since the palate and larynx are both capable of moving upwards, downwards, forwards and backward, it is this portion of the pharynx whose shape is the most variable. Movements and alterations in the shape of the tongue are significant in this section because this can alter the shape of the resonating space and obstruct the aperture of the oral pharynx and pharyngeal cavities [Bunch, 1997: 85–86].

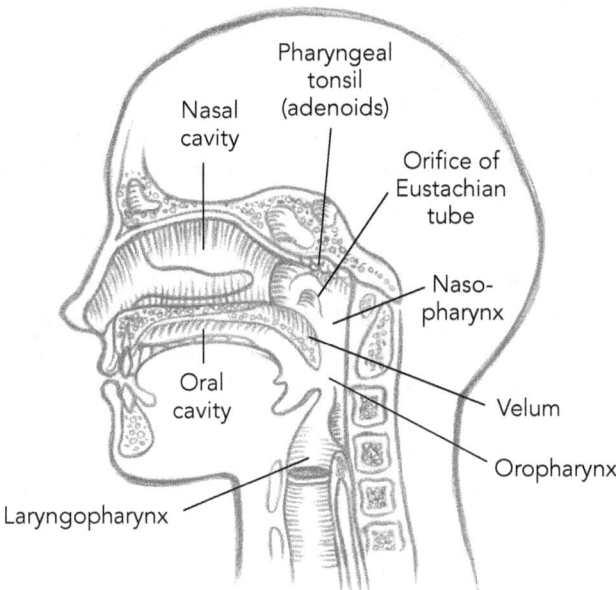

Figure 16 – Oral, nasal and pharyngeal cavities.

As previously discussed, the tongue has the complex connections to the larynx, pharynx and soft palate. When it contracts, it changes in shape affecting the size and spatial configuration of the vocal tract, which alters the size and shape of the cavity. Bunch Dayme, declares that if the lower connections of the palate, such as the tongue, are tense, it is virtually impossible for the palate to achieve sufficient elevation. This can create problems such as nasality and a garbled sound' [Buch Dayme, 2005: 77]. It is worth recalling that altering the tongue position and configurations inexorably alters the resonating space and consequently the formants of the vocal tract, which form the vowels. Altering the body of the tongue affects the second formant, whilst the tip of the tongue affects the third formant, and jaw position has a great deal to say about the first formant.

We can see from the above that the jaw has a very strong connection not only with the tongue but also with the pharynx and soft palate (velum). The mandible has been described by Seikel et al., 'as the unsung hero among articulators'. The reason for this accolade is that the mandible quietly and without fanfare does its important work of 'assisting the lips, changing its position for tongue movement, and tightly closing when necessary' [Seikel, 2010: 379].

In addition, as we saw above, the opening of the jaw plays a major part in raising the first formant so critical to the upper register of higher voices, in particular the soprano voice.

The laryngopharynx is continuous with the esophagus below and is limited above at the level of the hyoid bone. Anteriorly (posteriorly) it communicates with the opening of the larynx formed by the epiglottis and the aryepiglottic folds [Zemlin, 1988: 223].

The inferior or laryngeal portion of the pharynx extends from the inlet of the larynx to the base of the cricoid cartilage. The opening of the larynx, sometimes called the laryngeal collar, is formed by the epiglottis and aryepiglottic folds, the ventricular folds, and pyriform sinuses, all of which are thought to contribute to the area of resonance that gives the voice a ringing quality, often referred to as the 'ring' of the voice in the literature, or the singer's formant [Bunch, 1997: 86].

The orbicularis oris muscle is the principal muscle acting upon the lips. It is represented by an oval ring of muscle fibers located within the lips and completely encircling the mouth. The orbicularis oris acts as a sphincter that surrounds the mouth. Contraction of this muscle closes the mouth and puckers the lips.

The risorious muscle originates at the fascia covering the masseter muscle; its fibres courses parallel with and superficial to the buccinator muscle. Contraction of the risorious muscle helps to draw the angle of the mouth laterally.

The levator labii Superior muscle originates at the lower margin of the orbital bone, with some fibres arising from the zygomatic bone and the maxilla. Other fibres course downward to insert into the upper lip. Contraction of this muscle elevates the upper lip, and may evert it somewhat as well.

The levator labii Alaeque is a slender muscle originating from the from the frontal process and infraorbital margin. Its two slips slope downward to insert into the lateral cartilage of the nose and the orbicularis oris respectively. Contraction of this muscle elevates the upper lip and dilates the nostrils.

The levator anguli oris muscle seems to be the counterpart of part of the depressor anguli oris. Its fibres converge as they course towards the angle of the mouth: some insert into the upper lip, and others into the lower lip at the angle. Contraction of this muscle elevates the corners of the mouth and assists in closing the mouth by drawing them towards the midline.

The angularis oris is a depressor that originates on the lateral margin of the oblique line of the mandible, its fibres interdigitating with the platysma.

Contraction of this muscle may either depress the corner of the mouth, or help to compress the upper lip against the lower lip.

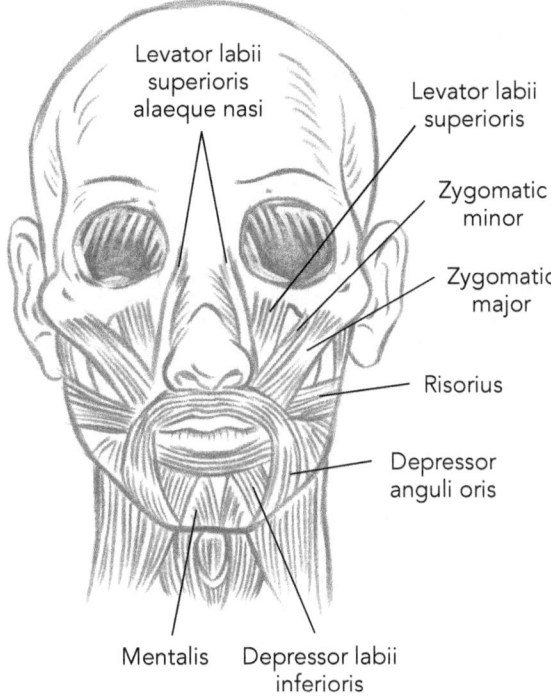

Figure 17 – Muscles of the face.

The buccinator muscle is the principal muscle of the cheeks. It originates on the pterygomandibular ligament, and courses its way to the lateral surface of the alveolar process of the maxilla to the posterior mylohyoid line of the inner mandible [Zemlin, 1988: 230–233].

These muscles collectively constitute the vocal cavity that is the human resonator. Consequently, they are subject to all the acoustic laws relating to cavities.

Bibliography

Adams, Brian (1986) 'La Stupenda ', Sydney: Random House.

Agricola, Johann Fredrich (1995) 'Introduction to the Art of Singing', New York: Cambridge University Press.

Agur, A.M. R. & Lee, J. Ming (1999) 'Grant's Atlas of Anatomy', Baltimore, Maryland: Lippicott, Williams & Wilkins.

Aikin, W.A. (1951) 'The Voice: An Introduction to Practical Phonology', London: Longmans Green.

Alderston, Richard (1979)'The Complete Handbook of Voice Training', New York: Parker Publications.

Alfred, John (1972) 'Manual of Sound Recording', London: Fountain Press.

Alton, Everest & Pohlmann (2009) 'Master Handbook of Acoustics', New York: McGraw Hill.

André, Naomi (2006) 'Voicing Gender', Bloomington & Indianapolis: Indiana University Press.

Appelman, D. Ralph (1967) 'The Science of Vocal Pedagogy': Translated by Julianne Baird. Bloomington: Indiana. University Press.

Ardoin, John (1988) 'The Calls Legacy', London: Gerald Duckworth & Co. Ltd.

Ardoin, John (1998) 'Callas at Juilliard: The Masterclasses', Portland, Oregon: Amadeus Press Inc.

Bacilly, Benigne de (1968) 'Commentary upon the Art of Proper Singing', New York: Institute of Medieval Studies.

Backus, John (1968) 'The Acoustical Foundation of Music', New York.

Bartholomew, Wilmer (1965) 'Acoustics of Music', Englewood: Prentice – Hall.

Bassini, Carlo (2008) 'Art of Singing', San Diego: Plural Publishing, Inc.

Batchelor, G. K. (2000) 'Introduction to Fluid Dynamics', New York: Cambridge University Press.

Battaglia Damiani, Daniela (2003) 'Anatomia Della Voce', Milano: Ricordi (BMG Publications.

Baudissone, Bruno (1989) 'Pricipessa turandot: La Voce e L'Arte di Gina Cigna', Parma: Azzali Editore.

_____ (1934) 'A Physical Definition of 'Good Voice-Quality', Department of Research, Peabody Conservatory of Music, Baltimore Maryland.

Bayly, Anselm (1771) 'A Practical Treatise on Singing and Playing with Just Expression and Real Elegance', London: J. Ridley Publisher.

Behnke, Emil (1881) 'The Mechanism of the Human Voice', London: Curwen and Sons.

Behnke, E. and Browne, L. (1895) 'A Practical Guide For Singers and Speakers', London: Sampson, Low, Marston & Company Limited.

Behrman, Alison (2008) 'Speech and Voice Science', San Diego: Plural Publishing Inc.

Benade, Arthur (1976) 'The Fundamentals of Musical Acoustics', London: Oxford University Press.

Berard, Jean-Antoine (1755) 'L'Art du Chant', Paris: Dessaint & Saillant.

Berg, Richard & Stork, David (2005) 'The Physics of Sound', New Jersey: Pearson, Prentice Hall.

Bisogni, Vincenzo Ramon 'Franco Corelli - Irresistibili Tenore', Varesi: Zecchini Editore.

Bjorling, Anna-Lisa & Farks, Andrew 'Jussi', Portland, Oregon: Amadeus Press

Bloem-Hubatka, Daniela (2012) 'The Old Italian School of Singing: A Theoretical And Practical Guide', North Carolina: McFarland and Company.

Boagno, Marina (1996) 'Corelli: A Man A Voice', Forth Worth: Baskerville Publishers, Inc.

Bonvicini, Candido (1992) 'My Friend Pavarotti', London: Omnibus Press.

Boone, Daniel R. et al. (2010) 'The Voice and Voice Therapy', Boston: Allyn and Bacon–Pearson Education.

Bouhuys, Arend (1968) 'Sound production in man: annals of the New York Acadamy of Science', New York: New York Academy of Science.

Bouhuys, Arend (1977) 'Physiology of Breathing', London: Gune & Stratton.

Boynton, Joan Frey (2003) 'The Private Voice Studio Handbook: A Practical Guide to All Aspects of Teaching", Milwaukee: Hal-Leonard.

Bozeman, Kenneth W. (2013) 'Practical Vocal Acoustics: Pedagogical Applications for Teachers and Singers', New York: Pendragon Press, Hillsdale, NY.

Brennan, Richard (2004) 'The Alexander Technique Manuel', London: Connections Book Publishing Limited.

Breslen, Herbert & Midgette, Anne (2004) 'The King & I' London: Mainstream Publishing.

Brewer, David J. MD (1964) 'Research potential in Voice Physiology', Syracuse: New York: University of New York.

Broad, David J. (1977) 'Topics in Speech and Science', Los Angeles: Speech Communication Research Laboratory.

Brodnitz, Fredrich S. (1988) 'Keep Your Voice Healthy', Austin, Texas: Pro-Ed Inc.

Brower, H. & Cooke, J. F. (1996) 'Great Singers on the Art of Singing', Mineola N.Y.: Dover Publications.

Brown, L. Oren (1996) 'Discover Your Voice: How to Develop Healthy Voice Habits', San Diego: Singular Publishing Group.

Brown, William Earl (1957) 'Vocal Wisdom: maxims of Giovanni Battista Lamperti', New York: Taplinger Publishing Company.

Bruno, Giovanna & Paperi, Valerio (2001) 'La Voce Cantata: Fisiologia, patologia e pedagogia del canto artistico', Roma: Verduci Editore.

Bukofzer, Manfred (1948) 'Music in the Baroque Era', London: J. M. Dent & Sons.

Bunch, Meribeth (1997) 'Dynamics of the Singing Voice', Wien: Springer-Verlag.

Bunch, Meribeth (2005) 'The Performers Voice: Realising Your Vocal Potential', New York: W. W. Norton and Comp. Inc.

Burgin, John Carrol (1973) 'Teaching Singing', Metuchen N. J.: Scarecrow Press.

Burney, Charles (1987) 'Viaggio Musicale In Italia', Torino: E.D.T. Edizione Torino.

Bybee, Ariel and Ford, James E. (2004) 'The Modern Singing Master: Essays in honor of Cornelius L. Reid', Marylands: Scarecrow Press, Inc.

Caccini, Giulio (1602) 'Le Nuove Musiche', Edited by H. Wiley Hitchcock. Madison: A-R Editions Inc.

Caesari, Herbert, E. (1963) 'Tradition and Gigli', London: Robert Hale.

Caesari, Herbert, E. (1965) 'The Alchemy of Voice', London: Robert Hale.

Caesari, Herbert, E. (1936 Reprint 1968) 'The Science and Sensations of Vocal Tone', London: J.M. Dent & Sons Ltd.

Caesari, Herbert, E, (1969) 'The Voice of the Mind', London: Robert Hale.

Callaghan, Jean (2000) 'Singing and Voice Science', San Diego, California: Singular Publishing.

Callaghan, Jean (2014) 'Singing and Science, Body, Brain, & Voice', Oxford, Compton Publishing Ltd.

Campbell, Agostini and Davis (1970) 'The Respiratory Muscles: Mechanics and Neural Control', London: Lloyd-Luke (Medical Books) Ltd.

Campbell, Agostini, Davis (1970) 'The Respiratory Muscles and Neural Control', London: Lloyd-Luke Ltd.

Campbell, E.J.M.(1958) 'The Respiratory Muscles and the Mechanics of Breathing', Chicago: Year Book (Medical) Publishers.

Cappelletto, Sandro (1995) 'La Voce di Farinelli: Vita di Farinelli Evirato Cantore', Torino: E.D.T. Edizione di Torino.

Carboni, Giancarlo (2017) 'Manuale Professionale di Dizione e Pronuncia', Milano: Ulrico Hoepli Editore.

Caruso, Enrico & Tetrazzini, Luisa (1909) 'Caruso and Tetrazzini on The Art of Singing', New York: Dover Publications Inc.

Casanova, Carlamaria(1885) 'Renata Tebaldi: The Voice of an Angel', Forthworth: Baskerville Publishers, Inc.

Castiglione, Baldesar ((1967) The Book of the Courtier', London: Penguin Books.

Celletti, Rodolfo (1991) 'A History of Bel Canto', New York: Oxford University Press.

Celletti, Rodolfo (2000) 'La Grana Della Voce', Milano: Baldini & Castoldi Publishers.

Chapin, Schuyler (1995) 'Sopranos, Mezzos, Tenors, Bassos, and Other Friends', New York: Crown Publishers, Inc.

Chapman, Janice L. (2012) 'Singing And Teaching Singing: A Holistic Approach to Classical Voice', San Diego: Plural Publishing Inc.

Christiansen, Rupert (1995) 'Prima Donna', London: Random House.

Christy, Van A. (1977) 'Expressive Singing', Dubuque, Iowa: Wm. C. Brown Company Publishers.

Cobelnzer, Horst and Muhar, Franz (2015) 'Respiro e Voce', Roma: Dino Audino.

Coffin, Berton (1960) 'Singer's Repertoire: Lyric and Dramatic Tenors', New York: Scarecrow Press, Inc.

Coffin, Berton (1980) 'Overtones of Bel Canto', Lanham, Maryland: Scarecrow Press.

Coffin, Berton (1987) 'Coffin's Sounds of Singing', Maryland: Scarecrow Press Inc.

Coffin, Berton (1989) 'Historical Vocal Pedagogy Classics', Maryland: Scarecrow Press.

Colton, Raymond & Caspar, Janina K. (1996) 'Understanding Voice Problems', Baltimore, Maryland: Williams and Wilkins.

Conati, Marcello (1984) 'Interviews & Encounters with Verdi', London: Victor Gollancz LTD.

Cooper, Morton (1999) 'Change your Voice, Change Your Life', Los Angeles: Voice & Speech Co. of America Publisher.

Cunelli, Georges (1973) 'Voice no Mystery', London: Staiber & Bell Ltd.

Curtis, Henry Holbrook (1896) 'Voice Building And Tone Placing: Showing a New Method of Relieving Injured Vocal Cords By Tone Exercises. New York: D. Appleton and Company.

Delle Sedie, Enrico (n.d.) 'A Complete Method of Singing: A Theoretical And Practical Treatise On The Art Of Singing', New York: G. Schirmer.

Dent, E. J. (1905) 'Alessandro Scarlatti: His Life and Works', London: Edward Arnold.

Di Stefano, Giuseppe (1989) 'L'Arte Del Canto', Milano: Rusconi Libri.

Domingo, Placido (1983) Placido Domingo: My First Forty Years', London: Weidenfeld and Nicolson.

Doscher, Barbara (1988) 'The Functional Unity Of The Singing Voice', Metuchen N.J.: Scarecrow Press Inc.

Douglas, Nigel (1992) 'Legendary Voices', London: Andrea Deutsch Limited.

Drake, James A. (1997) 'Rosa Ponselle: A Centenary Biography', Portland, Oregon: Amadeus Press.

Duey, Philip A. (1980) 'Bel Canto in Its Golden Age', New York: Da Capo Press Inc.

Ellis, Alexander (1898) 'Speech and Song', London: Novello.

Emmons, Shirlee (1990) 'Lauritz Melchior: Tristanissimo', London: Schirmer Books Inc.

Ezzu, Alberto (2009) 'Il Canto degli Armonici', Torino: Musica Pratica.

Fant, Gunnar (1970) 'Acoustic Theory of Speech Production', The Hauge: Mouton Press.

Fant and Kruckenburg (1996) 'Voice source properties of the speech code'.TMH-QPSR.

Fernandi, Franco (1994) 'Le Voci Piacentine: Due secoli di bel canto a Piacenza', Parma: Azzali Editori.

Field Hyde, F.C. (1950) 'The Art and Science of Voice Training', London: Oxford University Press.

Fields, Victor Alexander (1947) 'Training the Singing Voice', New York: King's Crown Press.

Fields, Victor Alexander (1970) 'Foundation of the Singer's Art', Reprint, 1984, 1984, New York: NATS Publications.

Fillebrown, Thomas (1911) 'Resonance in Singing and Speaking', Bryn Mawr: Oliver Ditson.

Fischer-Dieskau, Dietrich (1976) 'Schubert: A Biographical Study of his Songs', London: Cassell & Company Limited.

Fitzlyon, April (1987) 'Maria Malibran: Diva of the Romantic Age', London: Souvenier Press (E & A).

Flanagan, James. L. (1972) 'Speech Analysis Synthesis and Perception', New York: Springer Verlag.

Forman, Edward V. (1968) 'The Porpora Tradition', Milwaukee: Pro Musica Press.

Forman, Edward V. (2006) 'How to Sing Italian Baroque Music Correctly', Minnieapolis, Minnesota: Pro Musica Press.

Forman, Edward Phd. (2006) 'The Art of Bel Canto in the Italian Baroque', Minneapolis, Minnesota: Pro Musica Press.

Forman, Edward (2006) 'A Bel Canto Method', Minneapolis, Minnesota: Pro Musica Press.

Foster, Roland (1935) 'Vocal Success: A practical guide to the essentials of Good Singing', Sydney: Paling's Music.

Freitas, Roger (2014) 'Portrait of a Castrato'. New York: Cambridge University Press.

Frisell, Anthony (1968) 'The Tenor Voice', Massachusetts: Bruce Humphries Publishers.

Fuchs, Viktor (1967) 'The Art of Singing and Voice Technique', London: Calder Boyars.

Fucito, S. & Beyer, J.B. (1922 Reprint 1995) 'Caruso and the Art of Singing', Mineola New York: Dover Publications Inc.

Fussi, F. & Gilardone, M. (2009) 'Clinica della Voce', Torino: Edizione di Cortina Torino.

Fussi, F. & Magnani, S. (1994) 'L'Arte Vocale', Omega Edizione.

Fussi, F. & Magnani, S. (2003) 'Lo Spartito Logopedico', Omega Edizione.

Fussi, F. & Magnani, S. (2010) 'Le Parole della Scena', Omega Edizione.

Fussi, S. & Turli, E. (2008) 'Una Prospettiva per il metedo Estill VoiceCraft', Omega Musica.

Galignano, M. (2013) 'Pedagogia e Sceinza della Voce', Omega Edizione.

García, Manuel 11 (a compilation of the 1841 & 1872 edit.) 'A complete Treatise on the Art of Singing: Part One', New York: Da Capo Press (1984).

García, Manuel 11 (1847) 'A Complete Treatise on the Art of Singing: Part Two', New York: Da Capo Press (1975).

García, Manuel (1894) 'Hints on Singing', New York: Joseph Patelson Music House Ltd. (1982).

Gattey, Charles Neilson (1979) 'Queens of Song', London: Barrie & Jenkins Ltd.

Gauffin & Hammarberg (1991) 'Vocal Fold Physiology; Acoustic, Perceptual and Physiological Aspects Of Voice Mechanisms', San Diego, California: Singular Publishing Group Inc.

Gelb, Michael.J. (1995) 'Body Learning: An Introduction to the Alexander Technique', New York: Henry Holt & Company LLC.

Gilardone, M. & Fussi, F. (1998) 'Le Voci di Puccini', Omega Edizione.

Gilliland, Dale (2006) 'The teaching of Jean de Reske', Minneapolis: Pro Musica Press.

Goldovsky, Boris (1968) 'Bringing Opera to Life', New York: Appleton-Century-Crofts.

Gossett, P., Ashbrook, W., Budden, J., Lippman, F. Porter, A., Caner, M. (1980) 'The New Grove: Masters of of Italian Opera', London: Macmillan Press.

Gosett, Philip (2006) 'Divas and Scholars: performing Italian Opera', Chicago: University of Chicago Press.

Gray's Anatomy (1995) Peter L. Williams. Edinburgh: Churchill and Livingstone.

Grove, George (1973) 'Grove's Dictionary of Music And Musicians' in nine volumes and supplementary, Edited by Eric Blom. London: Macmillan Press.

Grove, George (1985) 'The New Grove's Dictionary of Music', in 20 Volumes, Edited by Stanley Sadie. London: Macmillan Press.

Grove, George (1992) 'The New Grove's Dictionary of Opera', Edited by Stanley Sadie. London: Macmillan Press.

Hardcastle, W. & Laver, J. (1999) 'The Handbook of Phonetic Sciences', Malden, Massachusetts: Blackwell Publishers.

Harpster, R (1984) 'Technique in Singing: A Program for Singers and Teachers', New York: Schirmer Books, a division of Macmillan Inc.

Hedington, C., Westbrook, R., & Barfoot, T. (1991) 'Opera: A History', London: Arrow Books Limited.

Helmholtz, Hermann (1877 Reprint 1954) 'On the Sensation of Tone', New York: Dover Publications.

Heriot, Angus (1956) 'The Castrati in Opera', London: Secker & Warburg.

Hiller, Johann Adam (1780) 'Treatise on Vocal Performance and Ornamentation', (Reprint 2001). New York: Cambridge University Press.

Hines, Jerome (1994) 'Great Singers on Great Singing', New York: Limelight Editions.

Hines, Jerome (1997) 'The Four Voices of Man', New York: Limelight Editions.

Hirano, Minuro (1981) 'Clinical Examination of Voice', Vienna: Springer-Verlag.

Hixon, Thomas J. (1991) 'Respiratory Function in Speech and Song', San Diego, California: Singular Publishing Group.

Holden, Amanda (2001) 'The New Penguin Opera Guide', London: Penguin Books.

Horne, Marilyn & Scovell, Jane (2005) 'Marilyn Horne: The Song Continues', Fort Worth, Teases: Baskerville Publishers, Inc.

Jeans, James (1968) 'Science & Music', New York: Dover Publications, Inc.

Joyner, James Richard (1998) 'Charles Amable Battaille: Pioneer in Vocal Science and the Teaching of Singing', Lanham, Maryland: Scarecrow Press, Inc.

Harrison, Scott (2010) 'Perspective on Teaching Singing: Australian Vocal Pedagogues Sing Their Stories', Bowen Hills Qld: Australian Academic Press.

Hemsley, Thomas (2013) 'Singing and Imagination', Oxford: Oxford niversity Press.

Henderson, W. J. (1921) 'Early History of Singing', New York: Longmans, Green And Co.

Hetherington, John (1973) 'Melba: A Biography', London: Faber & Faber.

Hopkins, Bart (1996) 'Musical Instrument Design', Tucson: Sharp Press.

Husler, F. & Rodd Marling, Y. (1965) 'Singing: The Physical Nature of the Vocal Organ', London: Faber & Faber Limited.

Jellinek, George (1986) 'Callas: Portrait of A Prima Donna', New York: Dover Publication, Inc.

Jones, David L. (2017) 'A Modern Guide to Old World Singing', David L. Jones.

Juvarra, Antonio (1987) 'Il Canto e le sue tecniche', Milano: BMG Ricordi S.p.A.

Juvarra, Antonio (2015) 'Il Canto e le sue tecniche', Milano: Casa Ricordi.

Juvarra, Antonio (2006) 'I segreti del belcanto', Milano: Edizioni Curci.

Juvarra, Antonio (2014) 'Canto Perduta Canto Ritrovato', Roma: Armando Editore.

Juvarra, Antonio (2014) 'La Tecnica Vocale Italiana', Padova: Armelin Musica.

Kay, Elster (1963) 'Bel canto and the Sixth Sense', London: Dobson.

Kayes, Gillyanne (2000) 'Singing and The Actor', London: A.C. Black (Publishers) Limited.

Kelsey, Franklyn (1950) 'The Foundation of Singing', London: Williams & Norgate.

Kendall, Alan (1992) 'Giocchino Rossini: The Reluctant Hero', London: Victor Gollancz Ltd.

Kennedy-Fraser, Marjory (1887 reprinted 2010) 'David Kennedy; The Scottish Singer', Memphis Tennessee: General Books.

Kennedy Scott, Charles (1954) 'The Fundamentals of Singing', London: Cassell and Company Ltd.

Klein, Hermann (1923) 'An Essay on Bel Canto and the Teachings of Manuel Garcia', London: Oxford University Press.

Klein, Hermann (1903) 'Thirty Years of Musical Life in London', New York: The Century Co.

Kolodin, Irving (1959) 'The Musical Life', London: Victor Gollancz Ltd.

Lablache, Luigi (1842) 'Metodo Completo di Canto' (Reprint 1997). Milano: Casa Ricordi, BMG Ricordi.

Ladefoge, Peter (1966) 'Elements of Acoustics Phonetics', Edinburgh: Oliver & Boyd.

Lamperti, Francesco (1864) 'Guida Teorica-Pratica- Elementare Per Lo Studio Del Canto', Milano: Ricordi.

Lamperti, Francesco (circa 1883) 'The Art of Singing' translated by G. Griffiths. New York: G. Schirmer.

Lamperti, G.B. (1905) 'The Techniques of Bel Canto', New York: G. Schirmer.

Lanza Tomoasi, Gioacchino (1934) 'Vincenzo Bellini', Palermo: Sellerio Editore.

Large, John PhD, (1980) 'Contributions of Voice Research to Singing', Houston Texas: College-Hill Press.

Last, R. J. (1984) 'Anatomy Regional and Applied', Edinburgh: Churchill Livingstone.

Lauri Volpi, Giacomo (1960) 'Voci Parallele', Blogna: Bongiovanni Editore.

Lehmann, Lilli (1902) 'How to Sing', (Reprint 1993). Mineola New York: Dover Publications Inc.

Lehmann, Lotte (1985) 'More Than Singing: The Interpretation of Songs', New York: Dover Publications Inc.

Love, Harold (1981) 'The Golden Age of Australian Opera', Sydney: Currency Press.

Love, Roger & Frazier Donna (1999) 'Set Your Voice Free', New York: Little, Brown and Company.

Lovegrove Graziano, Susan (1999) 'Oggi si Canta: La Voce e il Canto nella didattica musicale', Roma: BMG Ricordi.

Mackenzie, Sir Morell (1886) 'The Hygiene Of The Vocal Organs: A Practical Handbook For Singers and Speakers', London: Macmillan and Co.

Mackenzie, Barbara & Mackenzie, Findlay (1967) 'Singers of Australia, from Melba to Sutherland', Melbourne: Lansdowne Press.

Mackinlay, Malcom Sterling (1908) 'Garcia The Centenarian, and His Times', New York: D. Appleton & Company.

McCoy, Scott DMA (2006) 'Your Voice: An Inside View', Princeton, New Jersey: Inside View Press.

McKinney, James C. (1994) 'The Diagnosis & Correction of Vocal Faults', Long Grove, Illinois: Waveland Press Inc.

McMinn, R.M.H. (1998) 'A Concise Handbook of Human Anatomy', London: Manson Publishing Ltd.

Magiera, Leone (2008) 'Pavarotti Up Close', Milano: Universal Music, MGB Publications srl.

Magnani, S. & Fussi, F. (2015) 'Ascoltare la Voce', Milano: FrancoAngeli.

Magnani, S. (2017) 'Curare la Voce: Diagnosi e terapia dei disturbi della Voce', Milano: FrancoAngeli.

Magnani, S. (2017) 'Vivere di Voce: L'arte della manutenzione della voce per chi parla, rcita e canta', FrancoAngeli, Milano.

Major, Norma (1987) 'Joan Sutherland', London: Queen Anne Press.

Malmberg, Bertil (1968) 'Manuel of Phonetics', Amsterdam: North-Holland Publishing Company.

Mancini, Giambattista (1774–1777) 'Practical Reflections On Figured Singing', Champain, Illinois: Pro Musica Press.

Manén, Lucie (1974) 'The Art of Singing', London: Faber Music Ltd.

Manén, Lucie (1987) 'Bel Canto', Oxford: Oxford University Press.

Manfredini, Vincenzo (1775) 'Regole Armoniche', Venice 1775 [Facsimile], New York: Broude Brothers.

Marafioti, Mario (1922 Reprint 1949) 'Caruso's Method of Voice Production: The Scientific Culture of The Voice', New York: Dover Publishing Inc.

Marchesi, Mathilde (n.d. Reprint 1970) 'Theoretical & Practical Vocal Method', New York: Dover Publications, Inc.

Marchesi, Mathilde (1897) 'Marchesi And Music: Passages From The Life of a Famous Singing Teacher', New York: Harper & Brothers Publishers.

Marchesi, Blanche (1923 reprint 1977) 'Singer's Pilgrimage: An Autobiography' New York: Arno Press.

Marchesi, Blanche (1931) 'The Singer's Catechism And Creed', London: J.M. Dent.

Marek, Dan (2007) 'Singing The First Art', Lanham, Maryland: Scarecrow Press Inc.

Mari, Nanda (1970, Reprint 1987) 'Canto e Voce: Difetti Causati da un Errato Studio del Canto', Milano: BMG Ricordi Music Publishers.

Matheopouos, Helena 'Diva: Great Soprano's and Mezzos Discuss Their Art', London: Victor Gollancz.

Meano, Carlo and Khoury, Adele (1967) 'The Human Voice in Speech and Song', Springfield, Illinois: Charles C. Thomas Publisher.

Melba, Dame Nellie (1926) 'Melba Method', London: Chapell.

Menicucci, Delfo (2011) 'Scuola di Canto Lirico e Moderno: Indaggine sulla Tecnica di Affondo di Mario Del Monaco', Torino: Omega Edizione.

Mensah, Karin (2009) 'L'Arte Di Cantare: Manuale Pratico di Canto Moderno', Milano: Volenete & Co.

Miller, Donald Gray, PhD (2008) 'Resonance in Singing: Voice Building Through Acoustic Feedback', Princeton: Inside View Press.

Miller, Richard (1977 Reprint 1997) 'National Schools of Singing', Lanham, Maryland: Scarecrow Press Inc.

Miller, Richard (1993) 'Training Tenor Voices', New York: Schirmer Books, an imprint of Macmillan Publishing Company.

Miller, Richard (1986 Reprint 1996)'The Structure of Singing', New York: Schirmer Books, an imprint of Macmillan Publishing Company.

Miller, Richard (1996) 'On The Art of Singing', New York: Oxford University Press.

Miller, Richard (2000) 'Training Soprano Voices', New York: Oxford University Press.

Miller, Richard (2004) 'Solutions for Singers: Tools for Performers And Teachers', New York: Oxford University Press.

Miller, Richard (2008) 'Securing Baritone, Bass-Baritone & Bass Voices', New York: Oxford University Press.

Monahan, Brent Jeffrey (1978) 'The Art of Singing: A Compendium of Thoughts on Singing Published Between 1777 and 1927', Metuchen, N.J.: The Scarecrow Press, Inc.

Monahan, Brent (2006) 'The Singer's Companion: A Guide to Improving Your Voice and Performance', Pompton Plains, New Jersey: Limelight Editions.

Moore, Keith L. (1984) 'Clinically Oriented Anatomy', Baltimore: Williams & Wilkins.

Mori, Rachele Maragliano (1970) 'Coscienza Della Voce Nella Scuola Italiana Di Canto', Milano: Edizione Curci.

Myer, Edmund (1902) 'The Renaissance of the Vocal Art', July 2004 [Ebook #12856].

_____(1891) 'Vocal Reinforcement', Boston: Boston Music Co.

Osborne, Richard (2007) 'Rossini: His Life and Works', New York: Oxford University Press.

Palisca, Claude V. (1968 Reprint 1991) 'Baroque Music', Englewood cliffs, New Jersey: Prentice-Hall Inc.

Panofka, Enrico (1871) 'Voci E Cantanti', Florence: Arnaldo Forni Editore.

Parker, Roger (1994 Reprint 20001) 'The Oxford Illustrated History of opera', New York: Oxford University Press.

Peraro, Walter (2004) 'Esercizi di Pronuncia', Roma: Dino Audino.

Peri, Jacopo (1604) 'Le Varie Musiche And Other Songs', Edited by Tim Carter', Madison: A-R Editions, Inc.

Phillips-Matz, Mary Jane (2001) 'Rosa Ponselle: An American Diva', Boston: Northeastern University Press.

Pinksterboer, Hugo (2008) 'Tipbook Vocals: The Singing Voice', Milwaukee: Hal Leonards Books.

Pisk, Litz (175) 'The Actor And His Body', London: George Harrap & Co. Ltd.

Pleasants, Henry (1967 Reprint 1983) 'The Great Singers: From the Dawn of Opera to Our Own Time', London: Papermac, A Division of Macmillan Publishers Limited.

Plunket Greene, Harry (1912 Reprint 1979) 'Interpretation In Song', New York: Da Capo press.

Potter, John (2001) 'The Cambridge Companion To Singing', Edinburgh: Cambridge University Press.

Potter, John (2010) 'Tenor: A History Of A Voice', New Haven: Yale University Press.

Porter, J.C. (1999) 'Baroque Naples: A Documentary History, 1600-1800', New York: Italica Press.

Proctor, Donald F. (1980) 'Breathing, speech and Song', Vienna: Spring-Verlag.

Proschowsky, Frantz (1926) 'The Way To Sing', U.S.A: C.C. Birchard & Company.

Pullen, Robert & Taylor, Stephen (1994) 'Montserrat Caballe: Casta Diva', London: Victor Gollancz.

Punt, Norman (1979) 'The Singer's and the Actor's Throat', London: William Heinemann.

Raguenet, Francois (1709) (Reprint 1968) 'A Comparison Between the French and Italian Musick And Opera', London: Gregg International Publishers Limited.

Randegger, Alberto (nd) 'Novello's Music Primers & Education Series: Singing', London: Novello And Company, Limited.

Rasponi, Lanfranco (1994) 'The Last Prima Donnas', New York: Limelight editors.

Reid, Cornelius L. (1972) 'The Free Voice: A Guide to Natural Singing', New York: The Joseph Patelson Music House.

Reid, Cornelius L. (1974) 'Bel Canto: Principles and Practices', New York: The Joseph Patelson Music House.

Reis, Cornelius (1984) 'The Free Voice: A guide to Natural Singing', New York: Joseph Patelson Music House.

Righini, Pietro (2008) 'L'Acustica Per Il Musicista: Fondamenti Fisici Della Musica', Milano: Ricordi, BMG Publishing Scl.

Righini, Pietro (1980) 'Lessico Di Acustica E Tecnica Musicale', Milano: BMG Ricordi Music Publishing S.p.A.

Rohmert, Giselle (2003) 'Il Cantante in Cammino Verso Il Suono', Treviso: Diastemi Libri.

Rose, Arnold (1962 Reprint 1971) ' The Singer and the Voice', London: Faber and Faber Limited.

Roselli, John (1995) 'Singers of Italian Opera: The History of a Profession', Cambridge: Cambridge University Press.

Roselli, John (1996) 'The Life of Bellini', Cambridge: Cambridge University Press, Cambridge: Cambridge University Opera.

Rossing, Moore and Wheeler 'The Science Of Sound', San Francisco: Pearson Education, Inc., Publishing as Addison Wesley.

Rubboli, Danieli (1974) 'Le Voci Raccontate', Bologna: Bongiovanni Editore.

Ruopolo, G. Schindler, A., Amitrano, A. Genovese, E. (2012) 'Manuale di Foniatria e Logopedia', Roma: Societa Editrice Universo.

Ruopolo, G. and Amitrano, A. (2013) 'Disartria: Possiamo fare di Piu', Torino: Omega Edizione.

Rushmore, Robert (1971) 'The Singing Voice', London: Hamish Hamilton.

Sanchez Carbone, Maria Luisa (2005) 'Vox Arcana: Teoria e Pratica Della Voce', Milano: Rugginenti Editore.

Sanchez Carbone, Maria Luisa (2011) 'La Voce. Mille Esercizi e Vocalizzi per Educarla, Esercitarla, perfezionarla', Milano: Rugginenti Editori

Sanchez Carbone, Maria Luisa (2017) 'Il Mondo del Canto: Vivere e Sopravvivere', Milano: Rugginenti Editore.

San Carlo, Irene and Daniel, Patrick (1906) 'The Common-Sense of Voice Development', London: Bailliere, Tindall and Cox.

Sataloff, Robert Thayer (1998) 'Vocal Health And Pedagogy', San Diego: Singular Publishing Group Inc.

Sataloff, Robert Thayer (2005) 'Voice Science', San Diego: Plural Publishing Company Inc.

Schindler, O. (2010) 'La Voce: Fisiologia, Patologia, Clinica e Terapia', Padova: Piccin Nuova Libreria S.p.A.

Schindler, Oskar & Mari, Nanda (1986) 'Il Canto Come Tecnica La Foniatrica Come Arte', Milano: Universal Music Publishing Rocordi R.s.l.

Schnidler, O., Ruoppolo, G., and Schindler, A. (2011) 'Deglutologia', Torino: Omega Edizione.

Scholtz, Piotr O. (2001) 'Eunuchs and Castrati', Princiton: Markus Wiener Publisher.

Scott, Michael (1992) 'Maria Meneghini Callas', London: Simon & Schuster Ltd.

Scott, Michael (1993) 'The Record of Singing', London: Gerald Duckworth & Co.

Seghers, Rene (2008) 'Franco Corelli: Prince of Tenors', New York: Amadeus Press.

Seiler, Emma (1872) 'The Voice in Singing', Philadelphia: Lippincott's Press.

Seikel, J., King, D., Drumright, D. (1997) 'Anatomy and Physiology For Speech and Language', San Diego: Singular Publishing Group, Inc.

Shakespeare, William (1898) 'Art Of Singing', London: Metzler & Co. Limited.

Shakespeare, William (1924) 'Plain Words on Singing', London: G.P. Putnam's Sons.

Shaw, Bernard (1932) 'Music In London 1890–1894', London: Constable and Company Limited.

Somerset Ward, Richard (2004) 'Angels And Monsters', New Haven, Yale University Press.

Stanley, Douglas (1945) 'Your Voice: Applied Science of Vocal Art.' New York: Pitman Publishing Corporation.

Stark, James (1999) 'Bel Canto: A History of Vocal Pedagogy', Toronto: University Of Toronto Press Incorporated.

Stemple, Joseph et al. (2000) 'Clinical Voice Pathology: Theory and Management', New York: Delmar Cengage Learning.

Stendhal, (1823) 'The Life of Rossini', Translated by Richard N. Coe. Richmond, Surry: Alma Calssics.

Stevens, Kenneth N. (2000) 'Acoustic Phonetics', Massachusetts: MIT Press Cambridge Massachusetts.

Stockhausen, Julius (1884), 'Gesangs-Methode', Provided by Saxon State and University Library.

Stockhausen, Julius (1886) 'Singing Method', London: Dover Books.

Strunk, Oliver (1998) 'Source Readings in Music History', London: W.W. Norton & Company Ltd.

Sundberg, Johan (1987) 'The Science of The Singing Voice', Dekalb, Illinois: Northern Illinois University Press.

Sutcliff, Tom (2000) 'The Faber Book of Opera', London: Faber and Faber Limited.

Sutherland, Joan (1997) The Autobiography: A Prima Donna's Progress', Milson's Point: NSW, Random House Australia.

Talia, Joseph. (2017). 'A History of Vocal Pedagogy: Intuition and Science', Brisbane: Australian Academic Press.

Talia, Joseph. (2018). 'Vocal Science for Elite Singers', Brisbane: Australian Academic Press.

Taylor, David C. (1922) 'The Psychology of Singing', New York: The Macmillan Company.

Tilmann, Bernhard N. (2007) 'Atlas of Human Anatomy', New York: Mud Puddle Books.

Titze, Ingo (1994) 'Principles of Voice Production', Englewood Cliffs, New Jersey: Prentice Hall Inc.

Titze R. Ingo (2006) 'The Myoelastic Aerodynamic Theory of Phonation', Iowa City: The National Centre for Voice Speech.

Toft, Robert (2013) 'Bel Canto: A Performer's Guide', New York: Oxford University Press.

Tosi, Pier Franscesco (1723 English Edition 1743) 'Observations on The Florid Singing', Translated by Galliard. London: J. Wilcox.

Tosti, Francesco Paolo (1996) 'Il Canto Di Una Vita', Torino: Edizione Di Torino.

Trovato, Elio (1996) 'Anita Cerquetti: Umilta e Fierezza', Parma: Azzali Editore.

Vennard, William (1967) 'Singing the Mechanism and the Technic', New York: Carl Fisher Inc.

Veneziano, Corrado (2013) 'Manuale di Dizione, Voce e Respirazione', Abbruzzi: Salento Books.

Ulissi, Liliana (2000) 'Fedora Barbieri: Un Viaggio Nella Memoria', Trieste: Balletto Stampatore.

Walker, Frank (1972) 'The Man Verdi', New York: Alfred A. Knopf.

Ware, Clifton (1998) 'Basics of Vocal Pedagogy: The Foundation and Process of Singing', Boston Massachusets: McGraw Hill,

Watson, Celeste R. (1999) 'Teaching the Mechanical Art Of Song', South Minneapolis: Pro Musica Press.

Weiss, William (2002) 'Educare la Voce', Roma: Dino Audino.

White, Ernest G. (1908 reprinted 1950) 'Science And Voice', London: Boosey and Hawkes Ltd.

White, Ernest G. (1938) 'Sinus Tone Production', London: Dent & Sons Ltd.

Wilson, K.J.W. & Waugh, A. (1998) 'Anatomy and Physiology in Health And Illness', London: Harcourt Brace and Company Limited.

Wilson, Pat (1997) 'The Singing Voice: An Owner's Manual', Sydney: Currency Press Ltd.

Winckel, Fritz (1967) 'Music, Sound And Sensation: A Modern Exposition', New York: Dover Press, Inc.

Wright, William (1995) 'Pavarotti: My World', London: Chatto & Windus.

Zacconi, Lodovico (1592) 'Prattica Di Musica', Florence: Arnaldo Forni Editore.

Zemlin, Willard (1988) 'Speech and Hearing Science: Anatomy & Physiology', Englewood Cliffs, New Jersey: Prentice Hall.

Articles

Austin, Stephen (1996) 'Principles of Voice Science: Studio Applications.' ANATS, *Australian Voice*, 1996.

_____(1997) 'I Couldn't Understand a Single Word!' ANATS, *Australian Voice*, 1997.

_____(1999) 'Pedagogical Application of the Two-Register Theory', ANATS, *Australian Voice* 1997.

_____(2000) 'Nasal Resonance-Fact or Fiction?' *Journal of Singing*, Volume 57, No. 2, November 2000.

_____(2004) 'Register Unification-Give Me a Break', *Journal of Singing*, Volume 61, No. 2, November 2004.

Austin, Stephen (2005) 'Treasure 'Chest' – A Physiological and Pedagogical Review of the Low Mechanism', *Journal of Singing*, Volume 61, No. 3, January 2005.

_____(2005) 'Like the Squawk of A capon: The Tenor do di Petto', *Journal of Singing*, Volume 61, No. 3, January 2005._____(2005) 'The Voce Chiusa', *Journal of Singing*, Volume 61, No. 4 March 2005.

_____(2005) 'The Attack on the Coup de la Glotte', *Journal of Singing*, Volume 61, No 5, May 2005.

_____(2005) 'Two-headed Llamas and the lutte vocale', *Journal of Singing*, Volume 62, No. 1, September 2005.

_____ (2006), 'There is a Whole in the Middle, the Middle, the Middle', *Journal of Singing*, Volume 62, No. 3 January 2006.

_____ (2006) 'Words from William Shakespeare', *Journal of Singing*, Volume 63, No 1, September 2006.

_____ (2006) 'Flapping Jaws and Acoustic Laws', *Journal of Singing*, Volume 63, no. 2, November 2006.

_____ (2007) 'Herman Klein: A Contemporary: Link to Mozart', *Journal of Singing*, Volume 63, No. 4, March 2007.

_____(2008) 'Plugging the Holes', *Journal of Singing*, Volume 64, No. 4, March 2008.

_____(2008) 'Filling the Gap with Giuseppe Aprile', *Journal of Singing*, Volume 65, No. 2, November 2008.

_____(2009) 'Stockhausen's Method of Singing', *Journal of Singing*, Volume 65, No 3, January 2009.

_____ (2009) 'Stockhausen's Method of Singing', *Journal of Singing*, Volume 66, No 1, September 2009.

_____ (2010) 'Carlo Bassini's The Art of Singing', *Journal of Singing*, Volume 66, No. 5, May 2010.

_____(2012) 'Awsome Voices!' *Journal of Singing*, Volume 68, No. 5, May 2012.

Baer, Thomas (1981) Observation of Vocal Fold Vibration: Measurement of Excised Larynges. *Vocal Fold Physiology*, Edited by Stevens & Hirano, University of Tokyo Press, 1981.

Bartholomew, Wilmer (1934) 'A Physical Definition of 'Good Voice-Quality' in the Male Voice', *Journal of Acoustical Society of America*, Volume 6, 1934.

Bjorkner, Sundberg and Alku (2005) 'Subglottal Pressure and NAQ Variation in Voice Production of Classically Baritone Singers',

Bloothooft, Gerrit and Plomp, Reiner (1986) 'The sound level of the singer's formant in professional singing', The *Journal of Acoustical Society of America*, Volume 79, No. 6.

Bouhuys, Proctor & Mead (1966) 'Kinetic aspects of singing', *Journal of Applied Physiology*, 21(2) 1966.

Bozeman, Kenneth W. (2010), The Role of the First Formant in Training the Male Singing Voice. *Journal of Singing*, Volume 66, No 3 January 2010.

Brewer, David (1964) 'Research Potentials In Voice Physiology', International Conference: State University Of New York: Syracuse.

Broad, David (1979) 'The New Theories of Vocal *Fold Vibration*', *Speech and Language advances in Basic Research and Practice*, Volume 2, 1979.

Brodnitz, Friedrich (1975) 'The Age of the Castrato Voice', *Journal of Speech and Hearing Disorders* Volume 40, 322–326.

Brown, Oren L. (2003), *Register*. Volume 60, No. 2 December 2003.

_____(2002), Sensations. *Journal of Singing*, Volume 58, No. 3 January 2002.

_____(2002) 'Glottal Valving', *Journal of Singing*, Volume 59, No. 2, November 2002.

_____(2012) 'New Technology for Teaching voice Science and Pedagogy: The Madde Synthesizer (Svante Grandvist)', *Journal of Singing*, Volume 68, No/ 4, March 2012.

Bunch, Meribeth and Sonninen, Aatto (1977) 'Some Further Observation on Covered and Open Voice Qualities', *The Nats Bulletin*, October 1977.

Callaghan, Jean (1996) 'The Implications of Voice Science for the Teaching of Singing: Vocal Registers', *Australian Voice*, Volume 2, 1996.

Callaghan, Jean (1994), 'The Implications of Voice Science for Voice Pedagogy: The Singer's Formant', *The Nats Bulletin*, Volume 50, No. 5, May 1994.

Callaghan, Jean (1991) 'The Teaching of Vocal Technique for the twenty – first Century: current scientific Models Compared with Bel Canto Precepts', AMEL, 13th Annual Conference, Hobart, September, 1991.

Callaghan, Jean (1994), 'Projection: Interdisciplinary Connections in the Professional Education of Singing Teachers', AMEL, Proceedings of 16th Annual Conference, Melbourne, September 1994.

Callaghan, Jean (1996) 'The Implications of Voice Science for the Teaching of Singing: Vocal Registers. *Australian Voice*, ANATS, 1996.

Campbell, Agostinin & Davis (1970) 'The Respiratory Muscles: Mechanics and Neural Control', Lloyd-Luke Ltd, London 1970.

Casselman, Eugene (1950) 'The Secret of Bel Canto', Etude, September 1950.

Cavagna and Camporesi (1970) 'Glottic Aerodynamics and Phonation',

Chapman Byers, Margaret (1941) 'Sbriglia's Method of Singing.' *The Etude*, May 1942.

Childers, Yea, and Boccheri (1983) Source/Tract Interaction in Speech and Singing Synthesis.

Cleveland, Thomas (1993) 'Voice Pedagogy for the Twenty-First Century: Voice Classification (Part II)', *The Nats Journal*, March 1993.

Coffin, Berton (1976) 'Articulation for Opera, Oratorio, and Recital' *The Nats Bulletin*, February 1976.

Colton, Raymond (1973) 'Some Acoustic Parameters related to the Perception of Modal-Falsetto Voice Quality', *Folia Phoniatrica*, 25:302.

Colton & Hollien (1973) 'Perceptual Differentiation of the Modal and Falsetto Register', *Folia Phoniatrica*, 25:1973.

Collyer, Sally (2004) 'The Sound in Silence: Observations on Silent Singing as a Practice Technique', *Australian Voice*, Volume 10, 2004.

Collyer, Sally (2009) 'Breathing in Classical Singing: Linking science and teaching', Published by AEC.

Cyr, Mary (1977) 'On Performing 18th-Century Haute-Contre Roles', *The Musical Times,* Volume 118, April 1977.

Daniloff, Raymond (1980) 'Overview of Supraglottal Aspects of Voicing', Transcripts of the Ninth Symposium Care of the Professional Voice, Van Lawrence M.D. Editor, Published by the Voice Foundation.

Darwin and Gardner (1986), 'Mistuning a harmonic of a vowel: Grouping and phase effects on vowel quality. '*Acoustical Society of America,* 1986.

Delattre, Pierre (1958) 'Vowel Color and Voice Quality: An Acoustic and Articulatory Comparison', *The Bulletin,* October 1958.

Dellattre and Howie (1962) 'An Experimental Study of the Effect of Pitch on Intelligibility of Vowels', *The Nats Bulletin,* May 1962.

Draper, Ladefoged & Whitteridge (1959) 'Respiratory Muscles in Speech', *Journal of Speech and Hearing Research,* Volume 2.

Estill, Baer, Honda, and Harris (1988) 'Supralaryngeal Activity in a Study of Six Voice Qualities', Haskins Laboratories, New Haven, CT, USA. The City University of New York.

Evans, Thomas (1973) 'Singing History', *Groves Dictionary of Music,* Edited by Blom 1973.

Fant, Gunnar & Krukenberg, Anita (1996) 'Voice Source Properties of the Speech Code', The *Acoustical Society of America,* December 1996.

Fant, Gunnar & Lin, Q. (1988) 'Frequency Domain Interpretation And Derivation of Glottal Flow Parameters', STL-QPSR, Volume 29, No. 2–3].

Galliver, David (1974) 'Cantare Con La Gorga: The Coloratura Technique of the Renaissance Singer',

_____(1976) 'Cantare Con Affetto: Keynote of the Bel Canto',

Garcia, Manuel (1855) 'Observations on the Human Voice', The Royal Society, March 1955.

Gaufin, Jan and Sundberg, Johan (1980) 'Data on the Glottal Voice Source Behaviour in Vowel Production', Paper given in Sydney, Australia, STL-QPSR 2-3/ 1980.

Gauffin, Jan & Sundberg, Johan (1989), 'Spectral Correlates of Glottal Voice Source Waveform Characteristics', *Journal of Speech and Hearing Research,* Volume 32, September 1989.

Gould and Okamura (1974) 'Interrelationships Between Voice and Laryngeal Mucosal Reflexes', In Ventilatory and Phonatory control systems, Wyke, London: Oxford University Press.

Griffin, Woo, Colton, Caspar, Brewer 'Physiological Characteristics Of The Supported Singing Voice: A Preliminary Study.'

Gunter, Heather (2003) 'A Mechanical Model of Vocal-fold Collision with high Spatial and Temporal Resolution', *Acoustical Society of America*, 113. No. 2, 2003.

Gunter, Horst (1992) Mental Concept In Singing: A Psychological Approach', *The NATS Journal*, May 1992.

Hall, Karen (2007) 'Musical Theater and Classical Singing: at Odds Personally and Professionally', *Journal of Singing*, Volume 63, No. 5, May 2007.

Helding, Lynn (2007) 'Voice Science and Vocal Art, Part One: In Search of Common Ground', *Journal of Singing*, Volume 64, No. 2, November 2007.

Heman-Ackah, Yolanda (2005) 'Physiology of Voice Production: Considerations for the Vocal Performer', *Journal of Singing*, Volume 62, No. 2, November 2005.

Hertegård, and Gauffin (1995) 'Glottal Area and Vibratory Patterns Studies with simultaneous stroboscopy, Flow Glotttography and Electroglottography, *Journal of Speech and Hearing Research*, Volume 38.

Hirano, Minoru (1974) 'Morphological Structure of the Vocal Cord as a Vibrator and its vibrations', *Folia Phoniatrica*, 26 (1974).

Hirano, Minoru (1988) 'Vocal Mechanism in Singing: Laryngological and Phoniatric Aspects', *Journal of Voice*, Volume 2, No. 1.

Hirano, Gould, Lambiase & Kakita (1980) 'Movement of Selected Points on a Vocal Fold during Vibration', *Folia Phoniatrica*, 32: 1980.

Hirosi and Gay (1973) 'Laryngeal Control in Vocal Attack', *Folia Phoniat*, 25, 1973.

Hixon, T.J., & Weismer, G. (1995) 'Perspective on the Edinburgh Study of Speech Breathing', *Journal of Speech and Hearing Research*, Volume 38, Feb. 1995.

Hollien & Colton (1969) 'Four Laminagraphic Studies of Vocal Fold Thickness', *Folia Phoniatrica*, 21,1969.

Hollien, Girard, Coleman (1977) Vocal Fold Vibratory Patterns of Pulse Register Phonation', *Folia Phoniat*, 20, 1977.

Hollien, Brown and Weiss (1999) 'Another View of Vocal Mechanics', *Journal of Singing*, Volume 56, No. 1, September 1999.

Isshiki, Nobuhiko (1964) 'Regulatory Mechanism of Voice Intensity Variation', *Journal of Speech and Hearing Research*, Volume 7, 1964.

Jerold, Beverly (2005) 'Mystery in Paris, The German Connection and More: The Bèrard-Blanchet Controversy Revisited', Eighteenth Century Music: Cambridge University Press.

Joliveau, Wolf, and Smith (2006) 'Sopranos Tune Resonances of Their Vocal Tract When They Sing in the High Range', *Nature*, 427, 116.

Joyner, James R. (1983) 'The Garcia Legacy: Charles Amable Battaille', *The Bulletin*, Volume 39, No. 5, May 1983.

Kelman, A. W. (1981) 'Vibratory Patterns of the Vocal Folds', *Folia Phoniat*, 33.

Kelsey, Franklyn (1973) Voice Training: Mechanics — Technical History.

Groves, George, Blom Editor, Macmillan Press.

Kirkpatrick, Adam (2009) 'Chiaroscuro and the Quest for Optimal Resonance', *Journal of Singing*, Volume 66, No. 1, September 2009.

_____(2008) 'Teaching Methods for Correcting Problematic Vibratos: Using Sustained Dynamic Exercises to Discover and Foster Healthy Vibrato. *Journal of Singing*, Volume 64, No. 5, May 2008.

Kob, Alhauser, Reiter (1999) 'Time-Domain Model of the Singing Voice', Proceedings of the 2nd COST G-6 Workshop on Digital Audio Effects, NTNU, Trondheim, December 9–11, 1999.

Joiner, James Richard (1988) 'The Relationship of the Vocal Folds to Vowel Formation: A Study of Current Research', *Journal of Research in Singing* September 1988.

Kaburagi, Tokihiko (2008) 'On the Viscous-inviscid interaction of the flow passing through the glottis', The Acoustical Society of Japan.

Keenze, Marvin & Bell, Donald (2005) 'Teaching Breathing', *Journal of Singing*, Volume 61, No. 4, March 2005.

Kenaston-French, Karen (2009) 'The Teachings of Jean-Antoine Berard: Content, Context, and Legacy', *Journal of Singing*, Volume 66, No 2 November 2009.

Kennedy-Dygas, Margaret (1999) 'Historical Perspective on the 'Science' of Teaching Singing', *Journal of Singing*, Volume 56, No 2 November 1999.

_____(2000) 'Historical Perspective on the Science of Teaching Singing Part III: Manuel Garcia II (1805-1806)', *Journal of Singing*, Volume 56, No. 4 March 2000.

Kessler Price, Kathy (2011), Emma Seiler: A Pioneering Woman in the Art and Science of Teaching Voice, *Journal of Singing*, Volume 68, No. 1, September 2011.

Kiesgen, Paul (2005) 'Vocal Pedagogy: Breathing', *Journal of Singing*, Volume 62, No 2, November 2005.

_____(2006) 'Vocal Pedagogy: Resonance', *Journal of Singing*, volume 62, No. 4, March 2006.

_____(2006) 'Vocal Pedagogy: Registration', *Journal of Singing*, Volume 62, No. 5, May 2006.

Ladefoged and Loeb (2002) 'Preliminary Studies on Respiratory Activity in Speech', Linguistics Department, UCLA, Los Angeles 2002.

Large, John (1972) 'Towards an Integrated Physiologic-Acoustic Theory of Vocal Registers', *The Nats Bulletin*, March 1972.

_____ (1973) 'Acoustic Study of Register Equalization in Singing', *Folia Phoniatrica*, Volume 25.

Laukkanen, Lindholm, Vilkman Hataaja, Alku (1996) 'A Physiological and Acoustic Study on Voiced Bilabial Fricative / :/ as Vocal Exercise', *Journal of Voice*, Volume 18, No. 1.

Laukkanen, Titze, Finnegan, Hoffman (2002) 'Laryngeal Muscle Activity in a Tonal Scale: Comparing Speech-like to Song-like Productions in a Mezzo-soprano', *Journal of Singing*, Volume 59, No. 1, September 2002.

Leanderson, Sundberg and Von Euler (1987) 'Role of Diaphragmatic Activity During Singing: A Study of Transdiaphragmatic Pressures', PubMed 1987.

Lieberman, Philip (1968) 'Vocal Cord Motion in Man', New York Academy of Sciences, Volume 155.

Lucero, Jorge (1997) 'Optimal Glottal Configuration for Ease of Phonation', *Journal of Voice*, Volume 12, No. 2.

_____(2005) 'Dynamics of the Vocal Fold Oscillation.' National Congress on Applied Computational Mathematics CNMAC in Porto Alegre, September 2004.

McCoy, Scott (2003) 'Falsetto and the Male High Voice',

_____(2008) 'The Seduction of Nasality', *Journal of Singing* , 64 No 5, May 2008]. *Journal of Singing*, Volume 59, No. 5, May 2008.

_____(2010) 'Building the Foundation', *Journal of Singing*, Volume 67, No.1, September 2010.

McCoy, Scott (2012) 'Some Thoughts on Singing and Science', *Journal of Singing*, Volume 68, No. 5, May 2012.

McGowan, Richard, & Howe, Michael (2010) 'Comments on single-mass models of vocal fold vibrations', Journals of *Acoustical Society of America*, April 2010.

McIver, William and Miller, Richard (1995) 'A Brief Study of Nasality in Singing', *Journal of Singing*, Volume 52, No. 1, September 1995.

Mead, Hixon and Goldman (1970) 'The Configuration of the Chest Wall During Speech', LLOyd-Luke LTD. London: 1970.

Mewburn Levien, John (1939-1941) 'The Decline of Singing', Letters to the Editor of 'Musical Opinion'.

Miller, Bonnie & Alt, David (1989), 'Mathile Marchesi and the Ladies' Home Journal', *The NATS Journal*, Volume 46, No 2, November 1989.

Miller, D, and Schutte, H. (2002) 'Characteristic Patterns Of Sub-And Supraglottal Pressure Variations Within the Glottal Cycle.' PAS-Conference October 2002.

Miller, R.L. (1959) 'Nature of the Vocal Cord Wave', The *Acoustical Society of America*, Volume 31, No. 6.

Miller, Richard (1980) 'Supraglottal Considerations and Vocal Pedagogy', *Transcripts of the Ninth Symposium, Care of the Professional Voice*, Edited by Van Lawrence M.D., Published by the Voice Foundation.

Miller, Richard (1992) 'How Singing Is Not Like Speaking', *The NATS Journal*, Volume 48, No. 5, May 1992.

Miller, Richard and Franco, Carlos (1991) Spectrographic Analysis of The Singing Voice. *The NATS Journal*, Volume 48, No. 1, Sept. 1991.

_____(1992) A Brief Spectral Study of Vowel Differentiation and Modification in a Professional Tenor. *The NATS Journal*, Volume 49, No. 1, September 1992.

_____(1994) 'Feeling, Hearing and Seeing the Voice.' *The NATS Journal*, Volume 51, No. 2, November 1994.

_____(1996) 'What Does Humming Accomplish', *The NATS Journal*, Volume 52, No. 3, February 1996.

Miller, Richard (1998) 'The Garcia Position', *Journal of Singing*, Volume 55, No 2 November 1998.

Miller, Donald (2009) 'On Master Classes and the Olympic Games', *Journal of Singing*, Volume, 65, No. 4, March 2009.

Millhouse, Thomas (2012) 'Observation of the Higher Formant Structure in the Male Operatic Vowel', Macquarie University, Sydney, Australia.

_____(2013) 'Perceptually Motivated Auditory Interpretation of the Singer's Formant', *Australian Voice*, Volume X 2013.

Morozov, V. P. (1956) 'Intelligibility in Singing as a Function of Fundamental Voice Pitch', *Soviet Physics-Acoustics*, Volume 10, 1956.

Myers, Myron (2008) 'The Legacy of Garcia', *Journal of Singing*, Volume 64, No. 5, May 2008.

_____ (2008) 'The Legacy of Garcia, Part 2', *Journal of Singing*, Volume 65, No 1, September 2008.

Newsom, Davis & Sears, T. (1970) 'The Proprioceptive Reflex Control Of The Intercostal Muscles During Their Voluntary Activation', *Journal of Physiology*, (1970).

Nix, John (1995) 'The Vocal Method of Mathilde Marchesi: A Modern Evaluation', *The NATS Journal*, Volume 51, No. 5, ay 1005.

_____(1999) 'Lip Trills and Raspberries: 'High Spit Factor' Alternatives to the Nasal Continuants Consonants', *Journal of Singing*, Volume 55, No. 3, January 1999.

Nix, John (2004) 'Vowel Modification Revisited', *Journal of Singing*, Volume 61, No. 2 November 2004.

Pressman, Joel (1942) 'Physiology of the Vocal Cords In Phonation And Respiration', *Archives of Otolaryngology*, Volume 35, March 1942.

Pressman, Joel (1952) 'Sphincters of the Larynx', The Academy of Ophthalmology and Otolaryngology, Chicago, October 1952.

Pressman and Kelemen(1955) 'Physiology of the Larynx', Dept. of Otolaryngology, Harvard Medical School, Boston Massachusetts, 1955.

Department of Otolaryngology, Harvard Medical School, Boston, Massachusetts, 1955.

Proctor, Donald (1980) 'Breath, the Power Source of the Voice', *The Bulletin*, November 1980.

Radomski, Teresa (2005) 'A Bicentenary Reflection: The 'Christopher Columbus of the larynx', *Australian Voice*: December 2005.

Reid, Cornelius (1997) 'Vocal Mechanics', *Journal of Singing*, Volume 54, No. 1, September 1997.

Reid, Cornelius & Reid, Donna (2000) 'Eighteenth-Century Registration Concepts', *Journal of Singing*, Volume 56, No. 4, March 2000.

Rezhevkin, S. N. 'Certain Results of the Analysis of a Singer's Voice', *Soviet Physics-Acoustics*, Volume 2, 1956.

Rhodes Draayer, Suzanne (2007) 'Canciones de Espana: Manuel Garcia-Composer, Teacher, and Singer', *Journal of Singing*, Volume 64, No. 2, November 2007.

Robinson, Clayne (2001) 'Beautiful Singing: What It Is and How to Do It', *Journal of Singing*, Volume 58, No. 1 September 2001.

Rose, Arnold (1955) 'The Italian Method and the English Singer', *Musical Times*, 96, December 1955.

Rothenberg, Martin (1968) 'The Breath Stream Dynamics of Simple-Released-Plosive', www.rothenberg.org/breath-stream.

Rothenberg, Martin (1972) 'The Glottal Volume Velocity Waveform During Loose and Tight Voiced Glottal Adjustments', Congress of phonetic Science held at the University of Montreal and McGill University, Published by Mouton, The Hague 1972.

_____(1972) 'A new inverse-filter technique for deriving the glottal air flow waveform during voicing', *Journal of the Acoustical Society of America*, Volume 53, No.6, 1972.

Rothenberg, Martin (1977) 'Measurement of Airflow in Speech', Publications of Dr. Martin Rothenberg, March 1977.

Rothenberg and Zahorian (1977) 'Nonlinear Inverse Filtering for Estimating the Glottal Area Waveform', *Acoustical Society of America*, Volume 61, No. 4, April 77.

_____(1980)'Acoustic Interaction Between the Glottal Source and the Vocal Tract', Vocal fold Physiology, K. Stevens & M. Hirano, Eds. University of Tokyo Press.

_____(1981) 'The Voice Source in Singing', *Research Aspects of Singing*, Academy of Music, Stockholm, 1981.

_____(1981) 'An Interactive Model for the Voice Source', Conference of Vocal fold Physiology, University of Wisconsin, June 1981.

_____(1984) 'Source-Tract Acoustic Interaction and Voice Quality', The Voice Foundation, NY. 1984.

Rothenberg and Mahshie (1986) 'Induced transglottal pressure variations during voicing', *Journal of Phonetics*, Academic Press Inc., 1986.

Rothenberg, Miller, Mollitor, Leffingwell (1987) 'The Control of Air Flow During Loud Soprano Singing', *Journal of Voice*, Volume 1, No. 3, 1987.

_____(1988) 'Monitoring Vocal Fold Abduction Through Vocal Fold Contact Area', *Journal of Speech and Hearing Research*, Volume 31, September 1988.

_____(1988) 'Acoustic Reinforcement of Vocal Fold Vibratory Behaviour in Singing', In Vocal Fold Physiology, New York 1988.

Rothenberg, M. (1988) 'Acoustic Reinforcement of Vocal Fold Vibratory Behaviour in Singing', Raven Press, NY. 1988.

Rothenberg & Mashie (1988) 'Monitoring Vocal Fold Abduction Through Vocal Fold Contact Area', *Journal of Speech and Hearing Research*, Volume 31, September 1988.

_____(2002) 'Correct Low Frequency Phase Distortion', *Journal of Voice*, Volume 16, No. 1, 2002.

_____ (2004) 'The Control of Airflow during Singing', Conference on the Physiology and Acoustics of Singing, Denver Colorado, 2004.

_____(2006) 'Some relations between glottal airflow and Vocal Fold Contact Area', Rothenberg 2006.

_____(2008) 'The Source-Filter Model Lives (if you are careful)', The Voice Foundation, 37th Annual Symposium, May 2008.

Rubin, H., Hirt, C., & Le Cover, M. (1960) 'The Falsetto: A high Speed Cinematographic Study',

Ruty, N., Van Hirtum, Pelerson, X. (2005) 'A Mechanical experimental setup to stimulate vocal fold vibration', ZAS Papers in Linguistics 40, 2005.

Sanford, Sally (1995) 'A comparison of French and Italian Singing in the Seventeenth Century', *Journal of Seventeenth-Century Music*, Volume 1.

Saxon, K. & Berry, S. (2009) 'Vocal Exercise Physiology: Same Principles, New Training Paradigm', *Journal of Singing*, Volume 66, No. 1, September 2009.

Schipp, Tom (1980) 'Vertical Laryngeal Position in Sighing', Transcripts of the Ninth Symposium Care of the Professional Voice', Edited by Van Lawrence M.D., Published by the Voice Foundation.

Schutte, Harm (1984) 'Efficiency of Professional Singing Voices in Terms of Energy', *Folia Phoniatrica,* 36: 984.

Schutte, Harm K. (1989) 'Measurements of Vocal Function', *The NATS Journal*, Volume 46, No 2 November 1989.

Schutte, H. and Miller, D. 'Characteristic Patterns of Sub-And-supraglottal Phase Variation within the Glottal cycle', PAS-Conference, October 2002.

Schutte, Harm and Miller, Richard (1984) 'Breath management in repeated Vocal Onset', *Folia Phoniatrica,* 36, 1984.

Schutte, Stark and Miller (2003) 'Change in Singing Voice Production, Objectively Measured', *Journal of Voice*, Volume 17, No. 4, 495–501].

Shore, Joseph (1995) 'A Great Singer on Great Singing: Jerome Hines Challenges Voice Scientists and Singers', *The NATS Journal*, Volume 51 No 3, January 1995.

Sjoerdsma, Richard Dale (2011) 'Creativity and Imagination', *Journal of Singing*, Volume 67, No. 5, May 2011.

Stark, James A. (1991) Garcia In Perspective: His Traite After 150 Years. JRS 20, 1991.

Stemple, Joseph et al (1994), Efficacy of Vocal Function Exercise as a Method of Improving Voice Production, *Journal of Voice*: Volume 8, No 3.

Stevens, Robyn (2009) 'The Garcia Family: The Pedagogic Legacy of Romanticism's Premier Musical Dynasty', *Journal of Singing*, Volume 65, No. 5.

Stone, Morrish, Sonies and Shawker 'Tongue Curvature: A Model of Shape during Vowel Production', Folia Phoniat. 39. 302–315.

Stone, Cleveland, Sundberg, and Prokop (2002) 'Aerodynamic and Acoustical Measures of Speech, Operatic, and Broadway Vocal Styles in a Professional Female Singer', *Speech, Music and Hearing*, KTH, Stockholm, Volume 43, 2002.

Story and Titze (1994) 'Voice Simulation With a Body-Cover Model of the Vocal Folds', *Journal of Acoustical Society of America*, Volume 97, No. 2.

Story, Titze and Hoffman (1996) 'Vocal Tract Area Function From Magnetic Resonance Imaging', *Journal of Acoustical Society of America*, Volume 100, No. 1.

Story, B., Laukkanen, A. Titze, I. (2000), 'Acoustic Impedance of an Artificially Lengthened and Constricted Vocal Tract', *Journal of Voice*, Volume 14, No. 4, 2000.

Story, Brad (2002), 'An overview of the physiology, physics and modeling of the sound source for vowels', Department of Speech and Hearing Sciences, University of Arizona, *Acoustic, Science & Technology*, 23, 4 (2002),

Story, B. & Titze, I. (1994) 'Voice Simulation With a Body-Cover Model of the Vocal Folds', *Acoustical Society of America*, Volume 97, Feb. 1995.

Sundberg, Johan (1970) 'Formant Structure and Articulation of Spoken and Sung Vowels', *Folia Phoniatrica*, Volume 22, 1970.

Sundberg, Johan (1973) 'The Source Spectrum in Professional Singing', *Folia Phoniatrica*, Volume 25, 1971.

_____(1974) 'Articulatory Interpretation of the 'Singing Formant'', *Journal of Acoustical Society of America*, Volume 56, No. 4, April 1974.

Sundberg, Johan (1977) 'The Acoustics of the Singing Voice', *Scientific America*, March 77.

_____(1977) 'Studies of the Soprano Voice', *Journal of Research in Singing*, 1, 1977.

Sundberg, Johan (1981) 'Research Aspects on Singing', Publications Issued by the Royal Swedish Acadamy of Music No. 33, 1981.

_____ (1983) 'Chest Wall Vibrations in Singers', *American Speech-Language-Hearing Association*, 1983.

Sundberg, Leanderson, von Euler and Lagercrantz (1984) 'Activation of the Diaphragm During Singing: A study of Transdiaphragmatic Pressures',

Sundberg, Leanderson and von Euler (1988) 'Activity Relationship Between Diaphragm And Cricothyroid Muscles', *Journal STL-QPSR*, 1988.

Sundberg, Elliot and Gramming (1991) 'How Constant Is Subglottal Pressure in Singing? *Journal STL-QPSR*, 1991.

Sundberg, Johan (1998) 'Vocal Tract Resonance In Singing', *The NATS Journal*, March 1988.

_____(1990) 'What's So Special About Singers?' *Journal of Voice*, Volume 4, No. 2, 1990.

Sundberg, Elliot and Gramming (1988) 'How close is subglottal pressure in singing', STL-QPSR.

_____(1991) 'How Constant Is Subglottal Pressure in Singing', STL-QPSD, Volume 32, No. 1.

_____(1992) 'Phonatory Vibrations in Singers: A Critical Review', Music Perception Spring 1992, Volume 9, No. 3.

_____ (1993) 'Breathing Behaviour during Singing', *The NATS Journal*, Volume 49, No. 3, January 1993.

Sundberg, Johan, Skoog, Jorgen (1997), 'Dependence of Jaw Opening on Pitch and Vowel in Singers', Dept. of Speech, Music, and Hearing, KTH, Stockholm, Sweden 1997.

Sundberg, Johan (2001) 'Level and Centre Frequency of the Singer's Formant', *Journal of Voice*, Volume 15, No. 2, 2001.

_____(2003) 'Research on the Singing Voice in Retrospect', *Speech, Music and Hearing*, KTH-QPSR Volume 45, 2003.

Sundberg, Troven & Richter (2007) 'Sopranos with a singer's formant?', Historical, Physiological, and Acoustical Aspects of Castrato Singing. TMH-QPSR, KTH, Volume 49, 2007.

Sundberg, La and Himonides (2013) 'Intonation and Expressivity: A Single Case Study of Classical Western Singing', *Journal of Voice*, Volume 27, No. 3, 2013.

_____ (2013) 'Formant Tuning Strategies in Professional Male Opera Singers', *Journal of Voice*, Volume 27, No. 3, 2013.

Sutherland, Joan (1998) 'The Cornerstone of Singing: Breathing and Breath Support', *Opera News*, 63 No. 5, November 1998.

Thomasson, Monica (2003) 'Effects of lung volume on the glottal voice source and the vertical laryngeal position in male professional opera singers', Speech-Music-Hearing TMH-QPSR, KTH. Volume 45, 2003.

Timberlake, Craig (1989), 'Thee Case of Manuel Garcia 11', *The NATS Journal*, Volume 46, No 2, November 1989.

Timberlake, Craig (1989), 'The Case of Manuel Garcia 11, Part 11.' *The NATS Journal*, Volume 46, No 3, January 1990.

_____ (1990) 'Terminological Turmoil – The Naming of Registers', *The NATS Journal*, Volume 47, No. 1 September 1990.

_____ (1990) 'The Quintessential Lieder Singer: Julius Stockhausen', *The NATS Journal*, Volume 46, No. 4, March 1990.

_____ (1990) 'Julius Stockhausen and His Method of Singing', Nats Journal, Volume 46, No. 5, May 1990.

Timberlake, Craig (1991) 'Practica Musicae: Catching up on Caccini: Nuove Musiche', *The NATS Journal*, Volume 47, No. 3, January 1991.

_____ (1991) 'The Caccini Collections Part 1', *The NATS Journal*, Volume 47, No. 4, March 1991.

_____ (1991) The Caccini Collection Part 11. *The NATS Journal*, Volume 47, No. 5, May 1991.

Timberlake, Graig (1993), Practica Musicae: 'Maffei – Medico e Musica', *The NATS Journal*, Volume 45, No. 5, May 1993.

_____ (1994) 'Pedagogical Perspectives, Past and Present: Laryngeal Positioning', Volume 51, No 1 September 1994.

_____ (1994) 'Pedagogical Perspectives, Past and Present: Apropos of Appoggio', Volume 52, No. 2 November 1994.

_____ (1995) 'Pedagogical Perspectives, Past and Present: Apropos and Appoggio part II', Volume 51, No. 3 January 1995.

Titze and Strong, W. (1975) 'Normal Modes in Vocal Fold Tissues',

Titze, Ingo (1973) 'The Human Vocal Cords: A Mathematical Model, Part 1', *Phonetica* Volume 28, 129–170.

_____(1974) 'The Human Vocal Cords: A Mathematical Model, Part 11', *Phonetica* Volume 29, 1–21. *Journal of Acoustics Society of America*, Volume 57, No. 3, March 1975.

Titze, Ingo (1980) 'Comments On The Myoelastic Aerodynamic Theory Of Phonation', *Journal of Speech and Hearing Research*, September 1980.

_____(1981), 'Acoustic Interpretation of Resonant Voice', *Journal of Voice*, Volume 15, No. 4, 2001.

Titze, Horii, and Scherer (1987) 'Some Technical Considerations in Voce Perturbation Measurements', *American Speech-Language-Hearing Association*, Volume 30, June 1987.

_____(1988) 'The Physics of Small-Amplitude Oscillation of the Vocal Folds', *Journal of Acoustics, Society of America*, 83 (4), April 88.

_____(1988) 'Male-Female Differences in the Larynx', *The NATS Journal*, January 1988.

_____(1988) 'A Framework for the Study of Vocal Registers', *Journal of Voice*, Volume 2, No. 3.

_____(1989) 'Physiologic and Acoustic differences between male and female voices', *Acoustical Society of America*, Volume 85 (4) April 1989.

Titze, Luchesi, and Hirano (1989) 'Role of the Thyrorytenoid Muscle in Regulation of Fundamental Frequency', *Journal of Voice*, Volume 3, No. 3.

Titze, Ingo (1992) 'Glottal Resistance', *The NATS Journal*, Volume 48, No. 4, March 1992.

_____(1992), 'Acoustic Interpretation of the Voice Range Profile' (Phonetogram). *Journal of Speech and Hearing Research*, Volume 35, 1992.

_____(1992) 'Voice Quality: Part I', *The NATS Journal*, June 1992.

_____(1992) 'Voice Quality: Part II', *The NATS Journal*, September 1992.

_____(1996) 'Lip and Tongue Trills — What do they do for us?

_____(1996) 'Vocal tract area functions from magnetic resonance imaging', *Journal of Acoustical Society of America*, Volume 100, No. 1, July 1996.

_____(1998) 'The Wide Pharynx', *Journal of Singing* Volume 55, No. 1, September 1998.

_____(1999) 'The Use of Low First Formant Vowels and Nasals to Train the Lighter Mechanism', *Journal of Singing*, Volume 55, No. 4, March 1999.

_____(2001) 'Acoustic Interpretation of Resonant Voice.' *Journal of Voice*, Volume 15, No. 4, 519-528: The Voice Foundation.

_____(2002),'Regulating glottal airflow in phonation: Application of the maximum power transfer theorem to a low dimensional phonation model', *Acoustical Society of America*, Volume 111, No. 1, Jan. 2002.

Titze & Story (2002) 'Rules for controlling low-dimensional vocal fold models with muscle activation', *Acoustical Society of America*, Volume 112, No. 3, September 2002.

Titze, Laukkanen, Finnegan and Jaiswal (2002) 'Raising Lung Pressure and Pitch In Vocal Warm-Ups: The Use of Flow-Resistant Straws', *Journal of Singing*, Volume 58, No. 4, March 2002.

_____(2003) 'More About resonant Voice: Chasing the Formants but Staying Behind Them', *Journal of Singing*, Volume 59, No. 5, May 2003.

_____(2004) 'Theory of Glottal Airflow and Source-Filter Interaction in Speaking and Singing', *Acta Acoustical United with Acustica*, Volume 90, 2004.

_____(2004) 'The Search for Efficient Voice Production: Where Is It Leading Us', *Journal of Singing*, Volume 60, No. 4 April 2004.

Titze, Ingo and Storey, Brad (1997) 'Acoustic Interactions of the Voice Source with the Lower Vocal Tract', *Acoustical Society of America*, Volume 101, No. 4, April 1997.

Titze, and Talkin (1979), 'A theoretical study of the effects of various laryngeal configurations on the acoustics of phonation', *Acoustical Society of America*, Volume 66, No. 1, 1979.

Titze, Ingo (2004) 'The Search for Efficient Voice Production: Where Is It Leading Us', *Journal of Singing*, Volume 60, No 4 March 2004.

_____(2004) 'A Theoretical Study of Fo – F1 Interaction With Application to Resonant Speaking and Singing Voice', *Journal of Voice*, Volume 18, No. 3. 2004.

_____(2004) 'What is Meant by Nonlinear and Interactive in Voice Science?' *Journal of Singing*, Volume 60, No. 3 January 2004.

_____(2004) 'What makes A Voice Acoustically Strong?' Volume 61, No 1 September 2004.

_____(2005) 'Space in the Throat and Associated Vocal Quality', *Journal of Singing*, Volume 61, No 5, May 2005.

_____(2005) 'How Loud is My Voice Inside My Mouth and Throat', *Journal of Singing*, Volume 62, No. 2, November 2005.

_____(2006) 'The Fo-F1 Crossover Exercises', *Journal of Singing*, Volume 62, No. 3, January 2006.

_____(2006) 'About Vocal Fold Thinning', *Journal of Singing*, Volume 62, No. 4, March 2006.

_____(2006) 'Voice Training and Therapy with a Semi-Occluded Vocal Tract: Rationale and Scientific Underpinning', *JSLHR*, Volume 49, 2006.

_____(2007) 'Falsetto Register and Vowels', *Journal of Singing*, Volume 63, N0. 4, March 2007.

_____(2007) 'Belting and a High Larynx Position', *Journal of Singing*, Volume 63, No. 5, May 2007.

_____(2008) 'An Appeal for Patience and Long-suffering by Singing Teachers in Their Assessment of the Value of Voice Science', *Journal of Singing*, Volume 64, No. 5, May 2009.

_____(2009) 'How Are Harmonics Produced at the Voice Source', *Journal of Singing*, Volume 65, No. 5 May 2009.

_____(2009) 'What Signals Physical Strength in a Voice?' *Journal of Singing*, Volume 66, No. 2 November 2009.

_____ (2011) 'Introducing A Music Notation Scheme For Pitch-Vowel Interaction', *Journal of Singing*, Volume 68, No. 1, September 2011.

Titze, Worley, and Story (2011) 'Source Vocal-Tract Interaction in Female operatic Singing and Theater Belting', *Journal of Singing*, Volume 67, No.5, May 2011.

_____(2012), 'Why Do Classically Trained Singers Widen Their Throat', *Journal of Singing*, Volume 60, No 2, November 2012.

_____(2013) 'A Short Tutorial on Sound Level and Loudness for Voice', *Journal of Singing*, Volume 70, No. 2, November 2013.

Titze, Ingo (2003), 'More About Resonant Voice: Chasing the Formants But Staying Behind Them', *Journal of Voice*, Volume 59, No. 5 May 2003.

Troup, Gordon (1982), 'The Physics of the Singing Voice', *Journal of Research in Singing*, Volume V1, No 1.

Troup, and Luke (1988) 'The Epiglottis As An Articulator In Singing', *Journal of Research in Singing and Applied Vocal Pedagogy*, December, 1988, XII No. 1.

Thomasson, Monica (2003) 'Effects of Lung Volume on the glottal voice source and the vertical laryngeal position in male professional opera singers', *Speech, Music and Hearing*, KTH, Volume 45, 2003.

Thomasson, Monica (2003) 'Effects of Inhalatory Behaviour and Lung Volume on Voice Function in Male Opera Singers', *Speech, Music and Hearing*, KTH, Stockholm. TMH-QPSR-KTH, Volume 45: 61–73.

Thorpe, Callaghan and Van Doorn (1999) 'Visual Feedback of Acoustic Voice Features: New Tool for the Teaching of Singing', NATS, *Australian Voice*, Volume 5, 1999.

Troupe and Luke (1985) 'Some Radiological Observations of Vocal Source-Vocal Tract Interaction.'Stockholm Music Acoustics Conference, July 1983, Volume 1.

Troupe, and Luke (1988) 'The Epiglottis as an Articulator in Singing', *Journal of Research in Singing and Applied Vocal Pedagogy*.

Tunley, David (1984) 'The Union of Words and Music in Seventeenth- Century French Song-The Long and the Short of It', *Australian Journal of French Studies*, Volume 21, No. 3, 1984.

Van den Berg (1955) 'On the Role of the Laryngeal Ventricle in Voice Production', *Folia Phoniat.* 7, No. 2, 1955.

Van den Berg, Zantena & Doornenbal (1957) 'On the Air Resistance and the Bernoulli Effect of the Human Larynx', The *Acoustical Society of America*, Volume 29, No. 5, 1957.

Van den Berg, Janwillem (1958) 'Myoelastic-Aerodynamic Theory of Voice Production', Journal of Speech and Hearing, Volume 1, No. 3, September 1958.

_____(1956) 'Direct and Indirect Determination of the Mean Subglottal Pressure', Folia Phoniatrica, Volume 8, No.1, 1956.

_____(1963) 'Vocal Ligaments Versus Register', *The Nats Bulletin*, February 1963.

Van den Berg (1968) 'Register Problems', Croninigen, Laboratory of Medical Physics, University of Croningeng: 129–134.

_____(1968) 'Sound production in Isolated Human Larynges', Croningen: Laboratory of Medical Physics, University of Croningen: 18–25.

Vasta, Stephen Francis (1999) 'The Rise of Little Voice', *Opera News*, Volume 64 No. 4, October 1999.

Verdolini, Druker, Palmer and Samawi (1998) 'Laryngeal Adduction in Resonant Voice', *Journal of Voice*, Volume 12, No. 3.

Von Leden, Hans (1961) 'The Mechanism of Phonation: A Search for a Rational Theory of Voice Production', *Archives of Otolaryngology*, Volume 74, Dec. 1961.

Von Leden, Hans (1992) 'A Cultural History Of The Larynx And Voice.' In The Science and Art of Clinical Care, edited by Robert Thayer Sataloff. Singular Publishing Group Inc. San Diego.

Vennard, Hirano, and Ohala (1970) 'Laryngeal Synergy In Singing Chest, Head, And Falsetto', *The Nats Bulletin*, October 1970.

Vennard, William and Hirano, Minoru (1971) Varieties of Voice Production. *The Nats Bulletin*, February 1971.

Vennard, William, Minoru Hirano, and Bjorn Fritzell (1971) 'The Extrinsic Laryngeal Muscles', *Bulletin*, May 1971.

Vennard, William (1971), In Memorium. *The NATS Bulletin*, 1971.

Wadsworth, Stephen (1976) 'Bonynge on Bel Canto', *Opera News*, February 1976.

Watson, Peter (2002) 'What Have Chest Wall Kinematics Informed Us About Breathing for Singing', PAS-Conference October 2002.

Walker, Evan (2008) 'The Fable of Adolphe Nourit', *Journal of Singing*, Volume 64, No. 4, March 2008.

Westerman Gregg, Jean (1990) 'From Song To Speech On Support', *The Nats Journal*, September 1990.

Westerman Gregg, Jean (2001) 'Resonation and Articulation-A New Concept', *Journal of Singing*, Volume 58, No. 2, November 2001.

Winckel, F. (1969) 'Acoustical Foundation of Phonetics', In Bertil Malmberg.

Winkworth, Davis, Ellis and Adams (1994), 'Variability and Consistency in Speech Breathing During Reading: Lung Volumes, Speech Intensity and Linguistic Factors', Journal of Speech & Hearing, Volume 37, June 1994.

Winkworth, and Davis (1997), 'Speech Breathing and the Lombard Effect', *Journal of Speech, Language and Hearing Research*, Volume 40, February 1997.

Wolf, Stanley, and Sette (1935) 'Quantitave Studies on the Singing Voice', *Journal of Acoustical Society of America*, Volume 6, 1935.

Yanagisawa, Estill, Kmucha, and Leder (1989) 'The Contribution of Aryepiglottic Constriction to 'Ringing' Voice Quality', *Journal of Voice* Volume 3, No. 4, 342–350.

Zanartu, Mongeau, Wodicka (2007), 'Influence of acoustic loading on an effective single mass model of the vocal folds.' *Acoustical Society of America*, Volume 121 (2) February 2007.

Zaslaw, Neal (1974) 'The Enigma of the Haute-Contre', JSTOR: *The Musical Times*, Volume 115, No. 1581, November 1974.

Zenker, Wolfgang (1964) 'Vocal Muscle Fibers and Their Motor-End Plates', *Research Potentials in Voice Physiology*. State University of New York, Syracuse.

www.ingramcontent.com/pod-product-compliance
Lightning Source LLC
Chambersburg PA
CBHW071235300426
44116CB00008B/1051